WITHDRAWN FROM
EMORY UNIVERSITY LIBRARY

HEADING TO THE FLEADH: FESTIVAL, CULTURAL REVIVAL AND IRISH
TRADITIONAL MUSIC, 1951–1969

# Heading to the Fleadh: Festival, Cultural Revival and Irish Traditional Music, 1951–1969

MÉABH NÍ FHUARTHÁIN

First published in 2024 by
Cork University Press
Boole Library
University College Cork
CORK
T12 ND89
Ireland

© Méabh Ní Fhuartháin, 2024

Library of Congress Control Number: 2024945693
Distribution in the USA: Longleaf Services, Chapel Hill, NC, USA

All rights reserved. No part of this book may be reprinted or reproduced or utilised in any electronic, mechanical or other means, now known or hereafter invented, including photocopying and recording or otherwise, without either the prior written permission of the publishers or a licence permitting restricted copying in Ireland issued by the Irish Copyright Licensing Agency CLG, 63 Patrick Street, Dún Laoghaire, Co. Dublin, A96 WF25.

British Library Cataloguing in Publication Data
A CIP record for this book is available from the British Library.

ISBN: 978-1-78205-013-1

Printed by BZ Graf in Poland
Print origination & design by Carrigboy Typesetting Services
www.carrigboy.co.uk

www.corkuniversitypress.com

# Contents

| | |
|---|---|
| LIST OF ILLUSTRATIONS | vi |
| ABBREVIATIONS | vii |
| ACKNOWLEDGEMENTS | viii |
| INTRODUCTION | 1 |
| 1  Contexts and Precedents for the Fleadh | 6 |
| 2  A Fleadh Beginning, Mullingar, 1951 | 21 |
| 3  Becoming the Fleadh, 1952–5 | 38 |
| 4  Fleadh Proliferations and Place-making: Ennis, 1956 and Dungarvan, 1957 | 71 |
| 5  Songs and Stories: Reenactments of the Fleadh | 102 |
| 6  'The Right Kind of Traditional Music': Adjudication at the Fleadh | 130 |
| 7  'Strange Contrasts at the Fleadh': Sessions and Fleadh identity in the 1960s | 168 |
| AFTERWORD | 194 |
| NOTES | 198 |
| BIBLIOGRAPHY | 236 |
| INDEX | 255 |

# List of illustrations

| | | |
|---|---|---|
| Figure 1 | Map of Fleadh Cheoil na hÉireann, 1951–69. Copyright and courtesy of Claire Marrinan | ix |
| Figure 3.1 | Band of the Ceard Scoil, Cappawhite, County Tipperary at Fleadh Cheoil na hÉireann 1959, Thurles. ITMA ref 9927-JPG. Copyright Pádraig Ó Mathúna, courtesy ITMA | 42 |
| Figure 3.2 | Bobby Casey medal, Monaghan, 1952. Copyright Ben Taylor, courtesy Angela Casey | 51 |
| Figure 4.1 | Unidentified musicians at Swinford, 1961. ITMA ref 9563-PH. Copyright Fáilte Ireland, courtesy ITMA | 75 |
| Figure 5.1 | Ciarán Mac Mathúna, with Elizabeth Crotty and Johnny Pickering, Fleadh Cheoil na hÉireann, Dungarvan 1957. ITMA ref 3188-PH. Courtesy ITMA | 107 |
| Figure 6.1 | Unidentified fiddle competitor, with adjudicators gathered around the adjudication table, Fleadh Cheoil na hÉireann, Dungarvan, 1957. Copyright and courtesy of Fáilte Ireland | 137 |
| Figure 6.2 | Competition marking schemes summary, *Nótaí do Mholtóirí* (Comhaltas, 1967) | 157 |
| Figure 7.1 | Unidentified musicians at the Gorey Fleadh, 1962. ITMA ref 9567-PH. Copyright Fáilte Ireland, courtesy ITMA | 174 |
| Figure 7.2 | Musicians at Fleadh Cheoil Dungarvan, with Eddie Moloney (flute), Tommy Coen (fiddle), 1957. ITMA ref 9589-PH. Copyright Fáilte Ireland, courtesy ITMA | 177 |

# Abbreviations

(archive collections)

CTMA  Comhaltas Traditional Music Archive, An Cultúrlann, Monkstown, Co. Dublin*
IFA   Irish Film Archive, Temple Bar, Co. Dublin
ITMA  Irish Traditional Music Archive, Merrion Square, Co. Dublin
NLI   National Library of Ireland, Kildare St., Co. Dublin
NPU   Na Píobairí Uilleann, Henrietta St., Co. Dublin

* Where available, CTMA file numbers are provided.

# Acknowledgements

Lengthy acknowledgements are part and parcel of academic publications, confirmation of the it-takes-a-village reality of monograph writing. Particularly with a project such as this (researched over a long period of time) acknowledgement lists are also perilous, with the spectre of inadvertent omissions looming. I thank all the music, friends and academics who, through rich encounters during the long gestation of this book, helped me bring it to fruition. Thanks too goes to my family who will be as pleased as I am to see this in print.

Early research for the project in which this book gestated was aided greatly by an Irish Research Council Doctoral Scholarship, gratefully acknowledged here.

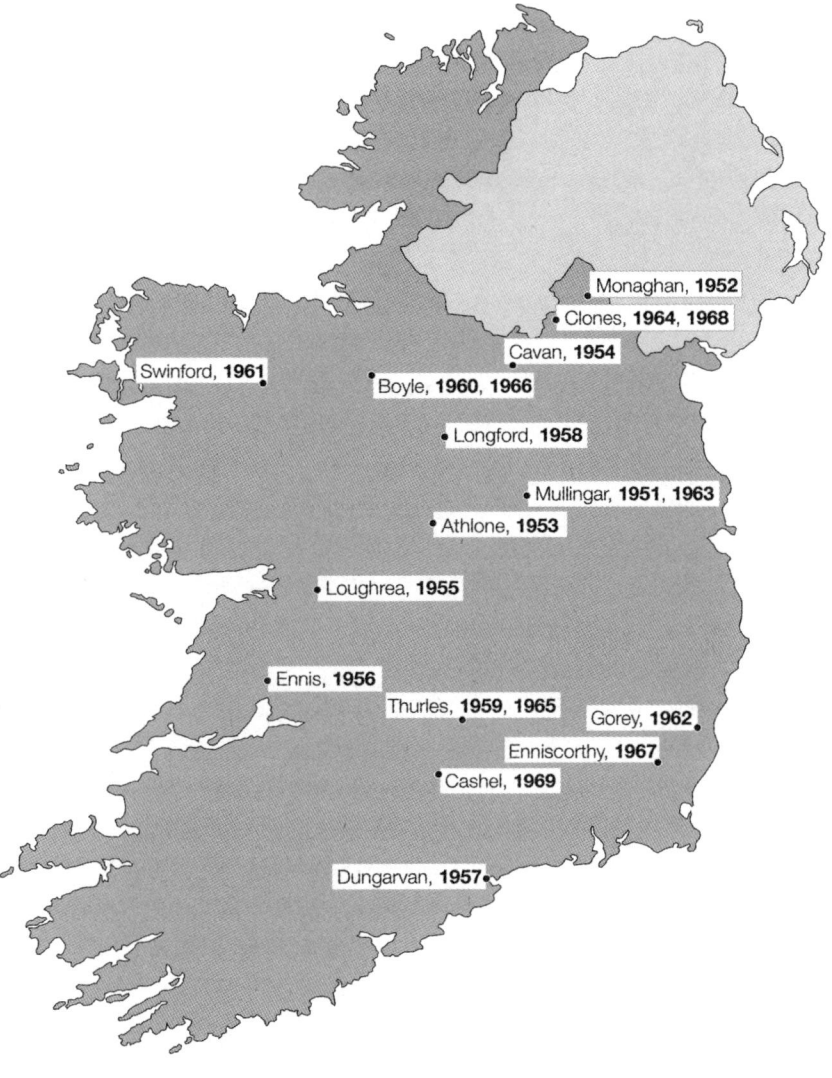

Fig. 1 Map, Fleadh Cheoil na hÉireann, 1951–69
Copyright and courtesy of Claire Marrinan

# Introduction

The All Ireland Fleadh, or Fleadh Cheoil na hÉireann ('feast of music of Ireland', Fleadh hereafter), is the single most influential, public manifestation of Irish traditional music revival from 1951 to 1969.[1] Today, at the time of writing, it is the largest music festival (or any kind of festival) in Ireland and among the biggest annual music festivals in Europe.[2] The festival was established by Comhaltas Ceoltóirí Éireann (Comhaltas), a traditional music revival organisation founded in 1951. The nascent organisation (so new it was yet to be named), hosted the first Fleadh at Whit weekend that same year, on 13 and 14 May. This inaugural Fleadh was held in Mullingar, County Westmeath, as a parallel event to Feis Lár na hÉireann, which was also running at the same time in Mullingar. Feis Lár na hÉireann was an extant annual competition-festival with a long history in the town. Like the Feis, the Fleadh (a term irregularly used in the early years of the festival) was modelled as a competition-festival and developed a core set of material and symbolic components, creating a distinct Fleadh identity. During the 1950s and 1960s, the Fleadh embedded itself in the social and cultural world of Irish traditional music, becoming a key driver in the revival during this period. A number of scholars have engaged with the Fleadh as site of inquiry, most often as part of broader discussions on Comhaltas. However, given its historical significance it is surprising that this book is the first full-length, critical study of the Fleadh as a transformative, cultural phenomenon.[3]

Researchers note the ubiquity of festivals and the cultural importance attached to festive forms across the globe, both contemporaneously and historically.[4] The Fleadh is an example of what Beverly Stoeltje describes as a socially based festival that serves the needs of group life and expresses group identity through a variety of symbolic vehicles.[5] Festivals, including the Fleadh, alter the social order and facilitate exchanges between participants that might not take place outside of festival time. Experienced as being 'outside time', festival time is where 'the world is turned upsidedown, the normal rituals of everyday life and the demands of work' are temporarily suspended.[6] Importantly, festivals can highlight skills that do not receive the same concentrated attention in the non-festive world.[7] At the Fleadh, Irish traditional music was fêted and validated, a circumstance not much found outside the Fleadh zone in 1950s Ireland. For traditional music and its music-makers, their artistic practice was at the apex of cultural value within the spatial and temporal confines of the Fleadh during these decades, inverting and subverting the cultural order in much of the non-Fleadh world.

The chronological bookending in this publication, from 1951 to 1969, was suggested by the subject matter. The Fleadh first took place in 1951 and therefore presents an obvious starting point. An analysis up to 1969 allows a full assessment of the impact of the Fleadh on Irish musical and cultural life in the intervening, contrasting decades of the 1950s and 1960s. Though this book is not a history of Comhaltas, the story of the Fleadh is necessarily intertwinned with that history. Between 1951 and 1969, Comhaltas made a significant shift organisationally from its exclusively grassroots, volunteerist beginnings to an organisation at the end of the 1960s with a professional, funded management structure supported by a grassroots base. The structural elements of the Fleadh were expanded and consolidated during the early 1950s, mirroring David M. Guss' assertion that, through festive form, disappearing worlds 'instead of simply dissolving into a market-driven global culturescape … may actually enlarge their semantic fields' through new contexts that are created and 'expanded audiences'.[8] In the 1950s, through the revival tools of the Fleadh and the development of a nationwide branch network, Comhaltas was elementally important in reconfiguring performance platforms for, and raising the public profile of, Irish traditional music.

This continued in the 1960s, but by then Comhaltas regarded itself as the facilitator and gatekeeper of Irish traditional music. The organisation navigated social and cultural challenges to its identity during this decade, but successfully expanded its 'embodied identification' as the authority on traditional music.[9] The apotheosis of that was the government grant awarded to Comhaltas in 1968 which legitimated the institutional authority of Comhaltas as tradition-bearing organisation. The end of the 1960s is a point of anticipated change within Irish traditional music (and in culture and society in Ireland more widely). Engagement with traditional music had vastly increased due to the undoubted influence of Comhaltas, the Fleadh and its wider competition-festival network. This increase was also due to:

> the world-wide upsurge of folk music, born of popular movements for emancipation and self-expression everywhere; a genuine affinity of spirit with the native mood and nuance; and in Ireland, the many good radio shows which have worked with the persistence of a drop effect to bring the native music to attention.[10]

But there were other developments emerging at the end of the decade reflecting the wider context of change in Irish traditional music. As Comhaltas moved toward the next phase of its maturation, it was entrenched in a contest for authority over the domain of traditional music, an authority that it had institutionalised from the mid-1950s. In the 1970s, traditional music moved into arenas over which Comhaltas had no direct responsibility or ongoing explicit input. The emergence of the new piping organisation Na Píobairí Uilleann, in 1968, and the establishment of Scoil Samhraidh Willie Clancy in 1973 (a joint initiative with Comhaltas in its first year, but not thereafter), diffused institutional power in the traditional music field, offering additional organisational and festive choices to Irish traditional music communities.[11] Also, building on Seán Ó Riada's 1960s vision of its possibilities, traditional music practice developed new modes of popular engagement in the 1970s.[12] After the Fleadh in 1969, which took place in Cashel, County Tipperary, the decision was taken to move the festival to a later summer date thereafter, away from the early summer Whit weekend that had been the Fleadh's calendar home from 1951 to 1969. All of the above taken *in toto* marks 1969 as a logical bookend for the discussions within these pages; it is the end of a chapter of Fleadh development and the beginning of another.

The methodological foundation of the work conducted for this book includes ethnographic fieldwork and archival research (conducted primarily between 2005 and 2010) in Ireland, though also in the USA. Archive research was carried out in international, national, local and indeed, private collections. This primary data is refracted through the interdisciplinary prism of Irish studies, drawing on cultural history and festival studies, ethnomusicology, anthropology, cultural musicology and folk music studies. In addition, literary and vernacular memoirs of the period are read as social histories as they include valuable descriptions and reflections on music and dance practice in Ireland at this time. I rely, gratefully and extensively, on the first-person narratives of fieldwork interviewees, time witnesses to the period.[13] Performers, Fleadh patrons and Comhaltas administrators (some individuals fulfilling all three roles) were generous with their time and memories. Taken in conjunction with contemporaneous reports in newspapers and journals, a rich story of the Fleadh experience emerges.

The opening chapter is a *mise en place* for Fleadh beginnings and growth, outlining the historical context of Irish traditional music at the mid-twentieth-century mark; the narrative of traditional music decline in the decades prior to that; and the broad social and economic changes in Ireland that took place from 1950 to 1969. This opening discussion also situates the Fleadh competition-festival model in music revival and festival criticism, a thread that continues throughout the book. The chapters that follow tell the story of the Fleadh and analyse its development using annual Fleadh case studies interpreted through literature of festival, exploring the 'intense social interaction' experienced by participants.[14] A number of Fleadh development phases can be identified in the 1950s and form the basis of early chapters: Fleadh beginnings (1951); becoming a Fleadh (1952–5); and Fleadh highs and lows (1956–7). Parsing Fleadh development in these phases traces a trajectory of the Fleadh as it becomes a symbolic touchstone for traditional music. The composition of the Fleadh is examined through the identification of constituent elements of Fleadh-time within the Fleadh zone: parades, pageants, competitions, concerts, céilís and, for a time, lecture presentations. The 1950s was a period of structural development and growth of the Fleadh during which an architecture and identity of the festival was created. In contrast, the 1960s was a period of consolidation, during which the identity of the Fleadh was challenged in various ways as it moved from a revivalist, alternative event towards the centre of mainstream culture, the subject of the final chapter. The challenges of the 1960s are framed through an analysis of the Fleadh object discussed in that last chapter, the session.

Fieldwork interviews offered two additional themes that warranted discussion in individual chapters: how the Fleadh is reenacted post-festival through story and song, and given its competition-festival mode, the thorny issue of performance competition and its adjudication. Music at festivals keys the emotions of the participants and opens up multiple layers of interpretation that are re-experienced, recounted and debated after the fact (including experiences of competition and adjudication).[15] Across all chapters, much of the interpretive commentary could equally be applied to provincial and county fleadhanna (pl.) as they developed during these same decades, but the singularity of the All Ireland Fleadh as an annually recurring totemic event is the key site of inquiry explored here.

As a very young musician, I participated in fleadh competitions, but truthfully had neither the constitution for competition nor the necessary virtuosity to thrive. As a result, my first-person knowledge of Comhaltas and the Fleadh was limited. Later, as a college student in the 1980s, there was a multitude of contexts to perform and engage with Irish traditional music: sessions (both paid and unpaid), concerts, and pilgrimages to Scoil Samhraidh Willie Clancy among others, not to mention the madcap, invigorating opportunities offered to traditional musicians in UCC by the inimitable Mícheál Ó Súilleabháin. Neither Comhaltas nor the Fleadh, quite frankly, featured too much in my youthful musical evolution. However, as my critical awareness developed, I realised what many others already knew, that the history of Irish traditional music must also include the story of the Fleadh. Recognising that there are many more stories yet to be told, this book is one story of the Fleadh in its first two decades.

CHAPTER I

# Contexts and Precedents for the Fleadh

In 1951, the newly formed Pipers Club in Mullingar announced that chief among its objectives was the organisation of a Fleadh or festival, to be held from 13 to 14 May, over the Whit public holiday weekend.[1] The festival in Mullingar would, over the course of those days, 'restore to its rightful place the traditional music of Ireland' and, as part of the festival, the committee hoped 'to bring to Mullingar the cream of traditional musicians from the four corners of Ireland'.[2] In addition to a formal lecture presentation there would be 'a concert featuring top-class artistes followed by a ceilidhe' and, furthermore, competitions for traditional music were to be 'organised in conjunction with the local feis committee'.[3] Most of these fundamental components of the Fleadh (including a parade), first set out in 1951, were retained and became constituent elements of the festival thereafter. Through the distinct composition of these elements (and others quickly added) new modes of practice for traditional music were created at, and by, the Fleadh. Within a matter of a few short years, the Fleadh became a key signifier for traditional music and associated culture.

This chapter sets out the national context in which the Fleadh began and subsequently developed. Key in this are the economic, social and cultural conditions of the mid-twentieth century in Ireland, with a particular reflection on rural Ireland. An intrinsic part of this discussion examines the rhetoric of cultural decline associated with the period and an exploration of Irish traditional music practice at the moment of Fleadh-beginning. As the Fleadh does not emerge in a vacuum but consciously responds to, builds on and references previous iterations of

Contexts and Precedents for the Fleadh 7

revival, competition-festival precedents to the Fleadh are also mapped out. Finally, the chapter contextualises the national story of Fleadh origins in the wider world of twentieth-century music revival and the theoretical field of festival, assembling the building blocks for the discussions in the chapters that follow.

IRELAND, POST-SECOND WORLD WAR TO 1969

The years from 1951 to 1969 span a particular watershed in Irish twentieth-century history. In the historiography of Ireland, the period is presented as two contrasting decades, with 1960 a convenient axis. Though these decades are described as the most recent modernisation drive, the narrative of the Republic of Ireland in the post-war period up to 1960 is more often one of an 'existence so grey, so monotonous and cheerless' that economic and cultural stagnation was inevitable.[4] And, though 'Ireland experienced an economic boom during the immediate post-war period', it was impressive only relative to what had preceeded it.[5] This false economic dawn was largely propped up by funds from the Marshall Aid programme, which contributed $149 million in grants and loans to the Irish state.[6] It was quickly forgotten in the 'profound national despondency' of the 1950s, brought on by unending economic tribulations.[7] A fanciful account of the island of Ireland losing its (geological) moorings and drifting out to sea in the *Capuchin Annual* in 1952 is perhaps illustrative of a national mood. Titled satirically 'The Emigrant Isle', the story's fictional would be captain-Taoiseach, in an address to the nation (at which point the island was 48 kilometres out to sea and heading for New York) declares 'We do not know where we are going ... or where this is likely to end'.[8] The storyline reflects the critical juncture at which Ireland found itself and indeed predicted the difficulties of the decade ahead. From 1953 to 1958, no growth of GNP was recorded, in fact, 'Ireland was the only country in the western world where the total volume of goods and services consumed' fell.[9] Between 1955 and 1958, two out of every five workers in the building industry lost their jobs and unemployment reached a record 78,000 in 1957. The chilling reality for those who were employed was that 'from 1949 to 1956 real national income rose by only 8 per cent, at a time when the average increase in Europe was 40 per cent'.[10] There are comparisons to be made with Northern Ireland during these decades too. Though there was some success 'during the 1950s in attracting British investment in the area of textiles, artificial fibres and other petroleum products', by 1960, the North's staple industries were in perpetual decline.[11] By the end of the 1960s, the Troubles were the frame in which cultural and political life was being experienced.

The impact of emigration from Ireland during the 1950s and 1960s, both at home and abroad, has been well rehearsed. Between 1951 and 1961, over 400,000 Irish citizens emigrated, peaking in 1957.[12] Following the war, Britain became the single most important destination for Irish emigrants due to tightening immigration laws in the USA; ease of travel between Britain and Ireland; labour needs in Britain; and a degree of (urban) cultural familiarity between the two islands.[13] The vast majority of these emigrants went directly to the industrial centres 'which fall on a line drawn from Liverpool to London' and in 1964 'more than one third of the people of Irish birth living in Great Britain' were in London.[14] Eamon de Valera delivered a speech in Galway on the exorbitant rate of emigration in 1951, but rather than propose how conditions might be changed to keep people from leaving Ireland, instead chose to 'tell how the exiles fared in Britain: of their bad lodgings, poor housing, overcrowded hostels and raw social life'.[15] When Paddy Maunsell, in 1954, attributed emigration in large part to 'the lack of an outlet for the Irish temperment [sic] and the importation of foreign rubbish' (musically and culturally speaking), he failed to recognise the significant push factors to leave Ireland such as unemployment, lack of prospects, and low living standards.[16]

There were, as mentioned, significant pull factors to Britain. In 1955, a working party and ministerial group reported to the United Kingdom cabinet in Whitehall that it unreservedly wished Irish immigration 'to continue because of labour shortage and its contribution to economic growth, and because of the fit young men and women being added to the population'.[17] Heinrich Böll wrote that in 1954 a young emigrant labourer in Britain could earn as much as £20 to £25 per week, with overtime.[18] In effect, a young fellow, even if he spends ten pounds a week on himself, will always send from two to fifteen pounds home, and there is many a granny living here on those two pounds sent to her by a son or grandson.[19]

Many of those who chose to travel across the Atlantic also fared better than their compatriots who remained at home. Thomas Gilrane, having emigrated from his native Leitrim to America, paid his aunt Catherine $15 a week for room and board, continued to pay off his passage, which she had advanced to him, and still faithfully mailed $10 per month to his father back home.[20] Such was the nature of the trend, that John O'Brien was compelled dramatically to comment 'Nothing in recent centuries is so puzzling or so challenging as the strange phenomenon being enacted before our eyes; the fading away of the once great and populous nation of Ireland' and he further predicted that if 'the past century's rate of decline continues for another century, the Irish will virtually disappear'.[21] Regardless of Dermot Keogh's assertion that 'Ireland was a very good place to live in the 1950s if one had a permanent and pensionable job', the 'dark shadow lying across the face of Ireland' was in sharp contrast to wider European and global patterns of population increase.[22] However, as Diarmaid Ferriter recognises, the 1950s was simultaneously a decade when the 'sanctification of deprivation' was challenged, 'not just by those emigrating, but by those left at home'.[23] When Ronan Fanning describes the late 1940s and early 1950s as a period of fermentation economically speaking, he might well apply the same analogy to spheres of cultural practice.[24] The establishment of the Fleadh is part of the cultural fermentation that took place, though noticeably absent from much of the historiography of the period heretofore.[25]

The 1950s gave way to economic and cultural transformation during the 1960s, a decade acknowledged as a turning point in Ireland and in Joseph J. Lee's assessment, 'one of those pivotal periods when a society swings on its axis to face a new direction' both from an economic perspective and with regard to general changes in society.[26] Importantly, the seeds of change were sown in the previous decade.[27] T.K. Whitaker, secretary to the department of finance from 1956 to 1969, produced the *First Programme for Economic Expansion* in 1958.[28] This is widely viewed as a catalyst (if not the catalyst) for the shift in policy and attitude leading to a new and open Ireland fiscally speaking, and was the driving engine behind 'the modernising mission'.[29] National output from mid-1959 to mid-1960 increased by 8 per cent, while exports rose by nearly 35 per cent.[30] Further economic programmes and the Anglo-Irish Free Trade Agreement in 1965 cemented the shift to an outward-looking economic policy, which culminated literally and symbolically in accession to the European Economic Community in 1973.[31] This political revision of economic policy was reflected in declining rates of emigration, when net emigration fell from the annual high of 43,000 between 1956 and 1961 to 16,000 between 1961 and 1966, and plummeted further between 1966 and 1971 to an annual net figure of 11,000.[32]

Seán Lemass, Taoiseach from 1959 to 1966, 'presided over the establishment of new procedures for economic and social decision-making', moving away from an isolationist and protectionist stance to a more open economy.[33] This was, in Andrew D. Devanney's words, 'a stunning reversal of nearly thirty years of protectionist economic policy, made more remarkable in that it was Lemass who had crafted the earlier policy in the first place'.[34] Still, John A. Murphy demarcates the 1950s and 1960s as 'two sharply contrasting periods, in respect of the economy and of Irish society generally' and he goes so far as to write that 'truly, it was the worst of decades followed by the best of decades'.[35] The 1960s, in contrast to the 1950s, witnessed faster and 'more sustained growth than in any previous period in Irish history'.[36] While Murphy is specifically referring to the political and economic conditions of the time, his analysis might be carried through to other aspects of Irish life during these years. Catherine Curran specifically notes the differentiation between both decades in traditional music terms as well.[37]

The 1960s brought not just a rise in living standards but also a growth in population of over 100,000 between 1961 and 1971. This growth was predominantly in Dublin, with internal migration contributing to that rate. With the exception of the west and north-west, all areas displayed some population increase, albeit small.[38] Many of the challenges of emigration to London or New York were common also to the newly arrived migrants from rural Ireland to the expanding capital. In Dublin, 'urban conditions of high population density, high social mobility and a wide and changing range of occupations' effected immediate change to previous patterns of living and social engagement.³⁹ Increasingly, and importantly for the purposes of this book, new urbanites experienced social relations through occupational and cultural organisations, not within kinship structures.⁴⁰

### IRISH TRADITIONAL MUSIC AND DECLINE

Looking to the past is a fundamental tenent of Irish traditional music.⁴¹ But traditional music, like any music, is also present-facing and responds to contemporaneous social, environmental and political conditions. With the inauguration of the Fleadh in 1951, the founding agents of Comhaltas took action within a particular set of circumstances: the economic stagnation of the post-war period; ongoing rural depopulation through emigration and internal migration (with a corrolating increase in an urbanised Irish experience); and the resulting 'decline of fixed social hierarchies' all of which collapsed the quotidian system of traditional music patronage.⁴² Consequently, the musico-cultural landscape of the post-Second World War period in Ireland is constructed as one in which Irish traditional music reached its nadir, in stark contrast to the late nineteenth century, described as the heyday of traditional music.⁴³ During those interstitial years, from 1900 to 1950, music was subject to modernising forces and a decrease in practice, as the balance of traditional music making (and dancing) shifted from the domestic to the public domain. This was arguably the most important contextual change traditional music experienced during this period. An editorial in the *Connacht Tribune* in 1955 opined that 'with the coming of the ballroom dance craze after the first war ... the young people turned to dance halls, and the kitchen scoraíocht [visiting] died'.⁴⁴

The narrative of traditional performance practice ascribed to the early twentieth century and up to the 1950s is framed in funereal terms, the bell of its demise perpetually tolling. Much later publications in the field of Irish music studies subscribe to this view, with comments such as 'the decline in domestic music making', 'lively house sessions where musicians gathered became a thing of the past', and 'live traditional music was now only heard at Christmastime and at weddings' scattered throughout commentaries.⁴⁵ A bleak picture is painted where:

there was little or no incentive for the young people, the lifeblood of the nation, to learn Irish music ... the fiddles were locked in their cases, the flutes were encased in their boxes, and the melodeons found a safe haven on the tops of dressers to gather dust.[46]

This is not just retrospective hand-wringing; commentators of the day also expressed this view. Joseph O'Connor declared, in the late 1950s, 'Here and now, with my hand upon my heart, I declare to the world at large, that we, the Irish, whose songs are sung by the world at large, are losing our gift of song'.[47] O'Connor includes both Irish and English-language song in his lament for the 'lost inheritance of vocal music'.[48]

Reflecting on all this, one might reasonably assume that these bleak prospects were wholly mirrored in mid-century Irish social life. However, Sean Shanagher urges caution regarding the 'narrative of oppression', as it ignores 'popular agency and a vibrant (social) dance culture' that underpinned social life in the mid-century decades.[49] Any number of organisations (the Gaelic League, the GAA, local parish organisations) and, increasingly, private commercial enterprise, provided all manner of possibilities for social activities. An array of newspaper advertisements for dances and other events, supporting Shanagher's claim. In addition to national contexts, incremental transnational processes of modernisation (economic, technological, socio-cultural and political) intersected with national and local conditions (symbolically and literally realised in the 1935 Public Dance Halls Act) which continued throughout the period under discussion here.[50] There was a resulting rationalisation of traditional music and dance. The exposition (and transmission) of traditional music was increasingly experienced in public forums (social dance events, competitions, concerts, on the radio and in recordings), often with an explicit function of cultural celebration. Rather than these practices being part of 'customary action' taken because it was what people did in a given group, an increasing voluntarism entered peoples' motivation for engagement with traditional practices.[51]

A complicated matrix of periphery-core social, political and cultural relationships informed the place of traditional music and dance practices found from independence to 1950. Though cultural nationalism at the turn of the twentieth century utilised music (specifically Irish-language song) and dance as key representations of Irish identity, the promise of regeneration was not realised for music in the period directly post-independence. As described, the continuing and debilitating rate of emigration, in particular that from rural Ireland, depleted the ranks of musicians substantially. During the 1920s and 1930s, what was Ireland's musical loss was Irish-America's (and also, the Irish in Britain's) gain: for P.J. Curtis, this is the golden age of Irish music 'should you happen to be living in New York or possibly London'.[52] All evidence supports the view that Irish traditional music and dance within its domestic setting experienced an inevitable decline, which without intervention, might have collapsed and, rather like the Irish language, resulted in a 'disorienting rupture in cultural continuity'.[53]

It is worth noting that there is an alternative experience recounted by musicians, dancers and listeners of the decades between 1930 and 1950, which recalls a life still centred on music making and dancing. Roger Sherlock remembers the musicians in his youth who he regularly heard, both through visiting houses and at house dances, when he borrowed 'his sleeping father's shoes to attend'.[54] Nicolette Devas described house dances in both the Aran Islands and Doolin as frequent and music-filled during the early 1930s, mirrored a decade later in Johnny O'Leary's experience in Knocknagree.[55] Meanwhile, both Sheila O'Dowd and Peter Horan separately recall their upbringing in Sligo as having music two or three nights per week, sometimes in their own houses and on other occasions at neighbouring houses.[56] Sean McNamara, who travelled from Liverpool to stay with family in Kilmihil, County Clare each summer gave this account of house dances during these years:

> The house dances were something marvellous. They'd start about eight or nine o'clock in the evening ... They'd start the evening off with the gramophone and the old people and young children would be entertained. But then, maybe eleven or twelve o'clock the dancers and the musicians would start coming in. And the dance would go on 'til morning. I mean seven or eight o'clock, when the sun would be cracking the flags, they'd be dancing the last set.[57]

Thus, for every account of the demise of traditional music during the 1930s and 1940s, when Michael Tubridy found it inordinately difficult to meet musicians such was the isolation in rural West Clare, there were also more hopeful experiences.[58]

## FLEADH PRECEDENTS: FEIS AND OIREACHTAS

In addition to the opportunity for playing at concerts and céilithe (pl. of céilí), traditional music performance in the public domain during the first half of the twentieth century was heard at festival-competitions such as feiseanna (pl. of feis), which were widely advertised. There were (and continue to be) various events titled feis, with important distinctions between them for the purpose of this discussion. Established in 1895, the Feis Ceoil Association (Festival of Music Association) inaugurated an annual feis in 1897, the first of which took place in Dublin. Soon after, there were other independent feis organisations set up, each administrating feis events: the Sligo Feis (1903) and Feis Lár na hÉireann in Mullingar (1904), are examples.[59] These events were part of the broader cultural project during the revival period. While acknowledging the importance of the folk music of the nation, the main body of these larger feis competitions was concerned with what Eamonn Ó Gallchobhair called 'cosmopolitan' music, by which he meant various presentations of Western art music.[60] Breandán Breathnach echoed these sentiments when he wrote:

> The Feis Ceoil continues to declare that the study and cultivation of Irish (traditional) music are among its primary aims but it has long since ceased to involve itself in such matters. It concerns itself almost entirely with West European art music.[61]

Within these non-Gaelic League larger feiseanna, categories of competitions ran the gamut from piano to choral singing to composition, but also included, to varying degrees, dedicated folk or traditional music categories and in particular, Irish-language singing. Singers were instructed for Irish-language competitions to make their selections from approved song collections, for example from Pádraig Breathnach's *Ár gCeol Féinig*.[62] Some singers continued to choose songs not necessarily previously published, leading Sir Richard Terry in his comments to declare: 'No manufactured or artificial thing could give one the thrill those songs gave me.'[63] At the Feis Ceoil in 1900, held in Belfast, competitors in the singing competitions were required to choose an Irish song (in Irish or English), in addition to their 'classical test piece'.[64] Traditional singing and instrumental practice at larger feiseanna were subject to a comprehensive series of regulations within the performance context and these regulations were sometimes also found at local feiseanna.

The most frequent appearance of a traditional instrument at the Feis Ceoil from its inception was uilleann pipes. As inheritor of the indigenous Gaelic instrument mantle from the Irish harp, this was not surprising. That being said, members of the Dublin Pipers Club, established in 1900, believed that though the annual Feis Ceoil, run by the Feis Ceoil Association, included Irish traditional music, the effect was 'sporadic and unsatisfactory'.[65] As the Feis Ceoil became increasingly less concerned with traditional forms, the uilleann pipes fell out of favour. Barry O'Neill notes that the uilleann pipes were no longer a Feis Ceoil category after 1935, due to low numbers of competitors.[66] Harping had an inauspicious start at the first Feis Ceoil, as 'not even one solitary harper entered for the wire-strung harp prize offered'.[67] In comparison, seven pipers entered, drawn from all four provinces.[68] On paper, all areas of presentation were highly regulated. This can be seen from the directives regarding costumry at Feis Athar Maitiú in 1925 where competitors were instructed that, while the costume itself could be modern or ancient (presumably in style rather than age), 'the material for the costume must be Irish made, including the buttons'.[69] No guidance is provided as to how this might be verified.[70]

The fortunes of the Feis Ceoil Association waxed and waned over the course of the first half of the twentieth century. As early as 1900, critics of the annual Feis Ceoil declared that the organisation would be better named 'The Itinerent German Philharmonic Society'.[71] This was a reference to the overwhelming predominance of non-Irish repertoire and practice found at the festival. The authors further commented that monies collected by the Feis Ceoil Association, ostensibly as a means of 'perpetuating and cultivating distinctly Irish music', were instead being utilised to parade 'the many young clever daughters of the well-got-on people of Belfast to perform ... a scherzo of some obscure German composer'.[72]

A much more ad hoc, autonomous system of rural feiseanna held throughout the island was organised by local branches of the Gaelic League with the earliest held in Galway in 1898.[73] These feiseanna were frequently held outdoors, with dancing and other kinds of performances taking place on temporary platforms.⁷⁴ O'Neill juxtaposes these local feiseanna with their Feis Ceoil urban counterpart when he wrote 'if the Dublin event was a night at the opera, this was a day at the country fair'.⁷⁵ At these feiseanna, Irish traditional dance competitions, introduced as early as 1898, were found in abundance. Much of the success of local Gaelic League feiseanna was due to the non-centralised nature of their administration, 'that pliability which enables them to mirror the changing circumstances of their localities'.⁷⁶ These small-scale feiseanna had the Irish language as core pillar, (in a review of the 1902 feis in Galway, Henry Fegan was impressed by the exclusive use of Irish throughout the proceedings), and were likely to have a wide variety of competitions and events as part of the festival.⁷⁷ The emergence of a feis system as a distinct competition event just for dancing was a later development, occuring during the middle decades of the century.⁷⁸

Local and regional feiseanna (of the non-dance-specific variety) continued up to the 1950s (and in that decade) to be an important site of competition, performance and community building. Feiseanna enjoyed high attendances, though the gradual shift of instrumental competition to the Comhaltas-sponsored Fleadh consolidated a divide between dance and instrumental competition, and their respective sites. Many traditional musicians, born during the 1920s and 1930s, recall that their first competitive outing was to a local feis. Peadar O'Loughlin, from County Clare, recollected travelling to Miltown Malbay for a feis in the late 1940s.⁷⁹ Ann Mulqueen, a singer from County Limerick, vividly remembers a three-county feis, drawing from Counties Tipperary, Limerick and Clare, held in Castleconnell, County Limerick every year and this too was her very first time singing in competition.⁸⁰ Willie Reynolds, a piper from Westmeath, who was central to the establishment of the first Comhaltas branch, attended Feis Misneach, in Athlone, in 1937 and 'came away with 1st prize – a lovely medal depicting the Bridge of Athlone'.⁸¹ This network of competitions was vital to the traditional music fraternity but particularly to uilleann pipers. Pipers, fewer and fewer in number, met and shared repertoire and listened to other pipers' music making. Reynolds met Leo Rowsome for the first time in 1950 at 'the great Aonach of the Midlands ... held in Tristernagh near Ballinacargy'.⁸² Reynolds previously heard Rowsome on Radio Éireann (RÉ), the national radio channel (established in 1926 as 2RN, it went through name changes over the years). Some forty years later, he recalled that Rowsome freely offered advice about playing the pipes, and 'promised to send me tunes, which he did'.[83] At the Walderstown Pipers' Club, 'the teaching of young pipers was undertaken from the beginning and pupils from the club won a number of prizes at Feis Átha Cliath'.[84] Feiseanna were also important among Irish emigrants. The twenty third annual New York Feis held at Fordham University in 1955 had a record attendance of 40,000 people.[85] Run by the Irish Counties Association, newspaper reports recorded that Scottish, Welsh, Cornish, Manx and Breton groups wore national costumes during the various contests.[86] Further drawing on the Gaelic League model of cultural revival, Comhaltas also hosted local feiseanna (though not frequently), for example in Templemore in 1959.[87]

An tOireachtas (the assembly), the annual Irish-language and culture festival run by the Gaelic League, premiered in 1897, the same year as the Feis Cheoil. Modelled on the Welsh Eisteddfod, the Oireachtas solely concerned itself with aspects of the 'native cultural traditions', with the Irish language central to proceedings.[88] In its inaugural year, the Oireachtas was run concurrently with the Feis Ceoil, but divested itself of any adjacency subsequently. Early Oireachtas competition-festivals also hosted instrumental competitions including uilleann pipes and harping. Similar to its coeval Feis Ceoil, the fortunes of the Oireachtas were inconsistent during the first half of the twentieth century: it was suspended after 1924 due to a lack of support but revived in 1939.[89] Seán Mac Néill enthusiastically noted the importance of the Oireachtas to Irish-language singing upon the occasion of the festival's revival.[90] He acknowledged, however, that there was much left to do, noting the complaints of choirs regarding the scarcity of newly published, Irish-language songs.[91] This reflects the place of Irish-language singing, rather than instrumental music, at the top end of a performance hierarchy within the Oireachtas.[92]

Piping was introduced in Oireachtas competition in 1899, though it was not the main event and 'the literary aspects of the Oireachtas dominated'.[93] Other instrumental competitions were also introduced in later years. By 1960, the spectrum of competitions at the Oireachtas included instrumental and singing categories also found at Comhaltas' Fleadhanna at the same time: 'amhránaíocht, fir' (singing, men); 'amhránaíocht, mná' (singing, women); 'comórtas don phíob uilleann' (competition for uilleann pipes); 'comórtas don bheidhlín' (competition for fiddle), 'comórtas don fheadóg mhór' (competition for flute); 'comórtas don acordán' (competition for accordion); 'comórtas do bhannaí céilí' (competition for céilí band); and the final competition, 'comórtas do cheol bheirte' (competition for duet).[94] While the Oireachtas was an important precedent for the Fleadh when it began, by the end of the 1950s a reciprocal influence was felt by the Oireachtas, with the Fleadh informing its competition categories.

Throughout the first half of the twentieth century, feiseanna and Oireachtais (pl.) were organised, suspended and reinstituted with varying degrees of success. However, the confluence of people, organisations and events provided the backdrop for the Comhaltas traditional music revival movement and the first Fleadh.

### MUSIC REVIVALS AND FESTIVAL

The festival format was a vital tool of revival during the 1950s and 1960s for Comhaltas and consequently Irish traditional music, creating and reworking modes of practice and experience.[95] Tamara Livingston confirms festivals and their associated activities as the material nuts and bolts of revival, and Chris Gibson and John Connell recognise that music is 'in the broadest sense the oldest and most common element of festivals'.[96] Those who attend festivals are searching for 'freedom from everyday life … socialization and its associated sense of belonging', in search of 'authentic experience'.[97] In the wider, international context of folk music revivals in the twentieth century this resulted in the proliferation of folk and traditional music festivals in the 1960s and 1970s.[98] Revivals had come and gone before, but there are particular factors at work in Western folk music revival of the mid-twentieth century and the lasting effects of the 1960s Anglo-American revival. R. Raymond Allen identifies these as threefold: 'media, transportation and the political atmosphere of the post World War era'.[99] The intersection of these developments with technological advances, mediated dissemination and popular music, saw folk and traditional musics garner wide attention from 1930 to 1965 and commercial success internationally from the late 1950s.[100] Folk music festivals emerged in the 1960s in Britain, more than a decade after the

## Contexts and Precedents for the Fleadh

first Fleadh. There is little evidence of conscious awareness in the early 1950s among Fleadh founders of these wider revival movements, though Paddy Maunsell in 1955 does comment that, regarding folk music, 'there was a time when the musical world failed to appreciate folk music ... But today, every civilised country realises its value'.[101] John Healy, reporting on the Fleadh in Longford in 1958, suggests:

> intellectuals will explain about it (the revival of traditional music) being a world-wide movement and point to America where the hill billy folk songs of the Tennessee mountains have stepped out of their environment ... and explain that the world's palate is growing tired of the commercial Tin Pan Alley product.[102]

Notwithstanding Healy's view, the expansion of folk music into the popular commercial sphere on both sides of the Atlantic from the late 1950s created a greater transnational revival awareness and did impact the Fleadh in terms of its popularity. The incentive for folk music revival in the years following the Second World War was commonly felt across many countries in Europe and the USA, irrespective of conscious awareness among participants of what their folk or traditional music counterparts were doing elsewhere.

Paradoxically, while relying heavily on tools of modernisation (in technology, transportation and media), music revivals commit to an idealised model of an historical past, often emphasising 'pre-commercial musical idioms'.[103] All revivalist social movements, including music revivals, are concerned with systems that are 'believed to be disappearing or completely relegated to the past'.[104] Comhaltas wished to restore traditional music through the Fleadh and other activities. Fleadh organisers were enthusiastic about the enterprise, as will be discussed in the chapters to come, but also believed they were working in opposition to contemporary, dominant structures, a belief shared across musical and cultural revivals internationally.[105] In the twentieth century, Western folk and traditional music revivals typically stemmed from outside mainstream political spheres, in opposition to dominant ideologies. As a revival gains momentum and gathers mainstream support, cultural and political domains can, and do, overlap. Revivals, and therefore festivals of revival, constantly reference the past and negotiate a consensual, accepted version of that past to which an allegiance is asserted. Revivialists 'align themselves with a particular historical lineage and offer a cultural alternative in which legitimacy is grounded in reference to authenticity and historical fidelity' inherently connecting with previous moments of interest in folk musics.[106]

## CONCLUSION

The genesis of the Fleadh was prompted by social, economic and cultural contexts of mid-twentieth-century Ireland. Emigration, migration, economic hardship and processes of modernisation all conspired to create a period of dramatic social change. Social upheaval after the Second World War in Ireland was experienced as a traumatic culmination of societal and cultural rupture, a context in which revival responses are typically triggered. The nature of social trauma can vary widely and a literal or symbolic displacement can prompt a revivalist reaction.[107] Traditional music, like much of the traditional way of life, was in crisis and its historical community of practice now much dispersed, was challenged to recreate new ways of being.

David M. Picard and Mike Robinson emphasise that festivals are the key revival response at times of dramatic social crisis: festival as cultural revival defibrillator, if you will.[108] This goes some way towards explaining the immediately enthusiastic response to the Fleadh from a community 'seeking to re-assert their identities in the face of a feeling of cultural dislocation'.[109] The Fleadh became an arena where participants and communities could innovate 'new markers of being and meaning' in the festive frame at this moment of cultural crisis and revival.[110] The particular ways in which that festive revival response was initiated and how that was manifest in its early years is the next chapter in this story of the Fleadh.

CHAPTER 2

# A Fleadh Beginning, Mullingar, 1951

An article in the *Sunday Express Reporter* in 1955 traces the genesis of the Fleadh, then in its fourth year, to much earlier gatherings:

> How did it all begin? Fifty years ago a band of six uilleann pipers met in a house in Thomas Street, Dublin. They called their sessions simply oiche ceol [*sic*]. Sometimes the musicians played at the house of Seamus Ennis in Finglas, at John Potts' in the Coombe, or at William Rowsome's in Harold's Cross.[1]

The account above recalls the historical and cultural primogenitors of the Fleadh as *oíche ceol* (night of music) 'which were held in the homes of well-known pipers during the early part of the century'.[2] These cultural conclaves were hosted by members of the Dublin Pipers Club.[3] The club was reconstituted in 1936, renamed as Cumann na bPíobairí Uilleann (CPU) and subsequently made a home at Áras Ceannt, 14 Thomas Street.[4] In 1950, members of the club expressed concern for traditional music (not just piping), for all the reasons described in the previous chapter. A meeting was held at Thomas Street where members adopted a motion to 'spread its ideals throughout Ireland'.[5] While operational details were vague, the principle was agreed that, as the first bold action in a wider revival strategy of Irish traditional music, a festival of traditional music would be held in 1951 – *de facto*, the first Fleadh.

PROPOSING A FLEADH

The proposal is unsurprising given that the tool of festival is central to any music revival.[6] Festivals come in many guises and the importance of the combined competition-festival event is significant. In Irish cultural history, the Belfast Harp Festival in 1792 is an iconic example of competition-festival; feiseanna and Oireachtais, as described, also fall along the competition-festival continuum. The Rowsome brothers, Leo and Thomas (Tom), stalwarts of the Dublin piping confraternity, are credited with being the 'originators of the scheme' to hold a fleadh, ambitious in their belief 'that an Irish bardic festival' could be 'made an annual event'.[7] The festival was understood to be the first action by an as yet unnamed new association for the revival of traditional music. A committee for the organisation was established, with Tom Rowsome as chairman, Art Mac Connaic as secretary and ordinary members Paddy McElvaney, Eamonn O'Gorman, Billie Nea and Seán Gannon to take on the challenge. The first meeting of this fledgling committee was held in January 1951 at the home of O'Gorman on East Arran Street in Dublin and arrangements were made for some committee members to travel to Mullingar, in County Westmeath, to meet with 'influential Gaelic enthusiasts in that town' with a view to hosting the festival there.[8] As part of festival deliberations, the Dublin envoys were tasked with discussing the formation of a new pipers club in the midlands and, aspirationally, a wholly new organisation to revive Irish traditional music.[9] A meeting was called in advance for 4 February 1951, at the Midland Hotel in Mullingar, over which Tom Rowsome presided. Rowsome had a long and well-respected lineage in traditional music circles, particularly in piping circles. Son of William, he was a piper himself and gained a reputation as an organiser through his work with the CPU. The Dublin contingent, which included fiddling siblings Kathleen Harrington and John Joe Gardiner (from Sligo originally), met in Mullingar with local members of Feis Lár na hÉireann (an annual Mullingar feis), the Gaelic League and GAA, together with other interested individuals.[10]

The choice of Westmeath (and its county town, Mullingar) as the possible location for a fleadh was due to a combination of factors. Willie Reynolds, a piper and revivalist from Westmeath, was well known to the Dublin pipers and instrumental in setting up a number of smaller piping clubs in Westmeath in the previous decade (Walderstown Piping Club, 1943–51; Moyvore Piping Club, 1943–51; and Lisdoughan Piping Club among them).[11] As part of the local scene, Reynolds taught through the piping clubs in Westmeath but was also part of the relatively tight-knit national piping network. In the late 1940s, members of Cumann na bPíobairí Uilleann travelled to Mullingar to compete in Feis Lár na hÉireann to play at céilithe, so were known to the Gaelic League committee members in Mullingar.[12]

Feis Lár na hÉireann first took place in 1906 and was described in 1917 as a decidedly 'Gaelic for a Galldacht Feis' (a Gaelic event for an English-speaking district).[13] Like many feiseanna, its history was potted, but Feis Lár na hÉireann had established a seasonal regularity at Whit weekend in Mullingar. The annual calendrical identity and time-limited nature of that identity at Whit are essential elements for any festival.[14] The Feis provided a calendar-tied structural framework to which the (new) Fleadh could conveniently attach itself with a ready-made select team of cultural revivalists. By 1951, Reynolds had close connections with the Rowsomes and other pipers of CPU, meeting and playing with them at feiseanna and other cultural events.

Additionally, the location of Mullingar in the midlands made it (theoretically at least) accessible from all corners of the island, further enhancing its suitability. The choice of a rural town setting was deliberate, notwithstanding the fact that the initial impetus for the event came from musicians based in the urban capital. The rural, in cultural imagination, often corresponds to indices of authenticity.[15] It follows that a rural Fleadh festival would 'reinforce the existing image' of the 'rural realm', but simultaneously could 'be used as a tool for reimagining rural communities in the minds of urbanites'.[16] The interlocking relationship of authenticity to rurality is a theme that is returned to repeatedly in Fleadh (and Comhaltas) history.[17]

A report on 10 February 1951, in the *Westmeath Examiner*, recounted that at the 4 February meeting, 'a branch of Cumann na bPíobairí Uilleann (Uilleann Pipers Association) was formed in Mullingar'.[18] Reynolds in his memoir disputes this, writing 'No Midlands Pipers Club was formed as a result', but he interprets the discussions which took place as the 'embryonic' stage of Comhaltas' formation.[19] Published some forty years after the meeting, Reynolds' recollections, at odds with contemporaneous press reports, demonstrate the conflation of the Fleadh as an event with the establishment of a pipers club branch and the interpretation of the relationship between the two. What is certainly the case is that this meeting was the first formal meeting in Mullingar at which the new festival was discussed. The new Piper's Club committee announced after the meeting was, in practical terms, a Fleadh committee, as the Fleadh was the only activity at this juncture. The assemblage also established a binary administrative architecture for the Fleadh, between the local committee and the national one (which became a Comhaltas national committee once the organisation was formally established). The local branch committee was, in effect, in charge of Fleadh operations and programme delivery. Also important is the shift in language; rather than club, new branches were formed, indicating the aspirational growth ahead. As was common practice across cultural organisations at the time in Ireland, a cleric, Rev. Dr Kyne, bishop of Meath, was appointed as patron of the branch.[20] Other officers announced were chairman, Very Rev. E.A. Crinion; vice chairman, Very Rev. Brother O'Farrell; and regular members, Rev. Fathers Dermody and O'Connor; Rev. Brothers Redmond and Dunne; Superintendent P. O'Sullivan; Cáit and Éamon Uí Mhuineacháin; Philip Mullaly (Feis Lár na hÉireann secretary); and, lastly, Seán O'Donoghue. The extended roll call of clerics found on this first committee was not repeated in subsequent committee formations, but the Fleadh retained the practice of having a cleric as a patron for many years. Many of the appointed clerical committee members were teaching staff at local schools and some were involved in the Feis Lár na hÉireann committee; other than Dermody, none are subsequently mentioned as having any active role in organising the Fleadh in Mullingar.[21]

The chief proposal approved at the auspicious 1951 February meeting was to hold a competition-festival (variously titled a Fleadh or Comhdháil in different advertisements and press reports) at Whit weekend, with its aim 'to restore to its rightful place the traditional music of Ireland and to arrest the decadent trend evident today in Irish life'.[22] The ever-present danger of the 'decadent trend' was reiterated in the years that followed.[23] At the suggestion of local Gaelic League members present at the meeting, it was agreed to hold the event in conjunction with Feis Lár na hÉireann, which was 'a leading event in the Gaelic circles in the midlands and always attracted a big attendance'.[24] Primarily, the new local organisation, technically still a sister branch of the piping organisation, wished to encourage the performance of Irish traditional music, the 'authentic' music of Ireland and, while doing so, would combat the encroaching, dangerous and modernising other. As part of the proposed festival of music in Mullingar, musicians would be drawn from all over Ireland: 'pipers, fiddlers and a host of traditional musicians, singers and dancers from the four provinces of Ireland will be present as the spearhead of the revival of our Irish culture'.[25]

As the festival was being run in parallel with Feis Lár na hÉireann, it was clarified that 'competitions for traditional music will be organised in conjunction with the local feis committee'.[26] Some later reports credited only the feis committee for organising the additional activities under the banner of the Comhdháil, such was the lack of clarity separating the two, at least in the public eye.[27] When it came to organising the Fleadh festival of traditional music, it was three locals who played the most active roles: wife and husband, Cáit Uí Mhuineacháin and Eamon Ó Muineacháin, and Philip Mullaly. All three were Irish-language enthusiasts, active members of the local branch of the Gaelic League and heavily involved in Feis Lár na hÉireann administration. In 1951, Mullally was secretary of the local Gaelic League branch. He was hoping the add-on value of the Comhdháil to Feis Lár na hÉireann would ensure that Feis Lár na hÉireann would 'surpass even the highest standards of pre-war years'.[28] Such was the enthusiasm for the project of running both events together that the Feis also added more traditional music competitions to its own roster of activities. The peculiar situation arose where, as part of the Fleadh-Comhdháil run by the Mullingar branch of the Pipers Club, there was uilleann pipe, fiddle and flute competitions (as well as others), but later that week, as part of Feis Lár na hÉireann, the *Midland Herald* reported, 'this year sees the introduction of a new feature in the way of competitions in the flute, whistle, accordion, fiddle and pipes – the common instruments of our countryside – in an effort to stimulate interest in our traditional music'.[29]

The *Midland Herald* further declared that the Fleadh would offer the 'successors of the Irish bards' an opportunity 'to congregate for the first time in two hundred years to inaugurate what is hoped to be a new era of Irish culture'.[30] The invocation of the bardic festivals connected the new festival to a past when music held high status within the social hierarchy: the *Irish Weekly Glasgow Edition*, on 29 April 1951, describes the Fleadh as an 'attempt to revive in Ireland the traditional bardic festivals'.[31] Evoking past customs and practices lent authenticity to new practices, suggesting that it was not new at all, circumventing the cultural suspicion that modern or innovative modes of engagement may have prompted. The utilisation of the past to legitimate the present provides symbolic support, creating authority in the new festival.[32] Traditional musics are particularly adept at deploying the past to embed authenticity in contemporary and future projects. The Fleadh in Mullingar is, in Paul Ricoeur's terms, a 'time of initiative', when 'the weight of history that has already been made, is deposited, suspended and interrupted, and when the dream of history yet to be made, is transposed'.[33] That the imagined music of the bards had little musical connection to traditional music practice in 1951 mattered less than the cultural authentication it provided for participants in the new revival. The harping tradition of the bards had suffered a cultural rupture during the turbulence of the seventeenth century in Ireland. Eighteenth-century harp festivals occurred at a time when the older harping practice they were celebrating, or commemorating, was already decimated. In the minds of music revivalists in 1951, a comparable rupture had occurred in Irish traditional music practice since the 1900. While the practice and repertoire of the music of this particular revival had never been the primary domain of the aristocratic orders, there was a fervent wish that it would become the dominant musical practice of the Irish nation across social groups. The belief was that this music could once again have widespread popularity, be held in high esteem and take its rightful place to the fore of Irish cultural life. For these supporters and practitioners, popular interest was not antithetical to authentic practice or integrity. Rather, the Fleadh was the Trojan horse to achieve that popularity.

The initial announcement of the new traditional music festival in 1951 identified the most immediate and pressing need, to create an opportunity for musicians to come together and play music.[34] Those opportunities would create festival communion, a key function and product of any festival.[35] Given the decline in performance platforms available to musicians over the previous decades, this was not surprising. The committee aspired to provide a variety of contexts in which music might be performed, both formal and informal. Specifically, this could be realised through concerts and céilithe at the first festival in Mullingar, with competition only mentioned briefly at the end of the press release. The final strategic element at the inaugural festival was to provide an academic convention where 'prominent speakers' would respond to a formal paper.[36]

Though the term Fleadh was used descriptively in various press accounts, the festival was announced in an open letter from Mac Connaic to all Cumann na bPíobairí members in 1951 as 'Comhdháil is Siamsa na gCeoltóirí' (Convention and Amusement of the Musicians).[37] Comhdháil, variously translated as 'convention', 'congress' or 'conference', foregrounds the studious element of the event, which Mac Connaic underscored. Concerts each night and a late-night céilí mór provided additional performance and engagement opportunities, the siamsa of the title.[38] In 1952 and 1953, 'National Festival of Traditional Music, Sean-Cheol na hÉireann' (Old Music of Ireland) was the headline title for Comhaltas' flagship event, but 'Fleadh' was also used to describe the event. By 1954, when Cavan was the venue, the festival had developed a recognisable public identity and the term Fleadh Cheoil na hÉireann or All Ireland Fleadh was used consistently in publicity for the festival that year. The latter was a term used in 1951 by Mullally in only one press release when he suggested that the Fleadh was 'an All Ireland final of musicianship', utilising the language of its sister organisation, the GAA and in Peroy A. Scholes' terms, 'harnessing of the spirit of sport to the chariot of art'.[39] The use of 'All Ireland' in the title situated the Fleadh in a national context, all the while remaining connected to the local through the sequence of small town locations, a fundamental part of the Fleadh festive experience.[40] Furthermore, as Sean Williams notes, 'All Ireland is not only inclusive of all of Ireland (both the Republic and Northern Ireland) but is also inclusive of people outside of Ireland'.[41] Beginning in Cavan, the All Ireland event was truncated in popular (and sometimes formal) discourse to the colloquial 'Fleadh', which became a signifier, both externally and internally, for and with, what Victor Turner terms a particular set of festive properties.[42] At the Fleadh these properties were centred on traditional music, specific modes of staging and presentating and an association with 'a particular physical and cultural environment'.[43]

FLEADH PROGRAMME

The first Fleadh ran on Sunday, 13 May and Monday, 14 May 1951, operating in practical terms as an opening pre-event for Feis Lár na hÉireann, the Gaelic League sponsored competition-festival that continued for two full weeks after that. The two events shared an opening public parade on Whit Sunday when 'members of the Cumann na bPíobairí in their tableaux as exhibited in the Saint Patrick's Day parade in Dublin' marched along the streets of Mullingar.[44] The importance of the tableaux is emphasised through reference to its prior outing in the capital. The implication is not that Mullingar was second best, but every bit as good as Dublin. The parade and tableaux (a costumed, representative cultural and/or historical scene) as recognisable elements of generalised festival format are notable; both activities are part of the active mode of festival experience.[45] They have an obvious structural function but are also part of a process of signification which happened at the Fleadh (see pp. 40–6). Other headline cultural events were also double-listed as part of the parallel Fleadh and Feis Lár na hÉireann schedule such as the cuirm cheoil (concert) and céilidhe mór, at which music was provided by members of Cumann na bPíobairí.[46] The performance 'of the massed musicians of Ireland' at both these functions on 'truly, a great day for the Gaels of Ireland as well as the Midlands', was simply 'proof that Ireland is very far from being "in the grave"'.[47] Here, the explicit assertion of both local (the midlands) and national (Irish) importance speaks to the delicate, but essential balance commonly found in festive narratives and encounters.[48]

The Fleadh weekend also hosted a convention: a meeting of those interested in Irish traditional music that took place on Sunday, at 3 p.m. in St Mary's Hall. The centre piece of the convention was a formal lecture presentation on 'Irish Music in Irish life' to be delivered by C.J. Harwood, D.Litt. (the honorific is always included) and to which 'prominent members from other national, cultural bodies' were scheduled to speak and respond.[49] It was hoped the inclusion of a formal paper would 'encourage the study of traditional music and folk tunes', an end to which the piping branch declared itself committed.[50] Not coincidentally, inviting scholars to 'lecture on the art and to debate the present state of traditional Irish music' could evoke enthusiasm for the project of regeneration and revival.[51] As it happened, Harwood was unable to travel to Mullingar and the paper was read on his behalf by Seán Óg Ó Tuama, a key figure of the Gaelic League and 'principle organiser of the choral movement An Claisceadal'.[52]

For any music festival, the programming of concerts is paramount. Though technically mid-way through the festival, the *cuirm cheoil* was declared a 'grand finale' scheduled for Sunday night of the Fleadh weekend.[53] The programme details illustrate a diversity of practice with traditional and not-so-traditional performers listed. Included in the line-up were Leo Rowsome, uilleann piper; Máire Ní Sheaghe, harpist; Leo Maguire, baritone; and Seán Óg Ó Tuama, also singing, but in Irish and in what was understood as a traditional style.[54] The diversity of styles and repertoire represented by these 'distinguished artistes' speaks to the reality of music practice and reception in Ireland at the time.[55] Traditional music repertoire and practice overlapped with popular practice, particularly through singing and in this way engaged with popular culture. The inclusion of Leo Maguire in the concert line-up is a case in point. A baritone singer, composer and broadcaster, his famous sign-off on his long running radio show on RÉ, *Walton's Programme* (1952–81) was, 'if you feel like singing, do sing an Irish song'.[56] Sponsored by the Dublin music shop Waltons, the show was a platform for popular Irish song. Among other songs, Maguire composed 'The Dublin Saunter' made famous by actor and performer Noel Purcell. In his youth, Maguire trained operatically with one of Count John McCormack's teachers, Vincent O'Brien, and was far removed in vocal style from traditional singing. Yet, he was one of the principal acts at the *cuirm cheoil* in Mullingar in 1951. In this case, the 'Irish' celebrity media element overrode any taint arising from the popular or Western art music aspect of his performance, a classification that seems at odds with the ethos of the Fleadh, but one that persists at early Fleadh concerts (see pp. 65–8).

As noted, music competitions as part of the new event were understood as one of a suite of activities that complimented rather than dominated concerts and céilithe. In a letter to potential competitors in 1951, Mac Connaic, then secretary of CPU in Dublin, shed some light on the relationship between Feis Lár na hÉireann and the simultaneous Fleadh in Mullingar.[57] He advised competitors to obtain entry forms for the Fleadh from the honorary secretary of the Feis committee in Mullingar (Mullally), as it was that committee that would administer all the competitions for the Fleadh. However, he also requested that members of CPU would return a detachable slip to him from the letter of promotion received, signalling their intent to attend.[58] This was a double-edged request. The unprecedented nature of the event meant that organisers wished to have some predictability on numbers attending for logistical reasons. Failure to return the slip of intent directly to Mac Connaic allowed him to make a direct plea to the member in question, urging attendance in Mullingar.

By 1951, such was the crucial importance of competitions at feiseanna, the Oireachtas and other similar, if sporadic, events, that there was an expectation for competitions to take place at any comparable cultural event.[59] Once the events of the Fleadh were over, Feis Lár na hÉireann instrumental and singing competitions continued, in addition to 'the usual heavy list of literary and drama competitions'.[60] Sporting fixtures were also a recurring feature of any local feis. In Mullingar, hurling and Gaelic football Feis Lár na hÉireann cup finals took place, which drew large crowds to Cusack Park, the local GAA field.[61] Local rivalries were played out on the pitch, giving 'a thrilling exhibition'.[62] Mullally predicted that it would take a full fortnight to conclude the Feis given the highest rate of entry since its inception: the *Westmeath Examiner* reported there were over 160 entries alone in the Feis dancing competition.[63]

Over the course of the previous fifty years, competition had become an essential intra-community tool of ascribing worth to Irish traditional musicians and the broader community of practice. This occurred during the twentieth century to many traditional and folk musics well beyond Irish borders, frequently intersecting with moments and movements of revival.[64] In the Irish context, this increase in status was also projected outward towards wider Irish society through newspaper reports and broadcast opportunities. The platform of competition was therefore an inevitable inclusion in the opening festival of the new Fleadh, as a music-focused event.

## COMPETITION CATEGORIES

A total of thirteen open competitions were run as part of the the joint Feis-Fleadh initiative on Whit weekend and 130 competitors took part.

Open competitions allowed entrants from near and far to compete, without restriction. The competition categories were as follows: piano, under 10 (u10); piano (u13); violin (u13); fiddle; senior pipes; intermediate pipes; junior pipes; flute; accordion; flageolet; violin and pipes duet; war pipes; and céilí bands. The *Midland Herald* applauded the introduction of these new competitions on what it described as 'the common instruments of our countryside', referring to fiddle, uilleann pipes, flute, accordion, flageolet and war pipes.[65] The same report acknowledged, again with some confusion, the role of the local piping club, and its Fleadh, in boosting entries, from 'places as far distant as Dublin, Belfast, Galway and Ennis'.[66]

The new branch of CPU's published list of objectives included the revival of an Irish harping tradition, yet there is no explicit mention of harp within any of the competitions in 1951, nor had Feis Lár na hÉireann previously included competitions for harping. An obvious explanation for the harp's omission was that, in 1951, the harp did not have a place within the world of traditional music practice comparable to flute, or fiddle, or uilleann pipes. Historically, the harp was an instrument of the aristocratic Gaels and maintained that elite association long after the demise of that patronage in the seventeenth century. The lingering, last gasp of the Gaelic harping tradition was lengthened by patronage from various families of landed aristocrats (both New English and Old Irish) in the new social order of the eighteenth century, but even they could not prevent its inevitable passing. Irish harping underwent a renaissance, of sorts, during the nineteenth century, heavily inscribed with the weight of its Gaelic past symbolically, but on a vastly modified instrument, with an utterly different performance technique and new repertoire.[67] It took until 1953 before harp was introduced as a competition category at the Fleadh and, when introduced, found itself without any entrants until 1957: the Fleadh in Dungarvan had harp competitors for the first time (see pp. 89–94).

The other instruments listed for competition at the inaugural festival include instruments that were, in the main, core to the instrumental dance tradition in 1951. Uilleann pipes had multiple competitions, with senior, intermediate and junior level contests listed. This was a familiar template used within the sports competition structure of the GAA and the precedent for its use in performance competitions had also been set in feiseanna and at the Oireachtas in piping competitions. In his opening address, Rowsome explicitly stated, 'that they could not do better than model their beginning on the system adopted by the GAA and the Gaelic League'.[68]

Additional solo competitions in accordion and fiddle (the latter was won by Paddy Kelly, from Tyrone) are included, as well as an underage category of violin (u13). The violin and fiddle are organologically identical but, at the time of writing, the use of 'fiddle' typically denotes its usage within traditional music practice. Violin's inclusion here references the wider system of the Feis Association, which always included stylistically classical violin competitions, for example at the Feis Ceoil, Feis Shligigh and Feis Maitiú. Given the shared administration between both Feis Lár na hÉireann and the competitions of the Pipers Club, both being run under the umbrella of the Feis in 1951, the 'violin' competition is a familiar (and convenient) moniker, not implying classical repertoire performance at the Fleadh.[69] In the use of 'violin' as a competition category at the first Fleadh, there is also an intersecting suggestion of youth performance rather than established, adult fiddle players. The secretary of both events, Mullally, used the same title as would be found in many feiseanna, for convenience. Incidentally, his daughter was the winner of this competition.[70] Likewise, the inclusion of an accordion competition also reflects wider practice. Ideally suited to playing for dancers in larger venues, the accordion was on the cusp of developing a highly virtuosic style, to which the platform of the Fleadh contributed significantly. By the 1950s, the accordion (variously termed the button box, button accordion or, simply, box) was well embedded in Irish traditional music and ideally suited to céilí band ensemble playing. A particular style of playing developed in response to dancers' needs in larger performance spaces from the 1920s and this also informed solo styles of playing. Accordion stars were emerging on both sides of the Atlantic during the 1950s – for example a very youthful Joe Derrane in Boston, an equally youthful Joe Burke, from east Galway, and Joe Cooley, also from Galway. Others, such as Paddy O'Brien from Tipperary and George Ross from Wexford, held a high profile among the traditional music fraternity. The melodeon was the simpler antecedent to the larger accordion, and it too in much later years had its own Fleadh competition category.[71]

The inclusion of war pipes, as a solo competition at the first Fleadh of the newly formed organisation, is notable. Often termed bagpipes, the mouth-blown marching band variety of pipes resided (like the harp) in parallel to rather than at the core of vernacular Irish traditional music practice in 1951.[72] War pipes are limited in their melodic range in comparison to their uilleann pipes relation and commonly found in a pipe band ensemble capacity. In a solo context, war pipes frequently lead parades or, in the revival period, announced the commencement of cultural events, such as feiseanna and aeríochtaí (open air entertainments, often with a competition element). The 1951 Fleadh winner was listed as P. Dunne, from Mullingar, with the second place going to another Mullingar local, P. O'Connor.[73] Given the published Mullingar addresses of these winners, the inclusion of this competition can be understood as a facilitation of specific, local musicians, on whatever instrument they played, to encourage participation. During the first decade of the Fleadh, as competition categories were developing, this practice of having competitions specifically tailored to local musicians continued to occur. In 1952, James Carolan, of Drumbrain House, Newbliss, County Monaghan had his war pipes 'overhauled and tested' in anticipation of the upcoming Fleadh to be held in Monaghan.[74] In 1957, the inclusion of a competition for orchestra, with only one competitor from the Mercy Convent in Dungarvan, the host site, was for the same reason.[75]

Flageolet is not a term in common usage within current traditional music parlance. In 1951, in Mullingar, it refers to a tin whistle.[76] Convention called for 'flageolet' to be used in formal or semi-formal contexts to describe the ubiquitous tin whistle but, adding to the lack of clarity, occasionally refers to recorder, or even piccolo. Many primary schools had a flageolet (tin whistle) band at that time. Áodán Ó Muineacháin surmised that it sounded more impressive to say 'we have a flageolet band in our school' rather than a tin whistle band and, in this way, flageolet adds status to the enterprise.[77] The tin whistle and flageolet confusion continued for many years to come, sometimes listed as separate instrumental competitions, when in fact they were one and the same instrument at the Fleadh. The flageolet competition in Mullingar, like many of the competitions at the first Fleadh, did not have age limiters. Records show that local competitor Hubert Magee, aged ten from the host town, came first, while P.T. Jordan was runner-up.[78] Jordan was principal teacher of the national school in Kilbeggin, just 20 kilometres from Mullingar.[79] Magee eventually became band leader of the Mullingar Brass and Reed Band, a position he held for over fifty years.[80] Jordan had a flageolet band in his school, which he regularly brought to competitions when the opportunity arose.[81]

The limited, local entry to some of the competitions was in contrast to the uilleann pipes competition, where winners were listed from Dublin (for example, Jim Seery, a member of Cumann na bPíobairí Uilleann), and County Clare (for example, Willie Clancy, who was first prize winner in the senior pipes). Clancy, one of the premier uilleann pipers of the twentieth century, was in regular contact with Leo Rowsome and the other members of CPU.[82] In all likelihood, it was at their invitation that he attended Mullingar. The runner up in that particular competition was the aforementioned Reynolds, coincidentally local.[83] Reynolds later wrote one of the few published first-hand accounts of the early days of Comhaltas.[84]

There were two ensemble competitions included in 1951: fiddle and pipes duet, and céilí band (see pp. 78–80 for a discussion of the céilí band competition). Though traditional music practice was historically a predominantly solo tradition, there was, since the early twentieth century, a precedent set in Oireachtas and at feis competition forums for duet playing. During the first half of the twentieth century, traditional musicians enthusiastically adopted the form at competition and concert venues. In addition, the dissemination of duet recordings, recorded in the USA and Great Britain during the 1920s and 1930s, also popularised the duet format.[85] The fiddle and pipes competition is also listed in some reports as a 'violin and pipes' contest, demonstrating the fluidity and slippage of language as some Fleadh elements were still in flux in this first iteration of the festival.[86] The winners of the duet competition in Mullingar were Kathleen Harrington on fiddle and the aforementioned Clancy on uilleann pipes. Each of these musicians also featured in the solo competitions. Harrington was a member of CPU, like many of the participants at the Fleadh.

Duet playing allowed the integrity of individual musicianship to be maintained, in a way in which céilí band playing was less likely to accommodate. Regardless of Seán Ó Riada's comparison of céilí band playing to 'the buzzing of a blue bottle in an upturned jam jar', céilí band playing has at its core an integrative aim to play for dancers, functionally distinct from the duet performances, and so was not aspiring to the heterophonic model.[87] The listed winner of the first céilí band competition as part of the new Fleadh was the Athlone B Céilí Band. As with several of the other competition results, a tie for runner-up was recorded between another local céilí band from Athlone, Gentex Athlone, and Ballinamere, from Tullamore, County Offaly. Gentex Athlone is telling in its naming. General Textiles (Gentex) was a textile industry in Athlone, and indeed the main employer in the area from 1938 to 1984, when it finally shut its doors. At the height of its trading, Gentex had over 1,200 employees and the factory had a lively social club, including a theatre space attached to the factory complex. The nomenclature of céilí bands in Ireland and England commonly emphasises the locality from which the band members come. For example, the Kilfenora Céilí Band, the Leitrim Céilí Band (actually from Leitrim, County Galway) and the Liverpool Céilí Band are place-making, locationary names and represent those places, both musically and culturally.[88] In an industrialised twist, identifying the cultural habitus of the factory floor (Gentex) as a social and cultural domain in Ireland, as well as Athlone (the local place), the céilí band title achieves double place positioning.[89]

## MULLINGAR: A FLEADH TEMPLATE

Following the success of the festival in Mullingar, and in particular the enthusiasm expressed for the event to become an annual one, CPU called a meeting to discuss, among other things, future festival plans. The meeting was scheduled to take place immediately after the annual Gaelic League Oireachtas in Dublin on 14 October 1951. Members of the Feis Lár na hÉireann committee and CPU assembled at CPU headquarters on Thomas Street and all present committed to continuing the campaign for Irish music revival through the new organisation that was formalised at the meeting.[90] In addition to the Rowsomes, Willie Reynolds recalls Paddy Maunsell, Jim Seery, Eamonn Ó Muirí (Eamonn Murray) (Monaghan), Art Mac Connaic (Arthur Connick), Brother Redmond, Paddy Kelly (Donegal), Michael McCarthy (Tipperary), Willie Hope, and husband and wife, Eamon and Cáit Uí Mhuineacháin

(Westmeath) being in attendance at the post-Oireachtas assembly.[91] Various private discussions that had taken place since the Fleadh in Mullingar bore fruit in a decision to launch a national movement of music revival. Cáit Uí Mhuineacháin was named as chair of Cumann Ceoltóirí Éireann (Fellowship of Musicians of Ireland), a name proposed by Éamon Ó Muineacháin, seconded by Tom Rowsome and adopted by the members present.[92] The name of the organisation was subsequently changed to Comhaltas Ceoltóirí Éireann at a further meeting on 13 January 1952, hence the dating of Comhaltas' formation to that date in many histories.[93] The locations of Fleadhanna to come in the next two years were announced: the 1952 festival would be held in Monaghan, and the following year it was scheduled to be held in Galway.[94] As events transpired, the 1953 festival was not held in Galway, but returned to County Westmeath and took place in Athlone.

The infrastructural foundations, laid in the first year of the festival, were the basis on which subsequent Fleadhanna developed. Hosting the Fleadh at Whit weekend became the annual practice. This worked in several respects. A festival depends upon seasonal consistency, creating an expectation among the attendees and then fulfilling it.[95] By quickly establishing the Fleadh Cheoil as a two-day Whit weekend event at the beginning of the summer, it allowed participants to make plans to attend, well in advance if they wished and from year to year. Additionally, for those in rural areas involved in farming, this was a seasonal window of opportunity right before the heavy summer duties began in earnest. Designated national holidays occuring on a Monday, such as was (and is) the case with Whit, made little difference to farming duties, but the wider occupational shift to a business-based calendar was reflected in the timetabling of the Fleadh.

Whit weekend had the bonus of being a shared holiday with Britain. The constituency for the Fleadh quickly expanded to include returning émigrés, particularly from England. The opening Fleadh piggybacked on the previously established Feis Lár na hÉireann, but Fleadh goers and organisers adopted the weekend as their own signature time, to great advantage. The imperative to hold the Fleadh at the same time each year was further emphasised by the fact that it would be in a different location each year (see Fig. 1). The Fleadh developed an expectation of moveability as part of its identity and created that expectation among attendees. This motility is unusual in a transnational festival context. Festivals rarely move location every year and, in fact, rely upon consistent place identity to build and bolster a festival's own success and identifiability.[96] The mobility of the Fleadh meant it did not develop a 'unique place-based socio-musical identity', tied to one place; rather its mobility resulted in an increased emphasis on a multi-locationary identity and increased emphasis on other structural invariants.[97]

The success of any festival depends upon establishing structurally invariant components, which are then balanced by spontaneous experiences. Fundamental invariant elements of the Fleadh were established in Mullingar: modes of music making such as competitions, concerts and céilithe, together with parades. These elements reflect both international and historical models of (music) festival, but were manifest in an Irish context, with particularities of time and place. Mac Connaic's urgent plea to musicians and the public, 'to play your part', was realised in the success of Mullingar, prompting the agreement to host the festival annually.[98] At the convention in Mullingar, Eamon Ó Muirí proposed, and it was agreed, that his home county, Monaghan, would host the Fleadh in 1952.[99]

From its beginnings in 1951 in Mullingar, the Fleadh entered a phase of development as it made its way over the next few years to Monaghan, Athlone and Cavan, and, in 1955, to Loughrea, all the while consolidating and building upon the Mullingar template. During this period, particular elements gained special significance, creating a structural and symbolic framwork of what a Fleadh should be. Part of that process was also leaving behind elements deemed no longer strategically useful or of value. The next chapter examines those elements during this period of the Fleadh story, focusing on becoming a Fleadh, from 1952 to 1955.

CHAPTER 3

# Becoming the Fleadh, 1952–5

Accepting Mullingar as the foundational Fleadh, it was followed by a period of Fleadh development as the festival wended its way through Monaghan (1952), Athlone (1953), Cavan (1954) and onto Loughrea (1955) in the subsequent years. The focus of this chapter is this period of Fleadh becoming, as the structure and identity of the Fleadh grew, bolstered by the expanding branch network of Comhaltas and increased public interest.[1] Branch activities at local level took place throughout the year; the Fleadh was the annual pinnacle of those endeavours. In this way, the Fleadh and branch network built a reciprocal relationship, mutually nourishing during these years. The festival motivated the formation of new branches, the expansion of established branches and, furthermore, encouraged festival attendees to become members of branches. Conversely, branches provided enthusiastic members to make the annual pilgrimage to the Fleadh.

An editorial in *The Northern Standard* on Friday, 30 May 1952 declared: 'Something was going take place in Monaghan town this weekend that never took place in Monaghan before. Something is going to happen that has only happened once before, and that was last year in the town of Mullingar'.[2] The event was scheduled to take place at Whit Weekend on Sunday, 1 June and Monday, 2 June. It was advertised as a Comhaltas festival, titled 'Sean-cheol na h-Éireann' (old music of Ireland), with a subheading of fleadh cheoil'.[3] By 1954, the name of the festival was fixed as 'Fleadh Cheoil na hÉireann', which was quickly shortened, by those involved and attending, to the colloquial 'Fleadh'. In advertisements, branding was inconsistent up to 1954 and a sub-heading with the translation 'National Festival of Irish Music and Singing' was still deemed necessary in 1954.[4]

Eamonn Ó Muirí's proposal that the Fleadh be held in Monaghan in 1952 was agreed in principle at the Fleadh in 1951. Before the first national meeting of Comhaltas in October 1951, held at the pipers club on Thomas Street, a Comhaltas branch was formed in Monaghan.[5] Similar to Mullingar in Westmeath, Dublin-based pipers had an established relationship with musicians in Monaghan prior to 1951. Paddy McElvanny, a member of CPU, hailed originally from Threemilehouse, in County Monaghan. Though working in construction in Dublin, at the weekends he often filled his car with traditional musicians, heading to Monaghan and gathering at the house of Johnny McCarvill, a melodeon player and dancer.[6] Ó Muirí (musician, national school teacher, journalist and cultural revivalist) was frequently in attendance at these gatherings and was at the helm of nascent Comhaltas activities in Monaghan subsequently. He was elected national chair of Comhaltas in 1952. Given that the Monaghan Fleadh in 1952 was the first autonomous Fleadh festival hosted by the now established organisation Comhaltas, it was a rebeginning of sorts, as the Fleadh was launched as an independent festival of traditional music.[7]

A week in advance of the Monaghan Fleadh, the *Northern Standard* confidently reported that the work of organising was completed 'and the programme covering both days is now finally arranged'.[8] Familiar and successful elements of the previous year's festival were retained. Advance press emphasised some anticipated highlights:

> A paper on Irish traditional music will be read in St. Macarton's Hall, and prominent speakers will address the assembly. At 4.15 (approximately) the convention of the Comhaltas will commence, at which officers for the coming year will be elected and the progress and policy of the organisation will be reviewed.[9]

Additional details of the programme were outlined, all of which had been constituent elements of the previous year's event:

> The grand concert of the Comhaltas will also be held in St. Macarton's Hall commencing at 8.30p.m. on Sunday evening ... Besides instrumental music there will be a feast of traditional

singing and step-dancing. As a finale to the proceedings there will be a Céilíidhe Mhór [sic] in Swan Park Hall. The competitions commence in St. Macarton's Hall on the Monday morning at 10 a.m. and will continue throughout that day.[10]

The same report connected with local and national identities, as well as historical and contemporary music makers, by listing adjudicators from Belfast and Dublin, and recounting the genealogy of piping in Monaghan.[11] The iteration of local and national elements was vitally important to the emerging identity of the festival and an enunciating strategy that continued throughout the 1950s and 1960s. Organisers, and those writing press releases, sought to bolster local support and involvement while accentuating the importance of the festival to those beyond the local borders of the annual designated site. Declaring that performers would be drawn to Monaghan from the four provinces of Ireland serves this very purpose.[12]

### PARADES, PAGEANTS AND LECTURE PRESENTATIONS

Parades and pageants are common devices used in festive spaces globally, and both elements became enduring performative and symbolic vehicles of the Fleadh.[13] Parades are an opportunity for festival patrons to transition from the external everyday into the internal festive space, creating a sense of belonging and place identity.[14] A parade empowers participants, those parading and onlookers alike, to process into festival mode and it expands the imaginative possibilities of the Fleadh in much the same way as pageantry. Political and religious parades have a powerful history in Ireland – witness the monster political processions of the early nineteenth century, the centuries old parade tradition in Ulster, and the processional rituals surrounding the celebration of saints' feast days and other religious calendar days.[15] Those attending any festival in 1950s Ireland could reasonably expect a parade: the role of parade participant and patron was a culturally familiar one. In this way, participants fulfilled prescribed roles, secure in the cultural insider knowledge required. Furthermore, the security of that shared cultural knowledge facilitates specific interpretations for specific occasions. As the parade gained popularity as a Fleadh festival component throughout the 1950s, the annual particularities of parade performance became more and more exaggerated. Parades transformed the significance of the space, leading and walking the paraders and viewers into bounded Fleadh time.

The Monaghan Fleadh parade was scheduled at 2.30 p.m. as the opening event on Sunday, the first day of the festival. The procession was led by the town's St Macarton's Brass and Reed Band and, following close behind, local school children marched in uniform.[16] The parade in Monaghan, though in its infancy as a festival element, displays the binarism of local and national identities at the festival. Following the school children was 'a tableau of Cumann na Píobairí [sic] Uilleann and a body composed of musicians attending the festival' announcing the presence of the new national movement and visitors to the festival from beyond Monaghan.[17] The *Northern Standard* observed that 'the event evinced much public interest and despite the sporting attractions elsewhere, large crowds joined in the procession and lined the route, which was gay with flags draped from windows and spanned by arches bearing inscriptions in Irish'.[18] At the Fleadh in Cavan in 1954, a Comhaltas memorandum circulated to all branch secretaries beforehand reminded them that 'delegates and members of the Comhaltas branches are expected to take part, with banners' in the 'spectacular parade' with 'various aspects of cultural and social Ireland'.[19] On the day, among the participants were 'Old I.R.A. [volunteers marching] with children in Irish costume and athletes. Floats carried céilí bands from Cavan, Monaghan, Leitrim and Fermanagh'.[20]

The parade became, for many, part of the Fleadh festive experience. The Liverpool Céilí Band was invited to participate at the parade in Thurles in 1959. Billy Greenall remembered:

> We were on the back of a trailer that was pulled by a tractor. We were seated on forms (benches). Behind us in the parade was a pack of hunting dogs – beagles I think. One of the Kilgallon lads leaned down and was calling the dogs for devilment. The dogs surged forward and the tractor took off! The band was thrown off their forms and the instruments scattered all over. It was a scene of chaos![21]

**Fig. 3.1** Band of the Ceard Scoil, Cappawhite, County Tipperary at Fleadh Cheoil na hÉireann 1959, Thurles
Copyright Pádraig Ó Mathúna, courtesy ITMA

The line between participant and onlooker was at times blurred, with some crossing that boundary and moving between the two roles. At parades and processions, particularly as the march drew close to its final destination, onlookers were encouraged to fall into parading themselves.[22]

Fleadh parades had participants beyond the musical fraternity. As an event of local importance, floats and paraders from community groups, schools and businesses took part (see Fig. 3.1). Though the parade was not a consistent feature of the All Ireland Fleadh in the 1960s, it persisted at county fleadhanna until the end of that decade. Amateur film footage from the Clare county fleadh in Kilrush in 1963 shows the streets thronged with people at the opening parade.[23] The same parade retained an element of pageantry with local and national identities side by side: St Senan led the monastic representation. Senan is the principal saint of the locality, with monastic sites close by on Scattery Island. Further emphasising the local, following Senan was the Little Ark of Kilbaha, a wooden wagon that functioned as a portable church on wheels in the nineteenth century in west Clare.[24] Again, the line between paraders and viewers is blurred, illustrating the reciprocity of that relationship.

The parade could not be a parade without those looking on and those that are looked upon, dependent upon each other for success and festive fulfillment.

Pageants also featured at Fleadhanna. As paratheatrical outdoor events that narrate and streamline a shared history, pageants recreate scenes of political, folkloric and historical importance. In Ireland of the 1950s and 1960s, pageants as cultural performances were popular entertainments during the summer months. In May 1955, for example, a pageant in Croke Park drew 14,000 in attendance.[25] Like successful theatre productions, pageants were often produced multiple times for different occasions: the *Pageant of the Fenian Rising* was performed at a Munster senior hurling final before its outing at a later Fleadh in Enniscorthy in 1967.[26] Parades and pageants at the Fleadh overlapped as the parade destination was often the pageant site with pageant actors marching in the parade. This intersection of parade and pageant redoubled the experience of the onlookers and participants as they paraded down streets into the pageant performance zone.

The growing spectacle of the parade and an incorporated pageant as a festive key to the Fleadh properly came to the fore in Cavan in 1954. The planned pageant in Cavan included characters and representations such as 'Miss Éire and [her] attendants; the ancient Irish Grianán … fairies and leprechauns, all on suitably decorated lorries'.[27] Twenty marching bands ('pipers, brass and reed, fife and drum, harmonica') from Belfast and Dublin and elsewhere took part and 'floats carried céilí bands from Cavan, Monaghan, Leitrim and Fermanagh'.[28] In addition to the programmed participants, 'a special section [was] open to the general public, for which prizes [would] be awarded to the best Irish costume'.[29] In this way, the attendees were drawn into the pageant (and Fleadh) zone. A front-page report in the *Anglo-Celt* gave a lengthy description of the 1954 Fleadh pageant in Cavan and declared: 'This was real Ireland that reached back to our ancestors at Tara and beyond'.[30] The tableau presented was of 'Miss Éire, played by Mary B. Fox and the roles of her "attendants" [recurring characters in pageants of the period], played by Gertie and Vera Farrell':

> All three were dressed in traditional costumes and surmounted by a crown, each holding a golden harp. On the second float the

fairy queen presided over a gathering of fairies and leprechauns. Representation of a Grianán, an old Irish summer house, was on the third float. On the fourth and last, that of the Irish Countrywomen's Association, a tableau depicting an Irish cottage industry with Peggy Magee working busily at a spinning wheel was seen.[31]

Some pageant actors stayed in costume throughout the Fleadh, such as the Cavan singer Margaret O'Reilly, who remained in pageant costume for the whole Fleadh, in and out of competition.[32]

In 1955, when the festival was held in Loughrea, the *Irish Independent* reported that the pageant would be filmed in technicolour, and 'will present scenes from Irish rural life in the eighteenth century' with participants 'clothed to the last detail in authentic dress of the period'.[33] Material details of the costumery was vital to the recognition of the symbolic order of a pageant and in a wider sense the Fleadh itelf.[34] In Loughrea, six lorries fanning out at either side of a wooden platform for dancers were required to exhibit the pageant scenes.[35] It was performed with the bucolic backdrop of 'sparkling sunlight' and 'the lake and the hills beyond'.[36] In Ennis in 1956, *The Pageant of the Four Green Fields*, written by Bryan MacMahon, embraced 'ten historical scenes from the time of Cuchulainn to the men of 1916'.[37] It too had previously been performed at half-time in Croke Park on the occasion of the 1954 Meath–Kerry All Ireland football final.[38] At the production in Ennis, the cast was drawn from local schools and the historical tableaux included the anthropomorphic four provinces; once again, Miss Éire was personated. Interspersed with these figures from the distant past were contemporaneous 'Knights of Malta, Ambulance Corps and Red Cross units' from Ennis 'illustrating blood transfusion' and other medicinal scenes.[39] Personations and events galloped through select touchstones of national and local history, including:

> the coming of St Patrick, Pádraic Pearse and the kilted pupils of Scoil Éanna; J.P Holland, the Liscannor-born inventor of the submarine; the return of the Fransicans to their Ennis Abbey, which was burned and sacked by Cromwellian soldiers; the growth of the G.A.A.; saints from the Golden Age of Irish history; and soldiers from the days of Brian Ború down to the Irish volunteers.[40]

In Ennis, it was a balancing act between a national model of identity (St Patrick, et al.) and the needs of the local (John Philip Holland) in the ambulatory Fleadh. Holland, from Liscannor, County Clare, is remembered as the inventor of the submarine. The return of the friars to their abbey in Ennis after Cromwellian displacement performs the same function. These scenes vitally engaged local identity in tandem with the national one. Later, the *Pageant of the Fenian Rising* was amended for the Fleadh in Enniscorthy, County Wexford (in 1967) to include representations of Vinegar Hill, a Wexford site of the 1798 rebellion, and other local points of historical and social reference.[41] The core dramatic elements, in terms of the thematic content, are maintained throughout repeated productions, but the local aspect is adapted and customised through inclusion of characters of particular local resonance, as described above. The pageant and parade were key tools in place-making and place-marking local landscape in national histories.

Pageants in wider society were not without their critics. Of another MacMahon pageant in 1956, the pseudonymous Conchubhar believed 'Is beag suime atá ag muinter Bhléa Chliath Cúchulainn a fheiceáil ag pocléimininigh i bPáirc an Chrócaigh' (the people of Dublin have little interest in Cuchulainn leaping about in Croke Park).[42] Notwithstanding that view, MacMahon's pageants were repeatedly performed all over the country. For example, *Pageant of the Flag* was premiered at the opening of Countess Markievicz Park, in Sligo, in 1957.[43] The next year, it was performed in Longford at the Fleadh, and again in Croke Park the following year. MacMahon was a school teacher and dramatist, and the appeal of his pageant writing was unrivalled. A script for the *Pageant of the Flag* from the Croke Park performance is replete with detailed stage directions: 'As the band plays the "Bold Fenian Men", the Fenians led by Devoy and Rossa enter the pitch from Corner C and move as indicated on Diagram having saluted the flag as they pass'.[44] Musical direction is also provided ('bugle blast' and 'roll of drums to crescendo, cut suddenly') and three criers are instructed to recite a passage 'jauntily'.[45] Anew McMaster (1894–1962) was later cast in the role of St Patrick for the 1959 Croke Park performance of *The Pageant of the Flag*, demonstrating the continued ability of pageants to attract recognised actors to a pageant cast.[46]

MacMahon incorporated a mixture of new writing with familiar, popular songs in all of his pageants. It was a formula especially suited to a Fleadh, engaging and holding attention in musical ways. Given the large, outdoor canvas in which pageants were produced, using songs from the popular folk song repertoire (often termed ballads) enhanced the narrative and allowed onlookers to insert themselves sonically into the pageant plot. In the *Pageant of the Flag*, as it reaches its dramatic chronological climax of 1916, the first male crier character is directed to 'with sudden passion' declaim 'in the dungeon grim, with brave MacSweeney and with peerless Ashe, or the boy, Barry, walking smiling to his fate?'. As a 'muted drum roll' begins, two verses of 'The Ballad of Kevin Barry' are to be 'sung with feeling' and followed with 'drum beats in marching time to restore buoyancy'.[47] Importantly, using familiar ballads from the popular repertoire acted as an aural magnet for the audience, drawing them back into the storyline, along familiar musical paths, thereby reconstituting the sonic, symbolic order.

Pageants and parades at Fleadhanna ritually recreated a legendary past and aligned ancient with modern, reframing and reconstituting folk memory.[48] The historical incongruity of Miss Éire side by side with Peggy Magee spinning or, in the case of the Fleadh pageant in Ennis in 1956, Cuchulainn marching with the men of 1916, moved the past into the present and strengthened immeasurably the symbolic order of the Fleadh, which was then recognised and shared by onlookers and participants. When performing Ireland and Irish identity, pageants drew on multiple pastnesses simultaneously, producing, in Joan Fitzpatrick Dean's terms, an 'unfettered inclusivity', which allowed all to participate.[49]

Unlike parades and pageants that incorporated music practice, the Fleadh festival element of a formal lecture on traditional music was far removed from music making, The lecture presentation was instituted in Mullingar (1951) and programmed annually up to 1957. In 1958, in Longford, there was an informal symposium event, after which the scholarly component was discontinued for decades.[50] As early as 1955, the *Anglo-Celt* proudly declared that Comhaltas was not very 'interested in [traditional] music as an academic subject'.[51] Typically given as part of the first day of the festival at early Fleadhanna, the lecture presentation offered an opportunity to Comhaltas, as a cultural revival organisation, to articulate its emerging identity and fulfil its own stated aim of promoting the study of Irish traditional music. Including Harwood's

1951 paper (as noted, delivered by Seán Óg Ó Tuama) speakers and topics were as follows:

| 1951 | Mullingar | C.J. Harwood, 'Irish Music in Irish Life' |
| 1952 | Monaghan | Seán O'Boyle, 'Ancient Irish Music' |
| 1953 | Athlone | Eamon Ó Muirí, 'Traditional Music' |
| 1954 | Cavan | Kevin Danagher, 'Ancient Irish Traditional Music' |
| 1955 | Loughrea | Paddy Maunsell, 'No Mean Heritage' |
| 1956 | Ennis | Kevin McCann, 'Turlough O'Carolan' |
| 1957 | Dungarvan | E.M. Wyley, 'Our Native Music Beyond Compare' |

These lectures, and any real-time responses to them, could serve 'as a site of debate and allow a testing of ideological waters, which was a necessity for the embryonic organisation'.[52] The eminent speaker in Monaghan was Seán O'Boyle, a collector, teacher and broadcaster from Armagh, and such was the popularity of the event, 'hundreds were unable to gain admission'.[53] The *Northern Standard* promised:

> It will not be surprising to those who know him intimately, if Seán makes a new approach to the question of old Irish music. He certainly is not afraid to hit straight from the shoulder, and hard facts rather than sentiment will predominate his address.[54]

Of interest were not just the speakers, but would-be respondents. Among those anticipated to respond to O'Boyle's paper were Fr Eamonn O'Devlin, president of the Ulster convention of the Gaelic League, a bilinguist of 'mellifluous Gaelic of Ulster and English', and also Dr Brian Galligan, an early committed activist for Comhaltas, who later rose in the ranks of Comhaltas administration.[55] Full honorifics for the contributors and respondents were always included, ascribing status to the proceedings. But, as Fleadh years went on, speakers were more likely to be Comhaltas insiders (for example, Paddy Maunsell in 1955), illustrating an increasing disinterest in inviting external speakers to deliver lectures at the Fleadh. The timing of this drift away from academic concerns is not coincidental. As the Fleadh grew in stature and attracted more musicians and patrons, the primary focus of the Fleadh was on performance, whether in parades or pageants, competitions or concerts. Unlike parades and pageants, which contributed to the festive collective experience, the lecture presentations were only useful in these early years of Fleadh development. Additionally, Comhaltas' waning interest in hosting the presentations correlates to the strengthening of the organisation's enunciated self-identity. It was an identity that found its authoritative voice increasingly in competition and branch activities (and, importantly, the administration of those), with less concern for scholarly engagement with traditional music and less still for providing any context for provocative cultural debate.[56]

## PIPES, FIDDLE AND ACCORDION: COMPETITION EXPANSION

The yearly growth of the competition menu, from Monaghan in 1952 to Loughrea in 1955, reveals correlations between an instrument's inclusion in competition, its contemporaneous position in cultural practice (regionally or nationally) and its symbolic importance. During these years, in solo instrumental competition, uilleann pipes, fiddle and box were the bedrock of competition structures as the Fleadh was coming into being. In each of these instruments, additional age or grade-level competitions were quickly added (in Mullingar in 1951 uilleann pipes was the only instrument with multiple competitions). Over time, a Fleadh-specific template of age divisions emerged. By the fourth Fleadh in 1954, held in Cavan, senior, 14–18 years and u14 were the broad delimiters used. However, up to then, and beyond in some cases, other competition grades appeared and disappeared from year to year (intermediate, junior and adult beginners in uillean piping for example), as do particular competitions. Some competitions were advertised but, due to lack of entries, disappeared from the programme on the day. In all cases, there was a process of trial and error underway informed by local and national customised responses. Fleadh committees attempted to cast the net of participation to where they believed there was interest and capacity. It took a number of years for age demarcations to be systematically applied and even longer still to be consistently offered in solo competition beyond the core pipes – fiddle – box trifecta. Unlike in other instruments, in the case of fiddle and box there was an established and growing pool of performers across all age groups in cultural practice, and additional competitions were introduced to cater to that.

Decoupled from Feis Lár na hÉireann, the Fleadh in Monaghan (1952) added new competitions to the Fleadh roster and competitor numbers increased. The *Northern Standard* reported 163 entries, a substantial increase from Mullingar in 1951 when 130 competitors were recorded.[57] The *Monaghan Argus* reported a larger number; according to its pages, 200 musicians participated in competitions.[58] Notwithstanding the numerical discrepancy between dispatches, entry numbers in Monaghan were not muddied by any other competition system running in parallel, as was the case in Mullingar with Feis Lár na hÉireann. At the Monaghan Fleadh (1952), the greatest number of entries came from Westmeath and Monaghan, with a combined entry of 118: a second competition venue was added, such was demand.[59] Local interest was obviously high, not to mention the convenience of competing if you were from the area. General attendance was also boosted by the fact that the main competition day, Monday, was also coincidentally the monthly fair day in the town, 'bringing the rural people, who had an ear for the music'.[60] St Macarton's, the town's parochial hall, was the main venue for the Fleadh, but additional rooms were mustered at local schools for underage competitions. The success of the previous year in Mullingar was still reverberating in Westmeath and with increased activity of new, local branches of Comhaltas, this was reflected in that county's competitor numbers, which were boosted by the relative accessibility to Monaghan from Westmeath. In addition to local Monaghan and Westmeath competitors, contestants registered from Dublin, Galway, Antrim, Fermanagh, Tyrone, Sligo, Roscommon, Armagh, Cavan, Clare, Leitrim and Offaly.[61]

Uilleann piping and fiddling competitions dominated at the Monaghan Fleadh in 1952. Due to the high number of pipers and fiddlers in attendance, both open and closed competitions took place. Open competitions, as the title suggests, were open to anyone (typically, though not always, with age and/or ability limitations); closed (or confined) competitions were restricted to local competitiors, usually demarcated along county lines. Feiseanna, and other competition-festival precedents, had long used open and closed competition systems. Introduced for the first time in Monaghan, a closed competition afforded local musicians a greater chance of winning a prize without pitching themselves against visiting virtuosos and were introduced for the first time in Monaghan. Closed competitions were maintained at the Fleadh until the establishment of full provincial qualifiers in 1959 (Munster, Leinster, Connaught and Ulster). In 1952, in Monaghan, open uilleann piping categories included senior, intermediate, junior (u16) and beginner uilleann pipes. The importance of uilleann piping as central to the Fleadh enterprise cannot be overstated. The centrality of members of CPU in the establishment of the Fleadh guaranteed the uillleann pipes' place. Just as significantly, the cultural resonance of the uilleann pipes as an indigenous, authentic representation of Irish traditional music was key to the Fleadh's early identity. The importance placed on the revival of uilleann pipes, an instrument 'so entwined with tradition, story, legend and poetic fancy' in the declared foundational aims of Comhaltas, assured the primacy of uilleann piping within the competition structure.[62]

At the Monaghan Fleadh, a number of recalls were reported in the press. Recalls allowed adjudicators to call back competitors who had tied marks to perform again, so that a final arbitration might be made. Over the years, as the Fleadh developed and entry numbers increased, recalls became more frequent. Cathy Larson Skye notes that Dan Collins, a Fleadh judge decades later, called recalls not only for his own benefit, but also to provide the parents of underage competitors a chance to 'hear the standard'.[63] Narratives of recalls constitute an important part in the telling, and retelling, of the Fleadh experience (see pp. 144–8). The very presence of recalls suggests, from a performance perspective, an elevated standard, with competitors so close it is impossible to designate a winner without one more hearing. From a practical point of view, recalls point to the difficulty for any adjudicator to listen to a successsion of musicians playing different tune selections, in often widely different styles and to arbitrate fairly.

Familiar names in the canon of twentieth-century piping are listed in the 1952 senior competition roll-call of winners. Willie Reynolds (second place winner in Mullingar) and Seán McAloon tied for first place.[64] McAloon was a piper from Fermanagh, who later emigrated to the USA and lived the latter part of his life in Belfast. The previous year's winner, Willie Clancy, came second and was one of only two competitors registered from County Clare at the Fleadh that year.[65] The drawn piping result was finally reached after two recalls failed to distinguish a clear winner.[66] Perhaps most importantly, in the construction of a narrative

Fig. 3.2 Bobby Casey medal, Monaghan, 1952
Copyright Ben Taylor, courtesy Angela Casey

of Fleadh experience, recalls provided dramatic moments, filled with suspense, where musicians, adjudicators and listeners are all complicit in the musico-cultural drama playing out before their eyes (and ears). Reynolds and McAloon, despite two recalls, were ultimately awarded a tied first place, such was the impossibility of adjudicating between them on the day. Further examples in later Fleadh years confirm the importance of the recall narrative. The 'long count' which took place between Seamus Connolly and Brendan McGlinchey, in the senior fiddle competition, in Swinford, in 1961 is widely remembered. After four recalls, both competitors finally went home in the small hours, neither knowing who had won. In Connolly's account, he read the papers the next morning with the headline 'Fleadh crux resolved in small hours', and discovered, only then, that he had prevailed (see pp. 144–8).[67]

Solo competitions for fiddles and accordions mirrored the quantitative frequency of these instruments within the community of practice in the early 1950s. Fiddle competitions drew large numbers of entries in Monaghan (1952) with four competitions available, ranging from u14 to senior. In the senior open competition thirty-eight competed and Bobby Casey, listed as a Dublin musician (but a Clare musician in origin and style), took top honours (see Fig. 3.2).[68] (Another Clare fiddler, Paddy Canny, won first place the following year in Athlone.)

Casey emigrated to London later in 1952 and is a key figure in twentieth-century traditional music practice both at home and among the diaspora. A tie was announced for third place, this time between Billy Coleman, Patrick McGuinness (both from Monaghan) and Johnny Pickering from Armagh (better known for his accordion playing in céilí bands).[69] Coleman's prowess and the 'wee figairies' he put in his playing of the jig 'The Hare was in the Corn', was described in a front-page column the following week in the local *Northern Standard*.[70] In the u14 fiddle competition in Monaghan, a young Liam Rowsome (Dublin) tied with Maureen McCabe from Clones, County Monaghan. McCabe is later referenced in Robbie McMahon's ballad, 'The Fleadh Down in Ennis' (see pp. 103–21). An additional closed fiddle competition, for Monaghan fiddlers 'who never won a prize', completed the fiddle competition inventory and attracted twenty-one participants: John McKenna from Emyvale carried the day.[71] The competition events attracted competitors and a listening public. An editorial in the local press following the festival in Monaghan in 1952 remarked that 'from beginning to end the Festival was crowned with success'.[72] The report, evocatively titled 'The Soul of Music', commented that 'there was something about the competitions which made a deep impression … St. Macarton's Hall was densely thronged, not with mere sightseers but with people intensely interested and intensely enthusiastic'.[73]

Particular Fleadh competitions quickly developed a star-making capacity in traditional music, accordion being a prime example (competition titles in English never used the vernacular 'box'; from 1954 onwards, all competition titles were typically in the Irish language, in this case 'bosca cheoil' (literal translation, box of music).[74] The senior open accordion competition drew twenty-one entries in Monaghan in 1952.[75] In 1953, at the Athlone Fleadh, Paddy O'Brien (Tipperary) took the senior accordion title signalling a shift in accordion competition participation, but also in the reputational importance accruing from winning a title at the Fleadh. O'Brien came to the competition with a reputation already in the ascendent. He had recorded a number of sides with Bill Stapleton's Irish Recording Company in 1949 and was a rising star in a new generation of accordion players during this period. Winning at the Fleadh confirmed and augmented that reputation (a dynamic benefit also shared by Galway's Joe Cooley, who placed second to O'Brien that year). By 1954 in Cavan, a wide complement of accordion competitions was in place to accommodate the growing competitor base: u14, 14–18, intermediate, senior open and senior closed. Solo competitions were a site where up-and-coming stars made public competition debuts and the accordion competition attracted underage entrants often noted for their skill during a period when accordion playing developed a stylised, virtuosic public profile. Paul Brock, who came first in the u14 competition at the Loughrea Fleadh in 1955, was one of the winning performers 'to gain most acclaim' that year and 'displayed extraordinary virtuosity'.[76] Loughrea in 1955 was a bumper year for young accordion players who launched national profiles following their Fleadh wins. Joe Burke, from Kilnadeema, Loughrea, placed third in the 14–18 accordion category, with Brendan Mulhaire, from Eyrecourt, also in Galway, also placing. Accordions were fundamental to the céilí band sound of the period, but the emergence of a solo aesthetic in accordion playing during these years is indebted to intra-Fleadh exposure and competition-winning status too. The Fleadh and non-Fleadh worlds acted reciprocally in generating solo accordion (and other instrumental) stars.

## GROWTH OF COMPETITION PROSPECTUS

The prospectus of competitions evolved from year to year. Other solo competitions at the second Fleadh, in Monaghan, included senior flute, which Paddy Treacy (Galway) won and in which Vincent Broderick (Dublin, but originally from Loughrea, County Galway) placed second. Broderick went on to win the title the following year in Athlone. Though flute was central to Irish traditional music practice from the mid-nineteenth century onwards, 'the flute did not achieve the same level of prestige or popularity as pipes or fiddle' during that century or in the first half of the next.[77] This was for a number of reasons, including limited availability of suitable instruments and its low status historically among the artisan musical class.[78] Additionally, while found throughout the island by 1900, the flute had a regional bias, with a 'strong heartland in … Sligo, Leitrim, and Roscommon, with south Fermanagh, east Galway, Clare and West Limerick also having a reputation'.[79] The lone (senior) flute competition from 1951 to 1955 and its title winners reflect the reality of flute practice at that time. It may not have had numerous competitions, or high entry numbers, but this did not preclude the *Connacht Tribune* in 1955 from exalting the playing of the senior competition winner in Loughrea, Peter Broderick (Vincent's brother), who gave a 'magnificent recital' of his own composition 'The Thatcher's Mallet' reel, playing 'an instrument fashioned by himself from a two-foot length of copper piping'.[80]

In comparison, tin whistle competitions multiplied at a much faster rate than flute. At the Cavan Fleadh in 1954, the familiar u14, 14–18, intermediate and senior contests were already in place. The tin whistle's beginner instrument reputation, in conjunction with it being embedded in many primary school classrooms (either solo or in a tin whistle band) goes some way to explaining this. This is further supported by the fact that winning entrants in tin whistle at early Fleadhanna are frequently listed with a school's name, rather than with a parish or Comhaltas branch of origin.[81] In early Fleadh years, tin whistle is also an outlier as it is the only instrument that has burgeoning underage entrant lists, but few senior entrants. An important pattern of Fleadh participation in these early years is the proportion of adults who competed (the pipers as discussed and the Brodericks above, for example). These were established musicians or, indeed, those encouraged to begin playing and compete as part of the process of engaging with traditional music culture during this period of revival. This mirrors Irish dance competition participation during broadly comparable years, as remembered by Marie Philbin.[82] This pattern of competition participation changed in the years that followed at the Fleadh (and indeed, in the parallel dance world too) when increasingly, underage competitions attracted the bulk of entries and repeated participation by established adult musicians decreased.

In the ebb and flow of competition inclusion, some instruments came and went from year to year, or were jettisoned entirely. The inclusion of piano competitions (u10 and u13) in 1951 at the Fleadh in Mullingar was due to its perennial insertion in Feis Lár na hÉireann. Untethered from the Feis, there were no dedicated piano competitions at the Fleadh from 1952 until 1957, when it reappeared in Dungarvan. In the interim, piano players were welcome to participate in a miscellaneous instrument category, though there is little evidence to suggest that this occured widely. Also in abeyance in 1952 was the war pipes competition, though a reporter noted that Paddy Meehan (one of the Monaghan organising committee) was seen carrying a box throughout the weekend that contained a set of war pipes, which Meehan confessed he could not play himself.[83] The war pipes intermittently reappeared in competition, in 1953 in Athlone (where there were open and closed war pipes competitions) and again in 1955 in Loughrea. Its inclusion in the first Fleadh in 1951 was to accommodate specific performers, often local talent, and it was likely the same reason for its inclusion in Athlone and Loughrea. Supporting this conclusion, the closed competition in Athlone in 1953, for Westmeath competitors, had (at least) three competitors, all listed as from Athlone, as local as was possible.[84]

Repurposing of non-purpose built venues for the duration of the Fleadh contributed to the experience of the Fleadh as all encompassing and transformative event, with its own temporal reality. The widening appeal and growth of the Fleadh, and the proliferation of Comhaltas branches in the early 1950s, contributed to a growth in competitor base with the competition catalogue expanded to match the pace. The number of competitions greatly increased after 1953. In Cavan in 1954 there were over thirty competitions listed (including ballad singing for the first time), which necessitated the use of eight different venues.[85] This was in comparison to the single competition venue required in Mullingar in 1951. By 1955, at the Fleadh in Loughrea, twelve venues were in use.[86] Before the 1954 Fleadh began in Cavan, the *Irish Independent* projected that over 500 competitors would take part, including 100 fiddlers.[87] Schools, courthouses, town halls and tennis pavillions were pressed in to Fleadh venue service.

Increased numbers of competitions and attendees necessitated increased administration and local Fleadh committees were filled with local Comhaltas branch members. Additional volunteers and Comhaltas members from further afield were also called upon during Fleadh weekend. The blossoming number of committees and offical titles reflects the growing size of the Fleadh, but also the growing administrative body of Comhaltas. The opening credits in the 1954 Cavan programme list the array of officers and committees involved in the Fleadh and indicates the months-long preparation for the festival. The Cavan programme was exclusively in the Irish language (much of it without any translation).[88] Listed within its hefty pages were committee positions of president, chair, vice-chair, treasurer and secretary (there were three secretaries in total, including two auxilliary secretaries) and the coiste feidhmiúcháin (executive committee), which had twelve members, drawn from the local established Comhaltas branch. An original programme includes four additional hand written names on that committee.[89] Full credit is also given to the various sub-committees, including the coiste cuirm cheoil is céilí (concert and céilí committee), coiste an mhór-shiúil (parade committee), coiste na maisiúcháin (decoration committee), coiste proinn is fáilte (meals and welcome committee), coiste airgeadais (finance committee), coiste na fógraíochta (publicity committee), and coiste stiúraithe (adminstrative committee).

Ensemble competitions appear under the 'Bands section' in the Fleadh programme in Cavan (1954). Duets and céilí bands (both were present from the first Fleadh in Mullingar, 1951), and trios (introduced in 1952 in Monaghan, but absent in 1953 in Athlone) are listed, but there are new competitions for quartettes, war pipes band (no winner is reported in the war pipes band category, indicating there were no entrants and the competition did not run) and, lastly, fife and drum bands (a fleeting appearance, it vanished the following year). The trio ensemble category (often pronounced try-ohs by this generation of musicians) made its debut in 1952 at the Monaghan Fleadh: Paddy Brophy (pipes), his son Mick Brophy and Joe Ryan (fiddle) took the inaugural first place. Trios were part of the céilí social dance soundscape in the 1940s and early 1950s, sometimes performing at smaller céilithe. Tom Brophy recalled playing at céilithe as part of a trio with his father (Paddy mentioned above, originally from Roscrea, County Tipperary, but settled in Dublin), which subsequently became the Pat Brophy and Sons Céilí Band, later the Brophy Brothers Céilí Band.[90] There were no entries in the trio competition in Athlone in 1952, resulting in Cavan being the next time the competition ran, after which it became a standard inclusion. The new quartette competition in Cavan was won by 'McNamara and others' from Tulla. Chris Keane identifies the membership of the quartette, which was drawn from the ranks of the competing Tulla Céilí Band that year, as Joe McNamara (accordion), Paddy Canny (fiddle), P.J. Hayes (fiddle) and Martin Talty (piper and flute player from Miltown Malbay).[91] The quartette competition had a sporadic future ahead of it, though it gained entrants (and popularity) in the latter half of the decade. In subsequent years, age grades within these ensemble categories were demarcated, but in Cavan in 1954 all were senior grade competitions.

The question of mapping a cartography of origin for ensemble winners is complicated with membership of any ensemble often being 'more widely derived' that the attached placename on Fleadh programmes.[92] For example, the first place in the duet competition in 1954 went to Kieran Kelly and Vincent Broderick, who are listed in the Fleadh programme as being from the Gentex branch in Athlone. Kelly had his own successful céilí band and worked at Gentex, but Broderick was from Galway, then residing in Dublin with no connection to Gentex. Broderick bumped into Kelly the night before the competition and they were one among twenty-five duets to compete. For Broderick, 'it was a mighty competition to win'.[93] Misleading as the Gentex origin listing is, this frequently occured, with the understanding that those interested would have the local place attachment knowledge to fill in the gaps. In the early years of the Fleadh, when there were no qualifying rounds, musicians often met casually at the Fleadh and decided spontaneously to enter duet and trio competitions together, an occurrence frequently remembered by those interviewed for this project.[94]

Singing competitions were first introduced in Athlone in 1953, with just two competitions, one English language and one Irish language, neither age or grade defined. Beginning in Loughrea in 1955, further age grades were included. However, the delineations of singing competition used in 1954, at the Cavan Fleadh, remain the broader categories at the Fleadh today and were constructed along two axes, that of language and gender. The 1954 singing competitions in Cavan were recorded as ballads in English (ladies); ballads in English (gentlemen); traditional singing in Irish (ladies); and traditional singing in Irish (gentlemen). Whistling and lilting were also tacked on, under the general section of solo singing competitions, a reflection of the difficulty in finding a suitable place anywhere else for these performers. In Cavan, Paddy Tunney, a singer and latterly a noted song collector, took second place in the ballads in English (gentlemen) category and won the senior lilting title outright.[95] Tunney won the lilting title again in Loughrea the following year where William Zilliacus, visiting from Finland to record a number of radio programmes, 'was fascinated with the traditional airs, but particularly so with the lilting. He had not, he said, heard anything like it in his travels all over Europe'.[96] Aside from the fascination with lilting, Zilliacus' attendance at Loughrea speaks to the wider attention the Fleadh was attracting among folk-traditional communities outside Ireland (see p. 178). Also noted in attendance at Loughrea was Rolf Dietrich Nath, a German film maker, who declared 'Ah, this is what I searched for', upon his arrival at the Fleadh.[97]

The final listed competition in the programme for Loughrea was *tomhas port*, translating as tune guess or tune sample.[98] This was a competition that required the contestants to identify tunes by name from a selection of ten that were played for them. The competition is an oddity across the competitive spectrum at the Fleadh. It requires no performance and the skill being judged is one of aural familiarity with repertoire. More than that, it expects competitors to marry dance tune titles with the melodies of the tunes themselves. Given the local, even individual, differenciations in naming tunes, judging the winner of this particular competition brought its own challenges.[99] *Tomhas port* was an attempt on Comhaltas' part to include a competition that allowed non-musician traditional music connoisseurs to participate. There was an increasing number of people attending the Fleadh and many were listeners, not performers; this competition afforded them the opportunity to compete. Moreover, non-musicians were finding their way in to Comhaltas administration, performing essential roles as secretaries, treasurers and other official positions. The competition could 'accommodate the person who is a musician at heart, but does not play, sing or lilt'.[100] In fact, practising musicians were explicitly barred from participation in *tomhas port*.[101] This had a marked similarity to the rules governing participation in the 1925 Feis Athar Maitiú, which precluded native speakers from participating in the Irish-language competitions.[102] Whatever the motivation, while *tomhas port* was advertised as a competition in the programme, it does not appear in the post-Fleadh published list of prize winners, suggesting that the competition did not take place at all. Clearly, at least in 1954, the interest of non-musicians was not sufficiently piqued and *tomhas port* quietly vanished.

### NATIONALISING PRACTICE: MISCELLANEOUS INSTRUMENTS AND CONCERTINAS

The miscellaneous competition was first introduced at the Fleadh in 1953 in Athlone, though termed the 'instrumental solo' competition on the published programme that year.¹⁰³ From its inauguration, entry was confined to any instrument that did not already have its own dedicated solo competition. On introduction in 1953, the published Fleadh programme lists possible miscellaneous instruments including banjo, guitar, piano, piano accordion and mouth organ, none of which had dedicated solo competitions at that time. Kitty Linnane, piano accompanist with the Kilfenora Céilí Band competed in the 'Any instrument' competition in Loughrea in 1955, before rogha gléas (choice of/miscellaneous instrument) became the standard title in 1956, and was awarded third place; L. Ó Donnachadha from Oughterard, 'whose mouth organ playing was really brillliant' took top honours in the same year.¹⁰⁴ A surprise inclusion in the pantheon of possible miscellaneous instruments at the Loughrea Fleadh in 1955 is saxophone (though there is no record of whether any sax player competed).¹⁰⁵ The competition was a 'mix-em gather-em of any instrument that there wasn't a competition for'.¹⁰⁶

The edges of the miscellaneous competition were capricious. For Comhaltas and the Fleadh, increasing competition participation was central to the festival ethos. The Fleadh added (or sometimes eradicated) competition listings from year to year in response to previous years' participation and domains of cultural practice at local and national levels. Paddy Murphy, noted concertina player from Kilmaley, County Clare, recalled playing in and winning the miscellaneous instrument competition at the Fleadh in Cavan in 1954. He participated in the miscellaneous competition in the absence of a dedicated concertina competition that year.¹⁰⁷ A smorsgabord of pianos, banjos and piano accordians, Murphy declared 'the standard wasn't great' at the competition, though he believed 'there was an advantage to playing the concertina, it was the most likely instrument to play a few tunes'.¹⁰⁸ Though Murphy's assessment, that 'the standard wasn't great', is suitably humble regarding his own playing, the low standard of much in the miscellaneous category was widely agreed. Murphy was given a mark of 98/100, 13 marks more than the second placed winner.¹⁰⁹ This was, incidentally, the highest mark given at the Fleadh that year in any competition.

His belief that the concertina was a more likely instrument to win the miscellaneous competition is also true. The other instruments represented in the miscellaneous category had a peripheral place and could not be classified as core melodic instruments in the tradition in 1954. The concertina was well within the instrumental nucleus of Irish traditional music in Murphy's cultural world in County Clare. So ubiquitous was the concertina in that county that when Junior Crehan, as a young boy in the mid-1910s, saw the fiddle case of west Limerick dance master, Pat Barron, the following exchange took place: 'So I [Junior] asked what was in the box. He [Pat O'Connor] said, "A fiddle" and I said, "Is that like a concertina?"'.[110] Crehan had only seen concertinas up to then. His error reflects the primacy of concertina in County Clare, one of the acknowledged strongholds of traditional music and makes the omission of the concertina from the spectrum of solo instrument competitions all the more puzzling at this, the fourth, Fleadh. Murphy sheds some light on this when he recalls that 'there wasn't another concertina in Cavan that day, and the most of the crowd that day had never before seen a concertina. It was a novelty, a bit of a surprise with most of the crowd'.[111] While the concertina was a relatively common instrument in County Clare and neighbouring east Galway, at that time it did not have the widespread usage and familiarity of fiddle, uilleann pipes or box.[112] In 1956, when the Fleadh came to Clare, Seán Shéamais asked and answered his own question:

> *Dar ndoigh [sic], mara dtiocfadh éinne chun na fleidhe ach muintir an Chláir, bheadh ár ndóthain araon den spórt ann ... Bean an Chrotaigh as Cill Rois agus an concertina léi. Níor chuala tú ceol concertina riamh? Well, is sa Chlár a chloisfir é, gan aon agó.*
>
> (Of course, even if the people of Clare alone came to the fleadh, we would both have our fill of sport ... Mrs Crotty from Kilrush and her concertina with her. You've never heard concertina music before? Well, it is in Clare it will be heard, without a doubt.)[113]

There is no mention of concertina in newspaper reports about the Fleadh prior to 1954 and certainly no broad outcry at its exclusion. The lack of a formal concertina competition, up to and including 1954, spoke to the relatively localised history of the instrument as a purveyor of Irish music, gaining popularity only during the latter part of the nineteenth century and, even then, only in some parts of the country. Murphy was, it seems, the first concertina player to present themselves for competition at the

Fleadh; with nowhere else to compete, the miscellaneous instrument category was the only option in 1954.

Instruments could graduate from miscellaneous to their own, newly introduced, solo competition. A number of factors lead to a dedicated concertina competition being finally introduced in Loughrea in 1955: Murphy's resounding win in Cavan's miscellaneous competition the previous year; the establishment of a Comhaltas county board in Clare, the concertina heartland, in April 1954; and the planned location for the 1955 Fleadh, in Loughrea, County Galway, adjacent to Clare. Murphy remembers ten or eleven competitors participating in Loughrea.[114] Though mostly from Clare, Connie Hogan, from Woodford in east Galway placed second in Loughrea. In the decade that followed, the competition was dominated by Clare competitors and winners. In Dungarvan, in 1957, all listed competitors in the progamme were from Clare.[115] Murphy won three titles – Loughrea in 1955, Dungarvan in 1957 and Longford in 1958. Chris Droney, from Bellharbour, in north Clare, emerged as another star concertina player, coming third in Loughrea, but winning his first senior concertina title (of many) in 1956. In the early 1960s, Jimmy Connors, another concertina player from Clare, won several titles (1962 and 1963). Between 1955 and 1970, only one concertina title went east of the Shannon, to Waterford in 1968, when Theresa White came first. The template for a nationalised winning style was set by these early successes, so that, arguably, a suite of Clare styles of concertina playing became the model against which all competitors would subsequently be judged.[116]

The miscellaneous instrument competition was maintained as a convenient tool of inclusiveness. It allowed the Fleadh (and continues to allow at the time of writing) to encompass a wider pool of competitors (and instruments) in solo competition, without ascribing the importance of a dedicated competition and the authenticity implicit in that. As in the case of concertina, other instruments graduated to their own competition slot. In 1957 a competition was introduced for mouth organ, which had previously languished in miscellaneous limbo. However, instruments that operated in some undefined nether space at the edges or outside of tradition continued to be accommodated in the miscellaneous category, awaiting annointment with their own competition.

## BECOMING A COMPETITION: CÉILÍ BANDS, 1952–5

In any discussions of traditional music during the twentieth century (and, indeed, since), the prevailing popularity of céilí bands looms large. The phenomenon of ensemble bands playing for dancing in built public performance spaces beginning in the early twentieth century is a response to social and cultural transformations of the period. The shift of dance from the domestic to public domain was not peculiar to Ireland, but rather a transnational phenomenon, with local particularities.[117] In the case of Irish cultural life, the consequences on traditional performance practice were played out in Ireland and also abroad among large diasporic communities in Britain, the USA and elsewhere. The shift from dancing at home to dancing in parochial halls, dance halls and marquees was inevitably transformative and not without challenges. Junior Crehan lamented:

> So, they barred the country house dance, and the priests was erecting parish halls ... the country house dance was knocked out then ... Then the emigration started. A lot of lads I used to play with went off to England and America, and there was no one but myself, Scully [Casey] was dead, and I used to go down the road, and I used ... Honest to God, I used to nearly cry. Nowhere to go, no one to meet, no sets in the houses. Nothing left but the hall.[118]

It is in this context that céilí bands took hold in Irish traditional music practice and were among the necessary material responses to larger public gatherings for dancing that reformed frameworks of social and cultural engagement.[119] By 1950, the céilí band genre was woven into the fabric of traditional music practice and socialisation structures in many parts of Ireland. It is no surprise then that céilí band competitions were embedded in the Fleadh from the outset in Mullingar (as discusssed in the previous chapter). In 1952, at the second Fleadh, the Williamstown Girls Céilí Band (a céilí band from Galway, put together by music teacher Leo Beirne) was announced as the winner, with Bellaghy Green Cross Céilí Band from Derry coming in runners up.[120] Both bands had previoiusly broadcast on RÉ (the Williamstown band was broadcast in 1951, on the basis of a feis success) and the Bellaghy band broadcast again on the national radio airwaves the week after their Fleadh appearance.[121]

Beginning in 1953, continuing to today, the céilí band competition has the highest profile of any Fleadh competition and is, in many ways, the climax of the Fleadh.[122] The 1950s saw a significant expansion of the cultural importance of céilí bands in the non-Fleadh cultural world. The dynamic relationship between the senior céilí band competition at the Fleadh from 1953, the mediation of céilí band sounds on radio and through recordings, and the popularity of céilí bands in the wider social milieu was a complex cultural web. Within a few short years, the competition established itself as a distinctly important part of the Fleadh, informing ceílí band culture outside the competition environs, in the non-Fleadh world.[123] In return, the Fleadh bolstered that importance, creating and accentuating a hierarchy of bands and band sounds. In the decade between 1952 and 1962, Clare bands took top honours six times (the Kilfenora Céilí Band in 1954, 1955, 1956, 1961; and the Tulla Céilí Band, 1957, 1960). Bands from the musically and geographically proximate Galway won four titles (the Williamstown Girls Céilí Band, 1952; the Aughrim Slopes Céilí Band, 1953; the Leitrim Céilí Band, 1959, 1962). The Kincora Céilí Band, based in Dublin, but populated by a number of Sligo expatriot musicians, were the only band to disrupt the clean streak (in 1958). Though distinct in style, each of the semi-professional bands from the west (the Kilfenora and Tulla, the Aughrim Slopes and Leitrim) contributed to a bulwark of céilí band sound that created a self-generating Fleadh bias.

For céilí band playing in Clare and Galway, 1953 is the beginning of Fleadh history. Regarded as 'the first seriously competitive (céilí band) contest of the early Comhaltas era', eight bands competed in Athlone in 1953, the highest entry number in any year up to that.[124] The Aughrim Slopes Céilí Band took first place, pipping the Breffni Céilí Band from Cavan by just one point, and the Ballinamere Céilí Band (County Offaly) took third.[125] The Tulla Céilí Band competed but did not place. Seán Óg Ó Tuama, the esteemed speaker that year (1953), noted in his opening remarks 'a weariness of mind that comes over those who listen' to céilí bands and their 'blaring ... shrill ... vulgarity'.[126] Ó Tuama did not believe that the 'noise' of céilí bands represented his vision of Gaelic music revival, but he was out of step with the growing enthusiasm for all things céilí band within and without the Fleadh zone. The Aughrim Slopes' win in Athlone marks the beginning of the reciprocally energising céilí band and Fleadh relationship. Originally the Aughrim Slopes Trio (confirming an earlier point), the Aughrim Slopes Céilí Band was frequently broadcast on national radio. The band drew its name from the site of the Battle of Aughrim in Galway and a reference to the battle in Thomas Davis' poem, 'The West's Awake'.[127] The Slopes came to the 1953 Fleadh with a local and national profile that was further enhanced by its first-place award. In 1954, three bands tied for first place: the Kilfenora Céilí Band, from County Clare; the Gentex Céilí Band, from Athlone, County Westmeath (the band that tied for second place in Mullingar, 1951); and the Mayglass Céilí Band, from County Wexford. This was the first time a band from Clare won a senior céilí band title. Another Clare band placed second, the Tulla Céilí Band, establishing a local derby rivalry on a national stage that continued for many years.[128] Winning a title added to the profile of a band outside of Fleadh settings, both symbolically and professionally, noted by céilí band performers.[129] This was further compounded by all annual Fleadh céilí band winners, from 1954 onwards, being recorded for broadcast on national airwaves: cultural and commercial capital were gained directly as a consequence.[130] There was brand name recognition for a winning céilí band, based on the the aesthetic of sound produced. The Kilfenora Céilí Band, with this its first Fleadh title in 1954, built upon its historical reputation, both in the name and in the sound already available to it.[131] After the first win, albeit a tie, a defined sound could be reiterated (or emulated) in the following years, and reasonably expect to do well. The Kilfenora Céilí Band was the first band to win three years in a row, in 1954, 1955 and 1956. In so doing, the band created a sonic template of how a winning céilí band sounded and secured for itself repeated success within Fleadh competition.

The Kilfenora was part of a wider influence of Clare céilí bands in developing a Fleadh céilí band style, which spilled out into non-Fleadh performance opportunities. In Loughrea, in 1955, the first, second and third places winners were all from County Clare: the Kilfenora, the Tulla and the Laichtín Naofa (very recently formed and first-time competitors from Miltown Malbay), in that order.[132] Such was the dominance of these Clare and Galway bands combined, that the 1951 and 1952 competitions are sometimes erased from the popular record. A 1998 history of the Tulla Céilí Band asserts that the céilí band competition began in 1953 with the Aughrim Slopes win, wiping Williamstown Girls Céilí band (from Galway) off the record.[133]

The accolade of winning the céilí band competition was brought with the band from the Fleadh space to the public dance space, in a way that was unique among prize winners because of the ensemble nature of the experience and the demand for céilí bands for dancing. Jerry Lynch noted that, when the Kilfenora Céilí Band won the competition in 1954, it was the catalyst for the band to immediately start touring all over the country.[134] At a time when solo professional or semi-professional instrumentalists were a rarity, céilí bands were inherently (semi-) professional and commercial (regardless of whether they actually made much money). Their raison d'être was to play for dancing crowds at social dances (céilithe), necessarily commercial spaces. Bands who won at the Fleadh observed a direct increase in profile, correlating with an increase in professional engagements.

Given the ensemble nature of bands, they experienced a number of acute challenges, not least of all the reality of emigration, internal migration and the ensuing effect on membership. Joe Cooley and Paddy O'Brien, both accordionists with the Tulla, emigrated in 1954 and this was a story repeated across many bands' experience.[135] The Liverpool Céilí Band, first winning in 1963 was itself an ensemble of emigrant musicians and the Kincora Céilí Band (winners in 1958), though based in Dublin was filled with many Sligo–Leitrim expatriots. A band's signature sound needed to weather and even transcend shifting individual contributions. Arguably, *e pluribus unum* prevailed and the place-making and professional capacity of the band was strengthened as a result.

## CONCERTS AND CELEBRITIES

The key goal in the establishment of the Fleadh was to provide opportunities for musicians to gather in musical communion, in the context of fewer occasions to do so by 1951, as discussed. Competitions were certainly an element in this matrix of expanded performance, but reports following the Fleadh in Cavan (1954) were at pains to point out that, while over 200 prizes were handed out, 'the winning of the competition was not the sole object of the Fleadh'.[136] Concerts (and céilithe) were formally organised as part of the Fleadh programme and quickly became central to Fleadh identity, providing a counterbalance to the competitive sphere. In Monaghan (1952) and Athlone (1953), the concert took place on Sunday night, after the day's parade and pageant and before the next day's competition. St Louis' National School Choir opened the Monaghan Fleadh finale concert in 1952 and the choir was followed by a slate of traditional musicians 'representative of the four provinces of Ireland'.[137] Among those playing the 'sweet music of the Gael' were pipers Leo Rowsome, Seán Seery (both members of CPU) and Willie Reynolds (first place in senior pipes the next day).[138] Rowsome's pupils gave a 'spirited rendering' of some 'rousing marches' and 'much interest was aroused ... by the graceful dancing of the St. Patrick's Dancing Club, Dundalk', arranged by Monica Clerkin.[139] In Athlone (1953), Leo Rowsome again headlined the concert, though it was reported that 'local and guest talent of a high order' would be joining him.[140]

In 1954 in Cavan, reflecting the growth of the Fleadh event, for the first time two concerts were scheduled, one on Sunday evening, 'a first class celebrity concert', the second on Monday evening, described as a 'celebrity and prize winners concert'.[141] 'Celebrity' indicated that the concerts would include stars of the stage and radio, those parachuted into the Fleadh concert space, but not necessarily embedded agents of Fleadh space in the same way as, for example, Rowsome. 'Celebrity' was also code for performers who were stylistically outside of traditional music practice but operated in a sonic and cultural wider world, where Irish, rather than traditional, was a key signifier of their performance, reception and reputation. The opening 1954 celebrity concert featured Delia Murphy, Leo Rowsome (as always), Denis Cox (baritone/tenor), Seán Maguire (a traditional fiddler, but also classically trained and recognisable from radio performances) and Sighle Ní Curtain [sic] (harpist). A step-dancing display by Brian Coleman was also scheduled and advance purchase of tickets was recommended, with the expectation it would be sold out.[142] Denis Cox was 'a classically trained singer of traditional songs ... who performed normally with a piano or orchestral accompaniment', in the formal concert tradition of performance dating to the late nineteenth century and Irish cultural revival.[143] Delia Murphy, in contrast, was a singer who stood at a particular intersection of traditional and popular. Her career illustrates the importance of the 'interface and interplay between traditional folk based elements and commercial popular products'.[144] She was celebrated as an interpreter of Irish ballads, achieving popular appeal in the 1930s, but revived her flagging career in the 1950s when she toured extensively in Ireland and Britain.[145] Distinct from the baritone Denis Cox model of Irish singer in style, training and repertoire, Murphy nonetheless often shared the formal, concert stage with singers of that practice and understood the complexity of her musico-cultural position in relation to an Irish traditional music community, as both insider and liminal agent at the same time. The inclusion of Sighle Ní Curtain [sic] on harp affirmed publicly the dedication of Comhaltas to the 'restoration of harp playing', in spite of the fact that a harp competition had yet to run at the Fleadh, something for which the Fleadh had been criticised (see pp. 89–94).[146]

In a bid to appeal to an additional audience constituency, the 'first class celebrity' of the advance press referred not to Fleadh competitors, or indeed the local acts that often also shared the stage, but rather to performers (mostly singers), who were in the national public eye as radio, recording and/or stage artists. Among the celebrity guest performers appearing in Cavan in 1954 at the final concert were Joe Lynch and Eamon Keane, both well known to radio and theatre audiences.[147] Lynch was a member of the Radio Éireann Repertory Company from 1947 and, additionally, had a number of hit records, such as the Leo Maguire-penned 'The Whistling Gypsy', which he sang in his trademark light baritone.[148] By 1954, he was host of the first comedy radio series on RÉ, *Living With Lynch*. Actor Keane was scheduled to recite poetry at the concert and his too was a voice familiar to the listening public. He was regularly heard as the seanchaí (storyteller) character on Din Joe's *Take the Floor* (1953–78), a hugely popular radio show on the national airwaves. The second concert, which was the penultimate programmed event of the Cavan Fleadh, was a first for the Fleadh and indicated an increased confidence in the identity of the Fleadh itself: musicians were advertised to appear on the concert stage by virtue of being competition winners at the festival. The concert bestowed formal acknowledgement on those who had achieved success within the competition frame.

In these formative years of the Fleadh, the interpretations of over-lapping edges between popular and traditional (and formally trained 'classical') sounds shifted, contracted and expanded, reacting to the circumstances as necessary. The prominence given to performers, particularly singers, who did not display traditional performance practice subsided as the Fleadh developed and gained its own confidence. Loughrea (1955) is the final Fleadh at which 'celebrity' musical guests of a non-Fleadh stripe were advertised during these decades. The headline performer at the Loughrea Sunday night celebrity concert was Michael Murphy, from Cork (with a tagline in pre-Fleadh advertising of 'runner-up in the All Ireland Caruso competition').[149] By 1957, in Dungarvan, the singers advertised for the concert were winners and competitors themselves, such as Angela Mulkere, from County Clare. This signals a significant and wider phenomenon within the history of the Fleadh: the Fleadh developed its own parameters and identity and it is those very parameters of identity that became the arbiters of what a Fleadh is and can be. The Fleadh began the process of looking inside the history of itself for definition in its seventh year in 1957, rather than outside itself to create definition. In this way, the particular dynamism and energy at Fleadhanna in the early 1950s is distinct from what followed. There is a cultural naivety perhaps, and an excitement related to that, which was subsequently muted. The enunciative authority of the early years was refined to become an institutional authority, which still relied upon symbolic support, but now imposed parameters of inclusion and exclusion, based upon the belief in its own authoritative voice.

Fleadh competitors became the celebrities of the Fleadh, and concerts became a full-blown prize-winners and traditional music stars' concert series. The prize-winners concert on the final night, first held in Cavan, became an embedded component of the Fleadh programme thereafter and, as the competition roster and the Fleadh grew, the need for non-Fleadh guests to fill the concert programme diminished. Throughout the 1950s and 1960s, the finale concert signalled the beginning of the shift back to the mundane, non-festive world. Done with the official business of designating the victorious and the defeated, the prize-winner's concert showcase prepared the participants to travel back, literally and metaphorically, with a new or renewed perspective. Ciarán Mac Mathúna began recording the prize-winners' concerts for RÉ in 1955 and its subsequent broadcast allowed listeners who had been at the Fleadh to reimagine themselves there. It also allowed those who stayed at home to listen their way in to that space, however briefly.

## CONCLUSION

The growth of the Fleadh in the early years, from 1952 to 1955, was reflected in increasing competitor entries, growing numbers of attendees, and developing structures of administration. In 1955, the *Irish Press* confidently declared the Fleadh 'the biggest musical event of the year'.[150] Through these years, the Fleadh consolidated and expanded as a competition-festival system, building upon the inaugural model in Mullingar. By the mid-decade mark, structural invariant elements, such as parades, competitions and concerts, were part of the reasonable expectations of festival attendees. These and other programmed components (céilithe) were also balanced with informal session playing (see pp. 169–77), and other spontaneous socialising, constituting what a Fleadh was and how it was experienced. In addition to these elements found annually, in any given year the identity of the Fleadh depended upon the particular location in which it took place and the specific experience of the Fleadh in that place. When the Fleadh arrived in Loughrea in 1955, it had stiff competition on the weekend in question, as Currach Day was scheduled to take place the same weekend in Salthill, Galway. The *Galway Observer* reported that 60,000 were in attendance at Salthill.[151] Nonetheless, an editorial in the *Connacht Tribune* predicted that 'Even the appeal of the National Currach Championships, and Galway has had evidence of the appeal, cannot reach as deeply into the hearts of the Irish people as can a festival of traditional music'.[152] Joe Burke clearly recalled the excitement beforehand in Loughrea, leading up to the Fleadh, and he knew it was 'a special thing for traditional music' and for Loughrea.[153] This was not just in terms of the festival programme itself. A distinction was felt among musicians that the Fleadh was focused entirely on traditional music (including song) and sought to promote an ever-widening variety of instruments. The Fleadh inverted the non-Fleadh social order, validated traditional music as being of the highest value. This was a transformative act, which spilled over into the non-festive world, increasing interest in, and creating a higher profile for, traditional music and dance beyond the Fleadh space.

The Fleadh was becoming an essential tool in the consolidation of the traditional music community, providing a locus for, and of, self-representation and identity. This resulted in each Fleadh having 'its own special atmosphere'.[154] The duality of expectations of structure, balanced against the mutability of location, added to the excitement of the Fleadh. Complicating Stanley Waterman's remarks that place identity of festivals is one of the most imporant lingering memories, in the case of the Fleadh, 'the valuation of place endowed by the festival' differed from year to year.[155] The multiple locations of the Fleadh altered the norm of festive attachment to place with the unexpected result of focusing attention on performativity in the first instance and on place location in the second, without compromising the identity of the Fleadh overall.[156] Rather than diluting meaning, each Fleadh developed a specific place character in a national Fleadh identity, layering meanings on the Fleadh superstructure from year to year. And on it goes, to the Fleadh down in Ennis in County Clare.

CHAPTER 4

# Fleadh Proliferations and Place-making: Ennis, 1956 and Dungarvan, 1957

In the intervening year between one Fleadh and the next, awareness of the festival grew, filtered through an expanding branch network of Comhaltas and the place-tied publicity generated by the festival as it moved locations. Festival popularity was reflected through augmented competition categories, rising numbers of attendees, and the introduction of county fleadhanna and provincial rounds of Fleadh competition. This proliferation and accompanying regulation throughout the 1950s are detailed in the opening sections of this chapter, preparing the ground for my primary concern, two specific place-making case studies. Not coincidentally, these two Fleadhanna, Ennis in 1956 and Dungarvan in 1957, take place one year after the other and both offer contrasting pre-Fleadh cultural identities and post-Fleadh legacies.

Arts festivals commonly occur in the same place every year and develop 'place-embeddedness' tied to that particular location.[1] The motile Fleadh had no such opportunity; rather the Fleadh cultivated place-identity tied to a sequence of host towns. In every Fleadh town, another layer of year- and site-specific festival place-making occured. In parallel, the Fleadh built an identity that transcended place, one that migrated with the festival from one town to the next through a series of recurring components such as competitions, parades and céilithe. Taken in concert, a bank of Fleadh identities accumulated. The decision as to where the festival would take place had high stakes for the Fleadh, for the town and for Comhaltas. Organisers,

Fleadh goers and competitors were all implicated in the place-making consequences of this expansion; ensemble competitions, such as céilí band, were vulnerable to dissatisfaction as will be demonstrated. Beyond the competition structure, the Fleadh céilí has particular significance for place-making legacies in Ennis but was a recurring (invariant) festive component embedded from the very first Fleadh in Mullingar. Control of Clare dancing bodies at céilithe was the subject of much debate in Ennis, where local (choreo-place-)practice collided with national Fleadh ideals.

National trends in performance (both within and beyond the Fleadh) were reflected in new competitions added each year, but during the 1950s competitions still retained the capacity to respond to local place practice. Expansion and rejection of competition categories as argued here, is also place-making. Harpers competed for the first time in Fleadh history in Dungarvan, but the place-making potential of this and other Fleadh milestones achieved in 1957 were overshadowed in what became Dungarvan's place legacy in Fleadh history.

The contrast of Ennis and Dungarvan festivals provides a useful axis in Fleadh history, when commercial considerations overwhelmed cultural ones. The Fleadh in Ennis came to be understood as the apex of Fleadh accomplishment within and without the community of practice, and held up as an exemplar of revival success during these decades, a reputation that continues today. Fleadhanna that followed were measured against the '*annus mirabilis*' benchmark of Ennis, as Gearóid Ó hAllmhuráin describes it, and deemed more, or less, successful by a set of place-attached criteria which were cultural and, by then, also commercial.[2] If Fleadhanna up to that point were Fleadh becoming, Ennis was Fleadh arrived. In comparison, the Fleadh in Dungarvan, a cultural success but commercial failure, was constructed in public discourse as the contrapuntal *annus horribilus* to Ennis, a contrast that layed bare the conflict between cultural and commerical stakeholders. The Fleadh, as the flagship of Comhaltas traditional music revival, was continuing to expand, but began to step beyond the embodiment revival phase towards maintenance of structures and identity.[3] The ensuing cultural flashpoints are found in the Fleadh highs of Ennis and Fleadh lows of Dungarvan discussed herein.

## FLEADH PROLIFERATIONS

The process of how sites were chosen for the Fleadh was in place by 1954, adjoined to the proliferation of Comhaltas branches then underway. If there were enough branches in existence within a county, a county board was created (a minimum of three branches were necessary). It was then the job of the county board to apply to Comhaltas' national executive (also later termed the central executive or central executive council) to host an All Ireland Fleadh, with the added caveat that the host town needed to have a registered Comhaltas branch. By 1961, provincial councils for Munster, Leinster, Ulster and Connaught were all in place, adding another layer of administration.[4] This hierarchical structure mirrored the long-established GAA system, which had a network of clubs, county boards and provincial councils, all reporting to a national executive. In the first few years of the Fleadh, the local Fleadh committee preceded the establishment of a county board and often morphed into a county board after the Fleadh.[5] In the afterglow of the 1954 Fleadh in Cavan, a county board was instituted and held its inaugural meeting on 4 October 1954, with Séamus Ó Dubhthaigh as chair, 'to coordinate matters within the county'.[6] Ó Dubhthaigh believed it was the first county board, but in fact Cavan had been pipped at the post. A county board was already in situ in County Clare and its first meeting was held on 11 April 1954, in Miltown Malbay.[7] An information sheet to all branch secretaries in 1955 records a third county board by then established in Monaghan.[8]

In 1957, interested Tipperary musicians and organisers proposed Thurles would be an ideal town in which to have the All Ireland Fleadh. However, there were few branches of Comhaltas in Tipperary at that time and none in Thurles. Dinny O'Brien, father of Paddy O'Brien the accordionist from Portroe, County Tipperary, contacted Paddy Hayes in Thurles and urged him to send out the call to musicians so that a branch might be formed.[9] The first meeting of the new branch was held on 27 November 1957, in the Confraternity Hall in Thurles, and the branch officers immediately applied to the Tipperary county board to host the All Ireland Fleadh in 1959.[10] The time from the notional idea of hosting a Fleadh to approval was remarkably short in this instance, the Fleadh came to Thurles in 1959. Lobbyists hoping to secure the Fleadh for

Swinford, County Mayo in 1961, claimed that people in smaller towns, such as Swinford, were more ambitious and interested in the success of the Fleadh than those in larger towns, hoping to sway the committee in their favour.[11] Seán Reid in response, 'with no ill feelings towards Swinford or the people in it', expressed grave concerns about the ability of the town to 'cater for the crowd', but was outvoted and to Swinford the Fleadh went (see Fig. 4.1).[12]

In the context of increasing branch level activity and numbers in attendance at the annual Fleadh (by growing numbers of Comhaltas members and interested others), proliferation of fleadhanna at sub-All level Ireland was inevitable. Where county boards were set up, a county fleadh was sure to follow, and this was the case when the first county fleadh in Cavan was held in August 1955.[13] Coming on the back of the success of the (All Ireland) Fleadh hosted by Cavan in 1954, Ó Dubhthaigh and the newly formed county board reasonably believed that a county Fleadh would be enthusiastically supported.[14] This pattern is repeated across the country. For example, following the establishment of the county board in Tipperary in 1957, a county Fleadh was held in July 1958. The county fleadhanna were independent from the Fleadh proper. In this respect, the first county fleadhanna were similar to local feiseanna; autonomous events and typically arranged during the summer months. Importantly, though organised at county board level, a county fleadh was nonetheless part of the administrative structure of Comhaltas. Coming after the Fleadh in Ennis, the first Clare county fleadh was held in Miltown Malbay in August 1957, while in Galway it took until 1960 before the first county fleadh was held, also the year Galway county board was formed. These early county fleadhanna followed the event pattern of its bigger All Ireland antecedent with competitions, parades, concerts and céilithe. Competitors were drawn not just from the county where the fleadh took place, but also from surrounding counties, if musicians cared to travel. In 1962, for the first time, a county fleadh was hosted in all six Munster counties, the earliest province to do so.[15]

The first fleadh in Donegal, in 1958, was organised at very short notice by a team under Paddy Tunney's stewardship. It 'made no claims to be a county fleadh', though to all intents and purposes it functioned as that and had approval from the national executive to be designated as a fleadh.[16] Tunney recollected that 'our fleadh incurred the wrath of

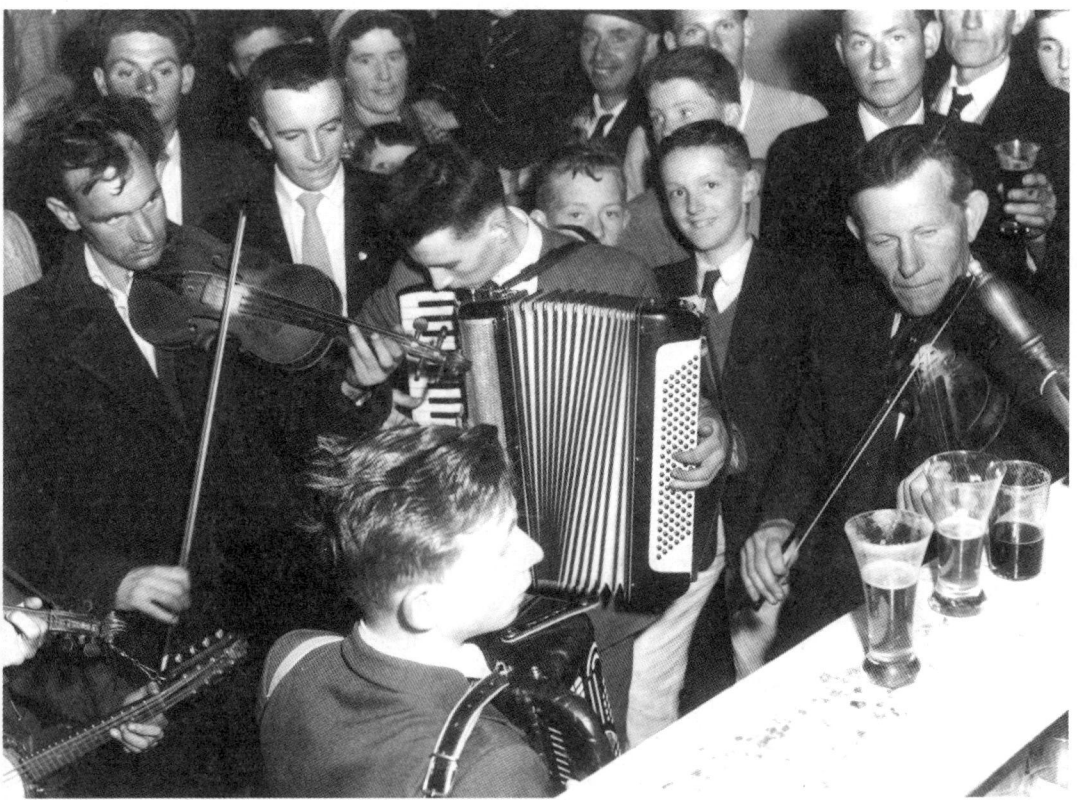

**Fig. 4.1** Unidentified musicians at Swinford, 1961
Copyright Fáilte Ireland, courtesy ITMA

Brian O'Donnell and Dr Brian Galligan', Ulster provincial Comhaltas officers, because they were not directly consulted.[17] A motion in 1959 reminded festival organisers 'all fleadh literature' should clearly indicate if any fleadh was 'sanctioned by Comhaltas'.[18] Among the large diaspora in Britain, John Burke remembers the first Comhaltas-hosted fleadh in London in 1959 at which there was no solo box or fiddle competitions: fiddlers and box players took their chances with everyone else in the miscellaneous category. Incidentally, banjo player Liam Farrell, originally from County Tyrone, won.[19] The inaugural Comhaltas Fleadh in the USA took place in 1964.[20]

As the national All Ireland Fleadh event grew in popularity, numbers of entries in key senior and some intermediate competitions (in fiddle, box, pipes, tin whistle and ensemble categories, including céilí band) were becoming unwieldy. The All Ireland Fleadh in Ennis was the first festival to include both confined county and provincial competitions in its weekend schedule. The County Clare confined competitions on Saturday remained as autonomous competitions and were not qualifiers for the Fleadh proper, continuing previous years' practice. The practice of having confined host-county competitions at the national Fleadh remained until 1965. During this period, the number of independent county fleadhanna, outside the Fleadh proper, also continued to increase. Newly introduced, a qualifying system of provincial rounds for some senior competitions was held on Monday morning, the main competition day at the Fleadh in Ennis. The top two placed competitors of the provincial competitions then progressed to All Ireland finals in the late afternoon.[21] Underage and singing competitions were still run as single All Ireland competitions in Ennis, as entry numbers did not warrant provincial qualifier rounds.[22] The saturation point for adult participation was still some years away and implementing a progressive qualifier system made sense administratively. Interest in Fleadh competition among adult musicians continued to increase up to 1960, as word of the Fleadh spread. The extent of sustained adult participation is also demonstrated by the intermittent appearance of both senior and intermediate categories of competition for pipes, flute and box up to 1963.

Across categories (provincial and All Ireland), some competitions lacked numbers to run (a familiar challenge at this stage) in Ennis. However, the Ennis Fleadh instituted a model of including provincial qualifiers at the Fleadh weekend, which continued for the years that followed, where numbers demanded. After the Fleadh in Dungarvan in 1957, a motion was formally approved at national executive level that provincial competitions would run only if the 'the overall entries … exceed(ed) twenty' and crucially, a new rule was introduced that only the first placed winner in provincial rounds would progress to the All Ireland, reducing the number of competitors going through to the finals, a change to previous rules (this was subsequently reversed in later years).[23] Limiting those who advanced to the All Ireland round heightened the Fleadh experience for musicians and patrons alike, but simultaneously created tension inside and outside the Fleadh zone. To complicate matters, and if numbers were sufficient, the 1957 motion provided for a provincial first round from which the top two placed competitors would proceed to the provincial final play-off. Only the first-place winner of the play-off for the provincial title went through to the All Ireland final later that day, creating an additional layer of dramatisation in the competition space.[24]

## EXPANDING REGULATIONS AND ENSEMBLE COMPETITION

New provincial qualifier rules were applied at the next Fleadh in Longford (1958) creating much discontent among céilí band competitors. Junior Crehan, then fiddler with the Laichtín Naofa band, described the first round of the Munster provincial qualifier:

> We won the first session ... in Longford and there was this rule that firsts and seconds could go in and compete again [at provincial level]. So, we were first ... in the heat, and we beat the Tulla and Kilfenora and the other bands that were in it. The Tulla were [sic] second.[25]

As Crehan described, in round 1 of the Munster céilí band competition, all top places were filled (unsurprisingly) with Clare céilí bands: the Laichtín Naofa came first, with the Tulla second and the Kilfenora third. But round 2 of the Munster provincial qualifier was to come, out of which only one band would progress to the final. While the Laichtín Naofa and the Tulla had another bite at the provincial cherry, the Kilfenora, in third place, was ineligible to compete in the newly introduced provincial play-off. The Kilfenora fans, and the band, were greatly displeased at this turn of events and loudly protested the perceived injustice in the competition hall. That the three-All Irelands-in-a-row band would be excluded from the provincial play-off, by virtue of a new rule that was not clear in advance to the band (or its disciples), was an outrage:

> It was discovered that the first two bands from each province were entitled to go on, which meant that, for the first time in the four or five years of rivalry between Kilfenora and Tulla, Kilfenora were knocked out of the final play-off. There was a bit of heckling and this whole thing was questioned from the floor by Kilfenora supporters, and there was great tension all around ... there was a fair bit of cut and thrust.[26]

The protests on Kilfenora's behalf from the floor took place as the Tulla band was sitting on stage waiting to play in the next round. Crehan recalled that the Laichtín Naofa 'had to go in again' against Tulla, in a first and second placed provincial play-off; the Tulla 'won that Munster part three'.[27] Laichtín Naofa, despite winning the first round at provincial level, was deposed by the Tulla who went on to compete as Munster champions in the (All Ireland) finals that evening.

Séamus Mac Mathúna remembered 'the worst of it was when the result was announced' of the All Ireland final later that day.[28] The Kincora Céilí Band from Dublin (primarily populated by Sligo–Leitrim musicians) took the All Ireland title and the Tulla came in second. There was uniform discontent among Clare céilí bands and their supporters. Mac Mathúna commented, only somewhat tongue in cheek, 'that was the end of the fleadhs now, when this kind of skulduggery was starting, when a crowd of wrenboys from the Kincora could beat two decent bands'.[29] This response emphasises the dominance of Clare céilí bands and the capital that was attached to winning the title. In Jimmy Ward's terms, 'twas nearly as exciting as fellas going out playing an All Ireland hurling or football match'.[30] Clare musicians felt particularly aggrieved in the céilí band category under the new rules. Despite the strength of céilí band practice and demonstrated winning capacity of Clare bands, the chance of a Clare prize-winning sweep at All Ireland final level was not possible with the new rules in place in 1958.

Ensemble music competitions are ritualised performances, where performance regulation and the value the music community places on the performance are closely intertwined.[31] As a ritual, the céilí band competition has deep meaning for participants. Roy A. Rappaport recognises that participants in ritual must 'establish a convention – a publicly recognised rule or understanding' and, furthermore, there must be acceptance of those rules, even if in private frustrations were disclosed.[32] In the case of the céilí band competition in Longford described above, objections were raised in private and publicly, from the competition floor. The ritual of céilí band competition, and indeed all the competitions at the Fleadh, were social contracts where a breach of obligation could have irreparable consequences. However, for the convention of competition to function, the participants, Clare céilí bands among them, accepted system rules (albeit begrudgingly) at the competition site. The céilí bands participated with a high degree of confidence, regardless of any reservations about the system itself. In theory, discontent with any Fleadh rule could be raised by a local branch by raising a motion for change through the central administration of Comhaltas at annual congress. Perhaps indicating continued disgruntlement by Clare céilí bands', Ennis Comhaltas branch proposed a motion in 1959 to the national executive that 'the provincial competitions be dispensed with at Fleadh Cheoil na hÉireann in future'.[33] The motion was not carried, nor did Clare céilí bands stop competing in the Fleadh.

Between 1958 and 1963, provincial competitions held at the Fleadh were in a stage of development and consolidation with rules were amended from year to year. At the Longford Fleadh (1958), a quartet from Liverpool found themselves unmoored from any provincial category upon arrival but were put in the Connaught round (which they won).[34] The next year, Ceoltóirí na Cathrach, the Miltown Malbay Comhaltas branch, one among those who proposed that an overseas category would be included at the Fleadh.[35] It was duly introduced in Boyle in 1960 for some senior and intermediate competitions, effectively operating as a fifth province at the Fleadh (resonating coincidentally with the Gaelic Ireland five-province order). The overseas céilí band competition in Boyle had bands from Liverpool, St Helens, Birmingham, London, Glasgow and New York. Like other provincial rounds, the overseas provincial competition was a qualifying level for the final round. In this period of competition system expansion (and consolidation), for several years from 1961, provincial qualifying rounds took place at the Fleadh and separately, provinces hosted a provincial fleadh later in the same summer, though these were not yet qualifier competitions for the All Ireland Fleadh. The provincial qualifier round at the annual Fleadh was retained until 1963 when, thereafter, it was declared that only 'those competitors who qualify at their respective provincial fleadhanna' could 'compete at the national Fleadh'.[36] Despite this, the Fleadh in Clones in 1964 included a full Ulster round of qualifier competitions. Play-offs (for provincial champions) continued to be hosted at the national Fleadh intermittently, but were fully regularised by 1965 in Thurles, with one exception. The overseas provincial round was retained at the annual Fleadh until 1967, when the All Britain Fleadh (which began as an autonomous event in 1963), became the qualifying round for the All

Ireland. The sequence of provincial to All Ireland qualification was also confusing. In any given year, the All Ireland Fleadh was scheduled for Whit weekend (in May or June) before provincial fleadhanna, which typically took place later in the summer. This created a situation where provincial winners qualified in one calendar year at a provincial fleadh during the summer and progressed to the national Fleadh the following year at Whit weekend. A motion to regularise this and move the Fleadh to August, with provincial fleadhanna to take place prior to that in the same calendar year, was rejected in 1962.[37] When the All Ireland Fleadh was finally moved in 1970 from Whit weekend to August, a correction in the progression from provincial to All Ireland qualification was made; both happened sequentially in the same calendar year thereafter.

The seemingly boundless expansion of the fleadh structure (and particularly competition propagation) was a source of concern to some in Comhaltas. Thomas P. Dempsey, public relations officer with the organisation, commented on Fleadh competition in 1963 that 'the very success of the Fleadh however may have resulted in its engaging too much of the attention of Comhaltas'.[38] Competition began to dominate the activities of Comhaltas and Dempsey believed the organisation's 'reliance on it [competition] as a way to popularise traditional music' was not positive.[39] In spite of any dissatisfactions, participants were clear about their roles and function and the Fleadh developed a highly codified and signified competition system.[40] It was a system that continued to attract more competitors each year, from county, to provincial, to All Ireland level, generating competition expansion and enabling Comhaltas consolidation as an authoritative body in Irish traditional music.

## CÉILITHE, CONTROL AND DANCING BODIES: ENNIS, 1956

> Making its leisurely way around the Green Isle, Fleadh Cheoil na hÉireann [National Festival of Irish Music] finds itself this Whitsun, for the first time, in the Province of Munster, with Ennis playing host to the musical sons and daughters of Erin, exiles as recalled by a magnet, and interested visitors from countries near and far.[41]

There are several co-related reasons for the selection of Ennis as the next stop after Loughrea in the Fleadh's odyssey. While Geraldine

# Fleadh Proliferations and Place-making 81

Cotter notes that Ennis, as the county town of County Clare, was not a centre for traditional music in the 1950s, or for many years thereafter, the broader picture of traditional music in the county's rural hinterland was far brighter.⁴² In the year prior to the Ennis Fleadh, Clare had increased Comhaltas branches from ten to seventeen, the highest number of branches in any county.⁴³ This branch growth can be explained in the first instance by the strength of traditional music practice in rural areas of Clare; but also by the number and popularity of Clare céilí bands; and finally, the dynamic effect of highly motivated individual musician-activists such as Seán Reid. Reid was a piper who moved to Clare in 1937 to take up a position as engineer with the county council and 'never stopped talking about traditional music ever since' according to Kevin Vaughan (chair of the 1956 Fleadh committee).⁴⁴ Finally, given that the Fleadh was in Loughrea in 1955, moving next door to the Banner county and bringing the Fleadh to Munster for the first time made sense.

Following the model first trialled at Loughrea, the Fleadh ran over three days at Whit weekend from 19 to 21 May 1956 in Ennis. The Loughrea Fleadh attracted approximately 15,000 people. Ennis surpassed all expectations where attendance was estimated up to 40,000, the 'biggest ever gathering since the days of Daniel O'Connell' in the town, according to the *Irish Examiner*.⁴⁵ The Fleadh programme illustrates the corresponding expansion in administrative and logistical planning. Familiar names within traditional music circles are found: Mrs Crotty from Kilrush, Martin Talty of Miltown Malbay, Seán Reid of the Tulla Céilí Band, Jimmy Ward from Kilfenora (though at that point resident in Miltown Malbay), Kitty Linnane (another Kilfenora stalwart) and the Mulcairs among them. Notably, most committee members were musicians.⁴⁶

Every available space in fourteen different competition venues was used across the townscape, among them the New Hall (colloquially known as Paddy Con's), the Scout Hall, the Maria Assumpta Hall, the courthouse, classrooms in various schools, the People's Park, the Queen's Hotel and even the Gaiety cinema, which was commandeered for the weekend. Perceived as an added benefit, a writer in the *Limerick Leader* noted that the use of the cinema coincidentally guaranteed that 'there will be no films or modern dances held during the festival'.⁴⁷ In competitions, entry numbers increased from the previous year. There were 330 solo entries, eighty-two duets, thirty-one trios, twenty-three quartets, seventy-five entries in singing and twenty-three céilí bands pre-registered.[48] Every county in Munster and Connaught was represented; Leinster and Ulster counties were amply deputised.

The céilí band competition was hotly contested and the atmosphere in the competition hall was tension-filled, with céilí band factions exchanging gibes: 'There's the Kilfenora now, ye've nothing like that back your side of the country' — 'Ah, wait until you hear Miltown (Malbay)'.[49] Following provincial qualifiers, the All Ireland final round, a recall and second adjudication, in the end the Kilfenora céilí band took home its third title in a row, with a score of 99/100.[50] The veneration of the Kilfenora began earlier at the festival's opening parade, when the band was 'borne on a laurel wreathed lorry' to Cusack Park (the GAA grounds) for the pageant.[51] In one published account from Ennis, the reputational dominance of Clare céilí bands overpowered the reporter. The Aughrim Slopes, third place winners (96/100), with an undisputed Galway place-identity and pedigree, were mistakenly reported as from Clare.[52] Replicating the order of winners the previous year, the Tulla came second (97/100). As the full complement of Tulla members 'trooped' onto the stage in the Munster qualifier, the band was greeted with a 'thunderous cheer': one audience member was heard to quip, 'what is this, the Hallé orchestra?'[53] Though céilí bands typically had from five to ten or eleven members, numbers of players in a céilí band had yet to be fully regulated in Fleadh competition; the Cill na Manach céilí band (Tipperary) had twenty-five musicians assembled on stage in Ennis.[54] A motion in 1959 proposed that céilí bands in any fleadh competition would comprise 'not less than five members and not more than nine'.[55] In 1964, a Donegal county fleadh programme reminded musicians that there should be a minimum of seven musicians. By 1966, the current five to ten musicians rule was finally settled on.[56]

The final Fleadh céilí, a significant object of the Fleadh structure, functioned as a counterbalance to the competitive space and was crucial within Fleadh festivity. Excitement built throughout the last day of competitions, with qualifying rounds and the céilí band finals programmed as the last competition of the whole weekend. Structurally and experientially the céilí band competition was a climax at the Fleadh. Winners of the céilí band competition were then invited to perform at the final céilí. Céilí band performances within competition and céilí band performances at Fleadh céilithe operated as dynamic coefficients, building festive meaning. Distinct from competitions, céilithe at the Fleadh were an opportunity for collective embodiment through structured participation for all. These social dance events allowed the relationship between attendee (dancer) and performer (céilí band) to be enacted in a particularly powerful way. Des Geraghty, when writing of the Fleadh during its early decades, notes that Fleadhanna 'had a combustive effect in releasing pent-up energy and a sense of enthusiasm and pleasure'.[57] This was realised fully at Fleadh céilithe, when the kinesthetics of the céilí released the energy of the comparatively controlled environment of the competition. Additionally, for many dancing at a Fleadh céilí their festive movement drew on internalised codes of movement experienced at céilithe outside of the Fleadh space. The combination of these factors produced a heady cocktail of festivity.

In 1952, at the second Fleadh, there were céilithe on both nights of the Fleadh and musicians came together 'to form the finest céilí band ever heard in Monaghan' for Sunday night's event.[58] Keenly anticipated in advance, 'the céilí mór in Swan Park' was 'one of the most outstanding attractions of the year' and eclipsed its promise, as it was 'the best attended and liveliest céilí ever held in a Monaghan hall'.[59] The next year in Athlone (1953) 'the biggest céilí band ever' was hosted, 'consisting of fifty artists' that provided music in St Mary's Hall for the opening céilí.[60] Journalistic hyperbole aside, such was the popularity of céilithe that in 1954 an open air, meterologicially optimistic céilí 'on the tennis court beside the town hall' was programmed in Cavan and 'although it was raining slightly, both adults and children enjoyed an hour's dancing to the music of the Breffni Céilí Band which was relayed from inside the hall'.[61] In 1955, to cater to the crowd at the Fleadh in Loughrea, a marquee was erected for one of the céilithe.[62] The popularity of céilithe at the Fleadh was anticipated to be even more in Ennis in 1956 and five indoor céilithe and one outdoor céilí were programmed.[63] The planning was well warranted: attendances at Fleadh céilithe in Ennis exceeded 4,500 across all venues.[64]

The hyper-experience and attached tension of the céilí band competition, where the collective dancing bodies of those in the hall were restrained from any dance response, could be fully indulged at Fleadh céilithe. There were additional tensions in Ennis where the Fleadh faced a divergence between local performance practice and national Comhaltas policy on sanctioned Irish dance practice. Set dancing, an autonomous, typically four couple dance in square formation, was rejected by the Gaelic League early in the twentieth century 'on the grounds that they [the set dances] were derived from the [French] quadrilles' and therefore 'foreign'.[65] Unsuitable for Irish dancing bodies, an alternative repertoire of approved céilí ensemble dances (sometimes termed figure dances) was developed by the League for dancing at céilithe.[66] In the transition from the domestic set dancing space of the nineteenth century to the twentieth century public dance space of the céilí, vernacular set dances were usurped by sanctioned céilí dance repertoire.[67] Up to and beyond the 1950s, the material effect of the Gaelic League's arbitration was that set dancing was banned at céilithe sponsored by the organisation. In Ireland and in the wider Irish transnational social world, other aligned cultural gate keepers (the GAA and Comhaltas) followed suit. Debates about what dance was suitable for Comhaltas céilithe continued until the late 1960s.[68] The language of advertised céilí titles could be indicative of what was allowed and what was not: a céilí without set dancing was ascribed the symbolically loaded title of 'fíor céilí' ('true céilí'). Also forbidden at fíor céilithe were waltzes, foreign too in this scheme of understanding. 'Céilí mór' (big céilí) advertisements were code for set dancing and waltzing prohibitions.[69] At a Fleadh, dancers understood that a fíor céilí was the default Fleadh event (even if the advertised title was not explicit) and céilí bands could expect 'to play for four or five hours with no waltzes', which was, as Jerry Lynch from the Kilfenora Céilí Band bemoaned, 'very severe' on bands and dancers all.[70]

Though céilí dance repertoire supplanted set dancing across the island in the first half of the twentieth century, there were pockets of resistance where set dancing was sustained in vernacular practice. Among them, County Clare and neighbouring east Galway were areas where 'ardent votaries, of an endless variety of sets, danced in country houses'.[71] In Ennis, Fleadh céilithe became a site of contestation between Fleadh céilí dance hegemony and vernacular set dancing publics. Prior to the Fleadh in Ennis, there had 'very nearly been a vicious row' at the Sunday night Fleadh céilí in 1955 in Loughrea, when set dancing insurgents took to the

*Fleadh Proliferations and Place-making* 85

floor, against Comhaltas *fíor* céilí policy.[72] With the Fleadh coming to Ennis and nightly céilíthe an embedded object of the festival, dissonance between local practice and 'hard-core céilí brokers' in Comhaltas led to robust debate in advance.[73] The *Evening Herald*, reporting on a Comhaltas national executive meeting held in Ennis in October 1955, recorded Donald Ó Lubhlaí's empassioned objection to sets. Class and cultural nationalism intersected with set dance opposition, when he decried that sets 'had come over with Cromwell and been danced in the drawing rooms by so-called lords and ladies of Ireland' before being relegated to 'Paddy the fiddler' in the kitchen.[74] P.J. McNamara, chair of Ennis Urban Council, in a stroke of ancient-equals-authentic one-upmanship, retorted that the sets in Clare were 'as old as the Cliffs of Moher and had been danced by the people of Clare from time immemorial'.[75] The national executive committee were treated to (or subjected to, depending upon the perspective) 'a display of the controversial dances' at the end of the meeting by 'teams provided by J. Hewsen from Ballinacally', a village south-west of Ennis.[76] Few on the national committee supported an exemption to allow Fleadh set dancing in Ennis, believing it an affront to national culture and a dangerous precedent. Brian Galligan said there would be a outcry against the inclusion of sets by céilí afficionados and Mary B. Fox (assistant honorary secretary) rejected sets as 'they had degenerated … into disgraceful exhibitions'.[77] This prompted Jimmy Ward, Kilfenora Céilí Band and Ennis Fleadh committee member, to defend the cultural credentials of Clare dancers, musicians and music. He said: 'That was not the case in Clare, where dancers would not take the floor unless real Irish traditional music was played for them. There was no danger', he added, that 'the sets would deteriorate in Clare'.[78] Malachy Sweeney from Armagh, a professional céilí band leader who had no compunction playing for sets or waltzes if an event required it, said the national committee would be 'guilty of an injustice to the people of Clare and Galway' if sets were banned in Ennis.[79]

The national executive took time to deliberate its final decision, but in anticipation that the dancers of Clare and Galway would be unable, or unwilling, to control their set dancing impulses, the Ennis Fleadh programme announced:

> In deference to the wishes of the people of Clare and Galway, who on account of proximity alone, will form a considerable part of the attendance of the Fleadh and who have their own figure dances [set dances], and are not familiar with the standard céilí dances taught by the Gaelic League, 'sets' will be allowed at one of the two céilís each night.[80]

Though the dispensation was granted, the diplomatic sheen is surface level. The readers of the Fleadh programme were reminded that the local dancers were not familiar with 'standard céilí dances'. In this, Clare and Galway dancers were deficient and would not, or could not, meet normative dancing requirements, unable to control their dancing bodies. Set dancers would be quarantined at two indoor céilithe (and one outdoor as well) thereby minimising dancing contagion.[81] The dancing guidelines of fíor céilithe would be strictly enforced at all other times.

At the céilí band competition, held in Paddy Con's on Monday of the Fleadh, those fortunate enough to gain access to the packed hall were deluged with sounds of Clare céilí bands through provincial and final rounds, as the Kilfenora took the crown. Mangaire Súgach described the scene:

> Time and again my eyes roved round that huge hall. From the front right back to the end it was one sea of faces and the balconies running down two sides of it were packed just as tightly. In the centre of the hall, hundreds of people were sitting in chairs. Further back, and along the entire length of the two sides of the hall, hundreds more stood, all eagerly interested. But what intrigued me the most were those who occupied the space between the stage and the first row of seats … these just sat in regular rows [on the floor]. That huge crowd that gathered in the new Hall [Paddy Con's] was as fine a cross section of Ireland as you would wish to see. Men and women were in about equal numbers and the young outnumbered the old by about two to one.[82]

Opened in 1950, Paddy Con's was well known for hosting set dancing céilís and set dancing competitions during the 1950s in Ennis, accommodating and encouraging local practice, in spite of national norms.[83] For that reason, it was designated by the Fleadh as the single venue for set dancing but with the caveat that it was only for a 'proportion' of the time at the nominated céilithe.[84] Releasing the festive pressure post-céilí band competition, chairs cleared from the floor, the set dancing began to the sounds of the winning Clare céilí bands. Once their apportioned time was over, preventing the set dancers from more set dancing proved to be a challenge for the national Comhaltas officials. Bríd Brody recollected:

> Ennis was my first outing in 1956. I was only interested in the competitions and going in and listening to the music. And the céilí bands took place in Paddy Con's Hall, and there was a céilí on that night with the winners. The powers that be … they didn't regard set dancing as Irish at all. And I know that we were dancing a set down at the end of the hall and someone came down with a Dublin accent and put us off the floor, because it was a fíor céilí and we didn't know what a fíor céilí was.[85]

Originally from Kilfenora, Brody was by then living in Dublin and a frequent patron of the Thomas Street club (run by the CPU), the Fiddlers Club on Church Street (officially the St Mary's Music Club) and the Clareman's club on Bridge Street.[86] Her assertion, that it was someone with a Dublin accent who put a stop to the set dancing is notable and reflects, among other things, some abiding cultural suspicion between rural and urban in traditional music's performative domain.[87] Dancing a set in Clare, her home county, trumped any organisational prohibition in the authenticity stakes. That a stop was put to their dancing in Paddy Con's, home to set dancing in Ennis, added to the cultural indignity for Brody and her set dancing cohorts. Though she asserts she was unaware what a fíor céilí was, as a set dancer she knew where set dancing was welcomed and the much more frequent occurrence of where it was not welcomed. Brody regularly attended particular céilithe in Dublin precisely because they welcomed set dancing.[88] Michael Tubridy, dancer and musician, also notes those set-dancer friendly céilithe in Dublin being full of, not coincidentially, Clare expatriots.[89] The Fleadh, as a mobile annual performance space, actively navigated the sharp edge between local practice and national benchmarks.

The set dancers in Ennis were ejected from the hall. However, the cultural centre was reclaimed by the exiled dancers. In an act of power restoration, Brody revealed the dancers 'opened the door and danced our set outside the door on the steps, and as we said, we knocked deatach [smoke] off the floor'.[90] In Brody's reflection, the set dancers reconstituted the liminal space between the dance hall inside where their dancing selves were unwelcome and the outdoors, by stepping to the fringe of the controlled space at the exit. They could still hear the music (of Clare céilí bands) from inside the fíor céilí. Between inside and outside, they danced their set and, in so doing, subverted the authority of the organisers inside, restoring themselves at the top of the dance hierarchy. The dancers at the edge challenged the nationally sanctioned fíor céilí dancing and articulated kinesthetically an alternative local identity.[91] The internal non-set environment was at odds with the external popular, traditional practice in Clare, but, as Brody interpreted her experience, the set dancers won the cultural battle on the day.

The wording of the dispensation for set dancing in the Fleadh programme is revealing in other ways. It is a pragmatic response to avoid conflict in the event of Clare and Galway set dancers being overwhelmed with festive emotion, when they would inevitably release their dancing selves in their own back yard. Nonetheless, there was nothing in the derogation's language that suggests cultural dance ecumenism at work. After all, the majority of the céilithe in Ennis did not allow set dancing and for those that did, it was for only some of the time. Where set dancing was permitted for a limited period at a céilí, set dancers were obliged to re-restrain themselves and view the fíor figure dancers around them. The arrangement at the Ennis Fleadh was a reluctant indulgence: a nod to the recaltricant locals, who refused to standardise their dancing selves. Should there be any confusion, Paddy Maunsell, secretary of the national Comhaltas Executive, wrote 'this arrangement is not to constitute a precedent for future Fleadhs' (a concern raised at the earlier October 1955 meeting).[92] The unwritten reprimand is that the set dancing Galwegians and the men and women of the Banner county should capitulate to céilí figure dancing or find themselves without a floor at future festivals.[93]

## HARPS AT THE FLEADH: DUNGARVAN, 1957

*Dúngharbhán na sean-bhád seolta* [Dungarvan of the old sailing ships] plays host to the greatest gathering of Irish traditional musicians ever seen at one time in the captial of Déise Mumhan. Already the vangaurd of this great concourse is arriving with the main influx expected on Saturday and Sunday when special excursion trains and buses are expected to bring record numbers to the town.[94]

Dungarvan in County Waterford as a Fleadh destination is immortalised in the final lines of Robbie McMahon's 'The Fleadh Down in Ennis' (see pp. 103–21). In his song, McMahon wishes the departing Ennis Fleadh goers in 1956 'good health and good luck' for the year ahead and looks forward to when 'we all meet in Dungarvan'. In Dungarvan, Kevin McCann and his fellow Comhaltas committee members, together with Humphrey Kelleher, lobbied for a number of years to bring the Fleadh to the Waterford town. The Dungarvan branch had bid unsuccessfully for the 1956 event, but were awarded the Fleadh for the following year, in 1957.[95] Kelleher, a fluent Irish speaker, hailed from Kilnamartyra, County Cork and, like other key Comhaltas activists (such as Seán Reid), was a civil servant, at that time working in the department of lands. With McCann, Liam Comerford, Jack Tobin and Joe Fahy (father of Matty Fahy, well-known flute player and adjudicator from Dungarvan), Kelleher formed the Dungarvan Comhaltas branch in 1953, the first in the county.[96] Similar to a growing number of other Comhaltas administrators, he was not a musician, but brought his civil servant skills, honed through his professional life, together with his commitment to traditional culture, to the organisation.[97] Kelleher was also the architect of the Comhaltas constitution in 1956 and became a member of Comhaltas' newly formed Comhairle na Mumhan (Munster Council) in 1960.[98]

The sustainability of any festival depends on a balance of structural knowns and yet-to-be knowns. By 1957, Fleadh attendees had reasonable expectations of what they knew would happen, together with the potential for localised experiences of the ambulatory Fleadh. The invariant components of competitions, a parade and pageant, concerts and céilithe were all scheduled to take place in Dungarvan. Competitions in expected solo categories appeared (fiddle, accordion, concertina, tin whistle, pipes, flute) as well as piccolo and war pipes, piano (reintroduced in Dungarvan), singing and mouth organ. All these were in addition to now familiar ensemble categories for duets, trios, céilí bands and, for Dungarvan, pipe bands. Fr John McGrath (from Carrickbeg, County Waterford) opened the Fleadh giving his speech in both Irish and English, a fact the *Munster Express* noted as fitting, given Dungarvan's proximity to the Waterford Gaeltacht, Ring.[99] The *Irish Press* reported:

> No more fitting setting could be found for a Fleadh than the historic town of Dungarvan. Essentially Gaelic in character and culture, the district is still known as 'na Déise' and here in the shadow of the Comeragh and Monavullagh mountains, by the ancient river of Colligan, a great hosting will take place … There will be a festive air abroad, for a meeting of true Gaels is always a joyous occasion and of course, there will be music and song and the swirl of Irish pipes and dancing in the square.[100]

While undoubtedly still developing, the Fleadh was no longer a novelty and was becoming less malleable and more fixed. Still, there was some agility available to respond to local interests on the principle of inclusion and the potential for reaching new cohorts. Saturday, the first day of the Fleadh, was full of a variety of events, including a drill display and maze marching. These events were tied to the local, as there was a maze marching band in Dungarvan at the time.[101] The inclusion of a competition for orchestra for the first time at the Fleadh (it was also the last time), with only one competitor from the Mercy Convent in Dungarvan, was for the same reason. This was followed by the familiar pageant performance, this time written by Kelleher. 'Breaking of Eire's Chains of Bondage' is described as a musical historical pageant; Maureen Clinch played the part of Éire (an ever-present character in Irish pageants) and it was produced by the local dramatic society.[102] In the lecture presentation later that day (the last such lecture to be presented for many years at the Fleadh), E.M. Wyley, from Cappoquin in Waterford, discoursed in his lecture 'Our Native Music Beyond Compare' on the importance of the Fleadh and the opportunities it presented.[103]

Dungarvan can claim a first in Fleadh history as the advertised harp competitions attracted competitors for the first time. Harp was

## Fleadh Proliferations and Place-making

not offered as part of the Fleadh-Feis Láir na hÉireann competition schedule in 1951. Nor did it appear in 1952, prompting editorial criticism in an otherwise complimentary report on the Monaghan Fleadh in the *Northern Standard*:

> What was missing? Why the musical instrument symbolic of the nation, the musical instrument immortalised by Moore in so many of his melodies, THE HARP [original capitals] ... What an abundance of native history and tradition it awakens! Alas, the harp is rarely heard today ... We commend to the Executive, on which Monaghan is now represented, the introduction of a competition for harpists at the festival to be held in Athlone next year.[104]

The impassioned case presented for the harp, 'the musical instrument, symbolic of the nation', was made on the basis of its undisputed Irish lineage, and its ability to 'transport to ecstasy' any 'Irish heart'.[105] However, harp practice was at a remove from the cultural and social world of pipers, fiddlers and box players. Not an instrument of the country house dance, the harp was historically an instrument of the aristocratic Gael, with 'a privileged position in Irish society', a position that was 'changed utterly by the seventeenth century' following the destruction of the Gaelic order.[106] The harp underwent a limited renaissance in the nineteenth century and became an instrument of the musically literate class. With a vastly modified instrument, a radically changed performance technique, and a new repertoire, the harp emerged as a 'fashionable ... drawing rooom instrument' gathering ideological and symbolic power along the way.[107] At the mid-twentieth-century point, harp repertoire was filled with nostalgic, sentimentalised songs, such as those of Thomas Moore. Formally trained, often as part of their convent school education, the mid-twentieth-century girl/woman singer-harpist (a gender shift from the harper of the Gaels) was seldom found at house dances or céilithe. All of these factors demarcated the harp as outside the habitus of instrumental, dance music tradition. Consequently, its exclusion from the 1951 list of competitions in Mullingar is predictable, notwithstanding the centrality of its symbolic place within the aims of the new organisation. The harp was simply not on the traditional instrument revival radar in 1951.

In the broader cultural arena, harpers performed in semi-professional presentational contexts on the airwaves or on stage. Máire Ní Sheaghe, harper, performed at the concert at the first Fleadh in Mullingar in 1951 and Síle Ní Curtín [sic] in Cavan in 1954, but otherwise, there is little trace of harp sounds at early Fleadhanna.[108] The material absence of the instrument did not prevent the harp as a symbolic touchstone holding high function for the Fleadh. The Belfast Harp Festival in 1792 is repeatedly mythologised as a predecessor of, and for, the Fleadh, drawing on its authenticating powers.[109] Comhaltas' first logo, designed in the early 1950s, has a harp centrally placed above broken chains of bondage, with a new sun dawning as background and the accompanying heraldic 'Comhaltas Ceoltóirí Éireann, Ceol agus Gaol' (music and kinship).[110] The rudimentary logo design relied on harp to communicate the music revival message, conveniently so, as the harp was long understood as an avatar for Ireland and collective identity building.[111] Harp also featured routinely in pageant paratheatrics, the meta-image of Mise Éire (Ireland), harp in hand (holding Ireland), evoking a centuries-old allegory for the nation.[112]

As part of its inaugural manifesto, Comhaltas declared in 1951 that the first aim of the organisation was 'to promote and encourage the playing of the uilleann pipes as our national instrument (with the harp)'.[113] The harp (then parenthetically included) is an afterthought and Tunney proposes that this revivalist aspiration was no more than a 'pious platitude' for Comhaltas until the 1970s.[114] Betraying its piping origins, Comhaltas activities and early Fleadhanna were a vehicle for potential uilleann piping revival rather than the harp. The second and third declared aims of the new organisation in 1951, to preserve uilleann pipes 'in the national life of Ireland' and 'uphold' the uilleann pipes 'to be the true and most ancient instrument, with the harp, in the history of our national music', confirmed the cultural order, with pipes having primacy for early Comhaltas revivalists.[115] Organologically, there were early 'ancient' pipes in Ireland, sharing a chronological past with early harp iterations, but the uilleann pipes, subject to the revivalist's gaze in 1951, were a much more recent invention, codified as late as the early 1800s.[116] The harp in 1951 was also a different instrument to the older Gaelic harp that revivalists symbolically invoked, looking back to a harping tradition that had been lost. However, the strategic inclusion of the harp reached back to the Gaelic past and ticked the checklist of authentic, Irish musical icons.

It was a source of embarrassment that harping was not included in the initial competition list, an omission that was glossed over in later years.[117] Reacting to the public criticism and 'following recommendations' from the Monaghan branch this was remedied in Athlone with 'an innovation … a competition for the harp, and for songs with harp accompaniment'.[118] Notwithstanding the competition's introduction, there were no actual entries for the 'novel feature' of harp competition either that year, or in the subsequent years in Cavan, Loughrea or Ennis.[119] No harpists (singing or otherwise) were heard in competition until 1957.

Staf Gebruers, in his capacity as harp adjudicator in Dungarvan, was disappointed at the presence of only three harpists, but this reflected the state of harping generally.[120] The harpists in the Dungarvan competitions were Philomena O'Keefe from Mallow, County Cork, Philomena Garvey (also listed as Treasa Ní Gharbhaigh), from Rialto in Dublin and Sile Ní Curtín, also from Cork (who had performed at a Fleadh concert at the Cavan Fleadh). Gebruers adjudicated that 'each had an understanding of the musical spirit of Ireland', emphasising the symbolic weight of their art; predictably, all three were women harpers.[121] Garvey won the trophy 'a solid silver replica of the O'Neill harp on a polished oak bass', worth £150 and sponsored by Guinness (whose logo was the same harp).[122] Guinness felt compelled to 'support the association in its efforts to revive harp-playing, which in recent years had tended to fall into disuse'.[123] Speaking to the visual, symbolic and sonic importance of the harp, two of the competing harpists were proudly to the fore performing outdoors in *Fleadh Cheoil*, an Amharc Éireann news reel produced by Gael Linn and filmed at the Fleadh in Dungarvan.[124]

Dungarvan made Fleadh history with its harp contestants. Not coincidentally, this also comes on the heels of the first published constitution for Comhaltas in 1956, largely authored by the Dungarvan revivalist, Kelleher. In the constitution, the order of harp and uilleann pipes in the restorative aims of the organisation were reversed, now reading 'to restore the playing of the harp and uilleann pipes in the national life of Ireland'.[125] This shift in hierarchical order, putting the harp (symbolically rather than sonically important at this point for Comhaltas and the Fleadh) ahead of the pipes (central to both the sound and identity of the Fleadh) is telling. The re-ordering of harp and pipes constitutionally spoke to the distance now gained from the pipers' beginnings of the organisation: the heft of the harp as figurative construct outranked the pipes as material reality, but at least Dungarvan had the sound of harps.

## COMMERCE AND CULTURE COLLIDE: ENNIS AND DUNGARVAN

Though the running of the harp competition is an important development in 1957, the Fleadh in Dungarvan is most often recalled for another reason, namely the conflict between cultural and commercial stakeholders that it exposed. In post-Fleadh reflections, invested parties including Fleadh administrators, the national executive, Fleadh patrons (performers and punters) and local business owners, robustly disagreed on the success (or failure) of what one front-page headline dubbed a flop ceoil in Dungarvan.[126]

Estimating Fleadh contestant numbers and patrons in advance was perilous for organisers every year and particularly so as the Fleadh began to attract significant numbers. For competitors, Fleadh organisers requested advance registration, arranged through local branch networks, though not consistently adhered to. Those who were members often decided to compete in additional categories spontaneously, depending upon which other musicians they encoutered on the Fleadh day.[127] Adding to this, many competitiors were not members of any local Comhaltas branch and arrived at the Fleadh to compete, without warning. Early Fleadhanna were responsive constructs (though less and less each year), balancing the logistics of the event with a wish to welcome all participants into the Fleadh fold. For Fleadh organisers, advance competition entries aided planning and also, importantly, provided much needed cash flow for the event as pre-registrations came with the competition fee enclosed. Several years before Dungarvan, a late announcement was made the day before the Fleadh in Cavan (in 1954) that 'entries will be accepted on the day of the competition', this in spite of entreaties (and warnings to the contrary) beforehand to submit entry forms, together with the appropriate fee.[128] In Cavan, organisers were anticipating 1,000 competitors, on the basis of the growth pattern of the previous three years, but the millennial of competing musicians

*Fleadh Proliferations and Place-making* 95

did not show up and careful plans for venues, adjudicators and facilities were wasted.[129] Without advance confirmation on contestant numbers, advertised competitions were sometimes without competitors (for example the harp competition, described above). Proinsias Ó Broin, secretary of the Ennis Fleadh committee in 1956, was exasperated at the lack of pre-registered entries to the Fleadh.[130] This was not just of passing concern, as he reported that it was causing him nothing less than alarm.[131] He wrote on 26 March 1956: 'I have sent *cláracha* [programmes] and entry forms to the secretaries of every cumann in the country, and I have received only *one* [Ó Broin's italics] entry to date'.[132] He made the Ennis Fleadh committee's position quite clear when he added: 'My committee have decided to adhere strictly to the closing date upon which we have decided, i.e. 18 April 1956', a month in advance of the Fleadh.[133] Ultimately, Ó Broin and his committee capitulated to the reality of walk-up registrations in Ennis.[134]

For all of Cavan's competitor woes and Ó Broin's in Ennis, from 1951 to 1956 the Fleadh was in an expansionist mode, a source of validation for Comhaltas and its revivalist principles. During this period, overall attendance projections were exceeded from one year to the next and the competitor base had an arc of overall growth in the 1950s. In Monaghan in 1952, there were 163 competitors. Beginning in 1955 at Loughrea, three days were necessary to accommodate competitor numbers and mushrooming competition categories. In Ennis, over seventy different competitions took place, with close to 1,000 competitors, a far cry from the thirteen competitions offered as part of the first Fleadh in Mulllingar. The numbers of competitors and attendees were frequently headline or opening statements of newspaper reports: 'Over two hundred competitors from all parts of the country' in Monaghan; 'Over five hundred traditional musicans participated' in Cavan; 'Up to ten thousand people packed into Loughrea on Sunday'; 'Into Ennis town this weekend will throng 20,000 people', emphasising the preoccupation with numerical growth.[135] As a destination festival event, patrons were part of Fleadh tourism and commercial expectations developed in tandem with cultural ones. The touristic importance of the Fleadh was (briefly) acknowledged in 1955 and 1956 by An Tóstal, the government tourist initiative, which coordinated festival events and was launched in 1953 by the Irish tourist board.[136] In the words of T.A. O'Gorman in 1956, chief officer with An Tóstal, the Fleadh was 'amongst the most significant (events) of the year in the country'.[137] The Fleadh in Ennis was lauded as the best so far and all indicators gave the next Fleadh committee in Dungarvan, its local business community, and the national Comhaltas organisation full confidence that the festival in 1957 would be a triumph, improving attendance even more. Not unreasonably, projections for Dungarvan were based on Ennis, where 14,000 people attended the pageant and the parade had 1,000 participants.[138]

One of the recurring heartaches for Fleadh committees was the challenge of accommodation. Calculating the number of beds needed was fraught with uncontrollable variables; finding beds for thousands of extra people, in small rural Irish towns, was not for the faint of organisational heart. In Ennis, the town and its vicinity were full to bursting. Remarked upon was the unusual tactic taken by hotelier Bobby Kerr who 'startled everybody by reducing his prices', though the opportunity was there to 'make a fat killing'.[139] With a sweeping characterisation, the *Irish Times* noted that 'fiddlers and ballad singers from Sligo and Donegal, Kerry and Antrim' were 'ordinary people with very ordinary pocket books'.[140] To cater for the huge swell of people invading Ennis, a Fleadh 'bed bureau', a subcommitte of the accommodation committee, was set up. The bed bureau worked with private householders to make an additional 600 beds available for the visitors to Ennis.[141] Kerr complimented one woman in the town who 'bought three beds so she could help' (an action benefitting her own household and festival alike).[142] Lena Bean Uí Shé recalled heading to Fleadhanna in the late 1950s and early 1960s, finding accommodation on arrival, sometimes sharing a room or even a bed with other Fleadh visitors, stangers to her beforehand.[143] In Longford, on the last day of the Fleadh in 1958, the bed bureau had long run out of options. Private houses close by in Tarmonbarry and Mostrim, and up to 35 kilometres away in Carrick-on-Shannon, County Leitrim, were all called upon to host guests if at all possible.[144] Householders were encouraged to welcome any passing Fleadh visitor to use their bathroom facilities, if someone in need presented themselves at their door.[145] In Thurles, in 1959, an appeal for beds was launched over the public address system in the town square, when all available beds were occupied early on the first day of the Fleadh. The *Tipperary Star* reported:

One woman took in six and her sons slept in armchairs in the sitting room ... Many had to find accommodation in farm-houses outside the town or in nearby towns and some even slept under the stars, the weather being so fine, or in the cars in which they had arrived. A group of An Óige members from Dublin camped out and the Longford group of folk dancers were in caravans on the outskirts of town.[146]

The Monaghan county board proposed a motion in 1959 that no town be selected for a Fleadh until the accommodation and the people who provided it had been 'thoroughly investigated and approved', but accommodation challenges were only set to worsen in the years that followed.[147] In Gorey in 1962, on the last day of the Fleadh, over 1,000 people were turned away by the Fleadh accommodation committee as it had already placed 2,000 last-minute guests in various beds around Gorey and beyond.[148] The *Irish Press* reported people sleeping overnight on the outdoor dance platforms in Mullingar in 1963.[149] When crowds far exceeded expectations, according to one account 'at nightfall, there were numbers of frightened girls pathetically seeking accommodation. Hundreds spent the night roaming the streets'.[150] In response to a Fleadh beds crisis in Clones, in 1964, the accommodation officer in Clones secured 400 army beds for use during the Fleadh weekend.[151]

Census records in 1956 count Dungarvan's population as 5,394. Forecasts of Fleadh numbers in 1957 predicted an eight-fold increase, with an estimated 40,000 to be there for the Fleadh weekend.[152] In preparation, business people in Dungarvan were shown films of the 'blackened streets of Ennis' from the previous year so that they might be fully ready for the anticipated onslaught.[153] It was reported that local hotels in Dungarvan were booked out from January 1957, prompting arrangements 'to accommodate visitors in nearby towns and holiday resorts. Places like Ardmore, Youghal, Cappoquin, Lismore, Clonea, Tramore and Waterford city have all rallied to the cause ... (visitors will be) assured of first class accommodation'.[154] An event on this scale necessitated buy-in from all stakeholders. The local urban council committed 'to purchase buntings and other materials to festoon the central square and streets of the town'.[155] The week before the Fleadh, the *Dungarvan Leader* described the scene: 'The town (is) *en fete* for the gala occasion, and myriads of multi coloured electrical light bulbs over the shops turn the town into a fairy land as darkness falls each night'.¹⁵⁶ Building community involvement further, prizes were offered 'for the best decorated houses and shops'.¹⁵⁷ In the days leading up to the Fleadh, newspapers carried details of extra Fleadh trains that would travel to Dungarvan from Kilmacthomas (in Waterford), but also Cork city, Ballyhooley, Mallow and Fermoy.¹⁵⁸ Longford was the Fleadh destination the following year and business owners, including hoteliers, were strongly urged to attend Dungarvan so they might prepare themselves. A bus was chartered from Longford (and subsidised by the Longford Chamber of Commerce) for 'enterprising local business men (to make) the trip to Dungarvan' to learn what it was all about.¹⁵⁹

The planning in Dungarvan was frenetic:

> All vacant shop space has been rented for the weekend and enterprising groups and individuals will sell minerals, teas and sandwiches, where ever space permits ... at least one shop has got in a big consignment of straw hats, while another has stocked in a big number of light macks. Rain or shine, the crowds can meet the situation.¹⁶⁰

The *Dungarvan Leader* reported that the 'ladies' of the town were occupied preparing food, 'the most necessary part of the festival', adamant that 'if the crowds are not adequately refreshed *"le nua gach biadh agus sean-gach dighe"* [the best of food and drink], the music they will discourse will not be as melodious as it might otherwise be'.¹⁶¹

All did not go according to plan. Following the Fleadh, the *Dungarvan Leader* led with a telling headline, 'Competitors pleased, traders disappointed'.¹⁶² The pilgrimage to the south-eastern town was not undertaken by the projected crowds and the unimpressive gathering 'could be compared to that seen at a county championship [GAA] final'.¹⁶³ Other accounts echoed these sentiments:

> Dungarvan was a town of music, song and dance yesterday and the day before, a town of colourful decoration and glorious sunshine, but it was a day of bitter disappointments for the people of Dungarvan and for the business people in particular. The big crowds that were expected did not show up.¹⁶⁴

## Fleadh Proliferations and Place-making

Of the 40,000 anticipated, it was estimated only 5,000 attended Sunday's activities.[165] Any suggestion that more were there was 'rubbing salt into wounds' of local traders.[166] The editorial in the *Munster Express*, 'Festival was a failure', was unequivocal.[167] In the same column, no mention is made of, or value given to, music making or what musicians thought of the festival. What is reported at length is the 'thousands of sandwiches, hundreds of pounds of ham and beef, chicken and mutton', that went to waste.[168] Preoccupation with the uneaten sandwiches was widespread, 'one observer stated that there were enough to feed the town for two days'.[169] Breweries agreed to take back 'unsold stocks of their products and collections were going on all day on Tuesday' after the Fleadh finished.[170]

Two particularly scathing reports by Tom Tobin appeared on 15 June in the *Dungarvan Observer* following the Fleadh: 'National festival "flopped" in Dungarvan, thirty thousand short' and 'The inside story, the flop that needn't have been'. Trying to solve the 'reasons for the flop', Tobin wrote that 'the weather was not to blame [as] glorious sunshine favoured the occasion'.[171] Liam Comerford, a secretary on the Fleadh committee, mused that 'Dungarvan being very far south may have been a bit out of the way for the big crowds that flocked to Ennis', which Tobin rejected, retorting 'Dungarvan is central enough for anything and well they know it'.[172] Location aside, more importantly Comerford said that Dungarvan did not have 'the strong backline of traditional musicians that Ennis had. West Clare, Limerick, Kerry and Galway were able to provide the great bulk' of those 'who supported the festival' there.[173] He realised, too late, that 'the people here [in Waterford] did not have sufficient interest in traditional Irish music to come [to Dungarvan] … they were leaving it to the outsiders'.

Journalist and editor, Tobin was personally vexed and the victual subplot continued when his report in the *Observer* noted that 'a festival dinner was held at the Convent of Mercy to which members of the press were not invited'.[174] The reporter showed no mercy as he provided a catalogue of the Fleadh 'fiasco': a céilí with few dancers; dancers but no céilí band; the 'abomination' of a platform necessitating the bishop use 'steel scaffolding as a support' to haul himself up; lack of cooperation with the press; and overpriced entry fees.[175] The irony of the visiting Keating family, who 'had to turn to the Sisters of Mercy in Dungarvan for food' though there were surplus sandwiches, was not noted.[176] Tobin called for an inquest, to which members of the press would be invited, writing 'Dungarvan's reputation has been injured … there is no good denying the fact'.[177] The final barb was delivered with a flourish: 'throughout the town' the Fleadh was 'being called "the flaw"'.[178] Between flop cheoil and flaw cheoil, the *Dungarvan Observer* found itself embroiled in a libel case in the circuit court brought by members of the Fleadh organising committee, the latter of whom prevailed.[179]

In the 1957 Comhaltas annual progress report, Paddy Maunsell recorded:

> This year's Fleadh Cheoil has come and gone since my last report and in its trail we have had many criticisms. It has even been referred in one periodical as a 'flop'. One wonders by what standards … Evidently they has come to expect some kind of fair day for the townspeople of Dungarvan who had been gulled by stories of big sales and fat profits. This aspect has never, thank God, entered into the deliberations of An Comhaltas.[180]

The argument was essentialised into righteous cultural anger on Comhaltas' part and vainglorious commercialism on the other. Maunsell advised Comhaltas followers to 'ignore the vapourings of a small but noisy group who never had, and I dare say, never will have the slightest interest in Irish music'.[181] In the next breath, Maunsell chastised branches for neglecting to pay affiliation fees, suggesting that financial concerns were part of Comhaltas moral order too, despite protestations to the contrary.[182]

## CONCLUSION

Rural festivals in particular 'act like glue, temporarily sticking together various stakeholders, economic transactions and networks', but what happens when the glue becomes unstuck?[183] The identity of the Fleadh in Ennis and then Dungarvan marks a point in the history of the festival when commercial concerns properly intruded upon how a festival was judged and identified as a success or failure. The perigrinations of the Fleadh did not limit the development of place associations for rural

## Fleadh Proliferations and Place-making

Fleadh towns, rather, as Gibson and Connell note in another context, towns became 'known through festivals, particularly if they attract national media attention'.[184] But place-making can have positive and negative associations. Place identities in public discourse of each Fleadh are clear; Ennis was a highpoint, Dungarvan (unfairly) was not.

Little acknowledgement is made of the fact that Dungarvan hosted the largest number of competing musicians at any Fleadh up to then, with in excess of 1,000 entries.[185] And, while overall attendance fell far short of expectations, many musicians travelled for the event. From Northern Ireland, Johnny Pickering and Malachy Sweeney were among the musical visitors, a large contingent from Clare, members of the Derry and Antrim Fiddlers Association, and expatriot musicians from the United Kingdom and the USA all arrived.[186] Even Tobin, in his bitter review (though buried in the middle of his criticisms), admitted that 'as a festival of traditional music, the event was an outstanding success ... what wonderful music was heard in the halls that Monday'.[187] For Tobin, and many others, that was not the priority. The Fleadh was no longer just about providing a musician-friendly meeting place, but by Dungarvan in 1957, the Fleadh identified itself to the host towns as a (potential) bonanza, at a time when small towns badly needed it. When that promise was broken, disappointment was articulated in no uncertain terms, disconnected from any aesthetic experience of musicians and attendees. In a post-Dungarvan Fleadh world, the Fleadh (and Comhaltas) were obliged to respond to the criticisms raised. The question remained as to what that response would be and how the Fleadh would manage competing cultural and commercial concerns. In addition, Dungarvan was the canary in the mine of overall attendance numbers in the late 1950s. Though competitor numbers continued to increase, there was a plateau in total attendance, with for example, 20,000 attending the Thurles Fleadh in 1959.[188] This too changed as the Fleadh rolled into the 1960s. There was a rapid acceleration in attendance: too few was not the challenge; in fact, too many became the problem, creating a whole other headache for Fleadh identity.

CHAPTER 5

# Songs and Stories: Reenactments of the Fleadh

Thus far, this book has charted the development of the Fleadh from modest beginnings in Mullingar in 1951, through the interim years of Fleadh development, to the highs of Ennis in 1956 and increased musicians' participation at the 1957 festival in Dungarvan (notwithstanding the Flaw/Flop Cheoil moniker). The Fleadh invigorated and validated the community of traditional Irish music practice and as the years went on, was an important tool of revival in the growth of that community. As a calendar-tied annual event, the Fleadh, like all festivals, was experienced as 'an autonomous temporal zone', where time is 'on its own terms rather than those of a clock bound world'.[1] Festivity at the Fleadh thrived on the encounters and rich exchanges between participants in Fleadh space, creating a web of social contracts and offering a bounty of opportunities to share music, renew social relations, and create new communion.[2]

Hyper-experience of the festival did not, however, begin merely on arrival at the Fleadh site. Real-time abandonment, moving from everyday temporality to the festive zone, began for Fleadh goers before they ever reached Athlone, or Cavan or Ennis. The anticipation of the event and the moment at which the physical journey to the Fleadh begins, when the musician caught the train or got in the car, or indeed mounted the bicycle, signalled the beginning of the shift into Fleadh time. Likewise, the end of the Fleadh, as the bunting was taken down and Fleadh goers took the road home back into ordinary time, did not neatly cauterise Fleadh experience. Rather, the communion experienced at the festival was revisited post-Fleadh by Fleadh goers in a process of ongoing

*Songs and Stories: reenactments of the Fleadh*

reenactment.³ In the case of music practice and celebration at the Fleadh, post-festival music making was a continuous enactment of the Fleadh experience. Tunes and songs heard at the Fleadh had reanimating possibilities in the post-Fleadh world. Repertoire and music making linked local, national and even diasporic communities together in a newly constructed community, bound by music practice and extending Fleadh experience beyond the festive space.

Just as music is shared and reshared after the Fleadh, in an ongoing extension of festive communion, the experience of the Fleadh was reenacted through Fleadh songs, poems and stories – the focus of this chapter. Spoken or sung, stories are a way in which people make sense of their world, creating new meaning with, and for, others. Fleadh stories, vital in a post-festival world, make it 'the experience of those who are (then) listening'.⁴ In Mary Mullaly's words, Fleadh stories just get 'better in the telling'.⁵ Thus, Fleadh interactions, musical and social, are vivified after the fact and the essence of the Fleadh experience is perpetuated at individual and community level beyond the Fleadh. Among the many stories gratefully heard during fieldwork for this book, journey stories were particularly abundant: heading to and leaving the Fleadh (moving in and out of festive time) was consistently recounted. There are also a number of poems written in response to the Fleadh, though, as will be clearly demonstrated, oral and sung narratives create post-Fleadh communion and sustain meaning for the community of Irish traditional music much more effectively than literary ones. The chapter begins with the most widely known of Fleadh story reenactments, Robbie McMahon's song, 'The Fleadh Down in Ennis'. So successful is the song in the post-Fleadh cultural world that it corroborates County Clare as 'home of traditional music' in the cultural imagination, a trope consolidated during this period and also explored in this chapter.

'THE FLEADH DOWN IN ENNIS'

'The Fleadh Down in Ennis' as sung and resung by its maker, Robbie McMahon, is the most iconic and revealing account of Fleadh experience in the 1950s.⁶ A Clare native and songmaker of note, McMahon, known as the King of Spancil Hill (due to his definitive version of the titular ballad) was deeply embedded in traditional music culture in Clare.⁷ Ennis was not his first Fleadh adventure, but McMahon was one of the many thousands attending in 1956. The song potently combines storytelling and music making, the two key modes of reenacting the Fleadh experience and it resonated powerfully with listeners. In this comic folk song, McMahon builds communion through acknowledgement of his social co-actors in the Fleadh while, at the same time, makes a spectacle of musicians and their music making. For McMahon and his listeners, these are complementary tactics.[8] Though it has the 1956 Ennis Fleadh as its subject, the song gathered additional layers of meaning in multiple performances thereafter and maintains current cultural relevance. In 1956, the Fleadh was still a once-a-year phenomenon but was already the single-most important and influential public manifestation of traditional music revival in Ireland. As discussed, Ennis was a watershed in the development of the festival (and of Comhaltas). McMahon's song captures the energy of that excitement and represents that moment of confident revival. As a socio-cultural narrative, it allows access to the engagement of music with festive life and is thick with meaning.[9] Here, the meaning is accessed by exploring the matrix of relationships found in folk song as described by Thomas McKean, between 'text and tune, text and context' and 'singer and audience', among others.[10] McMahon's song transforms the personal into an ethnographic collective account, while retaining ownership of that narrative for his own telling and retelling of the Fleadh experience.[11]

The full text is here below, transcribed from a version shared with me by McMahon:

> Will you sit back a while 'til I sing you a song,
> Tis not very short, nor it's not very long,
> It's about the Fleadh Cheoil down in Ennis you see,
> So, to me will you pay your attention.
> I'm not a great singer, but I know there are worse,
> I cannot help trying to sing you a verse,
> Or to let you all know how the Fleadh Cheoil got on
> And for you, now, who couldn't attend it.
>
> They came from the North and they came from the East
> From the West and the South, 'twas a thriller to see,
> With fiddles and bagpipes and piccolos too

And drumsticks to keep them in order.
They came down from Dublin, so hearty and gay
They brought Leo Rowsome to show them the way,
Himself and Seán Seery they played all the way
With their flute player, Vincent O'Broderick.
*Sciddery idle, dom diddery, dom die dee.*

They came down from Cavan so far, far, away,
I'm sure they were travelling for most of a day,
With singers and players, the best I can say
To compete at the Fleadh down in Ennis.
Their players were good, and their singers were keen,
But Margaret O'Reilly was the best of the team,
And big Dr Galligan, he wore the báinín,
Just to swank at the Fleadh down in Ennis.

From the Kingdom of Kerry, they all made their way
And brave Denis Murphy he started to play,
The 'Auld Floggin' Reel' and 'The Black Cup of Tay'
Sure, you'd feel ten times younger right after.
From Limerick's fair city they came by the score,
And Johnny McMahon he played an encore,
And the bould Andy Keane sure he played as much more
And to finish he played 'Colonel Frazer'.
*Sciddery idle, dom diddery, dom die dee.*

From Wicklow and Carlow, they all fell in line,
And up from Portarlington came Johnny Ryan,
He resined the bow and he watched every line
For he won the first prize on the violin.
From Galway they came every man and his wife,
With Eddie Moloney who played on the fife,
And young Kieran Collins would make the dead rise
When he played us 'The Lark in the Morning'.

There was music and song from all over Clare
The Macks of Crusheen and sure all the Mulkeres,
The Mike Preston Trio and Martin Mulhaire

Not forgetting the Mister Joe Leary.
Mrs Crotty, she came all the way from Kilrush,
She took a high note for the 'Bird in the Bush',
She played all the day and she never did blush
'Twas 'Good girl yourself, Mrs Crotty'.

Now Peter O'Loughlin from Connolly came,
He brought Paddy Murphy, sure 'twas all in the game,
They played a duet and they made a big name
For they won at the Fleadh down in Ennis.
And down from Bell Harbour Chris Droney he came,
He played on a matchbox, I thought 'twas that same,
'Til someone said, 'Robbie, what's that you're saying?
Isn't that his own small concertina!'

They came down from Quilty, to sing and to play,
With big Martin Talty from Miltown Malbay,
And the bould Willie Clancy, he gave a display,
Sure, we know he's the king of the pipers.
And someone said then 'Who's that man over there?
Isn't that Jimmy Ward from the North side of Clare?'
He plays on the banjo with music to spare,
For he plays with the great Kilfenora.

Our own Paddy Canny, he took oe'r the fair
He played through the streets and right up to the square.
Says Daniel O'Connell 'My life on you there,
And I think you're the best of them all, sure'.
And o'er from America more of them flew,
And Paddy O'Brien, he was one of the few,
He played on the accordion you'd swear there were two,
He got so many notes in together.

Now Ciarán McMahon was busy bedad,
Recording them all, sure the good and the bad,
But for him our music was gone to the bad
So 'tis 'Welcome Ciarán Mac Mathúna'.
'Tis all over now, but 'twas something to see

So, thanks to Seán Reid and the great committee,
So, I wish you good health now and good luck now from me,
Until we all meet again in Dungarvan.
Sciddery idle, dom diddery, dom die dee.[12]

Delivered in his signature, declamatory style, the song became a regularly requested one in McMahon's repertoire, and he knew when audiences cajoled him into singing, 'twould lift them up, twould wake them up'.[13] As songmaker and singer, the Clare native doubly inserted himself in the Fleadh by giving the song its first airing at the Fleadh in Dungarvan in 1957.[14] He was invited to sing on a temporary stage in the town square and was also recorded by Ciarán Mac Mathúna, who attended the Dungarvan Fleadh, for later broadcast on RÉ (see Fig. 5.1).

**Fig. 5.1** Ciarán Mac Mathúna (seated on right), Elizabeth Crotty and Johnny Pickering, Dungarvan, 1957
Courtesy ITMA

McMahon sang at the 1957 Fleadh, about the previous Fleadh, placing the song (and story) through its debut in Dungarvan in the crucible of festive celebration. Adding to the effect, the song is populated in 1957 by characters not in some dim distant past (though they may now be so), but in real time. Many of the song's characters were there in front of him in Dungarvan. McMahon says 'I remember that, I sang it outside on the stage, and it went down like a bomb'.[15] McMahon's performance secured the song's future in traditional repertoire as proprietorially McMahon's, while consolidating its signature importance in the narration of Fleadh experience.

By 1956, McMahon already had a reputation in County Clare, and further afield, as a singer and songmaker. He distinguished himself by composing both melody and lyrics for many of his songs (for example 'The Old Man on the Hob'), but for 'The Fleadh Down in Ennis' he used an extant melody, found in other traditional songs ('The Limerick Rake', 'The Wife of the Bold Tenant Farmer' and 'Fágaimid Siúd Mar Atá Sé').[16] Many songmakers within traditional music culture exploit this time-honoured practice of new lyrics set to existing melodies. McMahon's compositions lie squarely within the (Irish) folk idiom, utilising familiar tropes melodically, metrically and lyrically. Like much folk song repertoire, 'The Fleadh Down in Ennis' is an internal cultural commentary, originating from within a music community and is intended for that community's consumption and interpretation. It is a comic come-all-ye song in the recreational, contemporary mode following Hugh Shields' definition of come-all-ye as 'any Irish-made narrative song in English'.[17] These songs often deliver the narrative in the first person, as is found in 'The Fleadh Down in Ennis' ('Will you sit back a while til I sing you a song?') and, like other new ballads, 'listeners expect an explicit story: a sequence not just chronological but complete, accompanied by dates, places, names of persons'.[18] This corpus of song relies exclusively on internal cultural markers for meaning: the jokes and jibes are insider ones but, as Shields cautions, it is a mistake to dismiss a 'simply labelled' recreational or comic song as implicitly thin in meaning.[19] And though Shields contends the 'intention' of a (comic) ballad text 'produces effects too internalized to the listener to be related to a recognisable function', a close analysis relying on text and fieldwork with the songmaker McMahon, and others, elucidates function, use and contemporaneous reception.[20] Through the course of its nine verses, McMahon outlines the performative and participatory elements of the Fleadh in Ennis. He defines the parameters of the Fleadh as festive space and catalogues the Fleadh experience. The song purposefully emphasises aspects of the experience that reiterate shared meaning and hold relevance beyond the Fleadh narrative and space.

Metrically, the song is in jig time (6/8), the dance metre most frequently used in Irish comic (or lighter) song genre.[21] In common with other dance tune types within the Irish tradition, jig time has an underlying metrical and rhythmic structure of eight measures per musical part. The resulting sixteen measures, with each measure divided internally in triplets, provide the metrical structure, and upbeats are found in each line:

> Will you sit back a while 'til I sing you a song,
> Tis not very short, nor it's not very long,
> It's about the Fleadh Cheoil down in Ennis you see,
> So, to me will you pay your attention.
> I'm not a great singer, but I know there are worse,
> I cannot help trying to sing you a verse,
> Or to let you all know how the Fleadh Cheoil got on
> And for you, now, who couldn't attend it.

One of the recurring motifs throughout the text is the notion of symmetry, reflecting the essence of any festive experience. Though Joseph P. Gusfield and Jerry Michalowicz discuss symmetry at festivals in terms of the individual/collective and religious/secular, and the balance between them, the success of any festive event is based not just upon these.[22] Its success is also dependent upon a balance between the formal and informal, the controlled and the transgressive. The opening couplet of 'The Fleadh Down in Ennis' assures listeners that what they were about to hear would achieve the perfect balance: 'Tis not very short nor tis not very long'. The perception of balance is reiterated almost immediately: 'I'm not a great singer, but I know there are worse', McMahon demurs. The self-deprecation would not be lost on his listeners as McMahon was a powerful singer, confident in his own singing prowess.

Notwithstanding his self-declared mediocrity, McMahon 'cannot help trying to sing you a verse' (again, the question of balance arises) and is compelled, by his own assertion 'to let you all know how the Fleadh Cheoil got on'. The Fleadh itself is subtly personated, constructed as an independent entity with predilections and its own identifiable character. In particular, he sings 'for you, now, who couldn't attend it', extending the Fleadh experience to those who could not be there. By 1956, the Fleadh had grown substantially and musicians travelled increasingly longer distances to attend. Drawing from the four cardinal points of Ireland, nodding to older poetic practice, McMahon describes the pilgrimage to Ennis in the opening lines of the second verse: 'They came from the north and they came from the east, From the west and the south twas a thriller to see'. The song alerts the listener to the exceptional social context of the Fleadh at a time when music gatherings of this scale and nature were rare. With 'fiddles and bagpipes and piccolos' in hand, McMahon hints at Alessandro Falassi's necessary element of festival trespass, the uncontainable element of the Fleadh, when he sings of 'drum sticks to keep them in order'.[23]

One of the duties of the comic songmaker is to acknowledge the field of characters (people, places and events) in the story. McMahon moves on to the business at hand, naming key figures of Irish traditional music in 1956, narrating their origins and locating them in the Fleadh world of Ennis. In an interview, McMahon repeatedly pointed out the number of performers named in the song, emphasising the importance of this narrative device: 'I'd say there could be thirty five or thirty six names of musicians and singers in that song'.[24] In 'The Fleadh Down in Ennis', there are families of musicians and ensembles named (the Macks and Mulkeres, the Mike Preston trio, the Kilfenora), in addition to twenty-five individually named practitioners of Irish traditional music (including McMahon himself). For McMahon, the explicit naming of these indivduals, families and ensembles is an essential part of his role as songmaker, and he takes direct responsibility through their naming to secure these musicians and singers in cultural memory. McMahon lamented in 2008 that 'there's a world of them dead, but the Clare ones are still living', further mythologising a strength of Clare musical genetics and the county's reputation as the home of traditional music (see pp. 114–8).[25]

*Songs and Stories: reenactments of the Fleadh*

In light of the rural bias found in discourses of and on traditional music practice, what Adrian Scahill terms the 'fractious relationship' between 'the rural traditional musician and the more urbane and urban-based folk cadre', it is significant that the first musicians introduced to the listener are Dubliner(s) or urban Dublin-based:

> They came down from Dublin so hearty and gay,
> They brought Leo Rowsome to show them the way;
> Himself and Seán Seery they played all the way,
> With their flute player Vincent O'Broderick,
> Sciddery idle dom diddery dom die dee.[26]

Though the Fleadh has since taken place in small cities on the island (Derry in 2016, and Kilkenny in 1983, 1984 and 1988), the perception of traditional music making and its association with the rural is constantly promoted, particularly during the early decades of Fleadh history, mirroring early twentieth-century folk music revival discourse in the USA.[27] The belief that the landscape of the countryside was traditional music's true home and the terrain that had sustained it was at odds with the joint urban and rural genesis of Comhaltas in Dublin and Westmeath. Like their American music revivalist contemporaries, the bearers of the tradition came from both rural and urban sites.[28] However, for Comhaltas and, by extension, the Fleadh, 'the heart of authentic traditional music practice' was in rural Ireland ideologically if not in practice by 1956.[29] Leo Rowsome is a key example of urban revivalist. Already identified as a key teacher, activist and practitioner of uilleann piping, he held a flawless musical lineage. His musician grandfather was a native of Ballitore, County Wexford and a contemporary of the Cash piping family in that county; nonetheless Rowsome identifies as a Dubliner. Given his role in CPU in Dublin and as a leading authority on uilleann piping, in McMahon's narrative it naturally fell to Rowsome to direct his car-mates into the heartland of the rural and, metaphorically, into the heart of the Fleadh. In McMahon's reading, Seán Seery, another musician, Comhaltas activist and true blue Dubliner, accompanies Rowsome and they both play their way to Ennis. Performing on the way to the Fleadh acts as a transitional device, a movement towards Fleadh space and place.

The third musketeer on this pilgrimage to the Fleadh holy ground is 'Vincent O'Broderick', a flute player and tune composer originally from east Galway, but living by this time in Dublin. Adding the supplementary syllable to Broderick's name, thereby transforming him from Vincent Broderick into 'Vincent O'Broderick', is primarily poetic necessity, allowing McMahon to supplement the line syllabically. It also wryly references a variety of popular Irish(-American) song, where the repeated articulation of surnames with O'and Mc prevails.[30] McMahon's gentle poking of fun through the 'O' in 'O' Broderick' distances itself from that stage genre, asserting its authenticity of form in comparison, while still confidently operating as comic song.

The 'jaunty vocables' of 'Sciddery idle, dom diddery, dom die dee', are irregularly used at the end of the second, fourth and ninth verses and offset the anticipated eight-line verse length otherwise found throughout.[31] The absence of a fully independent chorus is common within the Irish folk song tradition, but the inclusion of a nonsense supplementary refrain at the end of some, but not all, verses is a familiar traditional song device often used in the comic genre. Vocables usually function as a mnemonic mechanism, used as an aid to memorise melody, but that is not their primary role in this song given the irregularity of usage. Within the strict structural framework, these audible surprises provide a relief from the undulating metre and voluble catalogue of names and place in the song, extending the verse length.

McMahon continues to list people and the various places from where they travelled to the Fleadh, articulating a living hagiography of Irish traditional music, intuitively using the praise poetry device of naming and recognising persons of note. From Cavan ('so far, far away') came singer Margaret O'Reilly (who came second to Angela Mulcaire at the Ennis Fleadh in the senior ballad competition) and her fellow county man 'big doctor Galligan':

he wore the báinín,
Just to swank at the Fleadh down in Ennis.

Brian Galligan, bedecked in his trademark aran jumper (báinín) was immediately familiar to contemporary listeners. A key figure in Comhaltas from early years, his administrative rank rose with the expansion of the organisation, and he ascended to national chairman of Comhaltas in 1956. Though this was a full four years before the Clancy Brothers and Tommy Makem formally adopted aran jumpers as their signature costume on the other side of the Atlantic, Galligan's attire represented a particular kind of enthusiasm in (and engagement with) traditional or folk music, something also seen in American folk music revival where afficionados would 'emulate rural ways in their dress'.[32] A writer in the *Irish Independent* in 1958 opined 'We don't have to wear outrageous outfits to show we are Irish. A man is not made an Irishman simply by donning an Arran bonnet, a bauneen or a *crios* [belt]'.[33] McMahon's description of Galligan's getup (the honorific 'doctor' who could 'swank' in his aran) recognises the sartorial staging of revival. For McMahon, the báinín and its associated identity is peripheral to the performative nucleus on which the tradition would flourish or flounder and noting this for his listeners.[34]

The song goes on to name-check Johnny McMahon (no relation to Robbie) from 'Limerick's fair city' (subtly commandeering the 'fair city' moniker from Dublin, as widely known from the come-all-ye, 'Molly Malone'). When interviewed, Robbie remembered Johnny as a 'beautiful fiddle player', though added with chagrin that Johnny would sometimes 'play with some modern band, the likes of Mike Delahunty'.[35] Delahunty and His Orchestra were one of most successful sit-down dance orchestras (as distinct from a céilí band) in the late 1940s and 1950s.[36] Johnny McMahon also played with his own dance band for a number of years and had a Christmas residency in Todds department store in Limerick. He was a member of the Irish Federation of Musicians (IFM), a union that purported to transcend the boundaries between traditional and popular practice representation, but in reality was focused on popular music dance bands.[37] While the world of the Fleadh was built on traditional music practice, the non-Fleadh cultural world of 1950s Ireland was one that was dominated by social dance accompanied in the early part of the decade by sit-down dance bands, and latterly by the emerging popular music genre of showbands. Despite that, McMahon (Robbie) remembered of Johnny McMahon: 'but he could play, play (traditional) slow airs' like no other.[38]

Other counties offered disciples to the Fleadh in the song:

> From the Kingdom of Kerry they all made their way
>
> ...
>
> From Wicklow and Carlow they all fell in line
> Up from Portarlington came Johnny Ryan
>
> ...
>
> From Galway they came every man and his wife
> With Eddie Moloney who played on the fife;
> And young Kieran Collins would make the dead rise
> When he played them 'The Lark in the Morning'.

Moloney and Collins were at the vanguard of traditional music practice from east Galway through their solo playing and also through ensemble performance with céilí bands (Moloney was in one permutation of the Ballinakill Céilí Band). As for Collins, a tin whistle player, he is given messianic powers, 'to make the dead rise'. The miraculous capacity of music making and musicians is a lyric device used several times in the song. He sings of Denis Murphy's playing that 'you'd feel ten times younger right after'.

McMahon includes numerous instrumental dance tune titles in the lyrics, 'The Lark in the Morning', 'The Ould Flogging Reel', 'Colonel Frazer', 'The Bird in the Bush' and 'The Black Cup of Tay'. All tunes cited in the song are part of the repertoire with which many Fleadh goers (musicians and non-) were familiar. Including the names of tunes in an insider-directed (song) commentary cleverly builds another layer of musical depth and memory. The tune names are cues for the tune melodies, an acoustic subtext to the primary song performance.

## CLARE, HOME OF TRADITIONAL MUSIC

In addition to the quality of song and songmaker, there are a number of interesecting contexts for the immediate success of 'The Fleadh Down in Ennis' and its sustained influence beyond the Fleadh zone. National recognition of traditional musicians was building through the recordings of Ciarán Mac Mathúna with the mobile recording unit of RÉ from 1955; through their subsequent broadcasting on the national airwaves; and, crucially, through those very same musicians' exposure at the Fleadh.

# Songs and Stories: reenactments of the Fleadh

Central to these developments was County Clare and its traditional music culture. Clare now describes and markets itself as 'the home of traditional music', an axiom laid down in the 1950s due in no small part to the Ennis Fleadh, the success of Clare musicians in its competitions, and the hugely popular Clare county fleadhanna that came in its wake.[39]

The opening verses of the song operate at a macro-national level, citing those who travelled furthest to the Fleadh, from Dublin and overseas. McMahon records the international character of the Fleadh singing that 'o'er from America more of them flew'. He provides more details on those who travelled furthest, from the USA:

> And Paddy O'Brien, he was one of the few,
> He played on the accordion you'd swear there were two,
> He got so many notes in together.

O'Brien, the Newtown, Tipperary musician, had a particular tie to County Clare musically as he played with the Tulla Céilí Band for a period before he emigrated to New York in 1954 (changes in membership of céilí bands due to emigration were frequent). A Fleadh winner in solo accordion in 1953 (in Athlone), the description of O'Brien's virtuosity, 'he got so many notes in together', is a cleverly veiled nod to O'Brien's ground-breaking chromatic acccordion style.[40]

McMahon moves concentrically closer and finally, in the sixth verse of the song, he arrives in the musical bread basket of Ireland: County Clare. In the fashion of a praise poem, he tabulates local Clare heroes, offering a genealogy of Irish traditional music, at the epicentre of the Fleadh and, for him, the centre of the traditional music world:

> The Macks of Crusheen and sure all the Mulkeres;
> The Mike Preston Trio and Martin Mulhaire
> Not forgetting the Mister Joe Leary.

Another verse continues:

> They came down from Quilty, to sing and to play
> With big Martin Talty from Miltown Malbay,
> And the bold Willie Clancy, he gave a display

> Sure we know he's the king of the pipers.
> And someone said then, "who's that man over there?"
> Isn't that Jimmy Ward from the north side of Clare,
> He plays the banjo with music to spare
> For he plays with the great Kilfenora.

The census of Clare places and musicians (all individual musicians named are men with the exception of Mrs Crotty later) is the seismic core to which McMahon has been guiding his listeners all along.[41]

The inevitable invocation of the Kilfenora Céilí Band as signifiers of an intra-community confidence in the importance of local musicians (and bands) on a national platform is cleverly judged. This reference is also notable, as in the first version of the song that McMahon made (and premiered at the Fleadh in Dungarvan in 1957) no mention was made of the Kilfenora Céilí Band explicitly. Shortly after that performance, McMahon received a postcard addressed to 'Robbie McMahon, Singer, County Clare'.[42] The postcard writer chastised McMahon for making a song about the Fleadh in Ennis but failing to mention the Kilfenora Céilí Band by name.[43] Demonstrating folk song's agility to continuously react (and McMahon's songmaking skills), he atoned for the mortal omission and revised the song to include 'the great Kilfenora', part of the song since. The dynamic relationship between Fleadh triumphs and the popularity of Clare céilí bands nationally is recognised by McMahon in the guise of Jimmy Ward, Kilfenora Céilí Band banjo player, whose musical cup overflows with 'music to spare'. When McMahon declares of Willie Clancy: 'Sure we know he's the king of the pipers', he builds consensus through presumptive first-person plural phrasing, a folk song tactic. Once again, these lines provide necessary symmetry of festive representation, with important local figures as counterbalance to the characters from further flung places indicated earlier. In these later verses, McMahon illustrates the intimacy of the local in his own interpretation of meaning at, and through, the Fleadh. Mrs Crotty ('Twas "Good girl yourself Mrs Crotty"'), grand dame of traditional music and chair of Comhaltas in County Clare at that time 'played all the day and she never did blush'. In an interview, McMahon asserted that at the Fleadh in Ennis 'you'd want to go before the courts to see her' such was the demand to hear Mrs Crotty play.[44]

## Songs and Stories: reenactments of the Fleadh

For McMahon, and other attendees, the competitions were an essential part of the proceedings, providing the containable balance to other music making at the Fleadh. The competition performance of Kilmaley natives Peadar (Peter in the song) O'Loughlin (flute) and Paddy Murphy (concertina) is recalled:

> They played a duet and they made a big name,
> For they won at the Fleadh down in Ennis.

Their winning performance in the Munster provincial final in Ennis makes a 'big name' not just for themselves, but for Clare as the home of traditional music.

'The Fleadh Down in Ennis' captured the imagination of contemporary and later listeners. In fieldwork interviews the song and McMahon's performance of it was repeatedly talked about by interviewees. One part of the song was most frequently pointed to by other musicians.[45] In the seventh verse, McMahon describes Chris Droney 'down from Bell Harbour' (in north Clare), using a typical folk song dialogue strategy between himself and an unamed observer:

> He played on a matchbox, I thought 'twas the same;
> 'til someone said, 'McMahon, what's that you're saying,
> Isn't that his own small concertina?'[46]

The importance of concertina in County Clare is given predictable deference. But the lines above also playfully critique the lack of concertina awareness in national music culture in 1956 (as discussed in a previous chapter). McMahon casts himself as the onlooker initially mistaking the concertina for a matchbox, raising an eyebrow at the concertina-ignorant. This is a blunder, McMahon knows, that no one from County Clare (the home of traditional music) would make.

McMahon further emphasises the Fleadh as musical miracle in his description of an exchange between Daniel O'Connell and Paddy Canny, east Clare fiddler and musical hero of the present as he played 'through the streets and right up to the square'. The square in question is the main junction of the primary thoroughfares of Ennis, including O'Connell Street, and it is understood locally as the centre point of the town. It is distinguished, like many town squares, by a statue of a historical figure; in the case of Ennis, O'Connell towers over the town's activities. O'Connell, founder of the Catholic Association, was the *de facto* nationalist leader of early-nineteenth-century Ireland and is commemorated in street names throughout the country. Though a Kerry native, O'Connell has a particular association with County Clare as he was first elected to parliament in the 1828 Clare by-election. The monumental O'Connell is so impressed by Canny and his music at the Fleadh that he is brought back to life and speaks directly to him, 'My life on you there, sure I think you're the best of them all, sure'. Cogent authenticity is bestowed from the past on the Fleadh in Ennis, on a Clare musician and on music in Clare through the Liberator himself.

## MEDIATING REVIVAL

A fundamental pillar in the wider revival of traditional music practice is the strategic use of mediating technologies. Contrary to any notion of cultural revivalists being anti-modern, they were committed to using the tools of modern society to further their cause.[47] Media (radio, recordings and latterly television) was an essential element in the success of traditional music revival facilitating the dissemination of repertoire, and the implicit attached cultural meaning, in a manner that would have been impossible otherwise. Deirdre Ní Chonghaile describes the post-war years as a 'boom period for the collection of Irish traditional music in Ireland' and Clare as 'musical mecca' (in Ó hAllmhuráin's words) was particularly important.[48] The role of media in music cultures across the globe increased exponentially from the late nineteenth century, beginning with the development of recording technology and the ability from the second decade of the century to mass produce those recordings. The intersubjective moment of live music no longer the only listening option, recording technology shunted listening along a continuum of active toward passive participation and made a dislocated listening experience possible.[49] Where previously hearing music involved being in the same physical space as the source of that performance, the development of recording changed that irrevocably, creating a distance between performer and listener heretofore unknown.

Commercial LP releases of Clare Fleadh winners in the years following the Ennis Fleadh further boosted Clare's home of traditional music reputation and extended Fleadh sounds beyond the Fleadh zone.[50] Dublin Records was established in 1956 by James and John O'Neill, with Sligo fiddler Paddy Killoran.[51] Though New York based, the O'Neill brothers were originally from Labasheeda, County Clare. Dublin Records' catalogue focuses on céilí bands and emigrant Irish dance bands (some with vocalists).[52] From 1956 to 1966, the label released a series of albums, many of which featured céilí band Fleadh prize winners (across All Ireland and other levels), a category in which Clare bands excelled. *Echoes of Erin* was recorded in New York in 1958 by the Tulla Céilí Band with 'All Irish Champions '57' emblazoned on the cover. Strategically using Fleadh wins to market the album demonstrates the status building capacity of the festival at this point. Similarly, *The Fabulous Kilfenora Céilí Band* album (c.1959) had the subheading 'All Ireland Champions for Three Consecutive Years' and the Laichtín Naofa Céilí Band, from Miltown Malbay, also recorded on Dublin Records, *Come to an Irish Dance Party* (1959).[53] Not coincidentally, some of these céilí band musicians are named in 'The Fleadh Down in Ennis': Mike Preston, Seán Reid and Martin Mulhaire, who played on the Tulla recording, and Martin Talty and Jimmy Ward, who both played on the Laichtín Naofa LP (Ward is more often associated with his membership of the 'great Kilfenora'). Clare musicians (and Fleadh winners in solo or ensemble categories) also anchored the album *All Ireland Champions Violin, Meet Paddy Canny & P.J. Hayes* (Dublin Records, 1959), headlined by the two Clare fiddlers Canny (named in the Fleadh song) and Hayes (both members of the Tulla Céilí Band). They were joined by O'Loughlin, the Clare flute player name-checked in 'The Fleadh Down in Ennis'. The only non-Clare-based musician on that album is the piano accompanist, Bridie Lafferty, from Dublin.[54]

While these albums were important at the end of the 1950s (and early 1960s) in consolidating the description of Clare as the home of traditional music, more significant were performances of Clare performers on RÉ. Developed in parallel with recording, radio had similar effects on music reception and performance. Rather than obtaining the material object (the record) and physically bringing it into the domestic domain, radio broadcasts came directly into the home and listeners did not know exactly what they would hear. In this way, temporally it was a listening experience closer to that of live performance, particularly in the early years of radio broadcasting (when all radio broadcasting was live performance) as was the case on RÉ.[55] Radio and commercial recordings developed an interdependency borne of necessity, with increased broadcast hours needing to be filled and a correlating decrease in live performance on radio. Field recordings were added to the radio broadcast mix internationally in the 1940s, expanding opportunities for folk and traditional musicians. In Liam Ó Murchú's words, radio shows of Irish traditional music worked 'with the persistence of a drip effect to bring the native music to attention' in the 1950s and 1960s.[56]

In January 1955, following RÉ's investment in a mobile broadcast unit, Ciarán Mac Mathúna 'began a month-long safari in village halls, country houses and pub kitchens in Clare. His immense collection was featured on Irish radio programmes for decades afterward'.[57] Described by Seán Reid at the time as 'a simple, decent, friendly young Limerick man and fond of the Irish music', Mac Mathúna was hugely influential in creating and cementing the home of traditional music reputation for County Clare.[58] Robbie McMahon welcomed Mac Mathúna on his travels to Clare and to the Fleadh in the final verse, using the English form of the broadcaster's surname on first mention:

> Now Ciarán McMahon was busy bedad,
> Recording them all, sure the good and the bad
> But for him, our music was gone to the bad
> So 'tis 'Welcome, Ciarán Mac Mathúna'.

The four-syllable 'Mac Mathúna' is too long for comfortable inclusion in the first line, explaining the use of the English surname form, but McMahon (Robbie that is) is also making another point. The full extent of Mac Mathúna's importance to traditional music is explicitly vocalised, 'But for him, Our music was gone to the bad'. Nonetheless, the possessive 'our' maintains an opaque construct of insider and outsider, the power residing with those on the inside, who graciously allowed Mac Mathúna access. The implication is that, while grateful for Mac Mathúna's intervention, the resource of the music itself is the basis on which that intervention could be made.

# Songs and Stories: reenactments of the Fleadh

Characteristically, the final verse of Irish (English-language) folk songs are recapitulations, using tried and tested motifs to summarise proceedings. McMahon uses the last four lines of text for exactly this purpose (with the added nonsense syllablic line to end):

'Tis all over now but 'twas something to see,
So thanks to Seán Reid and the great committee;
So I wish you good health and good luck now from me
Until we all meet in Dungarvan.
Sciddery idle, dom diddery, dom die dee.

The last individual name mentioned in McMahon's traditional music roll-call is Reid. A great friend to McMahon, and an unparalleled figure in traditional music in County Clare during this period, Reid 'rooted out the players in every parish and got them organised'.[59] As the last named actor of the Ennis Fleadh in the song, Reid is given pride of place. Naming Dungarvan locates the Fleadh in place, but also embeds the song in the Fleadh to come. The call to community is quintessentially vernacular, echoing bardic forefathers as he bids adieu to his fellow Fleadh goers, wishes them good health and good luck, and looks forward to the coming year's assemblage. McMahon reverts to lyrical type within the final lines, casting his glance backwards over the Fleadh in Ennis and forwards to the next Fleadh with collective salutations, before he skiddery-idles on his way.

### JOURNEY NARRATIVES: HEADING TO THE FLEADH

'The Fleadh Down in Ennis' is an example of a non-institutional narrative of Fleadh experience, providing a counterbalance to administrative inscriptions of the Fleadh offered through official channels of Comhaltas.[60] Fleadh stories are another way in which, in a process of ongoing exchange, the currency of Fleadh experience sustained value. With each telling, and each singing, the Fleadh experience is regenerated. Fleadh administrators reanimated their Fleadh experience through their own stories. Mícheál Ó Ceallacháin describes the céilí conundrum in Boyle in 1960. At the final céilí in St Joseph's Hall, Ó Ceallacháin found himself with lots of dancers at the ready, but no céilí band. The Liverpool

Céilí Band was scheduled to play but had been misinformed by some unknown 'authoritative' person upon arrival at the dance hall door that no céilí would take place: 'the members of the band had scattered throughout the town … and only one of them was to be found in their hotel'.[61] With a queue forming to get in to the céilí, eager to dance, Ó Ceallacháin and his organiser comrade (Michael Carty) went in search of a céilí band.

> Michael went one way and I went another. On the Crescent I saw a group and heard music. There before me was a whole band complete with drums, playing away for all their worth to the delight of a good crowd …
>
> There was no preliminary bargaining. I got straight to the point. Of course they would play at the céilí. The race back to the hall was the only time I led a band anywhere. Two minutes later the boys – from Annaghdown, and then known as the Primrose Céilí Band – were playing reels for all their worth and the now happy crowd of dancers were haring through a Siege of Ennis.
>
> I went back stage to wipe my brow and draw my breath.
>
> There was Michael Carty with a puzzled look on his face. 'I have a band here now', he told me. 'Well, I have a band on the the stage and that's the important thing now'. The second band – a great bunch of lads from several counties, were not a bit disappointed with losing this engagement and they decided to wait and relieve the Annaghdown boys, which they did. Then came another steward who had heard of the difficulty in the hall. He had recruited another band and had them with him. In his case, he had 'arrested' every man he saw with an instrument and conscripted him for band membership. They decided they would also wait and play a few tunes later …
>
> So there we were, with three bands and a hall full of dancers. Then I got a message to open the back door of the hall. I went down and did so. Who was there? Yes, you've probably guessed it – the Liverpool band.[62]

Ó Ceallacháin's story has humour, tension and a happy ending. When the drama of the story concludes, he ends with the reflection, that 'the

*Songs and Stories: reenactments of the Fleadh*

readiness of the three voluntary bands ... was fairly indicative of the spirit of generosity and co-operation which is common to all traditional musicians'.[63] Ó Ceallacháin draws the Fleadh narrative as an ethical tale, a testament to the character of traditional musicians, the communion of the Fleadh and traditional music culture.

In fieldwork for this book, multiple Fleadh stories were told that centred on musical and social encounters with other Fleadh goers, reanimating the Fleadh in the post-Fleadh world and creating a meta-narrative of Fleadh experience.[64] Among these Fleadh stories shared, a prevailing theme of heading to and from the Fleadh emerged, enabling participants to reenact and recreate moments of transition in and out of the Fleadh zone. O'Loughlin, mentioned in 'The Fleadh Down in Ennis', recalled travelling to Cavan in 1954 for the Fleadh. Though he had been at several small feiseanna in Miltown Malbay, a town 20 kilometres from his home, Cavan was by far his 'biggest outing to date'.[65] O'Loughlin remembered that, in his circle of musicians and interested friends, they 'made a bit of preparation in gathering a few bob together and getting a car'.[66] Ireland came 'late into the age of a car for most families' and renting a car (and sometimes a driver) for various social events at long distances was not unusual.[67] Buses were also hired for interested musicians to go to the Fleadh, usually organised through the growing Comhaltas local branch network. For example, in 1953, buses were advertised to go to Athlone (from Cavan and Monaghan with numerous stops along the way).[68] CIE, the national transportation network began running special buses and trains to Fleadh sites in the mid-1950s, mirroring the service it provided to GAA matches. In response to a query from Seán Reid, CIE priced the hire of a thirty-nine seater bus from Ennis to the Cavan Fleadh in 1954 at £39.10.0 for a day return, or £47 for a two-day trip.[69] CIE further advised that the journey would take four and a half hours, with an additional forty-five minutes for mass on the way.[70] Evidently, the price was unacceptable, as there was no bus or train advertised to go to the Cavan Fleadh from Clare in 1954. Musicians made their own transportation plans, hence O'Loughlin's recollection. Like many others, O'Loughlin travelled to Cavan for Monday, the main competition day, and he remembered that he 'was below [in Kilmaley] at the cross waiting for the car at six o'clock on Monday morning and when we came back ... it was nearly six o'clock the next morning'.[71] Patsy Herron and other musicians from Donegal hired a car to go to Loughrea in 1956: 'an auld Morris 8, it burned as much oil as petrol, as I told you, we didn't come home until Tuesday, sure we were all young'.[72] A late cancellation for car hire to go to the Dungarvan Fleadh from Clare in 1957 left taxi driver Frank McTigue still demanding reimbursement from Reid and the Ennis Comhaltas branch months later.[73]

The first journey to the Fleadh often remained one of the most vivid experiences in musicians' Fleadh memories. Michael Tubridy remembers the first fleadh he attended, a Clare county fleadh in 1957, in Miltown Malbay.[74] On that occasion, he travelled from his home in Kilrush, with a neighbour who was one of the few car owners in the locality. Several others travelled with them and the car was full to capacity. Tubridy clearly recalled learning a version of the tune 'Rip the Calico', as they all lilted their way to the Fleadh.[75] It was a tune that he played for many years afterwards with the Castle Céilí Band: 'you can imagine them all lilting that on the way up to Miltown. I'll never forget that. That was my first experience of the Fleadh, in 1957, my first contact ... but not the last!'[76] For Tubridy, the version of 'Rip the Calico' he learnt on the journey to the Fleadh operated for the rest of his life as a reconnecting sonic memory to that journey and experience: music is not 'something that simply happens in place, but rather as something that is productive of place'.[77] Tubridy is not alone in recalling the journey to and from the Fleadh in musical articulations. O'Loughlin recalled coming home and trying to remember the second part of a tune he heard at a Fleadh, which incidentally he could not, a source of frustration to him decades later.[78] Tubridy also tells a story of cycling from Dublin to a Clare county fleadh in Lisdoonvarna in 1959. It was a distance of over 300 kilometres and, by his own assessment, he was not well prepared for the second day of the journey through the stony uplands of the Burren limestone landscape. Temperatures soared on the August day, and Tubridy had neither a hat, nor water, on his person. He commented, only half joking, that he was lucky to survive that particular journey to a fleadh.[79]

Fleadh journey narratives are often populated with multiple identifiable characters, boosting cultural capital gained from their telling. The characters are familiar to many of the listeners and the story depends on the ability of the storyteller to weave the drama of the story around these already knowns.⁸⁰ Robbie McMahon recalled travelling with Reid on festival excursions. Mrs Crotty was a frequent companion on those trips. Crotty was an important and popular figure in musical and social circles (in addition to being a musician, she ran a pub in Kilrush). As Reid had a car, he was regularly contacted by fleadh organisers (All Ireland, provincial and county) to provide lifts to musicians, potential adjudicators and patrons from County Clare: 'bring Jack Mulcaire with you', 'bring a car load'.⁸¹ The recounting of who travelled in the car together to the Fleadh formed an essential part of the narrative of Fleadh journey experience. It is, after all, these characters who subsequently provided the dramatic elements of the story as it is devised and refined after the fact. Being one of Reid's travelling companions was also important for McMahon from a material perspective as he did not have a car himself. Far more important, however, was the potential for making a story with Reid in the driver's seat.

Of the Longford Fleadh in 1958, having travelled to the Fleadh with Reid, McMahon told this story:

> He was a most forgetful man, he forgot to bring myself home from the County Longford. I met this lad and he said 'Seán Reid's gone home'. And I said 'He isn't, sure amn't I with him'. 'He is', he says, 'he said goodbye there a good while ago'. And he was. And I was all day coming with buses [back to County Clare] … I was just walking over towards Seán Reid's at about eight o'clock, and he was coming out with his pipes, and he put them into the back of the car. 'Oh, hello', he says, 'You're a nice man', I said to him, 'Why?' he says to me, 'You left me above in the County Longford, I had to walk it home'. 'Oh dang it', said he 'I searched the place for Willie Clancy, I thought 'twas he I brought with me'.⁸²

In this story, McMahon uses reported speech, a key comic device in storytelling (and comic song making).⁸³ Through the words of the generic 'this lad' and McMahon's own responses, together with Reid's punch line (where the story is heading from the beginning) a careful balance of credibility (the already knowns of Reid, his car, Willie Clancy and McMahon) and improbability (that Reid would forget who he brought) is calculated.⁸⁴ The narrative frame provided by the Fleadh journey and

Reid's well-known character lend it veracity as truth is 'stretched to impossiblity' for comic effect.[85] Combined with McMahon's delivery, the story reanimates Fleadh meaning, extending the hyper-experience of the Fleadh beyond the Fleadh zone.

### POETIC REENACTMENTS AND THE SIEGE OF MULLINGAR

Other creative responses to the Fleadh are also found, for example in Patrick O'Neill's poem 'The All Ireland Fleadh', which appeared in the Clones (County Monaghan) All Ireland Fleadh programme in 1964.[86] Given its inclusion in the Fleadh programme, the poem is bestowed an institutional imprimatur, distinguishing its beginnings from many of the stories and the song discussed thus far. O'Neill was a native of Scotstown, County Monaghan, and the poem follows a typical come-all-ye arc (though there is no melody suggested for sung delivery), opening with the familiar present tense call to attention:

> All Irishmen from everywhere I pray you gather round,
> The All Ireland Fleadh will soon be held
> In dear old Clones town.

O'Neill summarises his version of Clones town's history, oscillating in time from monastic settlements to Cromwell, from the Danes to St Patrick (who 'stopped in Clones'). In later verses, O'Neill lands in the contemporary in 1964, when 'Clones lives anew'. He moves onto (typical) naming of recognisable living figures – piper Jack Wade 'For the cause an ardent worker' and Martin McCabe 'his trusted aide' – both Fleadh committee members in 1964 in Clones. Unlike 'The Fleadh Down in Ennis', there is little comedic sensibility to be found. Rather the poem uses the language and tone of a political ballad, a call to arms 'To rally round the Comhaltas flag', confident that Clones 'will play its part, In the cause of C.C.E.'. The foil of a political ballad suited the military language of war often used in institutional utterances by Comhaltas, 'invoking a moral advantage for traditional music' in the cultural battle it faced.[87]

The Fleadh poem above, and indeed other Fleadh stories and song discussed, emerged from the performance and/or institutional core of

## Songs and Stories: reenactments of the Fleadh

the Fleadh, but there are responses from other arenas, beyond the Fleadh centre during these decades. John Montague's poem 'The Siege of Mullingar', which reflects on the Fleadh in 1963, is a notable example.[88] Montague, the American-born Ulster poet, had a 'mythological slant' in a number of his poems, and such is the case with 'The Siege of Mullingar'.[89] The Fleadh returned to Mullingar in 1963 for the first time since 1951, touted as a triumphant homecoming to the town of its origins. Unfortunately, this was not to be. The Mullingar Fleadh in 1963 was a publc relations fiasco for Comhaltas, due to levels of public disorder and the national attention that disorder drew (see pp. 179–91). It was branded in the press as sordid and unruly, and by the editor of *Fonn* (an early Comhaltas magazine) as a crisis in the organisation's history.[90]

The provocative poem title, 'The Siege of Mullingar', is layered with political and social history meaning. From Comhaltas' perspective the Fleadh (and Mullingar) were under siege, from unwanted attendees at the Fleadh and negative press coverage as a result. But Montague's poem offers an alternative perspective on the Mullingar Fleadh in 1963, interpreting the festival as a portent of a 'new and more liberal age about to dawn in Ireland'.[91] Montague reads the Mullingar Fleadh as a transformative moment, where old Ireland expired and a new Ireland emerged. The Mullingar 1963 Fleadh, for Montague, was a revolutionary site, a theme that drives the poem.[92] The refrain (at the end of each of the three verses) references W.B. Yeats (italics in original):

> *Puritan Ireland's dead and gone,*
> *A myth of O'Connor and O'Faolain.*[93]

In this recurring couplet, O'Connor (Frank) and O'Faolain (Sean), both Cork-born, twentieth-century Irish literary figures, are imagined akin to the Fleadhanna of the 1950s, important but belonging to an Ireland now consigned to the past. In this telling, when 'young girls roamed the streets with eager faces, Pushing for men', at the 1963 Fleadh in Mullingar, a line was drawn in the cultural sand between the weight of the past and the provocative potential of what lay ahead:

> … Everything then,
> In our casual morning vision

> Seemed to flow in one direction,
> Line simple as a song:
> *Puritan Ireland's dead and gone,*
> *A myth of O'Connor and O'Faolain*

The cultural myth-making of O'Connor, O'Faolain and the Fleadh model of the 1950s, for Montague, was over. Mullingar sounded a 'ground bass of death and resurrection' in 1963, welcomed by the poet.

Montague was 'deep' into traditional Irish music, sometimes he thought too deep 'as another singer's head went back and some unearthly wail smote the night'.[94] He served for a time as director, with Garech Browne, of Claddagh Records, the Irish folk and traditional label and was part of a new listening constituency during the 1960s that was brought to Irish traditional music (and the Fleadh) in part through the Western folk music revival.[95] Montague's poetic response, 'The Siege of Mullingar', was published in the Autumn of 1963, just a few short months after the festival, in the London-based literary magazine *Arena* and quickly appeared again the following year in the Spring edition of *The Massachusetts Review*.[96] It is part of Montague's limited edition collection *Patriotic Suite*, which appeared in 1966, the fiftieth commemorative year of the 1916 Rising (and dedicated to Seán Ó Riada). Basil Payne writes that all nine poems in *Patriotic Suite* 'explore evocatively and/or provocatively the ideal of nationality'.[97] 'The Siege of Mullingar' proposes a new kind of nationhood, turning away from the past and to the future.

Montague's reflection on the Fleadh in Mullingar is distinct from McMahon's 'Fleadh Down in Ennis' song in any number of obvious ways, but in particular in the reception and afterlife of the poem compared to the song. Unlike McMahon's song, the poem was not directed inwards to musicians and Fleadh goers; rather, it was directed towards a different public, who may or may not have been within Fleadh cultural orbit. In contrast to the oral tradition's 'The Fleadh Down in Ennis', no fieldwork interviewees for this book mentioned 'The Siege of Mullingar' as a Fleadh reference point. In contrast to the other Fleadh stories and reenactments, it remained, and remains, largely unread and unremarked upon by musicians and Fleadh patrons, residing in a space untethered to their lived experience of the Fleadh.

## CONCLUSION

Narratives of the Fleadh serve multiple functions, as Turner notes 'celebrations end' and people then 'try to put into words ... what they have experienced'.[98] This chapter emphasises the potent endurance of Fleadh reenactment and, in the final example, the contradictory emphemerality of the written word for this community of practice. In the case of the Fleadh, non-institutional narratives successfully regenerate meaning in a way that the poems discussed, O'Neill's 'The All Ireland Fleadh' and Montague's 'Siege of Mullingar', do not. 'The Fleadh Down in Ennis' and journey stories, as described, retain places and people in folk memory. They (re)locate the narrators and other actors directly in the Fleadh story and Fleadh zone, guaranteeing continued cultural significance in a constant action of framing and reframing Fleadh experience.[99] McMahon's songmaking acts as a testimony to the importance of the Fleadh, but is simultaneously part of that importance, central to the embedding of Clare as home of traditional music. The telling of journey stories draws boundaries and lines around the community at the Fleadh but, following the event, offers a continued glimpse of the social catharsis enacted in Fleadh space.[100] Though the celebratory experience of being at the Fleadh is not wholly replicable in sounds, song and story, 'language can give an approximate rendering of it and some semantic perspective on its products, the symbols it uses and leaves behind'.[100] The stories Fleadh goers told after the Fleadh, about themselves at the Fleadh, were often as important as real-time presence at the Fleadh itself.[102]

CHAPTER 6

# 'The Right Kind of Traditional Music': Adjudication at the Fleadh

## INTRODUCTION

A newspaper report promoting the Fleadh in Athlone in 1953 declared the success of the previous year's festival proved 'that the right kind of traditional music is appreciated'.[1] Little detail is offered on what the right kind of traditional music might be in competition or, conversely, the wrong kind. Richard Blaustein observes that any traditional music institutionalisation through competitive events leads to 'elaborate, standardized contest or exhibition styles' and, furthermore, 'seemingly submerge(es) older, more localized repertoires and performance techniques'.[2] Blaustein's critique is one often levelled at Comhaltas, a criticism that Fleadh competition encourages the standardisation of practice, nationalises particular styles to the exclusion of others and creates an identifiable, homogenous Fleadh competition sound (by implication, a Comhaltas sound).[3]

Codes of competition develop and consolidate over time but while the competition space can be a highly formalised one, it is neither static nor consistent. Competitors, adjudicators, those in attendance at (and many beyond) the competition hall all invest in and engage with competition structures, processes and outcomes, each with an individual experience. Though Chris Goertzen writes that 'any contest needs a judge', in reality any contest needs a competitor, without which the competition is void, as happened at many early Fleadhanna.[4] Experiences in Fleadh competition during these first two decades suggest that, though competitors were sometimes frustrated, confidence in the competition structure increased

*'The Right Kind of Traditional Music': adjudication at the Fleadh* 131

and competitors voluntarily adjusted (or not) to developing structures and regulation.[5] Adjudicators, those who held the authority to bestow or withhold reward, were subject to inconsistently applied regulations at the Fleadh and, as Fleadh competitions multiplied, finding a full complement of adjudicators was difficult. Competition and adjudication were much debated. Surprisingly, therefore, the first autonomous guide to adjudication produced by Comhaltas, *Nótaí do Mholtóirí*, did not appear until 1967.[6] In addition to a discussion on competition and adjudication regularisation, this chapter offers an analysis on winning styles at the Fleadh, using two competition-specific case studies (fiddle and song). The process and outcome of both provide evidence of discernible Fleadh styles emerging, but also ongoing competitor agency. The influence of external music developments on Fleadh competition adjudications, specifically commercial mediation, are also explored. In combination, the chapter proposes a number of key ways in which 'the right kind of traditional music' was adjudicated during the 1950s and 1960s at the Fleadh.[7]

### COMPETITION AND COMPETITORS

Though not the first competition system for Irish traditional music, Fleadh competitions in the 1950s were dynamic sites where identity and authenticity were negotiated and then articulated in adjudication decisions. During this decade, Irish traditional music found little reward in the meta-social world beyond the Fleadh. In contrast, at the Fleadh, and particularly in competition at the Fleadh, excellence in traditional music performance held high value. Competition at Fleadhanna, unlike the public non-Fleadh sphere, was a domain in which standard bearers of Irish traditional music were elevated and then emulated. Judith Blau notes the need for any music organisation to publicly reward accomplishments; Fleadh competitions fulfilled that need in the most obvious way.[8] David Oakley asserts that competition is 'only part of a process' in a music culture, but that it can be 'a means, a part of becoming' of and in that music world.[9] Comhaltas articulated a related position in relation to Fleadh competition: 'it is not intended that competitions should be merely a means by which a competitor may gain a prize or defeat a rival but rather as a medium in which these competitors may pace one another on the road to excellence'.[10]

From the early 1950s, Fleadh competition quickly became a valued performance platform by the community of Irish traditional music. Competitions became their own validating framework, an internalised (and internalising) authority that gathered further momentum in the 1960s. Constituting or reconstituting what was deserving of reward within the framework of the competitions is, after all, the objective. Though writing of céilí band competition, Daithí Kearney's observation pertains to all competition categories: 'particular tunes, styles and approaches to playing go through cycles of popularity' that indicate 'tastes of competitors, adjudicators and audiences'.[11] Enunciating musical authenticity (and authority) through adjudication of competitions at Fleadhanna created and then reaffirmed the growing institutional power of the Fleadh and indeed of Comhaltas itself. Noted in other revival movements, issues of 'authenticity and tradition' were paramount.[12] Fleadh competition is an area where both were adjudicated, debated and declared.

Larson Skye contrasts Fleadh competition with the historical practice of house dances in Ireland:

> At competitions, the adjudicator provides all listeners with an external norm for excellence, implicit in the choice of winner ... In contrast, standards evolved gradually in traditional communities, in repetitions of social events such as at a dance gathering ... An entire interactive community created standards for what was good music, rather than one or two judges.[13]

While true in a general sense, the binary described between house dances and competitions is not absolute. Fleadh adjudicators took upon themselves the task of deciding winners, ascribing value according to a set of aesthetic markers (articulated or tacit), but they did not enter the process from a vacuum of cultural and musical experience. Particularly in the early years of the period under examination, adjudicators were themselves well-regarded practitioners of Irish traditional music. Many adjudicators were foundational musician organisers of the Fleadh, 'people on the inside, so to speak', who were ideally placed to carry out adjudications.¹⁴ For example, at the second Fleadh in 1952, adjudicators were listed in advance of competitions in local newspapers: Kathleen Harrington (Dublin), Jim Seeery (Dublin) and Seán Maguire (Belfast) presided over the fiddle competitions; Paddy Brophy (Dublin), Francie McPeake (Belfast) and Sean Seery (Dublin) judged the uilleann pipes; accordion had Sean Gannon (Dublin) and Frank McCann (Clogher, County Louth) in charge; and John Joe Gardiner (listed as from Sligo, he was Kathleen Harrington's brother) was at the flute adjudication table.¹⁵ All were respected musicians and therefore trusted, quite reasonably, to be qualified arbiters of traditional music practice, no matter how difficult that adjudication might be. Musical insiders, such as these listed, participated in the complex process of codifying a system of competition reward for traditional Irish music.

In competition, the thorny issue of assigning worth to performances (and therefore, by implication, to performers) results in a complex relationship between adjudicators and competitors. Competitors need to accept adjudicators' decisions in order for the competition system to be sustained. It is a social contract that may not always engender unanimous agreement, but nonetheless requires a consensus for continued engagement. As evidenced by the exchanges at the 1958 céilí band competition in Longford, discussed in an earlier chapter, the competitor–adjudicator relationship was often tested. Competitors' adjudication woes sometimes spilled over, outside the Fleadh zone. Singer Ann Mulqueen recalled her father accosting an unsuspecting adjudicator on a train, as the adjudicator failed to award Mulqueen first place at a Fleadh.¹⁶ Mulqueen's own victories, when they occured, did not go without challenge. Peig Ryan, one of Mulqueen's opponents, 'tackled the judge' about being placed second to Mulqueen in a competition in 1960.¹⁷ Ryan sang 'She Lived Beside the Anner', which, she recalled the judge said, was not traditional enough.¹⁸ (Given the inconsistencies in adjudication of singing styles, this is unsurprising: see pp. 159–65.)

Competitors developed an awareness of the individual tastes of particular adjudicators. Though Séamus Connolly beat Brendan McGlinchey in the final adjudication in 1961 in Swinford, nearly five decades later Connolly still believed that one adjudicator was not on his side: 'one of the adjudicators was Liam Rowsome and he was the one who was rooting for Brendan McGlinchey'.[19] Ann Mulqueen remembers the advantage different adjudicators afforded different singers:

> There was another adjudicator ... when I'd see him I'd be delighted, and think, I'm alright today, because he always chose the best looking woman, I'd be smiling at him and he'd be smiling at me. Until one competition, I arrived and there was this lovely blonde girl, and she was from Ballinasloe, and I took one look at her and before she opened her mouth at all I said, there's the winner, I'm finished today anyway. But you'd cop them all on.[20]

Conversely, when Bríd Bean de Brún, a Comhaltas administrator and adjudicator throughout the period, was judging singing competitions, Mulqueen believed she had no chance of winning, and indeed credits Bean de Brún with her abandoning competing: 'When I'd see Bean de Brún, I'd run, because I'd have no chance with her, no matter how I'd sing'.[21] Mulqueen was scolded publicly at a Fleadh competition by de Brún for changes in her style of singing, which de Brún blamed on Mulqueen singing with commercial céilí bands, critiquing Mulqueen's singing and commercial céilí band sounds simultaneously. Mulqueen recollected that it was similar to being called from the altar for errant behaviour by a priest. While Mulqueen denies any change in her style had occurred; de Brún was 'not for turning', and never awarded Mulqueen a prize in any contest she adjudicated subsequently.[22] Whether or not any stylistic change had occurred is less important in this case than de Brún's assertion that it had, and the recollected consequent loss of trust in the process by Mulqueen.

To what extent music competitions produce their own prescriptive practices, potentially limiting style and repertoire representation, is a subject of concern across folk and traditional music cultures, particularly those in revival mode.[23] Larson Skye identifies a 'perception of a Comhaltas style' which 'reveals fears' within the community of practice 'that competitions are threatening musical diversity'.[24] Many interviewed for this book shared this generic concern but, when questioned, any detail on what constitutes a Comhaltas competition style was difficult to articulate. Sheila O'Dowd believed: 'whoever wins the Fleadh this year, well, the whole country is going to try and play like him next year ... and

'The Right Kind of Traditional Music': adjudication at the Fleadh 135

the next thing you have people all over the country playing exactly the same'.²⁵ Adjudicators in any performance competition draw on a stock of 'associational references', where 'each performance is observed against previous expressive events'.²⁶ Previous Fleadh competition experiences are embedded as auditory references over time. Tomás Ó Canainn shared O'Dowd's fears, but admitted to being tempted as a competitor by what he believed was a preferred competition style:

> Mind you, I have to say that we got sucked in a wee bit to the competitive thing, I remember, in 1968, Matt Cranitch, Raymond O'Shea and myself used to play a good bit together, and we would be going to small Fleadhs ... I remember Sean Ó Riada, in 1966 maybe, introducing me to Denis Murphy at one of the small Fleadh down in Kerry or something ... we were into odd things ... we got into the final of the trio competition but we were turned down for first prize because they thought our music was too harmonic or something, we had harmony which was a sin in those days ... And then we went in 1969 again, and we got through to the final, same way ... and I remember saying to Matt and Raymond, look what's the point of doing our usual thing if they are just going to say the same thing? And you know, let's play it their way, and rattle away, no harmonies and stuff, and they were much more principled than I was and they said, no, we are going to play our music our own way, and I said ok, but we were lucky that year, and the adjudicators thought our playing was great that year, and they heaped praise on us, that was in 1969, in Cashel.²⁷

Ó Canainn's story is illustrative of the variability of performance adjudication and speaks to the 'seemingly incommensurable poles of the subjective expressivity of musical performance and the spectacle of rules-governed competition'.²⁸ The lack of consistency between adjudicators from year to year as to what was unacceptable in 1966 but awarded flying colours in 1969 speaks to the continuing subjectivity of performance adjudication in any competitive frame. Unlike at an athletics event, where the first to cross the line wins, in a music (or any cultural) performance competition, it is not so clear cut. Ó Canainn's admission that he considered playing to the competition ideal (or an imagined one), compromising his own musical creativity in doing so, is also indicative of a strategic approach to competition that musicians might take for a variety of reasons: the accrual of cultural status as Fleadh winner chief among them. Finally, Ó Canainn's story is framed in such a way that the creative ideal triumphed in the end, even within the strict confinement of the Fleadh competition. Adjudicators necessarily bring a subjective view to the proceedings and individually interpret each performance. In this case, it worked in a positive way for these competitors.

## 'ANY CONTEST NEEDS A JUDGE': ADJUDICATORS AND AUTHORITY

Goertzen's previously cited maxim that 'any contest needs a judge' might be attached to another truism, that adjudicators and controversy go hand in hand.[29] Motivation for performers to enter competition was to build community and gain status, a feature in music revivals across national borders in the twentieth century.[30] Competition structures preserve music and music making and 'by extension a way of life remembered'.[31] Adjudicators at Fleadhanna believed that they too were remembering that past life of traditional music and contributing to community building. In addition, the adjudicator is the 'keeper and enforcer of the standards'.[32] Consequently, acting as an adjudicator lent credibility not just to the revival movement itself, as Blaustein asserts, but also to the adjudicator.[33]

It was practice during the 1950s (and for a period in the early 1960s) to list adjudicators in the Fleadh programme. At the Cavan Fleadh in 1954, fifteen adjudicator names in total appear on the programme, many of them assigned to multiple competitions.[34] Most competitions that year had two adjudicators, but for tin whistle, flute and piccolo there was a panel of three, who divided the competitions between them: John Gardiner, Dan Treacy and Eamon Murray. In later years, a system was applied whereby 'one adjudicator shall adjudicate at all solo competitions, two at duet and trio competitions and three at céilí band competitions', but this was irregularly applied. In 1957, multiple adjudicators were assigned to the solo fiddle contest (see Fig. 6.1).[35]

# 'The Right Kind of Traditional Music': adjudication at the Fleadh

**Fig. 6.1** Unidentified fiddle competitor, with adjudicators gathered around the adjudication table, Fleadh Cheoil na hÉireann, Dungarvan, 1957
Copyright and courtesy of Fáilte Ireland

Many of the adjudicators in Cavan (1954) were drawn from the ranks of CPU: Leo Rowsome, Willie Reynolds, and Seán and Jim Seery for example. The only woman adjudicator listed in the programme is the fiddle player Kathleen Harrington (she and others reappear year after year), but in another archive document for Cavan, Mrs Kavanagh is noted as the ballads competition adjudicator, and Sighle Curtain [sic] as sole adjudicator in the harp categories (which drew no contestants, as discusssed).[36] Helpfully for attendees, there is also a list of named stewards included. Stewards were required to attend to the logistics of the competition: to shepherd competitors in and out; to ensure that correct registration procedures had been followed; and undertake any other tasks that guaranteed the smooth running of the competition. As the Fleadh grew in stature and size, the number of adjudicators grew accordingly and, by 1964, in Clones, County Monaghan, forty-five were listed, with just four from Munster, illustrating that the local Fleadh committee had secured adjudicators closer to home.[37]

Adjudicators were drawn from a panel compiled and approved by the national executive council, though unlisted adjudicators were commonly prevailed upon to step with little notice when the need arose. Judges were added to and taken off the panel for a variety of reasons. In a letter from Padraic an Chnoic to Seán Reid in 1958, he responded to a request from Reid about a particular individual adjudicating at an upcoming county fleadh. With regard to the proposed judge, he writes:

> *D'éirigh sé as an rúnaíocht ach dár ndóigh bhí air é a dhéanamh agus rudaí mar a bhí. Níl sé fíor ... gur 'ciceáladh amach é'. Pé ar bith scéal é níl sé ina bhall den Chomhaltas ar chor ar bith anois agus beidh sé iontach mí-rialta é bheith a dhéanamh moltóireacht ag an bhfleadh agaibhse agus faitíos orm ná beidh mórán moltóirí as an Ard-Chomairle ag gabháil ... más dóigh leo go mbeidh seisean taobh leo.*

> (He resigned from the position of secretary, but he had to do that and with things the way they were. It is not true ... that 'he was kicked out'. Whatever the case, he is not a member of Comhaltas at all now and it will be very much against the rules for him to be adjudicating at your fleadh, and I would be nervous that many adjudicators on the Executive Board would not travel ... if they were to know he was to be beside them.)[38]

The individual in question was rejected as unsuitable not because of his lack of muscial authority but because of the disputed circumstances of his resignation from a committee of Comhaltas. The administrative machine trumped any musical qualification and, indeed, the national committee trumped the wishes of a local fleadh committee in this case.[39]

For disgruntled competitors there were avenues for appeal. In the Fleadh programme for Gorey in 1962, the appeals procedure was outlined: 'objections regarding competitions must be made in writing within seven days after the Fleadh', with the requisite fee that would be refunded 'if the committee finds that the objection is in order'.[40] Unfortunately for Josephine McCreesh, she did not get her entry fee back in 1960 when the standing committee, having heard a report from Humphrey Kelleher, decided that her objection to the result of the senior fiddle competition in Boyle would not be upheld.[41] Patrick Maguire, appealing on behalf of his son in the u14 fiddle, also at the same Boyle Fleadh, fared much better: the competition was declared null and void and his money was returned.[42]

Adjudicators were also required to wear identifying badges: competitors and committee members were subject to the same stipulation. Underscoring the moral weight of an adjudicator's role, annual congress in 1962 passed a motion 'That adjudicators observe proper decorum in keeping with their standing and responsibilities' as representatives of the administration and authority of the organisation.[43] An adjudicator's 'failure to keep an accepted appointment on more than two occasions in any one year' would 'merit the removal of such an adjudicator's name from the official panel' (in practice this rarely happened).[44] At the Fleadh in Boyle, in 1960, the final céilí band competition was (optimistically) scheduled to be held outdoors, so that the Fleadh 'would end on a triumphant note with open-air entertainment for the huge throng which was now assembled on the spacious crescent'.[45] The first band took to the platform ready to start, but 'there was an empty chair at the adjudicators' table' and 'a message of urgency was sent to the Fleadh office'.[46] Mícheál Ó Ceallacháin remembers, 'unbelievable as it might seem', that this was the first adjudication 'glitch' all weekend:

> Over the loudspeakers came a frantic plea for the missing adjudicator. Again and again the message was repeated. There was a note of restlessness now amongst the crowd and the band on the platform was also getting a but restive … Then to add to the misery a dark cloud [loomed] over the Curlew mountains, darkening the sun. Frantic messages scurried around the town and just as a substitute adjudicator was being named the missing man appeared. Relief all around and a great cheer from the huge audience.[47]

While the adjudication crisis was averted, the storm clouds were not and, mid-way through the competition, céilí bands and listeners ran for cover to St Joseph's Hall where the competition continued and the Tulla Céilí Band took home the prize.

Adjudicators were obliged to travel the length and breadth of the country fulfilling their duties, for no great monetary reward. Eamonn Murray 'was in great demand as an adjudicator and acted in this capacity at the All Ireland Fleadh and many music festivals in Newry, Ballymena, Armagh, Dungannon and many other places in Northern Ireland'.[48] Seán Reid was inundated with requests to adjudicate, only refusing to do so if he had other engagements.[49] He acted as a vital proxy for, as already described, ferrying adjudicators and musicians to Fleadhanna. Adjudicators were paid expenses, not fees, and were entitled to room and board at the Fleadh (or fleadh) in question. In 1964, the princely sum was three pence per mile for adjudicators, as prescribed by the national executive.[50] Three years later, a motion to increase this expense payment was ruled out of order.[51]

Ó Canainn, who competed in Fleadhanna, also found himself at the other side of the adjudication table. In this account, the authority of Ó Canainn as adjudicator was contested:

> Yeah, I can remember I was adjudicating singing, Irish singing it was, I gave the prizes, and I believed they were ok, but there was one fella and he had quite a chip on his shoulder and he should have won and all this ... and he came up and sat down and said, do you know this one? And he started to hum a song, you see, and I said, yeah, that one is such and such. And that was alright, and then he said, do you know this one, and he sang another, and then another, and I said yeah, but I had to go away from him after a while because, he would keep thumping until he was determined to keep going until he had one I didn't know ... I passed the test but called an end to it myself just in case I wouldn't.[52]

Adjudication could be prejudiced with the best of intentions. O'Dowd recalled two adjudicators debating a particular result:

> It was held in the school just down the road, I went down to hear the youngsters play ...there was two adjudicators ... there was three families actually involved in this particular competition, and the two men were having a conversation about these two, a brother and sister, and he said 'I think it should go to these two'. And the other man said 'No, I gave it to them at such and such a

thing [another fleadh], so it is due to go to the other family' ... and I thought huh ... that did go on, maybe that they had other things in mind, maybe he thinks that would be a bit of encouragement ... but 'twas very unfair.[53]

In this story of Fleadh competition deception (the reasons perhaps noble), the adjudicator wished to spread the benefit and capital of winning at the Fleadh to more competitors. The ensuing unfairness to the other (better) competitor, not to say the integrity of the competition, was disregarded. Adjudicator bias came in many guises.

## WINNING INSTRUMENTAL STYLES

From 1955 onwards, adjudicators were required to deliver their adjudications orally and publicly, a practice already informally in place.[54] It was not uniformly welcome; as late as 1967, there were motions to Comhaltas congress to abandon this requirement.[55] However, archive oral adjudication sources together with (limited) organisational documentation, evidence how particular sounds, styles and repertoire were foregrounded within the Fleadh competition frame during these decades. Read in conjunction with the sounds of performers (winning and not winning), an understanding of how some performances were adjudicated to be the winning ones, and, by implication, others deemed to be non-winning, is possible.

Laura Olsen's account of federally sponsored folk music competitions in the Soviet Union, from 1920 to 1940, describes the success in promoting a pan-Russian folk music that sought to minimise local music accents.[56] Similar patterns emerged in Shetland, some twenty years later.[57] Though fear was expressed that Fleadh competitions could lead to homogenisation, early Fleadhanna did not expressly seek to present a generic instrumental style.[58] Winning styles, particularly in the early years from 1951 to 1955, strongly reflect competitors' local, county and regional origins, though are not in themselves determinants of winning. The number of competitors, though increasing each year, were still disproportionately drawn from particular counties, and therefore particular styles found in those counties, local or individual, predominate in lists of winners. As the number of competitors increased, so too did the range of winning sounds, but this was informed by previous years' (limited range of) winning styles. By the late 1950s, performances that had been adjudicated as 'winning' prompted emulation in both repertoire and performance style. Writing more broadly of music revival and competitions, Blaustein notes that music competition 'accelerates stylistic change and standardization'.[59] Furthermore, 'it is only natural that competitors should emulate the performances of winning contestants, but the unintended result is the restriction of the full range of styles and tunes to suit the criteria of the judges'.[60] In that sense, the template of success in competition was created by those early competitors and the presiding adjudicators. As the field of competitors widened, the synchronic model, the moment of a single winning performance, informed the diachronic blueprint for winning in subsequent years.

From 1953 onwards, many Fleadh competitions had a high rate of participation by County Clare musicians, further adding to its reputation as the home of traditional music. The commensurate representation of Clare musicians in competition can be explained by the strength of traditional music practice in the county and the radio air time afforded Clare music (mutally dependent factors), but also revivalist agitations in the county by Reid and others.[61] Céilí bands from Clare and Galway had a high rate of success in the first decade of Fleadh competition, consolidating a generic céilí band template codified in Fleadh winning and competition rules. However, within that generic template (which settled at no less than five players, no more than ten, and any instrument allowed) stylistic distinctions were heard between each of the bands.[62] Winning bands displayed a high degree of self-curation and competition strategising. Top-placed céilí bands were diligent in their pursuit of excellence for competition, practising two or three nights per week, and sometimes drafting in musical expertise beyond band members to prepare.[63] Additionally, in the wider cultural world, outside of the Fleadh, céilí bands experienced a period of significant growth in the 1950s. This was influenced by the popularity of the céilí band competition at the Fleadh (and its winners, such as the Kilfenora and Tulla céilí bands). There was a mutually invigorating benefit between the céilí band Fleadh domain and non-Fleadh domain, with a correspondence between winning an All Ireland céilí band competition and increased professional opportunities outside the festive competition frame. Jerry Lynch, of the Kilfenora Céilí Band, identifies the Fleadh win of 1954 as a key moment: 'after that, we started going all over the country playing'.[64] Unlike other individual instrumental traditions, céilí bands' *raison d'être* was to play for social dances and was inherently tied to commerce, taking place in a variety of public social dance spaces.[65] In a practice that continues to today, particular bands were formed explicitly to compete – for example, the Liverpool Céilí Band who first competed in 1959.[66] In this way, Comhaltas contributed to a (limited semi-) professionalisation of traditional Irish music practice specifically in céilí band performance in these early Fleadh years, with competition reconfiguring traditional practice.

The winning style of accordion playing at Fleadhanna was typical of accordion playing found in the popular céilí band domain, but hyperbolised in the Fleadh solo competition setting.[67] The experience of listening and playing are both exaggerated in this fashion. Button accordion was distinct from fiddle in obvious ways (it is a fixed pitch instrument). But it was also distinct from fiddle or pipes in that its primary role in Irish traditional music was in ensemble dance bands (including céilí bands) from the 1920s on; the wider evolution of solo styles came later.[68] The Fleadh was a key site where that solo style was honed and rewarded. Joe Burke's victory in an underage category in 1955 is an important moment in that development, and Paddy O'Brien's highly rhythmic, fully open sound with a syncopated bass, laid the foundations for Burke's viruosity to develop. On a recording of the winner's concert in Gorey in 1962, Burke's robust national anthem performance with the Leitrim Céilí Band illustrates his winning style, as he fills in cadential pauses with arpeggiac outlines to rousing applause.[69] As detailed, Clare concertina players monopolised the list of winners in solo concertina competition from 1955; indeed, the solo concertina competition was introduced to reflect Clare music practice and there were few concertina players from any other county competing, which made the Clare-dominated results inevitable. Also important to note is that, among those Clare concertina players, a wide variety of individual styles was heard, notwithstanding the conflation of traditional style in discourse to a county or regional level.

## DUELLING FIDDLES, COMPETITION AND VIRTUOSITY

The 1960s' fiddle competition Fleadh rivalry between Séamus Connolly and Brendan McGlinchey, both 'widely acknowledged as the young fiddle titans of their generation', provides a window into the process of competition adjudication.[70] Connolly won the senior fiddle competition in 1961 and 1963, McGlinchey won in 1962, with recalls the order of the day on each occasion. At provincial level, Connolly from Killaloe, County Clare, came through the Munster qualifying channel, while McGlinchey, from Armagh, came through Ulster. Earle Hitchner writes of the Fleadh competition encounters between Connolly and McGlinchey that 'the virtuosity of one seemed to spur the virtuosity of the other, creating an instense, mutually respectful duel of horsehair bows that is still recalled'.[71] Such was their rivalry at Fleadh competitions (and the interest it generated among the listening public) that Comhaltas introduced a Champion of Champions fiddle competition in 1964 for previous winners to battle it out. This was a specific response to the Connolly–McGlinchey fiddling jousts.[72]

Connolly was a frequent medallist at underage and then senior level in solo fiddle, his name conjoined forever with the tag of ten-time-All Ireland-winner. In addition to his ten first-place solo medals, he won four All Ireland titles in duet competition (with Peadar O'Loughlin). In 1961, Connolly had the distinction of winning both the 14–18 level and senior fiddle in the same year, at the Fleadh in Swinford, County Mayo. This prompted a rule change later that year to prevent competitors taking part in any solo competition outside their age categories.[73] A master of his instrument from a young age, Connolly consciously selected tunes for competition that fell squarely within the repertoire of traditional dance music, thereby avoiding any accusation of unsuitability.[74] Within that repertoire, Connolly carefully mixed his selections between common and more unusual tunes and, as with any virtuoso, chose tunes with his specific instrument in mind.[75] Connolly's contemporaneous style can be heard on a recording that Ciarán Mac Mathúna made at a county fleadh concert in 1964 in Scariff, County Clare (close to Connolly's east Clare home in Killaloe).[76] In this example, Connolly plays a number of his competition tunes from that year, the reels 'The Liffey Banks' and 'The Shaskeen', at a fast tempo. His devotion to Michael Coleman's Sligo fiddling style is clearly heard in florid runs and turns, much more so than what is typically constructed as an east Clare musical accent.[77] The performance is an illustrative example of what Tim Collins recognises as a 'much more complex geography' than regional or county style.[78]

The Armagh native's fiddle style, in comparison to his epic rival Connolly, was more northern in execution, with attacking bowing and, at times, a faster tempo than Connolly's. Like Connolly, McGlinchey employed a subsantial degree of melodic ornamentation, but shorter and sharper than his Clare counterpart. McGlinchey's first Fleadh was in Ennis in 1956 and, though only sixteen years old, he was broadcast by Ciarán Mac Mathúna on foot of his participation at the winners' concert. He won at underage level the following year in Dungarvan in 1957, and subsequently moved up to senior level competition. His Fleadh appearances garnered attention from professional céilí bands and he began touring with the Malachy Sweeney céilí band in 1956. McGlinchey did not like competition, 'but profited greatly from the advice and constructive criticism' of adjudicators.[79] On an archive recording of a Fleadh concert held in a marquee at the Swinford All Ireland Fleadh in 1961, a brief clip of McGlinchey playing with a piano accompanist is heard.[80] In the midst of this performance, the ghost of Coleman's musical presence is apparent, specifically in the shape and execution of some of the ornaments: McGlinchey exploits the full range of the tune, filling in intervalic gaps with runs and turns.

While concert and competition are two distinct performance modes, both of these fiddlers displayed a winning style. While vastly different, there are nonetheless some shared observations that might be made of both Connolly and McGlinchey's performances. Both are virtuosic, with a high level of technical skill. This mirrors traditional music revival processes more broadly, which Blaustein (referencing Peter Cooke) terms 'the westernization' of folk musics.[81] Fintan Valley also notes that the 'virtuosity and variety seen in [Irish] traditional music today in fact represents a classicisation of folk music', which can be viewed as 'the re-emergence of a once-suppressed indigenous classical tradition', therefore not wholly new.[82] Both Connolly and McGlinchey, at least in these Fleadh concert performances (from 1964 and 1961 respectively), use a driving tempo and a high instance of melodic ornamentation. And both nod to their mediated fiddling mentor, Coleman. The stylistic homage to Coleman reflects the generational reality of traditional music and its highly mediated state by the second half of the twentieth century. In addition to face-to-face transmission that Connolly and McGlinchey experienced in their musical development, musicians of their generation had access to radio broadcasts and were drawing heavily on recordings of their musical forefathers (there are few recordings of musical foremothers) when developing individual styles. Fiddlers, in particular, had recourse to an especially rich archive of recorded sound. Recordings of traditional fiddle players made in the USA in the early decades of the century were available and shared. Hugely influential within that body of work were the recordings of Coleman and his Sligo fiddling compatriots, Paddy Killoran and James Morrisson. The stylistic influences of fiddle recordings is inescapable in both Connolly and McGlinchey's music, albeit in different ways, as their styles evolved.

None of these elements, in themselves, define a Fleadh competition sound for winning fiddling. Rather, the common thread is the overall technical mastery and self-conscious polish of the performances. Goertzen notes the effects of competition on American old-time fiddling, one of which was an elevation of technical skill.[83] As early as 1957, Ernst Klusen recognised that in wider folk revival 'renewed tradition' is aimed at 'technical perfection'.[84] In an Irish context, Rachel Fleming also identifies one of the primary effects of competition as the aspiration to reach a theoretical ideal that the adjudicator has in mind.[85] But that theoretical ideal is shaped not just by the competition and the adjudicator, but also by the competitors themselves. Increasing technical virtuosity is a concrete goal, and technical matters and technicalities can be more easily adjudicated, compared and ranked. The competition context required the musicians to present a clean, unmuddied performance in order to win, and this spilled over onto other formal Fleadh performance platforms, such as the concerts found in these archive recordings of Connolly and McGlinchey. Once Fleadh competitions established themselves as an important site of status making within traditional music, technically impeccable performance presented in a polished delivery, expunged of environmental or stylistic noise (to whatever extent possible) became part of the winning Comhaltas competition sound.

What if the winning sound of more than one top-placed performer were equally masterful, equally polished, what then? At the All Ireland Fleadh in Swinford in 1961, Connolly and McGlinchey faced off in the senior fiddle solo competition. Both had won their respective provincial

### 'The Right Kind of Traditional Music': adjudication at the Fleadh

qualifiers and advanced to the final title-deciding round held on Monday of the Fleadh weekend. The final competition was, by any measure, an extrordinary series of musical encounters, as Connolly and McGlinchey were recalled again and again to the colosseum of fiddling to adjudicate the winner. A report in the *Nenagh Guardian* the following week reported Connolly's ultimate victory:

> [Connolly's] meteoric rise to fame must be as unique as it was spectacular, considering that for the past five years he has won the Under 18 championship and climaxed this consistent record by winning the premier award in his first entry to Senior competition.[86]

The *Nenagh Guardian* was one of several local newspapers on Connolly's home turf and it does not mention any of the complicating factors of how the title was decided. The result (and the many adjudications to get there) was the subject of heated discussion in real time among competition attendees packed into the competition hall, as the contest dragged on into the small hours of Tuesday morning. Connolly remembered he left after his final recall performance to get a lift home to Killaloe, not knowing who won.[87] The *Irish Press* reported:

> the Fleadh came to a close without the result of the All Ireland Senior traditional violin competition being declared. The three adjudicators could not come to a decision as to which of two recalled competitors, seventeen-year-old Séamus Connolly of Killaloe, County Clare, or twenty-year-old Brendan McGlinchey, from Armagh should be awarded the [Michael] Coleman cup, one of the top prizes of Fleadh.[88]

The next morning, Connolly read the national *Irish Press* headline: 'Crux Delays Fleadh Result'.[89] The crux in question arose because the team of three fiddle adjudicators found Connolly and McGlinchey's respective fiddling impossible to unanimously rank (necessary for an All Ireland final result). The *Evening Herald* declared the next day:

> One of the main talking points last night was the discussion which arose over the destination of the open senior traditional fiddle class title. Two adjudicators gave their votes to Séamus Connolly of Killaloe, while a third favoured a competitor from Armagh.[90]

The unnamed Armagh competitor is, of course, McGlinchey. The account of the Connolly–McGlinchey marathon discloses that 'an extraordinary general meeting of the Fleadh Ceoil Executive Committee' had to be called in the middle of the night to respond to 'a crux over the playing of a jig' which 'caused a sensation at the Fleadh Ceoil in Swinford last night'.[91] In 'Rules for Fleadhanna Ceoil' (1962), one part of an expanded Comhaltas constitution, competitors in senior solo competitions were directed that four tunes should be played in the first round of the final competition, the selection to include one slow air plus three others chosen from the following tune types: reel, jig (single, double and slip), hornpipe, march and (solo) set dance.[92] For senior competition recalls, competitors were required to play 'all the tunes specified in Clár na gComórtas (programme of competition) for that competition'.[93] In this case, each competitor should play a single, double and slip jig (in addition to the other tune types required). McGlinchey made a fatal error and omitted the single jig, playing another double jig instead, understood by the adjudicators to be a breach of repertoire rules in the recall:

> After a long delay, while two thousand people waited impatiently in the town hall, members of Comhaltas Ceoltóirí Éireann, at a specially summoned meeting, ruled that the decision of two of the adjudicators in nominating as the winner the competitor who had kept to the regulations should stand.[94]

Connolly, with his approved (single) jig, was declared victorious. When all other factors were equal, McGlinchey's failure to adhere to competition rules was the crux of the matter.

In 1961, the year of duelling fiddles, the All Ireland Fleadh programme listed the winners of the previous year's senior competitions within its pages, further cementing its internal system of authority and authenticity, with high cultural stakes. Competition encouraged and rewarded musicianship, technical excellence and clean performance. Connolly's assertion, some four and a half decades later, that he took particular care to select tunes unassailable in their competition virtue and suitability, subtly acknowledges the importance of also knowing the rules to play by.[95]

'The Right Kind of Traditional Music': adjudication at the Fleadh    149

## STANDARDISATION: 'RULES FOR FLEADHANNA CEOIL'

Beginning in the late 1950s, various pleas were made by adjudicators (and administrators) to the national executive to standardise and distribute guidelines on adjudication.[96] At a quarterly meeting in 1959, a branch motion was put forward:

> We propose that in future county and All Ireland Fleadhs accordeon [sic] competitions should be adjudicated by accordeon players; that violin competitions should be judged by violin players and each other musical competition should be judged in a similar manner.[97]

In this motion, the specific issue is that adjudicators were increasingly judging competitions for instruments on which they themselves were not proficient. Another underlying suggestion, though not explicitly stated, is that by the end of the 1950s adjudicators were not necessarily skilled musicians (or even musicians at all), but part of the growing bank of Comhaltas administrators. In the Fleadh administration's defence, the expansive number of competitions across solo and ensemble categories at multiple age levels, at All Ireland, provincial and county fleadh levels, presented a significant challenge to find enough adjudicators. Musicians graduated out of competition participation and became adjudicators themselves, but that did not fulfil the increasing demand.[98] In Monaghan in 1952, there were fifteen separate competitions; in 1958 in Longford, there were more than seventy-two. In 1966 in Boyle, a decade and a half after the first Fleadh, there were ninety-two competitions; but at that point in the Fleadh's history, county and provincial qualifying rounds (other than overseas) had been separated from the All Ireland Fleadh. Amassed together, competition categories at fleadhanna in the course of a year ran to a thousand or more competitions, all of which needed to be adjudicated.

A motion to Comhaltas annual congress in 1967 expressed 'dissatisfaction with the choice of some adjudicators, and as a result, the common occurance of bad adjudication', whatever that might mean.[99] The administrative balance of practitioner to non-practitioner, the shift that Burke described as 'when the lay people got involved', changed during the 1960s as the Fleadh and the organisation grew.[100]

In 1968, Breandán Breathnach confirmed that adjudicator ranks were no longer the preserve of expert musicians as had been the case in early Fleadh years: 'it should be unnecessary to say that a person appointed to adjudicate at a competition in traditional music should know what this music is, and that he must know the instrument he is about to judge'.[101] For Breathnach, Comhaltas criteria for adjudicators (membership of Comhaltas, music literacy and the capacity to deliver coherent adjudication comments) were redundant without a 'thorough appreciation of traditional music and a practical acquaintance with the instrument'; in fact, Comhaltas adjudicator criteria could be 'positively harmful'.[102] Over the course of two decades, as Comhaltas and the Fleadh developed an increasingly institutional framework, the organisation and festival in Breathnach's description was 'seized and … controlled by people who profess aptitudes in adminstration and organisation' rather than music.[103] Though overstated, there was a redistribution of adjudication power in the 1960s away from musicians in the organisation. Simply put, there were too many competitions and too few competent adjudicators.

Fleming points to 'the most obvious source of tension' in competition as being 'that Irish traditional music is based on diverse, individual interpretations of melodies, while objective judgment relies on constant clearly defined standards'.[104] Adjudicators' musical accents and preferences also impact their adjudications. Writing of Norway fiddlers and competition, Goertzen recognises that one of the primary bones of contention is whether judges from one area could adjudicate fiddlers from another, given the local accents of style that fiddlers display.[105] This was (and continues to be) also a concern for some Fleadhanna competitors and observers. Peadar O'Loughlin, himself a competitor during the 1950s, believed it very difficult to make any adjudication between distinct styles, assuming a parity of skill and musicianship. At the Cavan Fleadh in 1954, O'Loughlin heard five fiddle competitors all with distinct styles and believed any one of them could have won first place. He questioned how Joe O'Dowd, a Sligo fiddler, could be judged against Aggie White for example, a renowned fiddler from east Galway.[106] O'Loughlin's difficulty stems from the inherent individuality within the traditional Irish music aesthetic, which cannot be exactly measured on a comparative index between musicians.

### 'The Right Kind of Traditional Music': adjudication at the Fleadh

In 1962, with growing calls for standardisation of ad hoc adjudication practices, one part of an expanded Comhaltas *Bunreacht* (constitution), was dedidicated to 'Rules for Fleadhanna Ceoil'. The sections collated dispersed guidelines previously used and expanded the Fleadh regulation system.[107] The long list of rules in the section 'Rules for Fleadhanna Ceoil' was organised in four sub-sections (VIII Rules for Fleadhanna Ceoil; IX County Fleadhanna; X Provincial Fleadhanna; and XI Fleadh Cheoil na hÉireann). While 'Rules for Fleadhanna Ceoil' explicitly addresses the nuts and bolts of Fleadh competitions and their administration, little useful advice on how to adjudicate is offered among the 108 rules (many with sub-rules). Specific mention of adjudication is made only in relation to the administrative running of the competition (section VIII–17–27; in sections IX, X and XI readers are directed to section VIII). Adjudicators were required to give oral adjudication at the competition's end (no. 18), a practice that had been in place since 1954, and told to sit apart when marking the same competition (no. 19).[108] There were proposals over the years that adjudicators should adjudicate in a different building to the competitors to maintain objectivity (in 1962 and again in 1967), but these motions were defeated.[109] In 1962, at the annual congress of Comhaltas, there was a motion reiterating the necessity to strictly enforce the rules that were in place:

> the adjudicators shall be so separated that intercommunication, strictly forbidden from the commencement of the competitions to the completion of adjudication is impossible: and that instructions to the adjudicators in the course of the competitions shall be by public announcement.[110]

Three rules (out of eleven in total on adjudicators and adjudication) outlined the penalties that would apply if an adjudicator failed to appear at the appointed competition venue on time.

The question of how adjudicators might actually adjudicate is not outlined in 'Rules for Fleadhanna Ceoil', nor is any information provided on how marks should be awarded and distributed. Adjudicators remained without any guiding centralised statement from Comhaltas as to a marking scheme and there was no dedicated organisational forum in which these questions might be debated among members of adjudication panels. Given that the adjudication panels for instrumental competitions were largely made up of musicians themselves, though that was changing as noted, there may have been an assumption that these adjudicators would simply know the best performance when they heard it. Without discernible guidelines, adjudicators were expected to intuit what was valued. In the early years, with musician-adjudicators and limited competitor numbers, this may have generated confidence in adjudicator decisions, by the 1960s this was no longer guaranteed. A quarterly meeting motion to the national Comhaltas council from the Thurles branch in 1959 proposed that adjudicators' sheets be standardised across all competitions.[111] This same motion had already been passed in 1957, but clearly not implemented.[112] The 1959 quarterly meeting announcement notes that a sample adjudication sheet was attached for discussion and distribution (though, unfortunately, detached from the archive document cited here).[113]

Despite these motions and their approval, Michael Tubridy remembered that on the occasion of his first (and last) adjudication duty in 1964 he received no direction, guidelines or adjudication sheet.[114] He scribbled down some headings before the competition as a means to organise his own thoughts, but was dissatisfied with the haphazard process. More generally, Tubridy had reservations about music in competition and the hyperattachment of value to winning a Fleadh title. The lack of consistency and guidelines in adjudication and, in his view, the impossibility of objectivity, merely confirmed his suspicions about the unsuitability of the competitive frame for Irish traditional music.[115] Like Tubridy, other musicians were sceptical of competition and the very notion of adjudicating performance, even if they competed themselves. This supports Rappaport's claim that consensus and continued participation in cultural rituals (as competitions became) did not require unanimous agreement with the rules or outcomes.[116] When he travelled to Cavan for his first Fleadh in 1954, Peadar O'Loughlin attended the senior fiddle competition to hear the music and support his fellow Clare musician, Paddy Canny, who was competing.[117] Like Tubridy, O'Loughlin expressed discomfort about the very notion of music performance in competition. Though frequently asked, O'Loughlin adjudicated only a few times as the lack of clear guidelines was 'bothersome' to him.[118]

## 'The Right Kind of Traditional Music': adjudication at the Fleadh

By the early 1960s, the informal but eminently qualified adjudicator panel of musicians involved in the Fleadh in its first decade was shrinking as they moved towards a adjudication quasi-retirement. In an article in the Newry branch newsletter *Fonn* in 1964, Breathnach's later summations about the adjudicator pool were confirmed when a member of Comhaltas' national executive wrote:

> Adjudication is a problem, largely of our own making, which must be tackled. While there are more than a few good adjudicators, we need a new panel to which additions should be made cautiously. The increase in travel expenses might help to draw some of the veteran adjudicators out of 'retirement'. A small number of good, young traditional musicians might be selected for attendance at a two-weeks summer course conducted by acknowledged authorities and performers and dealing with the finer points of traditional music and singing. Whatever methods are used, care should be taken by the Music Committee to ensure that a panel of really competent adjudicators emerges.[119]

How adjudication was a problem of Comhaltas' making is not revealed but, despite pleas from the rank and file, the lack of comprehensive adjudication guidelines in an ever-expanding competition system remained a problem. Key in the advocation above is a demand for a judicious cross-section of 'veteran' adjudicators and young musicians, who could be given proper training in the art of adjudication by 'acknowledged authorities and performers'.[120] Interesting here is the separation of 'authorities' from 'performers', implying there were a cohort of non-performers who were also in a position to explicate on 'the finer points of traditional music and singing'. This inadvertently draws attention to a disquiet developing among performers that non-performers were exerting an undue influence on Comhaltas activites, prioritising administration above music making and making claims to authority in the performance domain. Clearly, expertise in music is not the preserve of performers alone, but 'acknowledged authorities' as adjudicators was a step too far.

## NÓTAÍ DO MHOLTÓIRÍ: CODIFYING PRACTICE IN COMPETITION

From 1959 to 1967 matters of adjudication were frequently debated at meetings, evidenced by items on agendas of the central executive council and other assemblies discussed above. In 1960, dedicated adjudication workshops were proposed, but there is no evidence that they took place.[121] The Offaly county board, in 1963, resolved to collect and publish ideas about adjudication but, again, no evidence is present to confirm this happened.[122] These were isolated initiatives and no action was taken at a national executive level until 1967. The secretary's report to annual congress that year records that a sub-committee was set up 'to consider the whole aspect of adjudicating at all Comhaltas competitions'.[123] This committee met six times and produced the booklet *Nótaí do Mholtóirí* (Notes for Adjudicators) issued in 1967.[124] This is the first autonomous publication on adjudication by the national executive. It took another two years before three seminars, one for potential adjudicators in particular, was announced.[125] On 1 and 2 March 1969, close to two decades after Fleadh competitions began, a weekend seminar on adjudication was held in Longford, the first of its kind organised by Comhaltas.[126]

Though a belated response, Séamus de Brún was confident that it would 'help our adjudicators to become more efficient and also standardise adjudication at the Fleadh'.[127]

*Nótaí do Mholtóirí* outlined the necessary qualifications for adjudicators:

> It is necessary that he should have listened to a great deal of first-class traditional Irish music, including pipe music, covering a varity [sic] of authentic styles, and have had his musical taste formed thereby. In addition, he should, himself, be a competent performer on the instrument, or instruments, on which he intends to adjudicate.[128]

That the adjudicator would be a skilled performer was a declared criterion from the first years of the Fleadh, but one that was not always adhered to. The requirement that adjudicators should be well versed in authentic styles through wide listening was previously implicit, rather than explicit. Additionally, it is pointed out that 'No amount of instruction or advice, nor rules of marking, can replace good taste, skill and balanced judgement on the part of the adjudicator'.[129] 'Good taste' and 'authentic styles' in this paradigm of correct adjudication are bound together, without any indicators of what constituted either. This perhaps also acts as a justification for the lack of instruction from central Comhaltas administration on adjudication up to that point. 'Good taste' is acknowledged as something fundamentally important, yet intangible and therefore difficult to describe to those who did not have it. Helena Rowsome, piper and Comhaltas activist, wrote in 1968 that traditional style was 'a style that is easily recognized when heard' even if 'it is impossible to define'.[130]

The second section of *Nótaí do Mholtóirí*, 'Suggestions for Adjudicators', enunciates the need for all adjudication to be based on the twin pillars of traditional repertoire and traditional style: 'the material must be traditional, the style of playing must be traditional'.[131] This requirement was established early in the Fleadh years. In the programme for the Fleadh in Cavan in 1954, under 'Coinníollacha' (Rules), competitors are advised only 'ceol fíor-ghaelach, sé sin ceol dúchasach na hÉireann' (true Irish music, that is native music of Ireland) was acceptable.[132] *Nótaí do Mholtóirí* advises the presence of traditional repertoire and style should be assessed under designated headings: command of instrument; rhythm and phrasing; time; interpretation; ornamentation; and overall effect of performance.[133] Where non-traditional performance was detected, adjudicators were instructed to disregard them in their assessments, though tact and discretion were to be used when communicating that to the errant performer.[134]

*Nótaí do Mholtóirí* reminds adjudicators that only 'proper' Irish tunes are allowed in instrumental competition. Though marches, slow airs and set dances are in the allowed column, adjudicators are cautioned to watch out for 'radical changes' and 'the use of notes foreign to the melodies' in these tunes, rendering them less authentic.[135] Polkas are specifically pointed out as tunes that might mistakenly be performed. Musicians who tried to substitute a polka for a reel, under the misapprehension it was truly Irish, 'should get no marking'.[136] Wending their way from Bohemia through England to Ireland, polkas were introduced to Irish traditional music in the latter half of the nineteenth century. Single polkas retained popularity in the twentieth century particularly, though not exclusively, in the south-west and are strongly tied to set dancing of that region.[137] Their relatively recent Bohemian origins, Saxon travels, and set dancing associations left polkas languishing with waltzes in reportoire limbo, unsanctioned for competition. A consequence is (potential) regional bias against polka-playing musicians.[138] Polkas do not appear on the approved list of tunes for instrumental competitions that had been sanctioned previously in 'Rules for Fleadhanna' in 1962 – a checklist that included slow airs, reels, jigs (single, double and slip), hornpipes and set dances (the tune and solo dance type, not the ensemble dance), in addition to marches.[139] All tunes should be thoroughly Irish, though it is noted that 'unless an adjudicator is very definite that a melody is not Irish he ought not condemn it. It may be of Irish origin' unbeknownst to him.[140] In Loughrea in 1955, Kevin Keegan, Martin Mulhaire and Kieran Kelly had a recall in the senior solo accordion competition. In the recall, Mulhaire played a march that the adjudicators declared Scottish and disqualified him.[141]

Precedents for the division of marks in adjudicating Irish traditional music were established well before the advent of the Fleadh.[142] For example, a *Clár Oireachtais* (Oireachtas Programme) from 1904 outlines the template of marks for the singing competition.[143] The list includes tone, tuning, interpretation, pronunciation and declamation, with a quarter of all marks ascribed to the usefully vague heading of Irish style. Though a uniform adjudication of marks sheet was not issued by Comhaltas before 1962, in practice many adjudicators utilised the general template established at feiseanna, Oireachtais and other competitions, with marks divided between choice of tunes; tone and tuning; rhythm and time; interpretation and phrasing; and, finally, traditional style and general effect.[144] Other adjudicators, as mentioned, spontaneously set criteria. The general division of marks above is almost identical to that utilised in American fiddle contests of the same period. Goertzen details the rules of fiddle contests 'in which judges were to evaluate performances on the bases of authenticity, rhythm and timing, and tonal quality and clarity (sometimes collectively called execution) as well as taste or creativity'.[145]

The 1967 guide provides marking schemes to be used henceforth (see Fig. 6.2), though it should not be assumed they were utilised at every fleadh, all of the time, thereafter.[146]

'The Right Kind of Traditional Music': adjudication at the Fleadh    157

|  | Uilleann pipes | Flute | Fiddle | Button accordion | Céili band | Duet/Trio | Singing |
|---|---|---|---|---|---|---|---|
| *Style & ornamentation* | 50 | 50 | 50 (*Traditional style & ornamentation) | 50 | 35 | 50 | 45 |
| *Quality & choice of tune/song* | 10 |  |  |  |  |  | 10 |
| *Tuning* | 10 |  |  |  |  |  | (*Quality of voice) 15 |
| *Tone & Tuning* |  |  | 10 |  |  |  |  |
| *Time* | 10 | 10 | 10 | 10 | 10 | 10 |  |
| *Rhythm & phrasing* | 10 | 10 | 10 | 10 | 15 | 10 | (*Rhythm) 10 |
| *Variation, control of tune* |  |  | 15 | 10 |  |  |  |
| *Command of instrument* |  |  | 15 | 20 | 15 |  | (*Phrasing & clarity) 10 (*Interpretation & expression) 10 |
| *Balance and blend* |  |  |  |  | 20 | 20 |  |
| *Arrangement & presentation* |  |  |  |  | 20 | 10 |  |
| *Regulators* | 10 |  |  |  |  |  |  |
| *Use of left hand* |  |  |  | 5 |  |  |  |

* Category wording is instrument specific.

**Fig. 6.2** Competition marking schemes summary, *Nótaí do Mholtóirí* (Comhaltas, 1967)

The devised adjudication headings would help adjudicators complete a more 'detailed analysis' and retain a sense of the overall standards.[147] Across all competitions (including singing), 'style and ornamentation' carry the bulk of marks with 50/100 marks awarded in uilleann pipes, flute, accordion, fiddle and duets/trios (termed 'traditional style and ornmentation' in fiddle and duet/trio guidelines). In singing, 45/100 marks were allocated to style and ornamentation, while in céilí band, only 35/100 marks were so designated. While slight variations are found in terminology and marking schemes from one solo instrumental competition to the next, the remaining 50 marks are distributed broadly thus: time (10), rhythm and phrasing (10), variation and control of tune (15 or 10, also termed tone and tuning in fiddle) and command of instrument (15 in flute and button accordion, 20 in fiddle). Duets and trio competitions have 20 marks for balance and blend (as do céilí bands) and all ensemble competitions also have marks for arrangement and presentation (10 in total for duets/trios, 20 in céilí band). Presentation in céilí band competition has 'no emphasis on dress of any form' (there is a caveat that dress presentation does matter 'at important controlled public functions').[148] Adjudicators are told to judge bands 'by listening, not looking':

> the best presentation will be given to the band that can start properly, perform as required ... and finish properly, which will seat its musicians so as to achieve the bext balanced results, and play exactly the same music ... one must be careful that the structure is not too weakened as this music is being played for dancers and a serious lapse from full instrumentation to one musician may break the rhythm and flow too much.[149]

Instrument materiality obviously affects marking; for example, fiddle is ascribed specific marks for tuning, where accordion is not. Uilleann pipes has 10 marks each for tuning and regulator use, while button accordion has 5 marks for use of the left (bass) hand. Within style and ornamentation marks (typically 50 marks), the adjudicator is advised that this marking divison allows marks to reflect 'anything that distracts the listener' and 'all faults not elsewhere provided for should be penalised here'.[150] This resonantes with John Bealle's comments on American old-time fiddle contests, contemporaneous to Fleadhanna, that 'contests could at times seem like prototypes of retributive justice, with complex rules of style that served as both restraint from and temptation for complex melodic improvisation'.[151]

Adjudicators were looking for guidance and, in the absence of any generic prescriptive language within the community of practice, it was necessary to co-opt another lexicon of description, illustrating the difficulty of codifying excellence in traditional performance practice. As Niall Keegan notes, 'the frontier where speech meets the reality of the aspects of performance' within the Irish tradition, can result in 'ambiguous' and even 'contradictory' interpretations.[152] Keegan further points to the fact that terms taken from other musical lexicons often lost their prescriptive value when crossing cultural lines and became descriptive instead, but only after the fact.[153] According to *Nótaí do Mholtóirí*, 'bad rhythm', where 'there is wrong grouping of notes or unnecessary breaks within any bar itself' and 'bad phrasing', where 'there are breaks after bar 1 and 3', should be easily detectable to the experienced adjudicator.[154] Mapping the term 'bar' on to traditional tune interpretations is not without difficulty, as many traditional musicians do not think of a bar as a significant gesture in performance.[155]

*Nótaí do Mholtóirí* contains the rules and regulations of Fleadhanna at county, provincial and All Ireland level and runs to twenty pages. Bealle concludes that the intention to ensure fairness within revival organisations often results in 'contest rules become increasingly complex', and this is the case with Comhaltas.[156] The motivation for *Nótaí do Mholtóirí* is two-fold. Firstly, Comhaltas is (finally) responding in a comprehensive way to the demands from its members to standardise the adjudication process, anticipating questions that may arise in the future. Secondly, it seeks to control the competition environment, direct the actors in the competition drama and assert the institutional power of Comhaltas within that space.

## SINGING FLEADH SOUNDS: REPERTOIRE, STYLE AND COMMERCIALISM

Even more than their instrumental adjudicator colleagues, singing adjudicators undertook the task of separating the popular song chaff from the authentic song wheat. Unlike the majority of their instrumental adjudicating peers in the 1950s, adjudicators in singing competitions at the Fleadh were often several times removed from traditional singing in a traditional context, without a direct relationship to historical traditional singing communities. Séamas Ó Dubhthaigh, for example, first began singing when he went to college but was a regular adjudicator at Fleadhanna in the 1950s and later.[157] Like instrumental music, traditional singing in both Irish and English had undergone several institutional and performance context transformations in the first half of the twentieth century. While it experienced a similar decline to instrumental music in traditional domestic contexts, singing (in both languages) had, nonetheless, been part and parcel of the turn of the century cultural revival. New contexts, albeit limited, for an older often altered repertoire had been created, for example at feiseanna and Oireachtais. Joseph O'Connor, an inspector with the Department of Education up to the 1950s, reports that, in select counties, there was a high incidence of Irish-language singing at primary school level.[158] Irish-language songs were also performed and taught as part of the embedded choral singing in convent secondary schools throughout Ireland and An Claisceadal, the Irish-language choral initiative, also afforded Irish-language repertoire a new context.[159]

Two singing competitions were initiated in 1953 at the third Fleadh in Athlone, the ballad singing competition (English language) and an Irish-language singing competition.[160] Male and female categories of singing competitions in both languages were introduced the following year in Cavan (1954), a gendered division inconsistently used for a number of years and not found in other competitions.[161] All singing competitions were solo and unaccompanied, two key attributes attached to traditional vocal performance, similar to solo instrumental competition. One of the main challenges facing Comhaltas in all competitions, but in particular in singing, was in establishing the delimiters of a winning sound, in both languages. O'Connor asserts that most people in Ireland, in 1956, came from non-singing households.[162] Added to that was the fact that exposure to singing, whether listeners ever became performers or not, was in the first instance often from radio and other recordings in the public domain, or written sources within a formal educational environment. Therefore singers competing in the Fleadh were frequently coming to singing from outside a traditional community of practice (in contrast to many of their instrumental counterparts). These singers become the authenticating voices of a new domain of traditional singing.

Singing competitions were subject to adjudications of authenticity (just as instrument comptitions were), but authenticity in repertoire for singing competitions was even more perilous. A large corpus of reels, jigs and hornpipes, all approved as suitable for competition, existed as a living tradition within the traditional music-making community. Additionally, there was a large body of published tune collections and recordings of traditional instrumental repertoire readily available for performance in competition. Even though the majority of those recordings had piano accompaniment, the piper, or fiddler, or box player was understood to be playing traditional music. In contrast, recordings of traditional (or folk) song repertoire, in traditional styles (solo, unaccompanied) in both English and Irish were much less abundant. Song recordings that were available were most often in a popular-traditional style, with piano or ensemble accompaniment, such as those recorded by, for example, Delia Murphy or Irish tenor singers, already discussed. Song repertoire was also available in various published collections, but inauthentic pitfalls awaited singers in their competition selections.

*Nótaí do Mholtóirí* describes the greatest difficulty in adjudicating singing as being the lack of expertise among singers and adjudicators as to what legitimately fell within traditional singing repertoire. In particular, regarding repertoire:

> there is considerable anxiety and uncertainty among competitors as to the songs and ballads in English that will be accepted as traditional by adjudicators ... The uncertainty is mainly due to a widely held, though erroneous, belief that all popular national songs and ballads, more especially those allied to old Irish airs by well known composers, must be deemed traditional. Such, of course, is not the case.[163]

Though unnamed, this warning is aimed at singers who might draw from written collections 'by well known composers', such as the nineteenth-century Thomas Moore.[164] Notwithstanding Moore's use of older melodies in some song settings, those did not meet the authentic standard required. That principle was clear, but the demarcations within 'popular national songs and ballads' remained ambiguous. A further refinement of authentic repertoire is offered, but brings little clarity to adjudicators or competitors: 'It should be remembered that arrangements, or adapted versions, of even the most authentic of our Irish airs are not necessarily traditional and cannot be accepted as such'.[165] Songs that were 'even the most authentic' might not be acceptable if adapted in any way. No clear definition of adaptation as it might corrupt an authentic song rendering it inauthentic is given, but songs that had undergone commerical recording and were released in the popular domain were the likely target of this cautionary note.

Rule no. 13 in the 1962 'Rules for Fleadhanna Ceoil' forbids recording at competitions but, usefully for my purpose, Ciarán Mac Mathúna, in his capacity as collector with RÉ (by that time RTÉ), recorded the men's English ballad singing competition at the Clones Fleadh in 1964, including the underage categories.[166] On that field recording the adjudicator's comments are also audible. The unnamed (male) adjudicator speaks to the difficulties for performers in distinguishing between 'ballad singing as ye hear' on the airwaves and 'ballad singing in the traditional style'.[167] In his adjudication comments, he laments that his opinion would be dismissed, 'Ye'll say they [adjudicators] know nothing'.[168] The adjudicator outlined to the competitors and competition attendees what the markers of traditional ballad singing were that Comhaltas would reward. Specifically, of the singers in the senior men's competition he was glad that 'there was no sign of waltz time', which is part 'of the commercial art arrived at today' and not authentically traditional. His adjudications are calibrated on 'voice, choice, traditional time and traditional style', adhering to the basic framework that was codified later in *Nótaí do Mholtóirí*. Donal Ó Nualláin, from Cappawhite, Tippperary won the senior title, as he sang in 'true traditional style' and 'had what was required'.[169] Ó Nualláin's voice was crystal clear, with a rich timbre. His competition song choices were considered traditional by the adjudicator's estimation. Ó Nualláin's first choice, 'Ballyneety's Walls', appeared in *Ballads of Irish Chivalry* in 1872 as the 'Song of Sarsfield's Trooper' set to the air of 'Here's Our Brave Lord Lucan'.[170] A political ballad, it describes the battle for Limerick during the seventeenth-century Jacobite wars. Ó Nualláin's second song, 'The Ballad of Seán Treacy', is also a political ballad, though much more recent in vintage. It commemorates Treacy, the Tipperary rebel who was killed in 1920 during the Irish War of Independence. Political ballads, with a nationalist perspective, were prevalent in Fleadh competition, regardless of their antiquity and even if they were in waltz time (as is 'The Ballad of Seán Treacy'). Both of these songs were popular choices in Fleadh competition, endorsed as traditional and authentic by virtue of their subject matter and delivery.

Though singers were warned to sing appropriately gendered songs, in practice much of the repertoire was a shared one across male and female competitions. During the 1960s, a winning repertoire emerged that was relatively narrow; among the songs, 'The Rocks of Bawn' was a repeated favourite. Local songs became national winners, which were then nationalised in repertoire performance; Ó Nualláin's 'The Ballad of Seán Treacy' is one example. Others include 'Where the Mulcair River Flows' and 'The Streams of Bunclody', which repeatedly appear as winning songs, in both male and female competitions.[171] Though writing of instrumental competitions at the Fleadh, Breathnach's observation that 'a handful of popular and factory-made tunes are grounded out at the sessions at the local branch and fleadh' resonates with song competition too.[172] Songs that were accepted and rewarded in Fleadh competition generated a competition repertoire, which was performed over and over again, without facing accusations of inauthenticity. Winning repertoire developed dynamically between Fleadh and non-Fleadh zones, with co-operation (and complicity) between singer, listener and adjudicator.

Still, confusion (or lack of experience) on what was acceptable and what was not continued. The singing adjudicator at the Clones Fleadh in 1964 goes on in his oral delivery of adjudication to compliment Eddie Byrne in the novice category (u14). Byrne's songs, 'The Rocks of Bawn' and 'Mountains of Pomeroy' were judged traditional in origin and delivery. He was awarded second place, in spite of the fact the adjudicator suspected Byrne was listening to too much radio. The third placed competitor was reprimanded for his first song choice, 'Noreen Bawn'. Written *circa* 1915, the lyrics of this song of emigration and loss are credited to Neil McBride, from Cresslough, County Donegal. In (*verboten*) swinging waltz time, belying its early-twentieth-century origins, Byrne's performance drew an additional criticism as the song was widely heard on radio and recordings at that time, sung by 'a young female singer' who sang in a 'pop' style.[173] The young female singer, whose name could not be uttered in the adjudicator's comments for fear of further contamination, was Bridie Gallagher. A Donegal native, Gallagher had an internationally successful concert and recording career beginning in the late 1950s. Her signature sound was Irish ballads with band accompaniment arranged for dancing, and 'Noreen Bawn' was a B-side single in 1959 that became popular.[174] Whatever her popularity, her mediated sound was not the sought-after one approved of in competition. Marks were accordingly deducted from the young singer, though a very high mark for the second song selection, 'The Blackbird of Avondale', secured Byrne the bronze medal.

Pity young A. McNeill in the same competition: both of his songs were deemed unsuitable. 'A Mother's Love's a Blessing' and 'The Men of the West' were not in the approved category for Fleadh competition for this adjudicator. Young McNeill would do very well if he 'was singing in a music hall, or at a bazaar, or singing at a concert, be the Lord he'd bring down the house, but that didn't count with us'.[175] The adjudicator made a clear distinction between competition and performance spaces beyond the Fleadh and was adamant that there was an appropriate style and repertoire for each. If songs were deemed ineligible, the adjudicator could award no marks at all, in this case he magnaminously deducted marks instead. McNeill could not be treated too lightly though: 'we must be severe, we must be harsh' the adjudicator is heard say.[176] Traditional song in the English language in Ireland was already thickly mediated. McNeill's first song, 'A Mother's Love's a Blessing', was composed by Cork circus performer and song maker Thomas P. Keenan in the early twentieth century and was widely recorded on both sides of the Atlantic in the intervening decades, including a popular rendition by the aforementioned Bridie Gallagher in 1959 (and reissued in 1962).[177] Gallagher's mediated association with the song was enough to make it competition-toxic. The lyrics of young McNeill's second selection, 'The Men of the West', were composed in 1898 by William Rooney, a Dublin journalist and Gaelic revivalist, for the centenary of the 1798 rebellion.[178] The circumstances of its lyrical and melodic origins (it was set to the melody of 'Eoghan Chóir', attributed to Ríocard Báiréad, himself a participant in the 1798 rebellion) might bolster rather than diminish its credentials in the suitability stakes. Crucially, overriding all that, it appeared on the Clancy Brothers and Tommy Makem's first album in 1956, *The Rising of the Moon* (and again on its reissue in 1959), putting it on the Fleadh competition pike.[179]

The first prize in the u14 competition in 1964 (Clones) was awarded to Seán Ryan. The adjudicator comments on Ryan's style and delivery; he 'put notes in where he should have put them in and we had to give him ninety marks'.[180] On the matter of his song choices, the adjudicator declared that 'The Rocks of Bawn' and 'The Cliffs of Dooneen' lent themselves well to 'the real style'. Both songs were popular numbers at Fleadhanna and the former was also played as an instrumental slow air with some success in Fleadh competitions.[181] The lyrics of the emigration ballad 'The Cliffs of Dooneen' are most often attributed to Jack McAuliffe, born in Lixnaw, County Kerry and most likely written in the 1930s. It is, therefore, a more recent composition than 'The Men of the West', but in contrast was declared competition-acceptable. In 1964, at the time of this competition, 'The Cliffs of Dooneen' had yet to be a commercial success with accommpanying radio play. That came later with Christy Moore's rendition on his 1971 *Prosperous* album and the subsequent recording by Planxty in 1975.[182] In this reading, authenticity in the Fleadh (English-language) song-world is not necessarily linked to the age of songs or their origins, rather the distinguishing marker is whether the adjudicator has 'associational references' with commercial renditions of the song.[183] If that was the case, the song was rejected.

All of the evidence above demonstrates the complex process of how competition informed a reconfiguration of repertoire and stylistic characteristics that are then rewarded. Through winning performances at Fleadhanna Ceoil, that style became a signature style of 'traditional' singing, at times supplanting older styles in winners' lists. Found inside and outside the competition zone it relegitimated itself with every Fleadh success. Mulqueen, in an interview, recognised her own place in the Fleadh and non-Fleadh singing worlds when she said, 'I wasn't a traditional singer really; I was a pop star', neatly encapsulating the complicated relationship between repertoire, style, competition and commercialism at the Fleadh.[184]

## CONCLUSION

The competitive arena created performance circumstances not experienced outside of that milieu. The enclosed competitive space, literally and metaphorically in the case of Fleadhanna, resulted in the emergence of what Bealle describes as 'competitive aesthetics'.[185] Certainly, Comhaltas, in common with other music revival agencies, 'selectively incorporate valued elements of an earlier culture into a formal bureaucratic structure that meets modern needs and conditions'.[186] Adjudicators of traditional and folk music performance were faced with the task of 'defining folk music by internal properties and geographical context' as well as 'its function and how it was cultivated', a continuing challenge nearly sixty years later.[187] Competitions are specific cultural performances, brimful with significance, and signification, as 'dramatizations that enable participants to understand, criticize, and even change the worlds in which they live'.[188] Within Fleadh competition, performances defined by Comhaltas as traditional were acceptable and the organisation refined its articulation of what adjudicators should look for after an initial silence on the subject. Particular styles, in singing and solo instrumental categories, were honed at the Fleadh, but were not sealed within that performance space. The decisions of adjudicators reflected a desire to enunciate a definition of traditional performance practice, but that adjudication was arrived at symbiotically, between adjudicators and competitors. Winning performances then became a delimiting framework themselves, informing subsequent adjudication decisions. These articulations of music heard on recordings and film attest to the stylistic refinements and variations found within performance practice.

Through adjudication, the Fleadh (and Comhaltas) defined acceptable sounds of traditional music in competition, which spilled over into other sites of performance. Fleadhanna were particularly influential in showcasing a solo style and aesthetic in English ballad singing, fiddling and accordion playing. Within the domain of ensemble, céilí bands used Fleadhanna to develop styles of practice. However, styles and preferences were negotiated between performers and adjudicators in the Fleadh zone and emerged out of those musical dialogues. Despite his own reservations on competition, Peadar O'Loughlin confirms the status attached to winning a Fleadh when he remembers Paddy Canny's win in Athlone (1953); 'we said, this is great, surely to God there must have been a lot of fiddlers there, and surely Paddy Canny must be a great fiddler'.[189]

Robbie McMahon remembered an early Fleadh competition, in which, after numerous recalls, the adjudicator finally tossed a coin to decide the winner.[190] It may well be, as O'Loughlin mused, that tossing a coin is as useful a way as any to decide, as a competition 'doesn't answer a question, truly'.[191]

CHAPTER 7

# 'Strange Contrasts at the Fleadh': Sessions and Fleadh identity in the 1960s

## INTRODUCTION

'**S**trange Contrasts at the Fleadh', an *Amharc Éireann* newsreel from the Gorey Fleadh in 1962, presents the viewer with a particular juxtaposition on screen.[1] It opens with a familiar Fleadh trope of on-street traditional music making, on this occasion with a fiddler, a bodhrán player, (an inaudible) banjo-mandolin performer and, to the right of the frame, a bones player. The camera then cuts to another musical scene at the same Fleadh, this time to a guitar player seated on the ground surrounded by rapt listeners. This hirsute balladeer is singing 'Jamaican Farewell, Kingston Town', a (folk) pop hit on both sides of the Atlantic for the Caribbean-American artist Harry Belafonte in 1956.[2] Onlookers join the refrain on 'Kingston Town' and Colm Ó Laoghaire narrates over the juxtaposition: 'bhí gach uile sort daoine ann, lucht traidisiún de agus lucht trad de' ('every sort of person was there, a traditional crowd, and a trad crowd'). The stylistic musical contrast of Ó Laoghaire's 'traditional crowd' and 'trad crowd' is replicated in Lennart Malmer's film *Porter Och Pipa* (1966) in a scene from a County Clare fleadh in Scariff in 1965, emphasising the point. In Ó Laoghaire's categorisations the 'traditional crowd' referred to those who played fiddles, bodhráns and the ilk, and whose repertoire sat comfortably within a traditional Irish music (session) mode by 1962. Unlike current vernacular usage, the 'trad crowd' here refers to the bearded balladeers on screen, aligned in musical interests and style to what was internationally termed folk in the 1960s. The same ballad-singing 'trad crowd' was excoriated by E. Stapleton the following year when he wrote of the Mullingar Fleadh (1963): 'these balladeers have created a cult ... Louder and louder it gets. New gimmicks will be thought up and ultimately gyrations employed to attract and hold attention'.[3] The music-making scenes detailed above and the responses from cultural gatekeepers are among the key elements for discussion in this final chapter.

I begin with an exploration of session as a symbolic and performed object of Fleadh structure, contextualising its development in wider traditional music practice in the post-war period and tracing the pathway of session into the lexicon of Irish traditional music culture. By 1960, the Fleadh, as an innovative model of music festival transnationally, was the embodiment of Irish traditional music revival and acknowledged as a key cultural (and economic) event.[4] A number of preceding chapters outline how Comhaltas built a structural and symbolic Fleadh framework in the 1950s through invariant (though not static) Fleadh objects such as céilithe and concerts, competitions and parades, consolidating the Fleadh domain. Part of any festival success is its ability to balance invariant with variant objects. At the Fleadh, sessions, music making by multiple musicians gathered in spontaneous ensemble indoors at pubs (typically) or outdoors on the street provided that balance. This chapter appraises the dynamic relationship between the development of the session as a mode of traditional music expression in Fleadh history. With session as a key driver of growth, the chapter then describes the expansion of festival constituencies in the 1960s beyond the traditional music fraternity of its beginnings, as the Fleadh extended its reach to other cohorts of cultural tourists. The final part of my discussion examines the resulting challenges to and for institutional authority within the festive frame.

## SESSION HISTORIES AND TERMINOLOGY

Music making, whatever the mode, was the most important element in a series of festive objects and practices from which meaning was derived at the Fleadh. How meaning is enacted through music making at the festival can be seen most obviously in two contrapuntal elements:

competition (much discussed in previous chapters) and sessions. Both are vital to the sustainability of the Fleadh, a binary of formal (invariant) and informal (variant) providing a necessary 'simultaneous coexistence of opposites'.[5] Picard and Robinson note:

> All types of festivity seem to include forms of stage and non-staged performances, and enactments, through which individuals and groups can discursively manifest their visions of the world and create meaningful frameworks of their being together.[6]

Sessions were the primary unstaged performance at the Fleadh, animating meanings and experiences that 'drew people together in solid and complete enjoyment'.[7] Additional binaries in the competition/session axis that heighten the festive experience for musicians and listeners are notable: competitions were indoors in classrooms and halls, and explicitly regulated, whereas Fleadh sessions were often outdoors or in pubs and implicitly regulated. Festivals resulted in increased group awareness and identities, and frequently this is 'realised by a performance which confirms the group as well as integrating new members'.[8] Sessions were an ideal vehicle for the development of Fleadh consensus, fulfilling a social contract of festive exchange in impromptu music making.

Often presumed to be an older practice, the session 'is a relatively recent import to Ireland' and to traditional music.[9] As described by Reg Hall, the (pub) session emerged in Irish emigrant communities in Britain beginning in the late 1940s, most influentially in London.[10] Sessions connect with historical domestic music practice but, crucially, favour ensemble playing. In 1951, when the Fleadh began, the predominant mode of traditional music in Ireland in the public sphere was also ensemble playing, but heard in céilí bands, not the pub session playing of their London emigrant kin. Though sessions developed in Britain directly after the war, as late as 1964 Luke O'Malley, on his first fleadh visit to Ireland from New York, noted that there were no comparable pub sessions in the USA at that time (they developed in the 1970s in Irish-American enclaves).[11] With some exceptions, ensemble playing in a session mode began in Ireland in the intervening decades, becoming 'the most accessible and popular space of musical practice, for both players and listeners' in the global world of Irish traditional music.[12] In addition to the influence of British emigrant contexts, other factors informed the development of sessions in Ireland: internal migration; the growth of the pub as accessible social space; Comhaltas branch development; increased domestic and international tourism; the international folk music revival of the 1960s; and, finally, the Fleadh itself. Jessica Cawley observes that sessions at festivals have a particular intensity and 'are important informal sites for musical participation, learning, and socialising. Vibrant, public displays of music making can fuel motivation and spark lifelong learning'.[13] The key aim of the Fleadh was to provide opportunities for musical communion. Gathered from near and far, musicians came to the Fleadh with the expressed purpose of playing traditional music with other musicians: the session was that communion experienced.

As a term, 'session' was added to the lexicon of Irish traditional music to describe the informal, spontaneous ensemble music making that emerged. Before its adoption by Irish traditional musicians, the word 'session' was employed to describe jazz jams beginning in the 1930s and 1940s primarily in the USA and in Britain. Distinct from staged performance, early jazz jam sessions were 'liberated from an address to, or a responsibility towards, the public audience' where the 'players become their own audience', similar to later Irish music sessions.[14] There is also a performative and chronological comparison between sessions in bluegrass music, which developed in the late 1950s, and Irish traditional music sessions.[15] In parallel, other folk music genres in the USA and Britain in the 1960s described informal, public music making as sessions. Direct routes between lexical worlds of American jazz (as the earliest twentieth-century example) and later mid-century Anglo/North American folk traditions such as bluegrass, to Irish traditional music are suggested, but not explicit.[16] Though music making took place in Irish emigrant homes in Britain in a limited way, and in isolated cases in pubs in Ireland before 1945, it was London pubs where the session aesthetic (and naming) took hold.[17] Hall's recollection of the first time he heard music making in a pub termed a session is significant. Uttered by fiddle player Michael Gorman in the late 1950s, Hall was 'taken aback' and concludes that 'some Irish musicians' had heard it 'referring to a free-for-all get-together of jazz and swing musicians' in London.[18] It may well be that returning emigrants to early Fleadhanna brought session terminology with them.

In a letter from F. Mulcahy to Seán Reid in 1960, Mulcahy uses the term session repeatedly, but each time in inverted commas ('session') as does a report on the Fleadh in Boyle that year.[19] Some years earlier, a newspaper account of the Ennis Fleadh in 1956 describes the 'bishop himself' at the Old Ground Hotel, who arrived 'for an official dinner and walked straight into a "session"'.[20] The qualifying punctuation in both cases suggests that the term session was being used increasingly to name the spontaneous music making found at the Fleadh, but still held some novelty. By extension, gatherings at Comhaltas branches throughout the year and beyond Comhaltas environs were also using the term. In the mid-1960s, Comhaltas and Fleadh documents consistently use the term session (with and without inverted commas) as the default descriptor of non-formal, spontaneous music making at the Fleadh.[21]

### SESSIONS AT THE FLEADH

Though the competition system and the competitor base expanded annually from 1951, Mackie Rooney writes that 'regimented competition [was] but a secondary consideration in the life-line of the Fleadh', a point demonstrated by the vast majority who attended but did not compete.[22] In 1954, the *Anglo-Celt* reported that 500 musicians competed at the Cavan Fleadh but was quick to counter with this:

> The winning of a competition was not the sole object of the Fleadh. These musicians came to Cavan to play and play they certainly did. They played in the streets, they played in the houses, they even played in the back yards when no other platform was available.[23]

Impromptu music making was vital sonically and symbolically, and the social contract of the Fleadh was realised not just metaphorically, but literally, through shared music making. In the non-Fleadh space of 1950s Ireland, many had limited opportunity to play with fellow musicians and were enthused by the opportunity the Fleadh provided. Vincent Broderick remembered his first Fleadh, in Monaghan 1952:

> Fleadhs of course were great, because when I went to the first Fleadh, well the first All Ireland Fleadh in 1952, I played in the competition. I was second that year. Well, we played that night outside, about nine or ten flute players, well it was very unusual to have flute players and nine or ten together.[24]

For Broderick, the excitement at meeting other flute players and playing with them was enriching and community building. These were flute players that he did not previously know, or certainly did not regularly meet, before entering the Fleadh space. The exchange of repertoire and cultivation of shared (musical) experience remained with him as meaningful, decades later. Patsy Herron from Donegal, resident in Sligo for much of his life, recalled the Fleadh as a chance to play with and meet musicians that he would never meet otherwise.[25] Herron, like others, noted the importance of meeting those musicians again at later Fleadhanna, building a mobile music community, moving from town to town with the Fleadh. Deborah Rapuano describes the process of emigrant musicians with different playing styles sharing repertoire in newly created session spaces, an observation that applies to all musicians meeting at the Fleadh in these early decades.[26] During the 1950s and 1960s the Fleadh was an important facilitator for session practice to develop in Ireland, with large groups of musicians meeting and making music together. It is an example of diverse local music accents coming together and the exchange moving towards a national sensibility of style. Returning to their parishes and towns, session playing was replicated through Comhaltas branch network meetings, and beyond, until the next Fleadh.

Outdoor session playing at the Fleadh was held in particularly high regard, the 'major thing', as Peig Ryan, a fiddle player and Comhaltas organiser in Tipperary and Limerick, described it.[27] The festival context also meant musicians encountered a festive public that was not always expert, even in these very early years. Broderick, in this Fleadh story, recalled:

> I remember one thing, I was left handed, I was standing on the outside of the group and we had about two hundred people listening to us and this fella said 'Tommy, will you look at your man on the outside and he standing on the wrong side of the flute'.[28]

Playing outdoors represents the untrammeled, transgressive side of festivity containing symbolic memory of historical festivity in Ireland, at pattern and fair days. Fr Clancy, chair of Wexford Comhaltas in 1964, was an outlier in his view that Comhaltas 'emphasised far too much the atmosphere of the impromptu concert [session]', but the *Free Press*

**Fig. 7.1** Unidentified musicians at the Gorey Fleadh, 1962
Copyright Fáilte Ireland, courtesy ITMA

looked forward in 1962 to outdoor sessions, which were promoted as creating a special atmosphere peculiar to the Fleadh (see Fig. 7.1).[29]

Healy describes a scene he witnessed at the Fleadh in Ennis, in 1956:

> I saw two fiddlers – complete strangers to each other – meet at three o'clock in the morning for the first time, though they had been playing together for two hours beforehand! After formally exchanging names they found they were to be competitors later in the day. One asked the other what he was going to play and the reply was to play it there and then ... 'Well now', said the man from Antrim, 'wouldn't it be great fun if the two of us went up with the same twist and leave the judges in a puzzle as to which of us was

the better?' And for an hour the two men played together, one to become as perfect as the other, and laughing to themselves at 'the steam' they'd have when they competed ... the men and women who come here are not medal hunters.[30]

Healy records part of the often-articulated attraction of the Fleadh, the conviviality of musicans meeting and playing spontaneously wherever the musical notion took them. Though he romantically asserts medal-winning did not matter (within the competition domain winning most certainly did matter to musicians, and it had currency in the post-Fleadh context), there is a more refined point to make. In the non-competitive Fleadh domain, competitors playing informally together contributed to a heightened experience of music making. Like sporting contests, the relational rules of behaviour which contestants adopted within the competition frame were relaxed outside that domain. The scene that Healy describes goes further than that. On the one hand, it illustrates a disregard for the structure of competition itself, and yet, on the other hand, places traditional musical performance and its implicit communitas squarely in the competitive frame, when the fiddlers are complicit in confounding the adjudicators.

Spontaneous sessions transformed other non-festive spaces into havens of temporary music making, where 'casual instruments supplied a symphony of music on the footpaths, or the steps of houses or the base of a handy statue'.[31] A session in Ennis (1956) took place late in the evening in the lingerie department of a shop that included, 'by the last chorus':

> ten fiddles, two jew's harps, a battered concertina, six concert flutes. Three tin-whistles, two melodeons and four raucous accordions are [were] thundering out the melody and the building itself seems to have cast aside its eighty-five years of dignity and respectability as singers and musicians raise the roof.[32]

The success of the Fleadh during the 1950s attracted returning emigrants from overseas, some of them subsequently setting up branches of Comhaltas in their diasporic locations.[33] Returning to Ireland for the Fleadh quickly became an opportune and fruitful early summer visit to Ireland, allowing emigrant musicians to meet with family and musical kin alike. These returning Irish were typically coming to a traditional practice already known to them. This was the music, song and dance of their youth (and increasingly of their diasporic experience) and the Fleadh allowed them to maintain that connection with a community of practice that was already familiar to them. While many competed, sessions were a key site of engagement. Tomás Ó Canainn, a member of the Liverpool Céilí Band, recalls in particular his first Fleadh session experience in Longford, in this case outdoors, in 1958:

> The atmosphere at that weekend (in Longford) was something that we had never before experienced. We started to play a few tunes on the street in Longford before a crowd that just kept growing until it completely blocked the street. We were enjoying it until we saw two gardaí making their way through the crowd. I said to Kit, 'We'd better stop'. 'Not at all' she said, 'Just keep playing' … Those early Fleadhs were like that … The first rapture of the Longford Fleadh lives long in the memory.[34]

Already established among emigrant musicians in Britain by 1950, the Fleadh was an early adaptor of pub sessions, at a time when the green shoots of session playing were only just surfacing in the non-Fleadh world.[35] Ryan encountered 'no such thing as pub playing' before she attended her first Fleadh in the 1950s.[36] In 1956, Seán Shéamais wrote: 'Agus mh'anam gur ins na tithe osta [sic] céanna a chloisfimid an ceol nuair a bheas deireadh leis an léiriú oifigiúil' (And on my soul, it is in those same pubs that we will hear the music when the official production is over) (see Fig. 7.2).[37]

Exchange and encounter, meeting friends old and new, the necessary festive symmetry actualised by sessions was eagerly anticipated:

> The crowds are already thronging the town and the 'sessions' have already started. It's a time for meeting old friends. Let's stop at this pub. The door is open and four fiddles and a flute are playing 'The Geese in the Bog'.[38]

Sessions filled 'every pub, guesthouse, and drapery shop', in Boyle (1960).[39] James Mulvaney's premises had music making until the small hours in the crowded space:

'Strange Contrasts at the Fleadh'

Fig. 7.2 Musicians at Fleadh Cheoil Dungarvan, with Eddie Moloney (flute), Tommy Coen (fiddle), 1957
Copyright Fáilte Ireland, courtesy ITMA

You had Boston-born Gearóid Lee … playing in the shoe department, with Dr Bill Loughnane, of Clare, and Joe Keegan, of Armagh, while two counters away, Richard Aherne, a friend of the late Margaret Burke Sheridan, calling for 'The Sligo Maid'. And Kitty Hodge, over from Liverpool, struck up the air. Seated on bales of suiting material, or sometimes on top of a draper's assistant's ladder, young Garech Browne fought, with some success, to impose order as the fear an tí [master of ceremonies], calling on Seán Ac Donncha, or Dolly McMahon to sing a song.[40]

Sessions quickly became a key attraction to the Fleadh zone, providing an informal counterbalance to formal competition. Importantly, the Fleadh was not divorced from wider changes happening in Irish traditional music practice; rather it coincided with and animated pub session playing in both the Fleadh and non-Fleadh zones, for performers and patrons alike.

## CULTURAL TOURISTS, FLEADH GATEKEEPERS AND MULLINGAR, 1963

The Fleadh is the earliest and most significant site of traditional music cultural tourism in twentieth-century modern Ireland. Those invested in traditional music travelled from all over Ireland and elsewhere to the Fleadh in growing numbers from the early 1950s, specifically because of their traditional music interests. As the profile of the Fleadh grew during the 1960s, the competition-festival attracted new cohorts of cultural tourists from within Ireland and overseas, changing the social composition of the festival. International visitors to the Fleadh were especially noted in reports, betraying a mindset simultaneously parochial, insular and othering. As late as 1970, Bryan McMahon wrote 'I've noticed there's always a foreigner about' at a Fleadh.[41] McMahon's foreigner designation does not refer to emigrées (returning cultural tourists themselves), but primarily to those with no emigrant attachment to the traditional music world. At the Fleadh in Boyle in 1960, two recently graduated occupational therapists from Germany, Wolf and Frau Stoltenberg, 'came because they had heard so much about traditional music' declaring the festival the 'most exciting thing of its kind' they had had ever seen.[42] Though not familiar with Irish traditional music, and not necessarily musicians themselves, the wider, international folk music revival and its incorporation into youth culture in the 1960s began to inform patterns of attendance and engagement at the Fleadh from near and far. It was noted that, among the 60,000 visitors to the Fleadh in Mullingar in 1963, many were drawn from continental Europe, as well as from Britain and the USA.[43] Manus Ó Domhnaill, at the Fleadh in Clones in 1964, observes the diversity of visitors:

> *Tá na Fleadhanna [sic] go breá, táid anseo ó gach áit san domhan, as Nigeria, as North Rhodesia, as Meiriceá, as Sasana, as Shéalann Nua, agus tíortha nach féidir liom ainm a chur orthu.*
>
> (The Fleadh is lovely, they are here from every place in the world, from Nigeria, from North Rhodesia, from America, from England, from New Zealand, and other countries that I can't put a name on.)[44]

'Strange Contrasts at the Fleadh'

International visitors (including visiting media) were invariably identified in reportage as a subject of curiosity and a warm welcome extended to them.⁴⁵

Close to 30,000 people were expected to make their way to Gorey for the Fleadh in 1962; estimates afterwards put the attending numbers at closer to 40,000.⁴⁶ The 'very decent' attendees are extolled in the local *People* newspaper:

> there was music here, there and everywhere in the town. On every street there were impromptu concerts and the dancing, singing and playing continued throughout the night. There was no such thing as bed, as hundreds, indeed it could have been thousands, made the sky their roof for the night. It was a weekend of round the clock enjoyment ... Referring to the people who attended the Fleadh, Mr. O'Connor (the town commissioner) said they were a very decent lot.⁴⁷

In contrast, the Clare county fleadh in Ennis later that summer anticipated problems that arose continually for the rest of the decade, when cultural tourists from closer to home were not so warmly received. A letter from 'Disgusted' to the *Irish Press*, on 25 August 1962, draws attention to the scenes of 'debauchery and drunkeness' on the occasion of the county fleadh.⁴⁸ 'A Traditional Teenager' from Galway agrees with 'Disgusted':

> When Fleadh Cheoils were first held they were wonderful. Only those with a genuine interest in Irish music attended and the result was a large gathering of good natured people ... all with a common interest in Irish culture. Of course, it couldn't last. People with no interest in any kind of culture began to come too. Any excuse to kick up a racket. Roaring mobs charged up and down the streets of Ennis on August weekend. They broke up attempts at organised céilí dancing, shouted down singers and threw bottles.⁴⁹

The response to the criticism from Comhaltas (by now self-appointed cultural gatekeeper) was robust. Labhrás Ó Murchú, at that time a Comhaltas administrator in County Tipperary, currently director-general of Comhaltas, writes that 'Disgusted' must have:

> failed to notice the 20,000 people who flocked to the town; the hundreds of musicians who came from all parts of the country;

the immense and wonderful organisation behind the Fleadh; the good clean fun derived by all from the function; the commercial significance to Ennis; the cultural and national importance of the Fleadh; the edifying and wholesome influence on the young.[50]

The defence of the Clare fleadh, as a cultural event of national import; as a tool of Comhaltas; and lastly as a bastion of good, clean fun, which could only be positive for the youth who attended, is asserted in no uncertain terms. Cormac Lankford questions also the logic of 'Disgusted', and points out that drunkenness and debauchery are found in lots of places; the organisers of the fleadh could not be held responsible for 'the actions of a few blackguards'.[51] Underpinning Lankford's view, Michel Peillon's notes that transgressive behaviours and 'breakdowns of order' are tolerated in any festive frame and can usefully 'reinforce' rules of engagement.[52] This also resonates with the reality of the festive space as one that encompasses 'multiple voices and understandings', with no simple identification of transgressive.[53]

Thomas P. Dempsey, the publicity officer of Comhaltas in 1962, does not deny unpalatable behaviour at the county fleadh in Ennis but, like Lankford, allows for a transgressive element. He writes that 'unfortunately, all such large gatherings attract an undesirable element' and going further identifies the culprits: 'judging by their hair, their dress and undisciplined behaviour, we may readily conclude they are not products of Gaelic culture'.[54] Dempsey uses a tried and tested essentialist defence that is employed repeatedly by Fleadh gatekeepers in later years: the infractions, though committed at a fleadh, are not approved by fleadh administrators or 'decent' people. The offenders are easily differentiated from the sanctioned and culturally authentic attendees by their appearance and behaviour. Any miscreant, in this scheme of logic, is not the fleadh's responsibility, precisely because they are not one of the insiders of Irish (traditional music) culture. In a letter to the *Irish Farmers Journal* later that year, 'Corca Baiscinn' laments 'the chaos and disorder in the streets, combined with the jostling and elbowing of the crowd in the competitions halls' as a 'gruelling and disillusioning experience'.[55] Furthermore, Corca Baiscinn suggests that the title of the festival should be changed from Fleadh Cheoil to Fleadh Óil (festival of drink).[56] The dissatisfied former Fleadh attendee stopped going to Fleadhanna in 1959, writing that the Fleadh became 'a camaflage [sic] for intemperate and riotous behaviour', something akin to the 'Roman scene in the days of Julius Caesar'.[57]

Immortalised in John Montague's 'The Siege of Mullingar', the Mullingar Fleadh in 1963 was hailed beforehand as a coming home of the festival, back to the site of its beginnings. Ireland in the early 1960s had positive, though cautious, economic growth and, for the first time in over a century, the population grew, particularly in the 14–24-year-old range.[58] Expanded interest from emigrant communities, combined with the international folk music revival and its ballad boom manifestation in Ireland, resulted in a significant expansion in numbers at all fleadhanna, but especially the All Ireland Fleadh. The Mullingar Fleadh in 1963 became a touchstone of cultural identity conflict, between gatekeepers of Fleadh identity and those who complicated and challenged that. Prior to the Fleadh, Cáit Uí Mhuineacháin, one of the organisers of the first Fleadh in Mullingar and founder member of Comhaltas nationally, expressed grave concern about the Fleadh coming back to Mullingar. In a letter to Reid in 1963, she wrote that there was little or no interest among the townspeople of Mullingar in traditional music.[59] Furthermore, the recent revival of the Mullingar Comhaltas branch was, in her view, a cynical act to host the Fleadh for commercial rather than culturally authentic reasons, echoing earlier debates on the clash between cultural and commerical interests.[60]

With an estimated attendance of 60,000 people, the Mullingar Fleadh was blighted by 'an unruly group who wended their way into Mullingar late on Saturday night, chanting songs and slogans', intent on 'causing real trouble at the Fleadh Cheoil' and 'in spite of repeated appeals by the organisers, they continued their campaign'.[61] Signs of trouble came early, on the first day of the festival:

> In the evening a voice was to be heard over a loud speaker reminding the public of the ancient Irish nation and asking with a slight undercurrent of desperation 'in the name of the Almighty to see that this festival gets the respect it deserves'.[62]

The public at which the plea was directed 'were the young people, the bright ones, all long legs in slacks and jeans, in high spirits and happy humours' distinct from 'legitimate ... music-lovers and the decent people who attend the Fleadh'.[63] One writer notes that fiddlers and pipers found themselves surplus to requirements:

> they were ousted by modern howlers and string-thumpers, to such an extent that they hid themselves from the public ear. Modern youth was out on top and at the height of the fun, boogie woogie, the rock and the twist defeated the simple rhythm of the reel.[64]

In a similar vein, the *Irish Independent* records that the same denim-ed youths:

> were also blamed for damage to public buildings, shops and houses and with interfering with cars. Street decorations were torn down, platform boards were ripped from their bases and several people were injured in beatnik rows.[65]

The national chairman of Comhaltas, Sylvestor Conway, defended the Fleadh and retorted that 'we did not send for them and we certainly do not want them'.[66] Extra Gardaí were drafted in from all over the Midlands to keep 'some semblance of order' among the crowds.[67] The *Irish Catholic* comments that 'an impartial observer is forced to the conclusion that the incidents of this year's Fleadh are not isolated ones' with 'radical reforms' necessary to address the problem and the 'Bohemian spirits' who were the cause had 'widespread disregard for traditional proprieties'.[68] The responses above combine a broad brushstroke of indicators (young, jeans-wearing, too much hair, exhibiting an interest in other musics rather than traditional) which, taken together, create a profile of those whose conduct was 'alien to the natural spirit of the Irish people'.[69] Though many felt the problem with the Fleadh lay in the size of the gathered crowds (one report declared that 100,000 attended the Fleadh in Mullingar), it is the profile of attendee that exercised critics most.[70] The 1960s in Ireland was a decade in which youth were an increasingly 'visible social group' with additional leisure time and resources to indulge their leisure interests.[71] Internationally, festivals in the 1960s attracted those for whom 'the social experience outweigh(ed) the music'; festivals were 'simply an enjoyable escape from routine'.[72] At the end of the decade, an article in the Muintir na Tíre's *Rural Ireland* reminded readers that 'leisure is going to be an increasingly large factor in the lives of everyone' and people would reasonably seek out opportunities to find 'honest joy in each other's company'. Rural dwellers needed to 'face [the] challenges' of that.[73]

The Fleadh benefitted from this demographic shift and these new economic actors but, simultaneously, youth were interpreted as dangerous 'harbingers of cultural change' by Fleadh gatekeepers.[74] Little distinction was made between those who may be guilty of social disorder and those youth who were simply partaking in festive experience. The *Irish Catholic* blames the ensuing trouble on 'the vast crowds attracted by the elaborate publicity' and further that, 'the extensive publicity attracted to the town an extensive number of beatniks, teddy boys and other bizarre and unwashed individuals'.[75] Blame for the Fleadh's fall from grace was laid at the feet of the corporeally, sartorially and spiritually unclean. The identity of the Fleadh and its gatekeepers was challenged by individuals who did not conform to the recognisable material components established during the 1950s. The recognisable, material components of Fleadhanna, in Turner's terms the 'set of properties' that identified the Fleadh, did not comfortably accommodate 'high-spirited, jeans-clad' youth, clean or unclean, 'twisting and jiving' in Mullingar.[76]

### DISORDER AND ORDER AFTER MULLINGAR

In the early years of the Fleadh, attracting larger numbers of patrons (musicians and listeners) was a clear goal; during the 1960s, the Fleadh became a victim of its own success as numbers attending increased to such an extent that the Fleadh became unstable within the established framework. The boundaries drawn around festival community can be inclusive and enriching but, for those who are not believed by cultural insiders to share specific affiliations or knowledge, the borders of festive community are less permeable.[77] The identification of unwelcome attendees, who purportedly distorted the Fleadh experience ('undesirables' in Uí Mhuineacháin's terms), was reiterated time and again, and there were whispers that that the All Ireland Fleadh should be abandoned until such time as the unruly elements could be rooted out.[78]

After Mullingar, Reid suggested that the Fleadh should be held on an island thereby controlling who had access; Uí Mhuineacháin agreed wholeheartedly – the suggestion gave her 'great hope that there are more genuine lovers of Irish music on the war path along with myself'.[79] Not for the first time, Whit weekend was criticised as an unsuitable time of year for the Fleadh, as it was a holiday weekend when everyone (and anyone) was free to travel to the Fleadh location. As early as 1959, delegates at the annual convention suggested that changing the date of the Fleadh was inevitable and necessary.[80] The primary motivation was a wish to control the increasing size of the crowds attending and the behaviour of patrons. Some within the administration, who favoured this, thought a shift away from the Whit holiday weekend would reduce the numbers.[81] If numbers were reduced, in particular the convenient revellers with little interest in traditional music as defined by Comhaltas, transgressive behaviour would decrease accordingly. Applying this litmus test, attendance would be restricted to those who demonstrated a genuine concern for Irish traditional music. The obvious difficulties of articulating and applying that standard was later summed up by Dempsey when he exclaimed 'if they come, we can't throw them out'.[82] In 1965, Demspey predicted that within a few years the Fleadh would be held in 'a confined space', perhaps in 'a Fleadh Cheoil village', over which 'Comhaltas will have complete control'.[83]

Throughout the 1960s several attempts were made at organisational level to move the Fleadh to a different weekend during the summer. The first of these motions was formally tabled in 1963 after the debacle of Mullingar and the motion was initially passed.[84] Five motions were quickly put forward to restore the Fleadh to the Whit weekend, one of which was tabled by the Clones branch (County Monaghan) already working towards hosting the Fleadh the following year, 1964.[85] The Clones contingent was opposed to moving the Fleadh for a number of reasons, not least of all the resistance of hoteliers to any change and 'the difficulty of keeping the Fleadh committees at a high pitch of preparedness and efficiency during the summer holidays'.[86] The deference to business interests was both practical and problematic, harkening back to concerns raised first in Dungarvan and prescient of Concubhar's comments after the 1967 Fleadh in Enniscorthy (County Wexford): 'Tá deireadh leis an bhFleadh mar a bhí sé [sic] sna blianta tosaí. Gnó atá anois ann' (The

'Strange Contrasts at the Fleadh'

Fleadh as it was in the first years is finished. Now, it is a business).[87] In addition, the knowledge among its supporters that the Fleadh always took place at Whit weekend secured it seasonally, partly explaining why repeated motions and suggestions to change it throughout the 1950s and 1960s were rejected.

In the wake of Mulligar (1963), problems of disorder were discussed at length and Comhaltas' executive council ruled that it would take a much more active role in the running of future Fleadhanna, enforcing rules already in place but inconsistently applied.[88] A centralised system of administration, which had always been a hallmark of Comhaltas aspirationally if not in reality, would weigh in to solve the problem. However, motions to move the Fleadh from Whit weekend were defeated, for now at least.[89] The need to enunciate the authority and cultural integrity of the Fleadh dominated Comhaltas meetings and discourse during this period. Stapleton commented that 'it is not simply a matter of controlling the crowds at the festivals. For Comhaltas it must be an enforcement of original aims and objects unadulturated'.[90] The Newry branch of Comhaltas published the first issue of its newsletter, *Fonn*, in the direct aftermath of the Fleadh in Mullingar. As one of the only published opinions coming from within the organisation, albeit at a local branch level, the views represented are stark:

> the Fleadh has reached a crisis in its history. The abject abandonment of the town to the hordes of vandals and hooligans ... has disgusted many sincere music lovers whom it will be difficult to entice back to future fleadhanna.[91]

As the commentator saw it, the problem was a public order one, but go on to write that with a sufficiently increased Garda presence, the Fleadh could be salvaged.[92] Over 200 extra Gardaí were drafted in for Clones in 1964 and combined with the 100-strong 'vigilance committee' (a formidable title) and other volunteers, a relatively uneventful Fleadh was recorded.[93] This was in spite of an estimated 70,000 in attendance (though inclement weather on the Sunday night of the Fleadh also contributed to the almost incident-free weekend).[94] A small number of cases were heard by the Clones district court during the week following the Fleadh, but all were for minor infractions.[95]

Though criminal charges arising from the Fleadh in Clones were few, at the annual congress of Comhaltas held in September 1964, numerous charges of crimes against Irish traditional culture were (again) levelled at the 'guitar bearing balladeers', with a front-page headline emphasising the now familiar facial-hair point, 'Beards at Fleadh Cheoil are criticised'.[96] So strong were the objections by Craobh an Phiarsaigh, the Dublin Comhaltas branch, to the direction the Fleadh was taking that the branch recommended an immediate discontinuation of the festival. The motion was not without its supporters and the call to abandon the Fleadh, or at least to take a hiatus of several years, was echoed later by others.[97] Dempsey responded that neither Comhaltas nor any Fleadh committee could prevent people from attending the Fleadh, even if they sported 'beards, jeans, and long hair or don't wash their faces' (in this instance, all gendered accusations: young men are the culprits).[98] All agreed that 'Fleadh Cheoil na hÉireann with its high quota of gimmicks, and functions and publicity had lost much of the homely spirit of the early fleadhanna'.[99] Here again is the assertion that 'commercial interests' were antithetical to the Fleadh's character, focused only on drawing more people to the festival year on year. Ironically, this was explicitly encouraged by 'pre-Fleadh publicity' at local and national Fleadh levels and by Comhaltas more generally.[100] It is not clear if the declaration at the 1963 annual congress that 'interference with open air music sessions by the public amplification of certain modern forms of music' would be 'regarded as prejudicial to public order by the Gardaí' was ever implemented, but the motion to suspend the Fleadh was defeated.[101]

Motions at Comhaltas annual congress meetings did not prevent the difficulties at the Fleadh in Thurles in 1965. Dubbed the 'Fleadh of the shattered glass', one commentator describes the antics as 'semi-organised hooliganism' and the Fleadh as a 'haven for blackguards'.[102] A solution was proffered that the Fleadh should be hosted in the most isolated town imaginable in Ireland 'so that the bowsie elements from the larger centres of population will find it even more difficult to get to them'.[103] The national chairman of Comhaltas in 1965, Micheál Ó Ceallacháin, issued a strongly worded attack on 'the lunatic fringe' who had been responsible for broken windows, scattered shards of glass, damaged cars, and general disorderliness.[104] At the same time, he recognised, without irony, that Comhaltas could not be the 'guardian of any person's morals'.[105] Though the Garda commissioner 'described reports of what happened as exaggerated', such was the level of disturbance in Thurles that a delegation of Comhaltas officers presented themselves at the Garda station in the middle of the night on Saturday of the Fleadh to appeal for help.[106] Evidently, the corps of 300 Gardaí was inadequate in the face of disturbances and many insiders, including the chairman himself, voiced concerns that this would, despite their best efforts, signal an end to the Fleadh. Raymond Smith wrote:

> It must not go on again. It must not be allowed to take place at a Whit weekend, or any holiday weekend at that, in its present form. Mullingar shattered its image. Thurles last weekend finally killed it. The young man who sounded the Last Post and Reveille in Liberty Square at 8am on Sunday morning was really sounding the death-knell of the Fleadh.[107]

Sheila O'Dowd, a fiddle player from Sligo, regarded the Fleadhanna during this period as 'not nice places to go to … the Fleadh was always held at Whit weekend, there was an awful lot of people at a loose end, people who had no interest in music at all'.[108] Eamonn Ó Muirí, Monaghan and national Comhaltas stalwart, writes that, with respect to the 'banjo-strumming, bearded exhuberance', it was not representative of the 'pulsating and vibrant revival get-together'.[109] Ó Muirí hints here at his own deeper understanding of festivity, and further comments that the youth with 'fleeces of face fungus' were merely seeking to 'escape from unreality', to one of the only places where 'the simple things that represent the culture of this ancient land' were accessible to them.[110] He carefully counsels that they were 'in search of something that neither progress not prosperity nor the cultural mediocrity of the new nation' could hope to offer.[111]

In addition to the disorder at the Fleadh in Thurles (1965), commentators bemoaned the lack of outdoor performance and spontaneous music making of the 1960s Fleadhanna.[112] Critics harkened back to the earlier Fleadhanna of the 1950s as exemplars of *al fresco extempore* performance. During the 1950s, this was a marker of Fleadhanna and one of the defining characteristics of non-structured performance at the festival. From musicians' perspective, session playing outside was exciting and a vital part of Fleadh festivity. However, during the 1960s this was balanced with teeming crowds and the vagaries of weather, elements that encroached on their festive experience.[113] Instead, most session playing retreated indoors to the still heightened environs of the pub or hotel bar, the spatial containment creating its own hyper-festivity. The proliferation of Fleadh sessions in pub venues also reflects changing contexts for music making in the non-Fleadh Irish music world during this decade. At the Fleadh, these confined spaces offered musicians a more intimate, acoustically preferable and physically safer vantage point. As a spontaneous, unstaged performance context, the 'communicative logic of the event', like early jazz sessions in the USA, inscribes the musicians themselves as 'auditors' and the public, however enthusiastic, as 'incidental participants'.[114] The short 1967 award-winning documentary, *Fleá Ceoil*, directed by Louis Marcus with Bob Monks, was filmed at a county fleadh cheoil in Kilrush, County Clare and chronicles the variety of spaces in which spontaneous sessions took place. Well-known traditional singers and instrumentalists (including Sarah and Rita Keane from Galway, and Willie Clancy from Clare) perform in various indoor and outdoor locations. The narration draws special notice to sessions in pubs, 'Is beag radharc ar domhan is teolaí ná tithe ósta lán de cheol tar éis titim na h-oíche' (it's few sights on earth are as cosy as pubs full of music after nightfall).[115]

For musicians and attendees, the spontaneity of sessions was crucial; for Fleadh committees, the visual and sounded signal of outdoor sessions was central to Fleadh identity. The decline in outdoor session playing in particular in the 1960s was a source of concern to Fleadh committees, being as it was a pillar of Fleadh identity. To counteract the decline, Fleadh committees responded in a number of ways, many of which were contrary to the spontaneous, informal essence of Fleadh sessions and reminiscent of the evolution of planned jazz jam sessions decades earlier.[116] A motion to the annual congress of Comhaltas in 1967 proposed that 'increased non-competitive attractions be made available at Fleadhanna: example, that prize winners at past Fleadhanna be featured at organised "sessions" in the town'.[117] At the Fleadh in Boyle, in 1966, the festival programme petitioned musicians directly, pleading with them to take on the responsibility for the life of the Fleadh through outdoor sessions:

## 'Strange Contrasts at the Fleadh'

> If you are a musician, why not start a music session on the streets? These impromptu street sessions are the essence of a Fleadh Cheoil. Strike up a tune on the street and very soon you'll be joined by many other musicians and you can play away to your heart's content. You will enjoy it and so will everybody else. The Fleadh committee depends on you to keep the spirit of the Fleadh alive.[118]

The incongruity of efforts to regulate spontaneous performance was not acknowledged by Fleadh or Comhaltas administrators. The inherent contradiction was not lost on musicians who resisted the growing organisational proclivity for session control.[119] In the absence of enthusiasm by musicians for these plans, a flurry of motions with other solutions were suggested. In 1967, Fleadh committees 'required to set aside at least one hall with adequate accommodation for music sessions'.[120] To placate the critics and disappointed listeners at the Fleadh, special platforms were erected to facilitate playing outdoors, some even trying to set particular times when this might happen. In Clones, for example, in 1968, 'trios and céilí bands' were 'encouraged to play' on wooden platforms outdoors.[121] It was unsuccessful for the musicians particularly, but also for many Fleadh goers, as staging session playing was symbolically understood as running counter to the composition of spontaneous music making.[122] There is a consequent deficit for listeners at the Fleadh who frequently found themselves left outside the confined and limited spaces of pubs and hotel bars, where music making was actually taking place, left without access to one of the core elements of the Fleadh festive experience, informal music making.[123] Spontaneous indoor session playing, rather than having a democratic aesthetic, could be an elite space, where musicians and connoisseurs self-prioritise.[124] Musicians emerged, at times under cover of darkness, if and when crowds had dispersed, to perform upon the outdoor constructed platforms, on their own terms.[125] Healy writes that, after the Monday night finale concerts and céilithe, musicians 'who have crowded and drowned this town with music' who are 'in no hurry home' will 'meet in hotel lobbies, public houses, park benches or in private houses to go on swopping songs and airs and playing for one another'.[126] In 1968, when the competitions ended in Clones, an adjudicator delivering his final comments urged competitors 'to go on out and give the crowds a bit of your music'.[127] The underlying suggestion is that musicians entrenched indoors are, at least partially, to blame for the disgruntled crowds gathered on the streets outside.

Due to disorder during the late 1960s, the Fleadh, the flagship event of Comhaltas, was not uniformly welcomed by rural towns. Following the public order difficulties in Thurles in 1965, Tuam (County Galway) withdrew its agreement to host the Fleadh in 1966 as it was considered too much risk for a small town. Boyle (County Roscommon) was prevailed upon to step into the breach, an action only possible by virtue of the fact that the incumbent chairman of Comhaltas, Micheál Ó Ceallacháin, was from Boyle (he was returned unopposed at a closed annual congress in September, 1966, when all other candidates withdrew their names).[128] Fleadhanna of the 1960s oscillated between being declared restorations of the umblemished Fleadhanna of old, for example, the uneventful Fleadhanna in Boyle in 1967 and Clones in 1968, to fiascos, such as 'the orgy that was the Cashel Fleadh' in 1969.[129] Despite that accusation, much of the immediate press coverage of the Fleadh in Cashel was positive, and Conchubhar remarks that there was little talk about the Fleadh until the members of the Irish Country Women's Association (ICA) in Cashel drew attention to conduct unbecoming at the festival.[130] A record number attended and no negative comment from Gardaí or local businesses immediately appeared in local or national press, a fact that was in equal parts surprising and suspicious to Sheila Crowe, secretary of the local ICA.[131] Crowe listed a litany of offences in a letter to the editor of the *Tipperary Star*, including the accusation that Fleadh goers broke the floodlights at the Rock of Cashel. Given the iconic significance of the Rock, this was a significant material and cultural transgression. Residents of the town were prisoners in their own homes, she wrote, afraid to venture out during the weekend, and furthermore, the letter writer demanded to know why the number of arrests was not published.[132] She went on to insist that she and fellow ICA branch members would do all in their power to prevent the Fleadh ever taking place again, not just in Cashel, but anywhere in the country.[133]

Crowe followed through on her threats to obstruct future Fleadhanna after Thurles. Enniscorthy (County Wexford) was scheduled to host the Fleadh in 1970. However, the ICA in Enniscorthy, on the advice of its

### 'Strange Contrasts at the Fleadh'

sister chapter in Cashel, launched a campaign to prevent the Fleadh from taking place in the town.[134] When the Vintners Association in Wexford added its voice to the objections, Comhaltas relented and abandoned the planned Fleadh in Enniscorthy. Not coincidentally, Comhaltas took this opportunity to finally sever the Fleadh calendrically from Whit weekend, moving it to August. The decision to move the Fleadh away from Whit was believed to be an important step in controlling the constituency of attendees. Furthermore, moving it all the way to Listowel, County Kerry, in 1970, far removed from the urban capital (and all those hairy youths), was strategically calculated.[135] Tony Meade, commenting upon the festival's move to Kerry in 1970, wrote 'The Fleadh has an unenviable reputation for drunkenness and debauchery, garnered in many of the other small towns of Ireland', but moving it to an August slot, and to Listowel, 'has broken the reputation utterly' and he was confident 'the dross has been shed'.[136] For Comhaltas, the Fleadh and its cultural gatekeepers, Listowel in August would restore Fleadh order.

Societal changes in the 1960s, including the explosion of pop music and increased mobility, brought people to the Fleadh who did not necessarily share the same vision of Ireland as those who attended during the 1950s. The wider folk music revival, in England and the USA, was a driving force in the 1960s ballad boom in Ireland, but, as demonstrated, its devotees had an uneasy relationship with the Fleadh hierarchy, overlapping but contesting a space between them.

#### CONCLUSION

From the outset, music making on streets and in pubs was a key Fleadh attraction and the contribution of the Fleadh in developing session playing as the default, informal performance practice of Irish traditional music in the late twentieth century is significant. Building on the Comhaltas constitutional aspiration of providing opportunities for musicians to play, sessions at the Fleadh were a material and symbolic touchstone of Fleadh identity becoming part of Fleadh fabric. There is a synchronic relationship between spontaneous music making in the developing Fleadh system as it expanded across All Ireland-provincial-county levels and contexts for session playing beyond the festive space during the rest of the year. In the 1950s, cultural tourists (musicians and patrons among them) found an opportunity to engage with traditional music practice at the Fleadh and the session was the core informal element of the festive experience. Returning emigrant musicians and those who lived in Ireland created a communion of practice at early Fleadhanna. Each brought their respective music and cultural experience with them to the festive space, but equally, they took the festive experience with them as they returned to their parishes and cities, where sessions were taking hold in pubs and as part of Comhaltas branch activities.

As seen in 'Strange Contrasts at the Fleadh', growing numbers of tourists in the 1960s beyond traditional musicians and (perceived) afficionados were also attending, drawn by informal music making as Fleadh object. As a tradition-bearing organisation, there was a need to clearly translate the organisational embodiment of tradition for new constituencies and in response to new challenges.[137] As demonstrated, this process was not a smooth one. In particular, spontaneous music making at the All Ireland event became a contested site of cultural stewardship, where transgressions of Fleadh order were the subject of robust debate. Stakeholders in this cultural tug-of-war, among them Comhaltas and newer constituencies of Fleadh goers, as well as those professing concern about public order and the mores of 1960s' youth, were exercised. Aspirationally, the Fleadh was open to all, but during the 1960s that aspiration was tested when Fleadhanna became the faultline between those who believed themselves cultural gatekeepers and those the gatekeepers viewed as disruptive interlopers and unwelcome guests.

As the Fleadh grew from its modest beginnings (a 'yearly exhibition of the work of Comhaltas') efforts to 'turn this homely, simple affair into something bigger, better and glamorous' resulted in, at least in Stapleton's view, 'a modern Donnybrook' in Mullingar.[138] Herein lies another complex faultline, the divide between commercial and cultural concerns, prompted by the collision between youth culture and Fleadh culture, with its well-established symbolic and material compostition. The expansion of the Fleadh was a critical factor in the public order challenges of the 1960s, but this growth was also a key measure by which the Fleadh's success was calculated, both internally by Comhaltas and externally by host sites and in public discourse. As Stapleton confirms, Comhaltas sought to grow the scale of the Fleadh each year, through competitions and other cultural events certainly, but also by expanding its patron base to new constituencies. Caught between cultural and commercial interests, the Fleadh and its organisational gatekeepers at the end of the 1960s knew that a recalibration of the All Ireland Fleadh was necessary, ideally without losing either cultural or commercial ground.

Ending the first two decades of development and consolidation, 1969 was the final year the Fleadh was held at Whit weekend. It is also, not conicidentally, the point at which this story of the Fleadh ends. The competition-festival moved to its new August calendar date in 1970, where it has remained since. This was the first step in the next phase of Fleadh Cheoil na hÉireann, the All Ireland Fleadh Cheoil.

# Afterword

In 2022, for the first time since 1963, the Fleadh returned to Mullingar, the site of its inception. Aptly titled 'The Homecoming', the competition-festival reappeared as an in-person event after an absence of two years due to the global Covid-19 pandemic.[1] In that context, Mullingar as Fleadh home in 2022 had a particular resonance. It attracted over 500,000 people between 31 July and 7 August, making it the single largest festival (musical or otherwise) ever hosted on the island of Ireland, and indeed one of the largest festival events in Europe. In 2023, when the Fleadh returned once again to Mullingar, over 5,000 competitors took part in 230 competitions. In the decades since 1970, the Fleadh has faced challenges and criticisms but the festival's importance to traditional music remains, demonstrated by an arc of increased participation and numbers attending.

When the Fleadh migrated to August from its Whit weekend date in 1970, it responded to the concerns of the 1960s outlined in the previous chapter. Retaining the cultural and financial capital of Whit weekend already earned, Comhaltas founded the Fleadh Nua (new) festival as a national event at Whit in 1970. Coinciding with that calendar move, the model of annual Fleadh mobility was revised and in its place, the principle of staying for at least two years (at times three) in the same place was agreed. With some notable exceptions, that has been implemented since 1972. The 1971 Fleadh was cancelled in Listowel, deferred on security grounds due to 'the extenuating circumstances' in Northern Ireland and in 'a gesture of solidarity with the people of the Six Counties'.[2] Political sympathies aside, there was much debate as to whether the traditional Fleadh model would (or should) return, though return it did, to Listowel in August 1972. Postponed competitions from 1971 were held at the Fleadh Nua that took place in Dublin in June 1972, resulting in the unusual happenstance of two sets of All Ireland Fleadh competitions taking place within a single calendar year. Since then, the

Fleadh has continued to favour rural towns or small cities over large cities as locations, disclosing residual ties of musical authenticity and rurality in the cultural imagination. Disproportionately, Fleadhanna have been hosted by towns in the southern province of Munster (twenty-seven times in total, to date) and has been hosted in Northern Ireland only once: Derry in 2013.[3] The Fleadh has responded to changes in Comhaltas' broader development since the 1970s. Scoil Éigse, instituted in 1973, is 'held in conjunction with the Fleadh' and offers a series of traditional music and dance workshops reflecting Comhaltas' central role in traditional music pedagogy since that decade.[4] In the early decades of Fleadh history, Comhaltas bewailed the scarcity of national media coverage received for the festival; in 2023, media saturation on national airwaves and digital platforms was achieved. Numerous competitions are now live-streamed and nightly performances are programmed specifically for broadcast on TG4 (the national Irish-language television channel). During the year, an RTÉ produced Fleadh series is broadcast from the previous year's festival, satiating Fleadh appetites until it comes around again. Among the constants in Fleadh history since the mid-1950s is the preoccupation with the intersection of culture and commerce. At the céilí band competition final in 2023 on the last night of the Fleadh, the Director General of Comhaltas listed the economic benefits to Mullingar and the wider area as a key outcome of the event.[5]

Internationally, the Fleadh is a singular model of mobile competition-festival, with a complex set of symbolic and material objects rooted for the most part in the early years of Fleadh development. Prompted in the first instance by a revival impulse, from 1951 to 1969 the Fleadh developed a symbolic and material structure that came to embody Irish traditional music. It was a meeting ground of past histories, present practice and future possibilities in a hyper-festive space. Peopled by musicians, administrators and patrons, the Fleadh can be situated in broader festival literature, as an attempt to collectively 'manifest' what 'it conceives(d) to be its essential life', within the distilled confines of the competition-festival frame.[6] Concerts, competitions, céilithe and sessions formed the bedrock of that essential life, in a delicate and sometimes fraught balance of invariant and variant, formal and informal Fleadh objects, all essential to the heightened concentration of the festive experience. The symbolic composition was not wholly static or fixed, and the expectation of the participants was framed and reframed *ad infinitum*.[7] At the Fleadh, musicians, dancers and singers were the 'makers', and articulators, of an 'otherwise inchoate celebratory spirit'.[8] This is recalled in music making, story and song after the Fleadh, breathing new life into the festival in a process of continuous reenactment.

Competition at the Fleadh over the course of these decades created an index of music makers who were bestowed with intra-cultural status. In many cases, competition prestige endured in the external post-Fleadh world, reanimated in other performance opportunities, those contexts themselves informed by Fleadh success. Discomfort with the emphasis on competition at the Fleadh or dissatisfactions in the ancillary minefield of adjudication processes did not unduly disrupt the centrality of competition as the Fleadh developed. While the Fleadh provided a space where collective identity was marked out, presented and highlighted, individual participants experienced this communion in different ways in the 'single time-space frame' of the Fleadh where the 'shared social reference' was Irish traditional music but festive experiences are polyvalent.[9] The Fleadh moved from one town to the next with a mobile core of embodied objects, but the locally enhanced place-making and place-marking of Fleadh sites occurred with disparate, residual ramifications in post-Fleadh histories. During the 1960s, tensions arose when (it was believed) the common interest of Irish traditional music was not shared by all Fleadh goers, challenging the authority of the Fleadh structure and Comhaltas in the process. Within the festive frame, a uniformity of collective consciousness gave way to the pluralistic nature of the festive form.[10]

Today, there is an abundance of Irish traditional music festivals that take place year round in Ireland and globally. Many offer an alternative to the competition-festival Fleadh model. However, the significance of the Fleadh to Irish traditional music during the 1950s and 1960s is unique. Vallely writes of Ireland in the early 1950s that Irish traditional music faced 'indifference, dismissiveness, and criticisms of "inferiority" at a national level'.[11] In 1967, Liam Ó Murchú declared that 'one of the most remarkable features of cultural life in Ireland over the past decade or so has been the development of interest in Irish traditional music'.[12] Without naming the Fleadh explicitly, Ó Murchú and Vallely both recognise the diverse circumstances for that remarkable change, which

# Afterword

'gave confidence and credibility to those involved' in Irish traditional music.[13] This book positions the Fleadh at the top of any taxonomy of traditional music revival and Irish cultural transformation in the 1950s and 1960s. The first Fleadh committee in 1951, aligned to Feis Lár na hÉireann in Mullingar, could scarcely have imagined the successes and tribulations of the Fleadh in the following two decades, nor the impact and scale of the enterprise. The Fleadh as festival, a tool of revival, achieved and surpassed expectations, creating a social and cultural world where the essential question for many in the traditional music world remains 'Are you heading to the Fleadh?'.

# Notes

**Introduction**

1   All translations author's own, unless otherwise indicated.
2   An estimated 600,000 people attended the Fleadh in Mullingar in 2023, https://www.rte.ie/news/leinster/2023/0814/1399734-fleadh-cheoil-mullingar/. For comparison, 200,000 attended Glastonbury in 2023, https://www.theatlantic.com/photo/2023/06/photos-glastonbury-2023/674527/#:~:text=More%20than%20200%2C000%20music%20fans,Ora%2C%20and%20many%20more%20artists. The Festivale Interceltique de Lorient attracted an estimated 850,000 over ten days in 2023, https://www.tourismireland.com/opportunities/opportunity-list/details/fr--festival-interceltique-de-lorient-2023.
3   For Comhaltas discussions which include Fleadh discussions, see Edward O. Henry, 'Institutions for the Promotion of Indigenous Music: the case for Ireland's Comhaltas Ceoltóirí Éireann', *Ethnomusicology*, vol. 33, no. 1, pp. 67–95; Daithí Kearney, 'Regions, Regionality and Regionalization in Irish Traditional Music: the role of Comhaltas Ceoltóirí Éireann', *Ethnomusicology Ireland*, vol. 2, no. 3, 2013, pp. 72–94; Méabh Ní Fhuartháin, 'Comhaltas Ceoltóirí Éireann: shaping tradition, 1951–1970', unpublished PhD thesis, NUI Galway, 2011; Ní Fhuartháin, *Chronicles of Comhaltas: enunciating and institutionalising authority in Irish traditional music, 1951–1970* (Cork: Traditional Music Archive, UCC, 2018); Rachel Fleming, 'Resisting Cultural Standardization: Comhaltas Ceoltóirí Éireann and the revitalization of traditional music in Ireland', *Journal of Folklore Research*, vol. 41, nos 2& 3, pp. 227–57. For Fleadh-focused research see Ní Fhuartháin, 'Fleadh Cheoil', in Harry White and Barra Boydell (eds), *Encyclopaedia of Music in Ireland* (Dublin: UCD Press, 2013), pp. 388–9; Adrian Devine et al., 'Reaching Across the Divide: the role of cultural events in peace building', *Event Management*, vol. 25, 2021, pp. 363–80; Daithí Kearney and Kevin Burns, 'Come Enjoy the Craic: locating an Irish traditional music festival in Drogheda', in A. Smith et al. (eds), *Festivals and the City: the contested geographies of urban events* (London: University of Westminster Press, 2022, pp. 231–47; Cathy Larson Skye, 'A Lot of Notes but Little Music: competition and the changing character of performance', *New Hibernia Review*, vol. 1, no. 1, 1997, p. 156–67; and Philip Duffy, *On the Night: Fleadh Cheoil na hÉireann – musicians and senior céilí band winners, 1951–2021* (Sligo: Philip Duffy, 2023).
4   Victor Turner (ed.), *Celebration: studies in festivity and ritual* (Washington: Smithsonian Press, 1982); David M. Guss, *The Festive State* (Oakland: University of California Press, 2000); David M. Picard and Mike Robinson (eds), *Festivals, Tourism and Social Change, Remaking Worlds* (Clevedon: Channel View Publications, 2006); Alessandro Falassi (ed.), *Time Out of Time: essays on the festival* (Albuquerque: University of New Mexico, 1987), pp. 5, 7.
5   Beverly Stoeltje, 'Festival', in Richard Bauman (ed.), *Folklore, Cultural Performances and Popular Entertainments* (New York: Oxford University Press, 1992), pp. 263, 261.
6   Aileen O'Carroll, 'Eight Hours for What We Will', in Roo Honeychild and Kate Butler (eds), *Mesh Net* (Dublin: Project Press, 2023), p. 5.

7   Noted by Stanley Waterman in another festive context. See Waterman, 'Place, Culture and Identity: summer music in Upper Galilee', *Transactions of the Institute of British Geographers*, vol. 23, no. 2, 1998, p. 256.
8   Guss, *The Festive State*, p. 3.
9   Kerry Dobransky, 'City Folk: survival strategies of tradition-bearing organizations', *Poetics*, vol. 35, 2007, p. 244.
10  Liam Ó Murchú, liner notes, *Rambles of Kitty* (Ceoltas, 1967).
11  Verena Commins, 'Scoil Samhraidh Willie Clancy: transmission, performance and commemoration of Irish traditional music, 1973–2012', unpublished PhD thesis, NUI Galway, 2013, p. 35. Muiris Ó Rócháin, a founder of Scoil Samhraidh Willie Clancy, was motivated to provide an alternative for musicians 'discomfited' by traditional music's 'festivalisation' at the Fleadh. Commins, 'Locating the Centre: Irish traditional music and re-traditionalisation at the Willie Clancy Summer School', David Doyle and Ní Fhuartháin (eds), *Ordinary Irish Life: music, sport and culture* (Dublin: Irish Academic Press, 2013), p. 118.
12  Seán Ó Riada's innovative development of a recording and concert-centred ensemble, Ceoltóirí Cualainn, was influential long after the last performance in 1970 in Cork. In the 1970s, building on Ó Riada's ensemble sound, the string and percussive arrangements of bands such as Planxty and the Bothy Band created the dominant ensemble template in traditional music for the next two decades. It was distinct in sound and sensibility from céilí bands. See, Seán Ó Riada with Seán Ó Sé and Ceoltóirí Cualann, *Ó Riada sa Gaiety* (Gael Linn, 1970); Planxty, *The Well Below the Valley* (Polydor, 1973); the Bothy Band, *Old Hag You Have Killed Me* (Mulligan, 1976). See also, Mícheál Ó Súilleabháin, *Ceol na nUasal: Seán Ó Riada and the search for a native Irish art music* (Cork: Traditional Music Archive, UCC, 2004).
13  Fieldwork interviews are used with permission. See Ní Fhuartháin, 'Comhaltas' (2011).
14  Michel Peillon, 'Irish Festivities in Comparative Perspective', *The Maynooth Review*, vol. 6, no. 2, 1982, p. 39.
15  See Stoeltje, 'Festival', p. 264; Roger Lyle Brown, *Ghost Dancing on the Cracker Circuit* (USA: University of Mississippi Press, 1997), xv.

## 1. Contexts and Precedents

1   *Westmeath Examiner*, 10 February 1951.
2   Ibid.
3   Ibid. Competitions are frequently found at festivals. See Peillon, 'Irish Festivities', p. 50.
4   Joe Cleary, 'Introduction: Ireland and modernity', in Joe Cleary and Claire Connolly (eds), *The Cambridge Companion to Modern Irish Culture* (Cambridge: Cambridge University Press, 2005), p. 14; John A. O'Brien, *The Vanishing Irish* (USA: McGraw Hill, 1953), p. 3.
5   Brendan M. Walsh, 'Economic Growth and Development, 1945–70', in Joseph J. Lee (ed.), *Ireland 1945–1970* (Dublin: Gill & Macmillan, 1979), p. 26.
6   Roy F. Foster, *Modern Ireland 1600–1972* (London: Allen Lane Penguin Press, 1988), p. 577; Diarmaid Ferriter, *The Transformation of Ireland 1900–2000* (London: Profile Books, 2005), p. 467. See also, Bernadette Whelan, *Ireland and the Marshall Plan* (Dublin: Four Courts Press, 2000).
7   John A. Murphy, '"Put Them Out!", Parties and Elections, 1948–69', in Lee (ed.), *Ireland 1945–1970*, p. 4.
8   J.P. Comyn, 'The Emigrant Isle, a Flight of Fancy', *Capuchin Annual*, 1952, p. 255.
9   Walsh, 'Economic Growth', p. 28; Fergal Tobin, *The Best of Decades: Ireland in the 1960s* (Dublin: Gill & Macmillan, 1984), p. 6.

10 Ferriter, *The Transformation*, p. 463.
11 John Bradley, 'The History of Economic Development in Ireland, North and South', *Proceedings of the British Academy*, vol. 98, 1999, p. 46.
12 Walsh, 'Economic Growth', p. 28.
13 Dermot Keogh notes that there was no restriction on travel to the United Kingdom from Ireland after 1947. Keogh, *Twentieth Century Ireland* (Dublin: Gill & Macmillan, 2005), p. 169; Jeremiah Newman, *The Limerick Rural Survey 1958–1964* (Tipperary: Muintir na Tíre Rural Publications, 1964), p. 159.
14 Newman, *The Limerick*, ibid.
15 Peadar O'Donnell, 'De Valera's Speech on Emigration', *The Bell*, vol. XVIII, no. 7, 1951, p. 54.
16 *Anglo-Celt*, 12 June 1954.
17 *Report of the Working Party on Coloured People Seeking Employment in Great Britain*, December 1953, NA, PRO, DO 35/5216. Quoted in Peter Hennessy, *Having it So Good: Britain in the 1950s* (London: Penguin Books, 2007), p. 369.
18 Heinrich Böll, *An Irish Journal*, 2nd edition (USA: McGraw Hill, 1967), p. 93.
19 Ibid.
20 Thomas Gilrane, *Just the Way it Was: Tommy Dan Tims, Derrinageer, Ballinaglera, a true story of a traditional farm life in County Leitrim, Ireland* (New York: iUniverse, 2007), p. 79.
21 O'Brien, *Vanishing Irish*, p. 3. Alice Curtayne, a contemporary reviewer, found in O'Brien's work 'a serious theme, mauled in the handling'. 'Review', *The Furrow*, vol. 5, no. 5, 1955, p. 32.
22 Keogh et al. (eds), *The Lost Decade: Ireland in the 1950s* (Cork: Mercier Press, 2004), p. 17; Katherine Edelman, 'Ireland, after Long Absence', *Capuchin Annual*, 1958, p. 54; Patrick J. McLaughlin, 'Ireland and the World Population Problem', *Capuchin Annual*, 1962, p. 171. Mary E. Daly identifies Ireland and East Germany as the only two European countries to experience population decline during the 1950s. *The Slow Failure: population decline and independent Ireland 1920–1973* (Madison: University of Wisconsin, 2006), p. 184.
23 Ferriter, *The Transformation*, p. 464.
24 Ronan Fanning, 'The Genesis of Economic Development', in John F. McCarthy (ed.), *Planning Ireland's Future: the legacy of T.K. Whitaker* (Dublin: Glendale, 1990), p. 85.
25 Keogh acknowledges visual arts practice as part of 1950s' counterculture, but not music. *Twentieth Century Ireland*, pp. 229–30. He also later mentions the musician and composer Seán Ó Riada, though in relation to the 1960s, rather than the previous decade. Ibid., pp. 261–8.
26 Lee (ed.), *Ireland 1945–1970*, p. 166.
27 A useful comparison is found in the work of Marilyn Silverman in her historical ethnography of Thomastown, County Kilkenny. In it, she cautions against the notion of a 'marked break' in social transformation, but rather advocates viewing change through a long lens. See Silverman, 'An Urban Place in Rural Ireland: an historical ethnography of domination, 1849–1989', in Chris Curtin et al. (eds), *Irish Urban Cultures* (Belfast: Institute of Irish Studies, 1993), p. 222.
28 This was not a completely new initiative. In 1949, the *Long Term Recovery Programme* was published as a white paper. This and Whitaker's earlier report in 1958 were the precursors to *Economic Expansion*. Murphy, *Ireland in the Twentieth Century* (London: Gill & Macmillan, 1975), p. 123.
29 Richard Breen et al., *Understanding Contemporary Ireland: state, class and development in the Republic of Ireland* (London: Gill & Macmillan, 1990), p. 37.
30 Tobin, *The Best of Decades*, p. 8.

Notes to pages 10 to 13

31  Ireland's first application for European Economic Community membership in 1961, unsuccessful at that particular time, was a clear indication of Lemass' political and economic outlook. See Lee and Gearóid Ó Tuathaigh, *The Age of de Valera* (Dublin: Ward River Press, 1982), p. 162.
32  Lee, *Ireland 1912–1985: politics and society* (Cambridge: Cambridge University Press, 1989), pp. 359–60.
33  Lee (ed.), *Ireland 1945–1970*, p. 20.
34  Andrew D. Devenney, '"A Unique and Unparalleled Surrender of Sovereignty": early opposition to European integration in Ireland, 1961–72', *New Hibernia Review*, vol. 12, no. 2, 2008, p. 15.
35  Murphy, '"Put Them Out!"', p. 3.
36  Walsh, 'Economic Growth', p. 33.
37  Catherine Curran, 'Changing Audiences for Traditional Irish Music', in Fintan Vallely et al. (eds), *Crosbhealach an Cheoil: the Crossroads Conference 1996, tradition and change in Irish traditional music* (Dublin: Whinstone, 1999), p. 59.
38  Ibid., p. 34.
39  George Homans, 'Foreword', in Alexander Humphries, *New Dubliners: urbanisation and the Irish family* (London: Routledge and Kegan Paul, 1966), p. v.
40  Terence Brown, *Ireland: a social and cultural history 1922–1985* (London: Fontana Press, 1985), p. 260.
41  Ní Fhuartháin, '"Mise Éire": (re)imaginings in Irish music studies', in Mike Cronin et al. (eds), *Routledge International Handbook of Irish Studies* (New York: Routledge, 2021), p. 323.
42  Christopher Whelan (ed.), *Values and Social Change in Ireland* (Dublin: Gill & Macmillan, 1994), p. 3.
43  Reg Hall, 'Heydays are Shortlived: change in music making practice in rural Ireland, 1850–1950', in Vallely et al., *Crosbhealach*, pp. 77–83.
44  *Connacht Tribune*, 28 May 1955.
45  Helen O'Shea, *The Making of Irish Traditional Music* (Cork: Cork University Press, 2008), p. 33; Sean Williams, *Focus: Irish traditional music* (New York: Routledge, 2020, 2nd edition), p. 82; Adam Kaul, *Turning the Tune: traditional music, tourism and social change in an Irish village* (New York: Bergahn Books, 2009), p. 39; Dorothea E. Hast and Stanley Scott, *Music in Ireland: experiencing music, expressing culture* (New York: Oxford University Press, 2004), p. 49.
46  Séamus Ó Dubhthaigh, *Survival, Irish Traditional Music and Song: a view* (Dublin: CCÉ, 2009), p. 13.
47  Joseph O'Connor, 'The Cold Chain of Silence', *Capuchin Annual* (1956/7), p. 95.
48  Ibid., p. 96.
49  Sean Shanagher, 'A Dancing Agency: jazz, modern and ballroom dancers in Ireland between 1940 and 1960', vol. 24, no. 2, *Irish Journal of Sociology*, p. 178; also, Ní Fhuartháin, 'Dance Halls, Parish Halls and Marquees: building and regulating Irish public dance space, 1897–1957', *Éire/Ireland Journal of Irish Studies*, vol. 54, nos 1 and 2, 2019, pp. 221–2.
50  Whelan, *Values and Social Change*, p. 3. For a detailed discussion of the Public Dance Halls Act see Ní Fhuartháin, 'Dance Halls'. For a localised study of dance practice as it moves to the public sphere, see Ní Fhuartháin, 'Genealogies of Irish Dance in Galway, 1922–1992', in John Cunningham and Ciaran McDonough (eds), *Hardiman and After: Galway culture and society, 1820–2020* (Melbourne: Arcadia, 2023), pp. 150–3.
51  Hilary Tovey and Perry Share, *A Sociology of Ireland* (Dublin: Gill & Macmillan, 2003), p. 15.
52  P.J. Curtis, *Notes from the Heart: a celebration of Irish traditional music* (Dublin: Torc Press, 1994), p. 58.

53 Ó Tuathaigh, 'Cultural Visions and the New State: embedding and embalming', in Gabriel Doherty and Dermot Keogh (eds), *De Valera's Irelands* (Cork: Mercier Press, 2003), p. 169.
54 Fintan Vallely and Charlie Piggot, *Blooming Meadows: the world of Irish traditional musicians* (Dublin: Town House, 1998), p. 192.
55 Nicolette Devas, *Two Flamboyant Fathers* (New York: William Morrow and Company, 1966), p. 143; Vallely and Piggot, *Blooming Meadows*, p. 162.
56 Interview with Sheila Dowd, 19 June 2008; interview with Peter Horan, 19 June 2008; Vallely and Piggot, *Blooming Meadows*, pp. 95–9.
57 Ray Rooney, *The Spirit of the Reels: the story of the famous Liverpool Céilí Band* (Liverpool: RayRoo Press, 2019), p. 17.
58 Michael Tubridy, interview, 13 January 2009; Peadar O'Loughlin, interview, 5 May 2008; Joe Burke, interview, 7 May 2006; Vallely and Piggot, *Blooming Meadows*, p. 169.
59 Feis Lár na hÉireann (Centre of Ireland Feis) has several spellings in contemporaneous advertisements: Feis Lár na hÉireann; Feis Láir na hÉireann (Feis of the Centre of Ireland) (*Midland Herald*, 17 May 1951); and even Feis Liar na hÉireann in the *Midland Herald*, 10 May 1951. Eamon Ó Muirí repeatedly refers to this event as Feis na hIar Mhidhe (Feis of Westmeath) in 'The Fortunes of Traditional Music', *Clogher Record*, vol. 1, no. 1, 1953, p. 30. 'Feis Lár na hÉireann' is used throughout the discussions here.
60 Éamonn Ó Gallchobhair, 'The Cultural Value of Festival and Feis', in Aloys Fleischmann (ed.), *Music in Ireland: a symposium* (Dublin: Cork University Press, 1952), p. 210. Ó Gallchobhair (1900–82) was an important figures in the revival of the Oireachtas in 1939 and played a central role in its administration over the following two decades.
61 Breandán Breathnach, 'The Feis Ceoil and Piping', *Ceol*, vol. 8, nos 1 and 2, 1986, p. 21.
62 *Ár gCeol Féinig* (Dublin: Browne & O'Nolan, 1920). Fr Pádraig Breathnach published numerous collections of Irish-language song as well as translations, which were constantly mined by revivalists. Other collections of his included *Ceol Ár Sinsear* (Dublin: Browne & O'Nolan, 1923) and *Songs of the Gael* (Dublin: Browne & O'Nolan, 1915).
63 T. Corcoran, 'An Issue Concerning Music', *The Irish Monthly*, vol. 61, no. 720, 1933, p. 338.
64 'Feis', *The Musical Times and Singing Class Circular*, vol. 41, no. 688, 1900, p. 402.
65 Ó Muirí, 'The Fortunes', p. 28. For an account of the Dublin Pipers Club, see Mick O'Connor, 'Dublin Pipers Club', in Vallely (ed.), *CITM* (Cork: Cork University Press, 2011), pp. 224–5.
66 Barry O'Neill, 'Piping Contests at the Feis, 1897–1935', *The Seán Reid Society Journal*, vol. 1, 1999, p. 1.
67 Robert Young, 'The Pipers' Competition at the Feis Ceoil', *Ulster Journal of Archaeology*, vols 3 and 4, 1897, p. 239.
68 Ibid. Interestingly, Young wrote that all pipers bar one was a professional. See also Breathnach, 'The Feis Ceoil and Piping', pp. 11–24.
69 *Feis Athar Maitiú 1925 Syllabus*. Feis Athar Maitiú was first held in Dublin, in 1909; a second feis (of the same name) was established in Cork, in 1927. Both were run by the Capuchin Order.
70 Kathleen M. Flanagan describes two 'stage Irish men' prevented from attending a Feis in Chicago in 1912 due to their inauthentic garb. See Flanagan, *Steps in Time: the history of Irish dance in Chicago* (USA: Macatar Press, 2009), p. 31.
71 Federigo and Sebastin, 'The Feis Ceoil Fraud', *All Ireland Review*, vol. 1, no. 26, 1900, p. 5.
72 Ibid.
73 *Tuam Herald*, 3 September 1898.
74 John O'Herlihy, *Footsteps, Fiddles, Flagstones and Fun* (Killarney: Comhaltas, 2004), p. 89; Tim Collins, 'Music Mountain: space, place and Irish traditional music practices in Sliabh Aughty', unpublished PhD thesis, NUI Galway, 2013, pp. 111–3.

75 O'Neill, 'Piping Contests', p. 1.
76 Ó Gallchobhair, 'The Cultural Value', p. 213.
77 Henry Fegan, 'A Feis', *The Irish Monthly*, vol. 31, no. 362, 1903, p. 464. In the same piece, Fegan reviewed an Irish-language play in which Douglas Hyde held the role of the Blind Fiddler, much to the delight of the audience. Ibid., p. 465.
78 Currently 'feis' is used to refer to several different events including dance competition and specific events such as the Feis Ceoil. By the 1950s, local feiseanna were focused largely on dance and organised by dance schools. This developed in parallel with and informed by the Coimisiún le Rince Gaelacha's progressive competition system for Irish dance. See Catherine Foley, *Step Dancing in Ireland: culture and history* (Farnham: Ashgate, 2013), pp. 141–51.
79 Interview, 5 May 2008.
80 Ann Mulqueen, interview, 5 June 2008.
81 Willie Reynolds, *Memories of a Music Maker* (Dublin: Comhaltas Ceoltóirí Éireann, 1990), p. 17.
82 Ibid., p. 26. 'Aonach' translates as a fair but here refers to a cultural event with music performances.
83 Ibid.
84 Ibid.
85 *Irish Independent*, 30 May 1955.
86 Ibid.
87 *Feis Templemore Clár*, 1959. NPU, SR F17 D41. The feis in Templemore was run by Comhaltas and had a variety of competitions in music, sport and other activities.
88 Ó Gallchobhair, 'The Cultural Value', p. 215. Eisteddfodau is a Welsh festival of literature and music. Drawing from an earlier model of Eisteddfodau, it was revived in 1792, the same year as the Belfast Harp festival in Ireland.
89 Éamonn Costello, 'Oireachtas na Gaeilge and Sean-nós Song Competition, 1940–2012: regionalism, nationalism and Gaelicness', *Éire-Ireland*, vol. 54, nos 1 & 2, 2019, p. 165.
90 Seán Mac Néill, 'An tOireachtas: smaointe fánacha', *Comhar*, vol. 8, no. 12, 1949, p. 28.
91 Ibid.
92 Lillis Ó Laoire, 'National Identity and Local Ethnicity: the case of the Gaelic League's Oireachtas sean-nós singing competitions', in Brian A. Roberts and Andrea Rose (eds), *Sharing the Voices: the phenomenon of singing* (Newfoundland: Memorial University, 1999), p. 161.
93 O'Neill, 'Piping Contests', p. 1.
94 *Clár, Oireachtas na Gaeilge 1960*. NLI, MS G 1,319/10.
95 In another music genre, but at the same time as the development of the Fleadh, the Wexford Festival Opera was established in 1951. It too began as a grass-roots response to a perceived cultural vacuum. See Bernadette Quinn, 'Symbols, Practices and Myth-making: cultural perspectives on the Wexford Festival Opera', *Tourism Geographies*, vol. 5, no. 3, 2003, p. 334–5.
96 Tamara Livingston, 'Music Revivals: towards a general theory', *Ethnomusicology*, vol. 43, no. 1, 1999, p. 69; Chris Gibson and John Connell, *Music Festivals and Regional Development in Australia* (Surrey: Ashgate, 2012), p. 7.
97 Chris Anderton, *Music Festivals in the UK* (UK: Routledge, 2019), p. 135.
98 Gibson and Connell, *Music Festivals*, pp. 14–15.
99 R. Raymond Allen, 'Old-time Music and the Urban Folk Revival', *New York Folklore*, vol. 7, 1981, p. 74.

100 The years from 1930 to 1965 could be viewed as a continuous period of Anglo-American folk music revival, but the commercial success of folk music from the mid-1950s is distinct from previous decades.
101 Paddy Maunsell, 'No Mean Heritage', CTMA.
102 *Irish Press*, 24 May 1958.
103 David E. Whisnant, 'Festivals, Folk Music', in Bill Malone and Charles Reagan Wilson (eds), *The New Encyclopedia of Southern Culture, Volume 12 Music* (Chapel Hill: University of North Carolina Press, 2009), p. 66.
104 Livingston, 'Music Revivals', p. 66. Anthony F.C. Wallace notes the same general pattern in religious revivalist movements. 'Revitalization Movements', *American Anthropologist* vol. 58, no. 2, 1956, p. 267. For a comprehensive discussion on Comhaltas as a revival organisation, see Ní Fhuartháin, 'Comhaltas', pp. 30–40.
105 Laura Olsen, *Performing Russia: folk music and Russian identity* (New York: Routledge Curzon, 2007), p. 8; Livingston, 'Music Revivals', p. 67.
106 Livingston, 'Music Revivals', p. 66.
107 Gillian Mitchell, 'Visions of Diversity: cultural pluralism and the nation in the folk music revival movement of the United States and Canada, 1958–65', *Journal of American Studies*, vol. 40, no. 3, 2006, p. 597; Richard Blaustein, 'Grassroots Revitalisation of North American and Western European Instrumental Music Traditions from Fiddlers Associations to Cyberspace', in Caroline Bithell and Juniper Hill (eds), *The Oxford Handbook of Music Revival* (Oxford: Oxford University Press, 2014), p. 562.
108 Picard and Robinson (eds), *Festivals*, p. 10.
109 Ibid., p. 2.
110 Ibid., p. 14.

## 2. A Fleadh Beginning

1 *Sunday Express Reporter*, 29 May 1955.
2 *Irish Independent*, 7 June 1954.
3 Both the Dublin Pipers Club and Cork Pipers Club (the latter was founded in 1898) were autonomous but analogous organisations, part of the cultural revival of the early twentieth century. For an account of the Cork Pipers Club see Mary Mitchell Ingoldsby, 'The Cork Pipers Club 1898–1930', in Tomás Ó Canainn (ed.), *Cork Review 1992* (Cork: Triskel Arts Centre, 1992), pp. 29–31.
4 Cumann na bPíobairí Uilleann (CPU) and Dublin Pipers Club are both used interchangeably by members and in press accounts during the 1950s and up to 1968. For the sake of clarity, CPU is used throughout here and Dublin Pipers Club only if contextually necessary.
5 *Westmeath Examiner*, 10 February 1951. See also, Reynolds, *Memories*, p. 64.
6 Picard and Robinson (eds), *Festivals*, p. 10.
7 *Glasgow Herald*, 29 April 1951.
8 *Anglo-Celt*, 18 September 1954.
9 Ibid.
10 Ibid. See also Reynolds, *Memories*, p. 5.
11 Ibid., p. 33.
12 Séamus de Brún, interview by Vincent Hearns, 16 December 1994, MIG.
13 *An Claidheamh Soluis*, 7 July 1917.
14 Corinne Berneman and Charlotte Petit, 'Festivals and Product Life Cycle: an exploratory study in the Rhône-Alpes region', working paper (2005), p. 2. Web. http://www.escpeap.net/conferences/marketing/2006_cp/Materiali/Paper/Fr/Berneman_Petit.pdf.

Notes to pages 23 to 28

15 Commins, 'Scoil Samhraidh', p. 90.
16 Robert L. Janiskee and Patricia L. Drews. 'Rural Festivals and Community Reimaging', in Richard Butler et al. (eds), *Tourism and Recreation in Rural Areas* (New York: John Wiley and Sons, 1998), p. 163.
17 Ní Fhuartháin, *Chronicles*, pp. 17–8.
18 *Westmeath Examiner*, 10 February 1951.
19 Reynolds, *Memories*, p. 5.
20 *Westmeath Examiner*, 10 February 1951. Kyne retained this position on the national executive of Comhaltas Ceoltóirí Éireann until 1955.
21 Reynolds, *Memories*, p. 68.
22 *Westmeath Examiner*, 10 February 1951.
23 Ibid. In a letter from Art Mac Connaic, secretary, to all Cumann na bPíobairí Uilleann members, he wrote 'It is the hope of the organisers that this Musical and Cultural Festival will help to arrest the decadent trend so evident today in Irish life'. Letter, 1951. CTMA. The phrase is repeated in Ó Muirí's lecture given at the 1953 Fleadh in Athlone, published as 'The Fortunes of Traditional Music', *Clogher Record*, vol. 1, no. 1, 1953, p. 31.
24 Reynolds, *Memories*, p. 67.
25 Mac Connaic, letter, 1951. CTMA.
26 *Westmeath Examiner*, 10 February 1951.
27 *Westmeath Examiner*, 10 May 1951.
28 *Midland Herald*, 10 May 1951.
29 Ibid.
30 Ibid.
31 *Glasgow Herald*, 29 April 1951.
32 For further discussion on this point, see Ní Fhuartháin, '"Mise Éire"', p. 235.
33 Paul Ricoeur, *Time and Narrative Vol. 3*, trans. Kathleen Blamey and David Pellauer (Chicago: Chicago University Press, 1988), p. 108.
34 *Westmeath Examiner*, 10 February 1951.
35 Peillon, 'Irish Festivities', p. 40.
36 Ibid. For a comprehensive discussion of lectures given at the Fleadh in the 1950s, see Ní Fhuartháin, 'Irish Music in Irish Life: articulating a vision of revival', in John Cunningham and Niall Ó Cíosáin (eds), *Culture and Society in Ireland since 1750* (Dublin: Lilliput Press, 2014), pp. 306–21.
37 *Westmeath Examiner*, 19 May 1951; Mac Connaic, letter, 1951. CTMA.
38 'Céilí mór' infers that set dancing and waltzing were not allowed.
39 *Westmeath Examiner*, 10 May 1951. This is the first time the phrase 'All Ireland Fleadh' is published, and pre-empts the general use of the term, which came later. Peroy A. Scholes, 'The Competition Festival', *The Observer*, 11 March 1923.
40 Recognised in another festival context by Michelle Duffy. 'Lines of Drift: festival participation and performing a sense of place', *Popular Music*, vol. 19, no. 1, 2000, p. 51.
41 Williams, *Focus*, p. 21.
42 Turner, *Celebration*, p. 12.
43 Ibid.
44 *Midland Herald*, 10 May 1951.
45 Stuart Henderson, '"While There is Still Time …": J. Murray Gibbon and the spectacle of difference in three CPR folk festivals, 1928–1931', *Journal of Canadian Studies*, vol. 39, no. 1, p. 151.
46 *Midland Herald*, 10 May 1951.
47 Ibid.

48 This idea expands Turner's discussions on balance and the festive experience. Turner, *Celebration*, p. 21. See also Ní Fhuartháin, 'Comhaltas', pp. 204–5.
49 Mac Connaic, letter, 1951. CTMA.
50 *Glasgow Herald*, 29 April 1951.
51 Ibid.; Ní Fhuartháin, 'Irish Music in Irish Life', pp. 306–21.
52 Ibid., p. 310. An Claisceadal began as 'informal choral group of Irish-language enthusiasts' in 1928 and in the years that followed Colm Ó Lochlainn edited and published sheet music and collections of Irish-language songs under the Claisceadal banner. Some contained text only, some tonic solfage or staff notation for the melody line, and later, arrangements for choral singing of Irish songs. See 'Colm Ó Lochlainn's Claisceadal Songsheets, 1940s', ITMA, https://www.itma.ie/features/printed-collections/claisceadal-songsheets.
53 *Glasgow Herald*, 29 April 1951.
54 *Midland Herald*, 10 May 1951.
55 Ibid.
56 *The Irish Times*, 14 November 2001.
57 Mac Connaic, letter, 1951. CTMA.
58 Ibid.
59 Additionally, *aeríocht* and *aonach* (both used as terms for open-air entertainment events, and often interchangeably) included competition. For example, Reynolds describes an *aeríocht* being run as a fund raiser for the Walderstown Piping Club in Westmeath in the 1943 and an *aonach* in 1950, in Tristernagh, County Westmeath (*Memories*, p. 26), both with uilleann piping competitions. Reynolds, *Memories*, pp. 61–2, p. 26.
60 *Midland Herald*, 10 May 1951.
61 Ibid.
62 Ibid.
63 *Westmeath Examiner*, 19 May 1951. The range of dance competitions at Feis Lár na hÉireann was interesting. Competitions were 'open' (where anyone could compete) or 'closed' (limited participation was allowed, the criteria of being a local competitor often being the requirement). Listed winners were frequently the same in both categories. Solo and ensemble dance competitions took place. For example, solo reels, slip jigs and set dances were listed, and the Humours of Bandon, Four Hand Reel, and the Three Sea Captains as ensemble dances. The set dances in question were not the older four-couple ensembles, but solo, exhibition dances. For a catalogue of Irish céilí dances (excluding ensemble set dances) see John Cullinane, *Aspects of the History of Irish Céilí Dancing 1897–1997* (Dublin: John Cullinane, 1998). For a catalogue of solo set dances see Orfhlaith Ní Bhriain and Mick McCabe, *Jigs to Jacobites: 4000 years of Irish history told through 40 traditional set dances* (Dublin: Independent Publishing Network, 2018). Dance competitions were added later to the Fleadh competition list.
64 Peillon, 'Irish Festivities', p. 50. For international comparisons, see Chris Goertzen, 'The Transformation of American Contest Fiddling', *The Journal of Musicology*, vol. 6, no. 1, 1988, pp. 107–29.
65 *Midland Herald*, 10 May 1951.
66 Ibid.
67 Helen Lawlor, *Irish Harping 1900–2010* (Dublin: Four Courts Press, 2012), pp. 16–41. On the broader topic of changes in harp patronage see Mary Louise O'Donnell, 'The Bengal Subscription: patriotism, patronage and the perpetuation of the Irish harp tradition in the early nineteenth century', in Sandra Joyce and Helen Lawlor (eds), *Harp Studies* (Dublin: Four Courts Press, 2016), pp. 75–89.
68 *Westmeath Examiner*, 19 May 1951.

69 Tes Slominski interprets the use of violin/fiddle terminology in the early twentieth century through a gendered lens. *Trad Nation: gender, sexuality and race in Irish traditional music* (Connecticut: Wesleyan University Press, 2020), p. 77.
70 Ibid.
71 For a history of accordion in Irish traditional music, see Máire Ní Chaoimh, 'Journey into Tradition: a social history of Irish button accordion', unpublished PhD thesis, University of Limerick, 2010.
72 For further details on the socio-historical relationship between war pipes and uilleann pipes in modern Irish culture see Commins, 'Éamonn Ceannt, the "Union" Piper', *Sound Post*, Winter 2016, p. 8; Commins, '"The Crustiest and Most Unbiddable of Instruments": Éamonn Ceannt and the pipes', *An Píobaire*, 2016, pp. 19–22.
73 *Westmeath Examiner*, 19 May 1951.
74 *Northern Standard*, 30 May 1952.
75 *Clár na Fleidhe 1957*. Fleadh commemorative programmes, CTMA, FCNE1-7.
76 Organologically, flageolet is the tin whistle's historical predecessor but also refers to any fipple flute. See Colin Hamilton, 'Whistle', in Vallely (ed.), *CITM*, p. 748. Tin whistle and flageolet continued to create confusion in Fleadh competition. In 1955, at the Fleadh in Loughrea, flageolet is listed as a competition and there is a separate tin whistle competition. In 1967, a motion at the annual congress of Comhaltas asked 'When did the tin whistle and the flageolet become one instrument, and if they are, why is there a separate competition for each in the clár?'. Motions for Annual Congress 1967, 17th Annual Congress Agenda, Comhaltas, personal library.
77 Aodán Ó Muineacháin, personal communication, 31 March 2009.
78 *Westmeath Examiner*, 19 May 1951. Though listed in the roll-call of winners as McGee, his preferred spelling was Magee.
79 Ó Muineacháin, personal communication, 31 March 2009.
80 Mullingar Town Band, https://www.mullingartownband.ie, [Accessed 1 August 2022].
81 Ó Muineacháin, personal communication, 31 March 2009.
82 Pat Mitchell, *The Dance Music of Willie Clancy* (Cork: Mercier Press, 1976), p. 15.
83 In the *Westmeath Examiner*, 19 May 1951, Willie Reynolds is listed among the winners as L. Reynolds, indicating the Irish form of his first name, Liam, on his entry form. This was common practice. In the *Midland Herald*, 17 May 1951, the winner is recorded as W. Reynolds.
84 See Reynolds, *Memories*.
85 The very first 78 rpm recording made of Irish traditional dance music was a duet of accordion and banjo, by John Kimmel and Eddie Wheeler, released in 1916 on Columbia Records.
86 *Midland Herald*, 17 May 1951 and *Westmeath Examiner*, 19 May 1951.
87 Seán Ó Riada, *Our Musical Heritage* (Dublin: Dolmen Press, 1982), p. 74. Ó Laoire, in a reassessment of Ó Riada, proposes that Ó Riada made provocative statements to encourage discussion and debate, and he may not have held these views with much conviction after all. See Ó Laoire, *Re-imagining Tradition: Ó Riada's musical legacy in the 21st century* (Cork: Traditional Music Archive, UCC, 2009), p. 3. Regarding playing for dancers, Goertzen notes a parallel in American fiddling, where the fiddler sought not to 'distract the dancers unduly from their physical and social undertaking'. Goertzen, 'The Transformation', 1988, p. 111.
88 The use of a saint's name in céilí band naming can have the same place-marking function. For example, the Laichtín Naofa Céilí Band, from Miltown Malbay, County Clare, is a place-marker for that locality through the use of Laichtín, an historical patron saint of the parish.

89  Though not in the competition in 1951, another occupational céilí band name example is the Garda Céilí Band (also known as the Dublin Metropolitan Garda Céilí Band), formed in 1936. There are also céilí bands that are named after the band leader (the Johnny Pickering Céilí Band from Armagh), use a family name (the McCusker Céilí Band) or use a generic Irish trope in the naming, for example the Siamsa Céilí Band. The latter was much less likely to be found in the west of Ireland.
90  Press release from Comhaltas Ceoltóirí Éireann, 30 May 1954. CTMA.
91  Reynolds, *Memories*, p. 64.
92  Mackie Rooney (ed.), *Eamonn Murray: Monaghan troubadour and mountainy man* (Dublin: Comhaltas, 2008), p. 30.
93  Minutes of Central Council, Cumann Ceoltóirí Éireann, 13 January 1952, reproduced in Rooney (ed.), *Eamonn Murray*, p. 31. The change was prompted by the fact that the Irish Federation of Musicians union who argued that Cumann Ceoltóirí Éireann was too close to the Irish-language version of the union's name. See Ní Fhuartháin, 'Comhaltas', p. 103.
94  Rooney (ed.), *Eamonn Murray*, pp. 31–3.
95  Berneman and Petit, 'Festivals and Product Life Cycle', p. 2.
96  See Ann-Kristin Ekamn, 'The Revival of Cultural Celebrations in Regional Sweden: aspects of tradition and transition', *Sociologia Ruralis*, vol. 3, no. 39, 1999, pp. 280–93.
97  Ray Hudson, 'Regions and Place: music, identity and space', *Progress in Human Geography*, vol. 5, no. 30, 2006, p. 628.
98  Mac Connaic, letter, 1951. CTMA.
99  *Anglo-Celt*, 18 September 1954.

**3. Becoming the Fleadh, 1952–5**
1   Ní Fhuartháin, 'Comhaltas', p. 106.
2   *Northern Standard*, 30 May 1952.
3   Ibid.
4   *Anglo-Celt*, 29 May 1954.
5   The other two counties with branches were Dublin and Westmeath. *Anglo-Celt*, 30 May 1954.
6   Rooney (ed.), *Eamonn Murray*, p. 28.
7   The Fleadh in Mullingar in 1951 is sometimes erased in Fleadh histories precisely because of its association with Feis Lár na hÉireann. For example in P.S. O'Neill, 'Traditional Music, Song and Dance', *Landmark*, January 1962, p. 17.
8   *Northern Standard*, 23 May 1952.
9   Ibid.
10  Ibid.
11  Ibid.
12  Ibid.
13  Henderson, '"While There is Still Time"', p. 151.
14  Kelly A. McClinchey, 'Contributions to Social Sustainability Through the Sensuous Multiculturalism and Everyday Place-making of Multi-ethnic Festivals', *Journal of Sustainable Tourism*, vol. 29, nos 11 and 12, 2021, p. 2037.
15  Gary Owens, 'Nationalism without Words: symbolism and ritual behaviour in the repeal monster meetings of 1843–5', in James S. Donnelly Jr. and Kerby A. Miller (eds), *Irish Popular Culture 1650–1850* (Dublin: Irish Academic Press, 1999), pp. 252–9; Neil Jarmen, *Material Conflicts: parades and visual displays in Northern Ireland* (Oxford: Berg, 1997), pp. 23–61; Róisín O'Gorman, 'Addressing the Bones: parades, photography and pedagogy', *Performance Research*, vol. 23, nos 3 and 4, 2018, pp. 232–6; Danielle L. Blaylock et al., 'From I to We: participants' accounts of the development and impact of shared identity at

largescale displays of Irish national identity', *Irish Political Studies*, vol. 36, no. 1, 2021, pp. 92–108.
16  *Northern Standard,* 6 June 1952.
17  Ibid.
18  Ibid.
19  Memorandum, 'Programme of competition centres, list of adjudicators, stewards and hours of various competitions, 1954', CCÉ. Personal library.
20  *Anglo Celt,* 12 June 1954.
21  Rooney, *The Spirit of the Reels,* p. 41.
22  *Anglo-Celt,* 29 May 1954.
23  The footage was filmed by the local chemist, James A. Doyle. http://clarelibrary.blogspot.com/2010/07/fleadh-cheoil-in-kilrush-1963-and-1966.html.
24  The Little Ark of Kilbaha regularly appeared at parades in County Clare during these decades, for example at the Munster Fleadh in Ennis in 1962. *Fleadh Cheoil na Mumhan, Clár na Fleidhe 1962,* personal library. See also, Little Ark of Kilbaha. https://www.clarelibrary.ie/eolas/coclare/history/kilbaha.htm.
25  *The Irish Times,* 21 May 1955. The event was run by An Tóstal, the government sponsored tourist festival enterprise. An Tóstal was launched in 1953 by the Irish Tourist Board (also called Fógra Fáilte, later rebranded as Bord Fáilte Ireland).
26  *Enniscorthy Guardian,* 3 June 1967.
27  *Irish Independent,* 5 June 1954.
28  *Irish Independent,* 7 June 1954; *Irish Independent,* 5 June 1954.
29  *Anglo-Celt,* 29 May 1954.
30  *Anglo-Celt,* 12 June 1954.
31  Ibid.
32  Personal communication, Gearóid Ó Tuathaigh, 13 April 2011.
33  *Irish Independent,* 21 May 1955.
34  As noted by Richard Dorson in another context. 'Material Components in Celebrations', in Turner, *Celebration,* p. 55.
35  *Irish Independent,* 30 May 1955. In the same column as this Fleadh report appears, 40,000 are reported to have attended a feis in New York. Competition systems for Irish cultural pursuits were popular at both sides of the Atlantic in 1955.
36  Ibid.
37  Letter from Francis Burns to Mary B. Fox, 24 March 1956. CTMA.
38  Joan Fitzpatrick Dean, *All Dressed Up: modern Irish historical pageantry* (Syracuse: Syracuse University Press, 2014), p. 229.
39  *Irish Independent,* 21 May 1956.
40  Ibid.
41  *Enniscorthy Guardian,* 3 June 1967.
42  Conchubhar, 'An Chaint sa tSráidbhaile', *Comhar,* vol. 15, no. 4, 1956, p. 30.
43  Fitzpatrick Dean, *All Dressed Up,* p. 229.
44  *Pageant of the Flag,* 1956. Unpublished. CTMA.
45  Ibid.
46  McMaster was an actor, theatre producer and director. He is subject of the documentary, *Anew McMaster: a theatrical life* (dir. Niall Matthews, RTÉ, 30 December 2008).
47  *Pageant of the Flag.*
48  Noted in other festive contexts by Dorson, 'Material Components', p. 55; Henderson, '"While There is Still Time …"', p. 151.
49  Fitzpatrick Dean, *All Dressed Up,* p. 194.

50 Formal lectures and presentations were re-introduced in the new millennium at some provincial and All Ireland Fleadhanna. For example, when the All Ireland Fleadh took place in Ennis, in 2016 and 2017, a series of lectures on matters musical, historical and cultural were scheduled.
51 *Anglo-Celt*, 28 May 1955.
52 Ní Fhuartháin, 'Irish Music in Irish Life', p. 308.
53 *Northern Standard*, 7 June 1952.
54 *Northern Standard*, 30 May 1952. The Irish and English forms of his surname are used to advertise the talk: O'Boyle and Ó Baoghaill.
55 Ibid.
56 Ní Fhuartháin, 'Irish Music in Irish Life', p. 309.
57 *Northern Standard*, 6 June 1952; *Midland Herald*, 17 May 1951.
58 *Monaghan Argus*, 7 June 1952.
59 Ibid.
60 O'Neill, 'Traditional Music, Song and Dance', p. 17.
61 *Northern Standard*, 6 June 1952.
62 Francis O'Neill, *Irish Minstrels and Musicians: the story of Irish music* (Chicago: Regan Printing House, 1913), p. 150.
63 Cathy Larson Skye, 'A Lot of Notes but Little Music: competition and the changing character of performance', *New Hibernia Review*, vol. 1, no. 1, 1997, p. 158.
64 *Monaghan Argus*, 7 June 1952.
65 *Northern Standard*, 6 June 1952.
66 Ibid. Reynolds also describes this in his memoir, though in his recollection he was the sole winner. *Memories*, p. 68.
67 Interview, 12 June 2008.
68 *Northern Standard*, 6 June 1952.
69 Ibid.
70 Ibid.
71 *Monaghan Argus*, 7 June 1952.
72 *Northern Standard*, 6 June 1952.
73 Ibid.
74 In 1963, the Fleadh was held in Mullingar and, for the first time, the official Fleadh programme demarcates this further using Bosca Cheoil (dhá shreathach) (accordion (2-row)) as the competition title. *Fleadh Cheoil na hÉireann Muileann Cearr 1963 Clár*. However, the competition was inconsistently titled in the years to follow.
75 *Northern Standard*, 6 June 1952.
76 *Connacht Tribune*, 4 June 1955.
77 Desi Wilkinson, 'Flute', in Vallely (ed.), *CITM* (Cork: Cork University Press, 2011), p. 275. Wilkinson identifies the emergence of virtuosic flute recordings from the 1980s as being a turning point. In comparison to fiddle, there are far fewer early-twentieth-century recordings of flute players.
78 Ibid.
79 Ibid. Junior Crehan's recollection confirms the strength of late nineteenth century presence of flute playing in west Clare. Local flute players, nine in total, gathered at Markham's Cross, in Mullagh, County Clare to play on Sunday nights in the summer. Tom Munnelly, 'Junior Crehan of Bonavilla', *Béaloideas*, vol. 66, 1998, pp. 88–9.
80 *Connacht Tribune*, 4 June 1955.
81 *Irish Independent*, 31 May 1955.

82  Marie Philbin, interview, 17 April 2019. There are differences in dance competition participation, not least of all that by the mid-twentieth century there was a comprehensive system of Irish dance competition and instruction well established. See Ní Fhuartháin, 'Genealogies of Irish dance', pp. 150–3.
83  *Northern Standard*, 6 June 1952.
84  *Westmeath Independent*, 30 May 1953.
85  *Anglo Celt*, 12 June 1954.
86  *Connacht Tribune*, 28 May 1955.
87  *Irish Independent*, 7 June 1954.
88  *Clár na Fleidhe 1954*. Fleadh commemorative programmes, CTMA, FCNE1-4.
89  Ibid. This programme copy has detailed marginalia; the note-taker is unknown. From the notes, a member of the national executive is the most probable author.
90  Tom Brophy, interview with Brian Lawler, 23 July 2001. ITMA, 1783-ITMA-MP3. Junior Crehan also remembered during the late 1930s playing with 'a kind of a trio ... at country dances and dance halls'. Munnelly, 'Junior Crehan', p. 101. Dick Smyth's Céilidhe Trio played a weekly céilí hosted by the Dublin Pipers Club (later CPU) on Thomas Street, Dublin before 1922. Leo Rowsome, 'The Origin of Our Ceilidhe Bands', *Bliain Iris Comhaltas Ceoltóirí Éireann* (Dublin: Comhaltas, 1968), p. 58.
91  Chris Keane, *The Tulla Céilí Band 1946–1997, A History and Tribute* (Clare: McNamara Printers, 1998), p. 53.
92  Niall Keegan, 'Traditional Music in County Clare', in Matthew Lynch and Patrick Nugent (eds), *Clare History and Society: interdisciplinary essays on the history of an Irish county* (Dublin: Geography Publications, 2008), p. 648. County affiliation in ensemble competition participation only vaguely describing county affiliation of the band members is ongoing.
93  Vincent Broderick, interview with Brian Lawlor, 23 June 2001. ITMA, 12064-BL-CDR.
94  Michael Tubridy, interview, 13 January 2009; Peadar O'Loughlin, interview, 5 May 2008; and Barry Looney, interview, 5 June 2008. Vincent Broderick recalled the same. Broderick, 2001.
95  *Clár na Fleidhe 1954*.
96  *Connacht Tribune*, 4 June 1955.
97  Ibid.
98  Ibid.
99  On the naming of tunes, see Breathnach, 'The Nomenclature of Irish Dance Music', *Sinsear*, vol. 3, 1981, pp. 12–6. See also O'Neill, *Irish Folk Music: a fascinating hobby with some account of allied subjects including O'Farrell's treatise on the Irish or union pipes and Touhey's hints for amateur pipers* (Chicago: The Regan Printing House, 1910), pp. 128–44.
100  Fleadh flyer, 1954. CTMA.
101  'Fleadh Cheoil na h-Éireann', press release, 1954. CTMA.
102  Feis An Athar Maitiú 1925 Syllabus. Personal Library.
103  The first use of 'miscellaneous' in a Fleadh competition title was in 1954 in Cavan and 'miscellaneous' or *rogha gléas* was the default competition title from 1956.
104  *Irish Independent*, 31 May 1955. Mrs K. Creagh, Rosenaillis, County Laois, is also listed in third place.
105  The tenor saxophone has an interesting place in the history of ensemble playing in Irish traditional music throughout the twentieth century. Though the sax has fallen in and out of favour, its appearance during the 1920s with various Irish dance bands and céilí bands showed an early predisposition towards its popular music properties. Many flute players tried their hand at saxophone as well, playing for two-steps, fox trots and other popular dance numbers, and reverted to flute for traditional dances. This was still the

case with some céilí and old-time bands in the 1950s, for example the Gallowglass Céilí Band and indeed the Kilfenora Céilí Band for a time.
106 Paddy Murphy quoted in Gearóid Ó hAllmhuráin, liner notes, *Paddy Murphy in Good Hands*, CD (Celtic Crossings, 2007).
107 Ibid.
108 Ibid. A designated competition for banjo was formally proposed and approved in September 1972 (motion nos 25 and 26), *Comhdháil Bhliantúil 1972* (Dublin: Comhaltas Ceoltóirí Éireann, 1972).
109 *Anglo Celt*, 12 June 1954.
110 Munnelly, 'Junior Crehan', p. 80.
111 Ó hAllmhuráin, liner notes.
112 Geraldine Cotter, *Transforming Tradition: Irish traditional music in Ennis, County Clare 1950–1980* (Clare: TM Office Supplies, 2016), p. 24; Ó hAllmhuráin, 'Clare: heartland of the Irish concertina', *Papers of the International Concertina Association*, vol. 3, 2006, pp. 1–20.
113 Seán Shéamais, 'An mBeidh tú ar an bhFleadh?', *Irish Press*, 12 May 1956. The landscape of concertina playing has been transformed in the late twentieth- and early twenty-first centuries. Concertina playing is in rude health globally in both solo and ensemble contexts. At the 2023 Fleadh in Mullingar, concertinas were abundant in the Senior céilí band competition; button accordions, sonic lynchpins of the same competition in the 1950s and 1960s, were noticeably few in the same bands.
114 Ó hAllmhuráin, liner notes.
115 *Clár na Fleidhe 1957*.
116 No one definable style exists among Clare concertina players, as musicians would be quick to point out.
117 Ní Fhuartháin, 'Dance Halls', pp. 218–50.
118 Barry Taylor, 'Junior Crehan of Ballymakea Beg', *Musical Traditions*, vol. 10, 1992, p. 29.
119 For more on the history and development of céilí bands, see Seán Corcoran, 'Céilí Bands', in White and Boydell (eds), *Encyclopaedia of Music in Ireland* (Dublin: UCD Press, 2013), pp. 180–4; Vallely, 'Bands–céilí', *CITM*, pp. 45–9.
120 *Westmeath Independent*, 30 May 1952; Duffy, *On the Night*, pp. 28, 31. Williamstown had many competitive successes during these years. The Williamstown Girls Céilí Band and Williamstown flageolet band both won first prize in the céilí band competition at Feis Lár na hÉireann in 1953 in Mullingar.
121 *Connacht Tribune*, 6 June 1952.
122 *Irish Independent*, 22 May 1958; Kearney, 'More than Buzzing Bluebottles: new contexts for céilí bands in Ireland', Liz Doherty and Fintan Vallely (eds), *Ón gCos go Cluas: from dancing to listening* (Aberdeen: Aberdeen University Press, 2019), p. 128.
123 An ongoing dynamic relationship in the new millennium. See Kearney, 'More than Buzzing'.
124 Duffy, *On the Night*, p. 49.
125 *Westmeath Independent*, 30 May 1953.
126 Ibid. This presages Seán Ó Riada's comparison in 1962 of the sound of céilí bands to 'the buzzing of a bluebottle in an upturned jar', previously mentioned. Ó Riada, *Our Musical Heritage*, p. 74.
127 Collins, '"Take Off Yer Boots": céilí bands, 2RN and sounding the nation', *Irish Review*, vol. 54, 2017, pp. 27–8.
128 Ó hAllmhuráin, *Flowing Tides: history and memory in an Irish soundscape* (New York: Oxford University Press, 2016), p. 176.

129  Jerry Lynch, interview with Brian Lawlor, 26 June 2001. ITMA, 12079-BL-CDR.
130  Céilí bands had long been heard on radio, their appearance often prompted by winning competitions. For a full discussion see Collins, '"Take Off Yer Boots"'. An early iteration of the Tulla Céilí Band won first place at Féile Luimní in 1946 and was invited to audition for radio broadcast on that basis. Keane, *The Tulla Céilí Band*, p. 26.
131  *In the Blood: one hundred years of the Kilfenora Céilí Band*, dir. John O'Donnell (RTÉ, 2009).
132  Keegan notes (in 2008) that Clare céilí bands won more All Irelands than other county since the beginning of the Fleadh. Keegan, 'Traditional Music in County Clare', p. 648. For a history of the Laichtín Naofa Céilí Band see Taylor, *Music in a Breeze of Wind: traditional music in West Clare, 1870–1970* (Kilrush: Danganella Press, 2013), pp. 286–95.
133  Keane, *The Tulla Céilí Band*, p. 52.
134  Jerry Lynch, interview with Brian Lawlor, 26 June 2001. ITMA, 12079-BL-CDR.
135  Ó hAllmhuráin, *Flowing Tides*, p. 187.
136  *Anglo-Celt*, 12 June 1954. Thomas Dempsey, publicity officer for Comhaltas, expressed concern in 1963 that, by then, the Fleadh, and competitions specifically, engaged 'too much of the attention of Comhaltas'. See Dempsey, 'Twelve Years A'Growing', *Fleadh Cheoil na hÉireann Muileann Cearr 1963 Clár*, p. 48.
137  *Northern Standard*, 30 May 1952.
138  Ibid.
139  *Monaghan Argus*, 7 June 1952.
140  *Westmeath Independent*, 23 May 1953.
141  *Anglo-Celt*, 29 May 1954.
142  *Connacht Tribune*, 28 May 1954.
143  'Denis Cox, County Meath Singer, 1930s'. ITMA, https://www.itma.ie/features/playlists/cox-denis.
144  G.H. Lewis, 'Folk and Traditional Elements in an Emerging Professional Art World: regional music in the American state of Maine', *International Review of the Aesthetics and Sociology of Music*, vol. 21, no. 2, 1990, p. 208.
145  Aidan O'Hara, *I'll Live Till I Die* (Leitrim: Drumlin Publications, 1997), pp. 162–70.
146  *Irish Independent*, 5 June 1954; *Northern Standard*, 5 June 1952.
147  *Anglo-Celt*, 12 June 1954.
148  Written in 1950, Lynch recorded it in 1952 for the Glenside Label, which had been set up in the same year by Martin Walton in Dublin. Lynch's voice has a Howard Keel resonance in timbre, range and delivery, demonstrating his popular music credentials and appeal. In addition to Walton being sponsor of Maguire's radio show (1952–80), he was owner of Waltons music shop and music publishing company. Michael Mary Murphy, 'A History of Irish Record Labels from the 1920s to 2019', in Áine Mangaoang et al. (eds), *Made in Ireland Studies in Popular Music* (UK: Routledge, 2021), pp. 21–2.
149  *Connacht Tribune*, 28 May 1955. The Caruso competition was an international tenor singing competition which ran Irish 'District elimination contexts' and an all-island Irish final in 1952. Over 500 singers took part. *Sunday Independent*, 23 March 1952.
150  *Irish Press*, 27 May 1955.
151  *Galway Observer*, 4 June 1955. The currach festival began in 1954 as a Tóstal initiative.
152  *Connacht Tribune*, 29 May 1955.
153  Joe Burke, interview, 7 May 2006.
154  *Fleadh Cheoil na hÉireann 1956*. Fleadh commemorative programmes, CTMA, FCNE1-6. See also Janiskee and Drews, 'Rural Festivals', p. 158.
155  Waterman, 'Carnivals for Élites?' p. 58.
156  Duffy, 'Lines of Drift', p. 59.

## 4. Fleadh Proliferations and Place-making

1. Marie Mahon and Torsti Hyyryläinen, 'Rural Arts Festivals as Contributors to Rural Development and Resilience', *Sociologica Ruralis*, vol. 59, no. 4, 2019, p. 614.
2. Ó hAllmhuráin, *Flowing Tides*, p. 175.
3. Dobransky outlines the steps of revival in tradition-bearing organisations. 'City Folk', p. 240.
4. Comhairle na Mumhan Secretary's Report, 1963. NPU, SR F34 D44.
5. This was not the case in Galway. Though the Fleadh took place in Loughrea in 1955, the county board was not formed until 1960.
6. Ó Dubhthaigh, *Survival, Irish Traditional Music and Song*, p. 114.
7. NPU, SR F37 D20. The next meeting of the Clare County Board was on 14 June 1954. NPU, SR F37 D31. Another quickly followed on 25 June 1954. NPU, SR F37 D7.
8. Information Sheet 7 to All Branch Secretaries, 1955. NPU, SR F36.
9. *Tipperary Star*, 23 May 1959.
10. Ibid.
11. CCÉ Quarterly Meeting Report, 12 April 1960. NPU, SR F34 D49.
12. Ibid. Decisions on Fleadh host sites continued to generate debate. Clones was approved as the 1964 site, but then the decision was reversed. Following multiple objections to how the Comhaltas executive treated Clones members ('acting *in ultra vires*') the Fleadh was re-awarded to Clones. NPU, SR F28 D7; NPU, SR F34 D72; NPU, SR F34 D73.
13. Though Ó Dubhthaigh records that the first Cavan Fleadh was held in 1954 (*Survival*, p. 106), newspaper reports record it being held in 1955 (*Anglo-Celt*, 20 August 1955).
14. *Anglo-Celt*, 29 January 1955.
15. Comhairle na Mumhan Report 1963. NPU, SR F34, D44. Limerick hosted its first county fleadh in 1962, the last county in the province to do so.
16. Paddy Tunney, 'Comhaltas Ceoltóirí Éireann in Donegal', in *Comhaltas Ceoltóirí Éireann in Donegal* (Dublin: Comhaltas, 1991), pp. 3–4.
17. Ibid., p. 4.
18. Comhaltas Ceoltóirí Éireann, Quarterly Agenda, 1959. NPU, SR F34, D44.
19. John Burke, interview, 19 September 2009.
20. NPU, SRF17, D17.
21. *Clare Champion*, 26 May 1956.
22. After 1963, age levels were standardised as u14, 14–18 and senior when sufficient numbers presented for competition.
23. Comhaltas Annual Report 1957. NPU, SR F35 D24. It was reversed again to the top two placed winners going through from the provincial qualifiers.
24. Dramatisation happens across festival contexts as part of the festive experience. Guss, *The Festive State*, p. 9.
25. Munnelly, 'Junior Crehan', p. 102.
26. Séamus Mac Mathúna, quoted in Ó hAllmhuráin, *Flowing Tides*, p. 183.
27. Munnelly, 'Junior Crehan', p. 102.
28. Séamus Mac Mathúna, quoted in Ó hAllmhuráin, *Flowing Tides*, p. 183.
29. Ibid.
30. Ibid., p. 182.
31. Denise Odello, 'Ritualised Performance and Community Identity: a historical examination of drum corps competition in the United States', *International Journal of Community Music*, vol. 13, no. 1, 2020, p. 71.
32. Rappaport, 'Ritual', p. 254.
33. Comhaltas Ceoltóirí Éireann, Quarterly Agenda, 1959. NPU, SR F34, D44; see Rúin (Motions), 1959. NPU, SR F34.

34 Rooney, *The Spirit of the Reels*, p. 36.
35 Comhaltas Ceoltóirí Éireann, Quarterly Agenda 1959. NPU, SR F34, D44.
36 *Souvenir Programme Fleadh Cheoil Cuige Laighean*, 1962. Personal library; letter from Tomás (Thomas P.) Dempsey to Seán Reid, 13 July 1962. NPU, SR F36, D33.
37 NPU, SR F36 D34.
38 Dempsey, 'Twelve Years A'Growing'. CTMA, FCNE1-13.
39 Ibid.
40 This is not always the case. At some festivals, participants are confused about the roles. Richard Bauman and Patricia Sawin, 'The Politics of Participation in Folklife Festivals', in Ivan Karp and Steven Levine (eds), *Exhibiting Cultures* (Washington: Smithsonian Books, 1991), p. 292.
41 *Fleadh Cheoil na hÉireann 1956*.
42 Cotter, *Transforming Tradition*, pp. 25–6.
43 Secretary's Annual Report, Ennis Comhaltas, 1956. NPU, SR F37 D57; Agenda, Coiste Chontae, 14 June 1954. NPU, SR F36. Branches continued to multiply in Clare. A branch was formed in Ennistymon in 1958. Enda Byrt, *Sound Your A: the story of the céilí and dance bands of Ennistymon* (Lahinch: Corcomroe Publishing, 2022).
44 Cotter, *Transforming Tradition*, p. 32; John Healy, 'Ennis Welcomes Traditional Musicians', *Irish Press*, 12 May 1956, p. 8. Reid's believed his devotion to traditional music (playing and organising) was contentious for his employer due to traditional music's ongoing low social status. Council management directed him not to perform with the Tulla Céilí Band and reprimanded him when he travelled with them. Cotter, *Transforming Tradition*, pp. 34–5.
45 Ó hAllmhuráin, *Flowing Tides*, p. 180; *Irish Examiner*, 21 May 1956, p. 6.
46 Breathnach notes that Comhaltas (and by implication the Fleadh) was 'unique among societies founded to preserve Irish music … Its members were practitioners, and the music was part of their life'. 'As We See it', *Ceol*, vol. 2, no. 3, 1963, p. 61. A survey conducted in 1964 by Comhaltas Ulster provincial council showed that 60 per cent of members 'enrolled in the branches were musicians and singers'. *Fleadh Cheoil na nÉireann Clár Cuimhneacháin 1964*. Fleadh commemorative programmes, CTMA, FCNE1-14.
47 *Limerick Leader*, 9 May 1956.
48 *Limerick Leader*, 26 May 1956. There were also walk-up registrations on the day; therefore final numbers are most likely higher.
49 *Limerick Leader*, 26 May 1956.
50 *Irish Press*, 23 May 1956.
51 *Irish Independent*, 21 May 1956.
52 *Irish Press*, 23 May 1956. The Aughrim Slopes always identified itself as a Galway band.
53 *Limerick Leader*, 26 May 1956. The Manchester-based Hallé orchestra performed several times in Ireland, as recently as 1953 in Cork as part of a Tóstal event, an event that became the Cork Choral Festival thereafter. See Ruth Fleischmann, 'Cork International Choral Festival', in White and Boydell (eds), *EMIR* (Dublin: UCD Press, 2013), p. 248.
54 *Tipperary Star*, 26 May 1956.
55 Comhaltas Ceoltóirí Éireann Quarterly Meeting, 1959. NPU, SR F34 D44.
56 *Clár Fleadh Cheoil Dhún na nGall 1964* and *Fleadh Cheoil na Breataine Syllabus 1966*. Personal library.
57 Des Geraghty, *Luke Kelly, A Memoir* (Dublin: Basement Press, 1994), p. 56.
58 *Monaghan Argus*, 7 June 1952.
59 *Northern Standard*, 30 May 1952; *Northern Standard*, 6 June 1952.
60 *Westmeath Independent*, 23 May 1953.

61 *Anglo-Celt*, 12 June 1954.
62 *Anglo-Celt*, 28 May 1955.
63 *Clare Champion*, 19 May 1956.
64 Curran, 'Changing Audiences', p. 59.
65 Barbara O'Connor, *The Irish Dancing: cultural politics and identities, 1900–2000* (Cork: Cork University Press, 2013), p. 28. Set dancing was the default traditional ensemble dance form in rural cultural life in the latter part of the nineteenth century and into the early twentieth century.
66 Foley, *Step Dancing in Ireland*, pp. 131–47. Céilí dance and figure dance are often used interchangeably to describe the repertoire.
67 Beyond the authenticity bar that the Gaelic League applied, O'Connor identifies class, revival strategies, changing patterns of rural living, and complex intersections of body and nation also having an effect. O'Connor, *The Irish Dancing*, pp. 27–33. See also Helen Brennan, *The Story of Irish Dance* (Kerry: Brandon, 1999), pp. 31–43. In Thomas Turino's terms, céilí dances are adopted by the Gaelic League to 'serve as the basis for socialising citizens to inculcate national sentiment'. Turino, 'Nationalism and Latin American Music: selected case studies and theoretical considerations', *Latin American Music Review*, vol. 2, no. 24, 2003, p. 175.
68 Sadie Walsh notes in Liverpool that the GAA and the Gaelic League 'would not permit non-Irish dances at their céilís', in contrast to the parish clubs that had waltzing and old-time dances. See Rooney, *The Spirit of the Reels*, p. 23. In 1967, the Ulster Council expressed 'alarm at the introduction of old time waltzing to Fleadh Cheoil na hÉireann céilí'. 17th Annual Congress agenda, 1967, personal library. As late as 1969, another motion to annual congress advocated that only 'Irish' dances be allowed at Comhaltas events. *Comhdháil Bhliantúil 1969* (Dublin: CCÉ, 1969), p. 14.
69 Joe Burke, interview, 29 April 2008; May McCann, 'Belfast Ceilidhes – the hey-day', *Ulster Folklife*, vol. 29, 1983, p. 61.
70 Jerry Lynch, interview with Brian Lawlor, 26 June 2001. ITMA, 12079-BL-CDR.
71 *Clare Champion*, 19 May 1956. Set dancing was also maintained strongly in west Cork and Kerry.
72 *Evening Echo*, 4 October 1955. A letter published just before the Ennis Fleadh, provides a counternarrative. The writer asserts that set dances were not the problem in Loughrea, rather the music was the bone of contention. The letter writer said 'was not in keeping with the policy of Comhaltas', which expected 'Irish music at an Irish event'. This suggests the band was playing waltzes, or other unsanctioned music. *Irish Press*, 20 April 1956.
73 Ó hAllmhuráin, *Flowing Tides*, p. 178.
74 *Evening Echo*, 4 October 1955.
75 Ibid.
76 Ibid.
77 Ibid.
78 Ibid.
79 Ibid. For a discussion on the tensions between the organisation as it developed and challenges to its authoritative voice, see Ní Fhuartháin, 'Comhaltas', pp. 143–6.
80 *Fleadh Cheoil na hÉireann 1956*.
81 *Clare Champion*, 19 May 1956.
82 *Limerick Leader*, 26 May 1956.
83 Bríd Brody, interview, 13 May 2008. Paddy Con's hosted a wide range of social dance events, including showbands and skiffle bands. Cotter, *Transforming Tradition*, p. 23.

84 *Clare Champion*, 26 May 1956.
85 Bríd Brody, interview, 13 May 2008.
86 Geraghty, *Luke Kelly*, p. 55. Vincent Broderick remembered his first time at the Thomas St club. He asked at the door 'is there music here?', to which the man on the door responded 'there is, but 'tis Irish music. So if you're not interested, you needn't come in'. Interview with Brian Lawlor, 23 June 2001. ITMA, 12064–BL–CDR.
87 *Monaghan Argus*, 26 May 1956; Ní Fhuartháin, *Chronicles*, pp. 17–8; Scahill, 'The Album in Irish Folk and Traditional Music, ca. 1955–70', *Éire-Ireland*, vol. 54, nos 1 and 2, 2019, p. 22.
88 Bríd Brody, interview, 13 May 2008.
89 Michael Tubridy, interview, 13 January 2009. Vincent Broderick also points to the Thomas St club as a haven for Clare set dancers and musicians. Interview with Brian Lawlor, 23 June 2001. ITMA, 12064–BL–CDR.
90 Interview, 13 May 2008.
91 See Bryan S. Turner, 'Introduction–Bodily Performance: on aura and reproducibility', *Body Society*, vol. 4, no. 11, 2005, p. 8.
92 *Fleadh Cheoil na hÉireann 1956*; *Evening Echo*, 4 October 1955.
93 The tide would later turn in favour of sets and set dancing. In 1969, 'Save the Sets' was unanimously approved by the Comhaltas Coiste Cheoil, 'as a first step' (*Treoir*, no. 9, 1969, p. 5). In 1970, Labhrás Ó Murchú, in his role as president of Comhaltas, mused that the country sets were a way of 'involving more young people actively' in Comhaltas and would be attractive to those who 'can't sing or play an instrument'. *Kerryman*, 5 September 1970.
94 *Dungarvan Leader*, 8 June 1957.
95 Information Sheet no. 6, 1954. NPU, SR F34 D3.
96 The first branch in Waterford city was founded in the early 1960s, 'when a small group of Irish music enthusiasts met at Breen's hotel'. Nóra Byrne Kavanagh, *Music and Memories: Waterford City branch of Comhaltas Ceoltóirí Éireann* (Waterford: Nóra Byrne Kavanagh, 2020).
97 For more on profiles of earlier Irish cultural revivalists, see John Hutchinson, 'Cultural Nationalism, Elite Mobility and Nation-building: communitarian politics in modern Ireland', *British Journal of Sociology*, vol. 38, no. 4, p. 485; Timothy G. McMahon, *Grand Opportunity: the Gaelic revival and Irish society, 1893–1910* (Syracuse: Syracuse University Press, 2008), pp. 85–126.
98 Ní Fhuartháin, 'Comhaltas', pp. 134–7.
99 *Munster Express*, 14 June 1957.
100 *Irish Press*, 7 June 1957.
101 *Dungarvan Leader*, 7 June 1957.
102 *Munster Express*, 14 June 1957.
103 *Irish Independent*, 10 June 1957.
104 *Northern Standard*, 6 June 1952.
105 Ibid.
106 Joyce and Lawlor (eds), *Harp Studies*, p. 19.
107 Ibid., p. 20. Ruan O'Donnell, 'The Irish Harp in Political History', in Joyce and Lawlor (eds), *Harp Studies*, pp. 121–8.
108 *Midland Herald*, 10 May 1951; *Anglo-Celt*, 29 May 1954.
109 *Westmeath Examiner*, 19 May 1951; *Fleadh Cheoil na hÉireann 1958*. CTMA, FCNE1-8.
110 'The Rise of Comhaltas', *Treoir*, vols 2 & 3, 1971, p. 8.
111 Barra Boydell, 'The United Irishmen, Music, Harps and National Identity', *Eighteenth-Century Ireland*, vol. 13, 1998, pp. 44–51.

112 L. Perry Curtis, 'The Four Erins: feminine images of Ireland, 1780–1900', *Éire-Ireland*, vols 33 & 34, nos 3 & 4, 1988, pp. 70–102; Boydell, 'The United Irishmen', pp. 44–51.
113 *Westmeath Examiner*, 10 February 1951.
114 Tunney, 'Comhaltas Ceoltóirí Éireann in Donegal', p. 9. See also Mícheál Ó hAllmháin, 'A Case for the Harp', *Treoir*, vol. 2, no. 3, 1971, p. 11, p. 22. Harp sounds became much more common and central to Comhaltas from the 1970s for several reasons. The work of the harping organisation Cairde na Cruite, formed in 1960, was positively affecting harp playing and in the 1970s, Comhaltas developed a more structured system for teaching Irish traditional music on many instruments, including harp. Additionally, when Comhaltas began tours in the USA and Britain, harp became central to the ensemble.
115 *Westmeath Examiner*, 10 February 1951.
116 Nicholas Carolan, liner notes. *The New Demesne: field recordings made by Alan Lomax in Ireland, 1951* (Dublin: ITMA, 2021), p. 8.
117 In 1956, the harp competitions advertised for Ennis were cited as extant *'le sé bliana'* (for six years), claiming a start date, incorrectly, at the first Fleadh. *Irish Independent*, 3 May 1956.
118 *Monaghan Argus*, 9 May 1953.
119 *Fleadh Atha Luain 1953 Programme*. NPU, SR F36 D20.
120 *Munster Express*, 14 June 1957. Gebruers was an organist, carillonneur, composer and choral conductor in Cobh, County Cork.
121 Ibid. At the Belfast Harp Festival in 1792 out of a total of eleven harpers, only one female attended, Rose Mooney.
122 *Dungarvan Leader*, 8 June 1957.
123 *Irish Press*, 3 June 1957.
124 Disappointingly, the sound of the harps (or any other traditional instrument featured on screen) is not heard, as the film is scored with the Gael Linn-commissioned Amharc Éireann theme music, composed by Gerald Victory. *Amharc Éireann* (Gael Linn, 1957), IFA, MV264/AA912; Mairéad B. Pratschke, 'A Look at Irish-Ireland: Gael Linn's *Amharc Éireann* films, 1956–64', *New Hibernia Review*, vol. 9, no. 3, pp. 17–38.
125 *Comhaltas Ceoltóirí Éireann Bun-Reacht* (Dublin: Comhaltas, 1956), p. 4.
126 Tom Tobin, 'National Festival "Flopped" in Dungarvan, Thirty Thousand Short', *Dungarvan Observer*, 15 June 1957, p. 1.
127 Peadar O'Loughlin, interview, 5 May 2008.
128 *Irish Independent*, 5 June 1954; *Anglo-Celt*, 29 May 1954.
129 *Irish Independent*, 7 June 1954.
130 Letter from Prionsias Ó Broin (Francis Burns) to Mary B. Fox, 23 March 1956. CTMA.
131 Ibid.
132 Ibid.
133 Ibid.; Peter Horan, interview, 18 June 2008.
134 When provincial qualifiers became independent events from the All Ireland Fleadh, the problem of unknown competitor numbers at the All Ireland Fleadh was resolved.
135 *Westmeath Independent*, 23 May 1953; *Anglo-Celt*, 12 June 1954; *Irish Independent*, 31 May 1955; and *The Irish Times*, 19 May 1956.
136 *The Irish Times*, 26 May 1958. See Dean, *All Dressed Up*, pp. 201–25.
137 Letter from T.A. O'Gorman to Brian Galligan, 13 December 1956, CTMA. For a full discussion of the Fleadh and An Tóstal see Ní Fhuartháin, 'Comhaltas', pp. 143–7.
138 *Irish Press*, 21 May 1956 and *Irish Independent*, 21 May 1956.
139 *The Irish Times*, 19 May 1956.
140 Ibid.

141 *Irish Press*, 12 May 1956.
142 Ibid.
143 Lena Bean Uí Shé, interview, 5 June 2008.
144 *Anglo-Celt*, 31 May 1958.
145 This was formally included as a note for visitors in the Fleadh programme in 1966, but was widespread practice before that. *Fleadh Cheoil na hÉireann, Mainistir na Búille 1966 Souvenir Programme*. Fleadh commemorative programmes, CCÉÁ, FCNE1-16.
146 *Tipperary Star*, 23 May 1959.
147 Comhaltas Ceoltóirí Éireann, Quarterly Agenda, 1959. NPU, SR F34 D44.
148 *Irish Press*, 14 June 1962.
149 *Irish Press*, 3 June 1963.
150 Ibid.
151 *Irish Independent*, 14 May 1964.
152 CSO 1956 https://www.cso.ie/en/media/csoie/census/census1956results/volume1/C_1956_VOL_1.pdf; *The Nationalist*, 8 June 1957.
153 *Dungarvan Leader*, 15 June 1957.
154 *The Nationalist*, 8 June 1957.
155 Ibid.
156 *Dungarvan Leader*, 8 June 1957.
157 *The Nationalist*, 8 June 1957. This initiative was first introduced in Loughrea in 1955; Hickeys on Dunkellin Street won. *Connacht Tribune*, 4 June 1955.
158 *Dungarvan Leader*, 1 June 1957; *Irish Examiner*, 4 June 1957.
159 *Longford Leader*, 8 June 1957.
160 *Dungarvan Leader*, 8 June 1957.
161 Ibid.
162 *Dungarvan Leader*, 15 June 1957.
163 *Munster Express*, 14 June 1957.
164 *Irish Examiner* 10, June 1957.
165 Ibid.; *The Irish Times*, 10 June 1957.
166 Tobin, 'National Festival "flopped"', p. 1.
167 *Munster Express*, 14 June 1957.
168 Ibid.
169 *Waterford News and Star*, 14 June 1957.
170 Tobin, 'National Festival "Flopped"', p. 1.
171 Ibid.
172 Ibid.
173 Ibid.
174 Ibid.
175 Ibid., p. 5.
176 Ibid.
177 Ibid.
178 Ibid., p. 1.
179 Humphrey Kelleher Jr., interview, 17 March 2009. The description of the 1957 Fleadh as a 'flop Cheoil' was long-remembered with residual rancour in the area. Ann Mulqueen, interview, 5 June 2008; Delia Kelleher, interview, 14 March 2009.
180 Progress Report, 1957. NPU, SR F36.
181 *Longford Leader*, 27 July 1957.
182 Progress Report, 1957. NPU, SR F36.
183 Gibson and Connell, *Music Festivals*, p. 9.

184 Ibid., p. 23.
185 *Irish Independent*, 10 June 1957. Comhaltas Annual Report 1957. NPU, SR F35 D24.
186 *Fleadh Programme*, Dungarvan 1957. Fleadh commemorative programmes, CTMA, FC1-7.
187 Tobin, 'The Inside Story, the Flop that Needn't Have Been,' *Dungarvan Observer*, 15 June 1957, p. 5.
188 *Irish Independent*, 18 May 1959.

## 5. Songs and Stories

1 Falassi (ed.), *Time Out of Time*, p. 8.
2 Peillon, 'Irish Festivities', p. 40.
3 For an exploration of institutional narratives within Comhaltas during the 1950s and 1960s see Ní Fhuartháin, *Chronicles*.
4 Walter Benjamin, *Illuminations* (New York: Schocken, 1969), p. 87.
5 Quoted in Rooney, *The Spirit of the Reels*, p. 69.
6 Robbie McMahon, *Last Night as I Lay Dreaming: Robbie McMahon of Spancil Hill* (Comhaltas, 2012); version is found on Robbie McMahon, *Old Man in the Hob* (2014) using field recordings by Fr Joe McMahon at St Flannan's College; other archive field recording versions are available, for example by Fr Lyons, 1958 (CTMA, T061 and ITMA, 1268-ITMA-MP3).
7 For a full biography of McMahon, see *Last Night as I Lay Dreaming* (Comhaltas, 2010).
8 John P.R. Schaefer sees the social actor and spectacle as opposing in festival context. See 'Frontstage Backstage: participatory music and the festive sacred in Essaouira, Morocco', *Western Folklore*, vol. 76, no. 1, 2017, p. 75.
9 Clifford Geertz, *The Interpretation of Cultures: selected essays* (New York: Basic Books, 1973), pp. 3–30.
10 Thomas McKean (ed.), *The Flowering Tree: international ballad studies* (Utah: Utah State University Press, 2003), p. 7.
11 Bruner, 'Ethnography as Narrative', p. 143.
12 Available on Robbie McMahon, *The Black Sheep* (Audiotape, Robbie McMahon, n.d.).
13 Interview, 14 May 2008.
14 Ibid.
15 Ibid.
16 Ibid. Songs identified by John Moulden. Personal e-mail communication, 5 March 2009.
17 Hugh Shields, *Narrative Singing in Ireland, Lays, Ballads, Come-All-Ye's and Other Songs* (Dublin: Irish Academic Press, 1993), p. 85.
18 Ibid., p. 91.
19 Ibid., p. 101.
20 Ibid.
21 Jig time is also an indicative metrical trope of 'Irishness' in international film scoring in the twentieth century. John O'Flynn, *Music, the Moving Image and Ireland, 1897–2017* (Surrey: Ashgate, 2022), p. 22, p. 44, p. 51.
22 Joseph R. Gusfield and Jerzy Michalowicz, 'Secular Symbolism: studies of ritual, ceremony, and the symbolic order in modern life', *Annual Review of Sociology*, vol. 10, 1984, p. 428.
23 Falassi (ed.), *Time Out of Time*, p. 7.
24 McMahon, interview, 14 May 2008.
25 Ibid. It is also worth noting that at the time of my interview with McMahon (2008), many of the Clare musicians named in the song were still alive, but not all. Since that time, many more have died.

26 Scahill, 'The Album', p. 22. The alignment of rurality with folk music practice and a correlating stamp of authenticity was codified by Johann Von Herder in the late eighteenth century and is embedded in his folk song writings. *Stimmen der Voelker in Ihren Liedern* (1789). See also Commins, 'Scoil Samhraidh', pp. 95–7.
27 Stephen Petrus and Ronald D. Cohen, *Folk City: New York and the American Folk Music Revival* (New York: Oxford University Press, 2015), p. 44.
28 Ibid., p. 305.
29 Ní Fhuartháin, *Chronicles*, p. 18. Janiskee and Drews recognise this paradox elsewhere in their study of festivals, see 'Rural Festivals', pp. 158–75.
30 A typical example is Ruby Murray's rendition of the Johnny Patterson-penned song, 'Shake hands with Your Uncle Dan', on *When Irish Eyes Are Smiling* (Columbia Records, 1955), track 4. This version has a final codetta added in which thirty-two surnames, all identifiably Irish, are listed in strict jig time, including eight with the prefix of Mc or O'.
31 Shields, *Narrative Singing in Ireland*, p. 88.
32 Petrus and Cohen, *Folk City*, p. 58.
33 27 May 1958. The *crios* is a woven belt worn by fishermen and is particularly associated with the Aran islands. It became popular as a cultural reference to traditional Irish life in the late 1950s and 1960s as part of the folk revival.
34 See also Duffy, *On the Night*, p. 161.
35 Interview, 14 May 2008.
36 Sit-down dance bands (often termed orchestras, mirroring international dance band-naming practice) were found throughout Ireland from the 1920s to the 1950s, preceding showbands that emerged in the mid-1950s. Rebecca Miller, 'Hucklebucking at the Tea Dances: Irish showbands in Britain, 1959–1969', *Popular Music History*, vol. 9, no. 3, 2016, p. 226.
37 For a discussion on IFM and céilí bands see Ní Fhuartháin, 'Comhaltas', pp. 154–9.
38 McMahon, interview, 14 May 2008.
39 Increased broadcasting of Clare musicians on the national airwaves also bolstered this claim. See Commins, 'Scoil Samhraidh', pp. 95–7.
40 Ní Chaoimh, 'Journey into Tradition', p. 252.
41 The highly gendered nature of McMahon's hierarchy of traditional music icons is not surprising and reflects the broad historical occlusion of women in the tradition. See Slominski, *Trad Nation*; Verena Commins and Ní Fhuartháin, 'Ageing Masculinities and Irish Traditional Music on Screen' in Michaela Schrage-Früh and Tony Tracy (eds), *Ageing Masculinities in Irish Life and Culture* (London: Routledge, 2022), pp. 220–33.
42 Frank Whelan, personal communication, 22 March 2022.
43 Ibid.
44 Interview, 14 May 2008. Mrs Crotty is the subject of a documentary which uses the song line in its title. *Léargas, Good Girl Yourself Mrs Crotty* (RTÉ, 2001).
45 Mícheál Marrinan, interview, 1 May 2008; Mick O'Connor, interview, 7 January 2009; Michael Tubridy, interview, 13 January 2009; Séamus Connolly, interview, 12 June 2008.
46 The accented delivery of these lines, and the cadential emphasis of the last two syllables of 'concertina', echo a stylistic device found in the singing of Micho Russell from Doolin, in north Clare. For example, Russell's renditions of 'John Philip Holland', on *The Man From Clare* (Claddagh Records, 2003) and 'The Flip Flop Song' on *Micho Russell Whistling Ambassador* (CD, Pennywhistler's Press, 2005).
47 Daniel J. Walkowitz, 'The Cultural Turn and a New Social History: folk dance and the renovation of class in social history', *Journal of Social History*, vol. 39, no. 3, p. 795.

48 Deirdre Ní Chonghaile, 'Séamus Ennis, W.R. Rodgers and Sidney Robertson Cowell on the Traditional Music of the Aran Island', in Nessa Cronin, Seán Crosson and John Eastlake (eds), *Anáil an Bhéil Bheo: orality and Irish Culture* (Newcastle Upon Tyne: Cambridge Scholars, 2009), p. 67; Ó hAllmhuráin, *Flowing Tides*, p. 1.

49 Michael Chanan, *Repeated Takes: a short history of recording and its effects on music* (London: Verso. 1995), p. 7.

50 For a discussion of the album in Irish traditional music see Scahill, 'The Album', pp. 17–45.

51 The label became defunct after 1966. Albums on the Dublin label subsequently appeared under the Shamrock label, and some have now been reissued on CD on Rego Records and indeed by Comhaltas itself. Thirteen albums in total were issued, as well as numerous singles and a limited number of EPs. Joe Burke asserted that others recorded material for Dublin Records, but the material was never released (Burke, interview, 16 June 2005). With the launch of its own label, Ceoltas, in 1967, Comhaltas took over the mantle of recording Fleadh Cheoil winners and other traditional music stars. Only one album was released under the Ceoltas label, *The Rambles of Kitty* (Ceoltas, 1968), which presented Fleadh winners, past and present, including Joe Burke, Ann Mulqueen, Séamus Connolly and the Bunclody Céilí Band. All subsequent records by Comhaltas appear under the label Comhaltas Ceoltóirí Éireann or CCÉ.

52 The O'Neills also released their own music on the label. John O'Neill and His Irish Dance Band, *Irish Folk Music* (Dublin Records, 1958); John O'Neill and His Irish Dance Band, *Irish Ballroom Dancing* (Dublin Records, 1960); James O'Neill, *Ireland in Song* (Dublin Records, 1959).

53 Dublin Records recorded the Leitrim Céilí Band (from Galway and Fleadh winners in 1960), *It's Irish Dance Time, Current All Ireland Champions* (Dublin Records, 1960). Joe Burke recalled that the band was not satisfied with the standard of recording or the take that was used when released. Joe Burke, interview, 16 June 2005.

54 For a discussion of the recording session, see O'Shea, *No Better Boy, Listening to Paddy Canny* (Dublin: Lilliput Press, 2023), pp. 117–20.

55 For more on traditional music and radio in Ireland see Peter Browne, *Tuning the Radio: the connection between radio broadcasting and traditional music* (Cork: Traditional Music Archive, UCC, 2007); Carolan, 'From 2RN to International Meta-Community: Irish national radio and traditional music', *Journal of Music in Ireland*, vol. 5, no. 1, pp. 9–13; Collins, '"Take Off Yer Boots"', pp. 23–33.

56 Ó Murchú, liner notes.

57 Ó hAllmhuráin, *Flowing Tides*, pp. 23–4. Clare musicians featured on the national airwaves from its establishment in 1926. The 1955 visit of Mac Mathúna was much anticipated. A letter from Thomas O'Connell on 31 December 1954 to Seán Reid, who was helping Mac Mathúna coordinate his trip, asked if a specific fiddler in Quilty, west Clare, might be added to the list of musicians to be recorded: 'it is difficult to get him to play. He lives alone in the village and when all are asleep he takes down his violin and there alone he plays for a considerable time ... [but] he may be in the mood to play for you'. NPU, SR F37 D26.

58 NPU, SR F37 D30. Ó hAllmhuráin, *Flowing Tides*, p. 24. The home of traditional music title is one that has sustained currency and is constantly refilled. See the reverential, but nuanced recent documentary, *The Job of Songs*, dir. Lila Schmitz (2021).

59 Healy, 'Ennis Welcomes Traditional Musicians', p. 8.

60 For a fuller discussion, see Ní Fhuartháin, *Chronicles*.

61 Mícheál Ó Ceallacháin, 'My Memory of a Fleadh', in *Bliain Iris Comhaltas Ceoltóirí Éireann 1968* (Dublin: Comhaltas Ceoltóirí Éireann, 1968), pp. 48–9.

62 Ibid., p. 48.
63 Ibid., p. 49.
64 Resonant with transnational festival experience. See Turner, *Celebration*, p. 19.
65 Interview, 5 May 2008.
66 Ibid.
67 Myles Wright, *The Dublin Region: advisory regional plan and final report* (Dublin: Stationary Office, 1967), p. 18. In 1949, there were 15,000 new car registrations in Ireland, which rose to 348,000 in 1968 (Ireland 2050, http://ireland2050.ie/past/transport/, [Accessed 7 March 2022]). The bulk of that expansion took place from the late 1950s and in the next decade. Cormac Ó Gráda, 'The Irish Economy During the Century After Partition', *Economic History Review*, 2021, p. 19.
68 *Anglo-Celt*, 23 May 1953; *Northern Standard*, 8 May 1953.
69 NPU, SR F14 D37.
70 Ibid.
71 Interview, 5 May 2008.
72 Interview, 21 April 2008.
73 Letter from Frank McTigue to Seán Reid, 18 February 1958. NPU, SR F29 D13.
74 Interview, 13 January 2009.
75 Ibid.
76 Ibid.
77 Aileen Dillane, 'Crossroads of Art and Design: musically curating and mediating Irish cultural artifacts in Chicago', *Éire-Ireland*, vol. 54, nos 1 & 2, 2019, p. 84.
78 Interview, 5 May 2008.
79 Interview, 13 January 2009.
80 'Already knowns' adopted from Kevin Donnelly, *The Spectre of Sound: music in film and television* (Ann Arbor: University of Michigan Press, 2005), pp. 4–10.
81 Letter from Pádraig Duffy to Seán Reid. NPU, SR F36 D31; Letter from Austin Sheahan to Seán Reid. NPU, SR F36; See also, Cotter, *Transforming Tradition*, p. 35.
82 Interview, 14 May 2006.
83 Richard Bauman, *Story, Performance and Event: contextual studies of oral narratives* (New York: Cambridge University Press, 1986), pp. 54–5.
84 On the balance of credibility and improbability see Mary Hamilton, *Kentucky Folktales: revealing stories, truths and outright lies* (Lexington: Kentucky University Press, 2012), pp. 63–4; Bauman, *Story*, pp. 11–2.
85 Hamilton, *Kentucky Folktales*, p. 11.
86 *Fleadh Cheoil 1964*, CTMA, FCNE1-14, p. 9.
87 Ní Fhuartháin, 'Irish Music in Irish Life', p. 310.
88 John Montague, 'The Siege of Mullingar', *The Massachusetts Review*, vol. 2, no. 5, 1964, p. 365.
89 Douglas Sealy, 'The Sound of a Wound: introduction to the poetry of John Montague from 1959 to 1988', *Irish University Review*, vol. 10, no. 1, 1988, p. 14.
90 *Irish Press*, 3 June 1963; *Fonn*, vol. 1, 1963, p. 1.
91 Sealy, 'The Sound of a Wound', p. 14.
92 Frank L. Kersnowski, 'The Poet and Politics: John Montague', *South Central Bulletin*, vol. 4, no. 32, 1972, p. 225. pp. 224–7.
93 Italics original. The refrain references Yeats' 'September 1913', which declares 'Romantic Ireland's dead and gone, It's with O'Leary in the grave'. See *WB Yeats Selected Poetry* (London: Macmillan, 1962), p. 55. The poem also precedes Montague's own later work 'A New Siege', with Northern Ireland as its subject. Montague, *The Rough Field* (Dublin: Gallery Press, 1972).

94  Montague, 'We Were Dazzled by the Arc of his Genius and then Stunned to Sorrow by the Signs of his Decline–Seán Ó Riada', *Irish Independent*, 1 August 2019; *The Pear is Ripe* (Dublin: Liberties Press, 2007), pp. 127–38; ibid., pp. 191–205.
95  Montague, *The Pear is Ripe*, pp. 127–38; ibid., pp. 191–205.
96  Sealy, 'The Sound of a Wound', p. 365.
97  Basil Payne, 'Review', *Studies: An Irish Studies Quarterly Review*, vol. 57, no. 226, 1968, p. 212.
98  Turner, *Celebration*, p. 19.
99  Guss, *The Festive State*, p. 6.
100 A.W. Sadler, 'The Form and Meaning of the Festival', *Asian Folklore Studies*, vol. 28, no. 1, 1969, pp. 8–9.
101 Ibid.
102 Sidsen Karlsen, *Festspel i Pite Älvdal: a study on the festival's impact on identity development* (Luleå: Luleå Techniska Universitet, 2005), p. 7.

## 6. 'The Right Kind of Traditional Music'

1  *Connacht Tribune*, 31 January 1953.
2  Blaustein, 'The Organization of Traditional Music Revival Activities from the Eighteenth Century On', in Caroline Bithell and Juniper Hill (eds), *The Oxford Handbook of Music Revival* (New York: Oxford University Press, 2014), p. 559.
3  See O'Shea, *The Making of Irish Traditional Music*, p. 45; Marie McCarthy, *Passing it On: the transmission of music in Irish culture* (Cork: Cork University Press, 1999), p. 136; and Séamus Tansey, *The Bardic Apostles of Innisfree* (Belfast: Tanbar, 1999), p. 14.
4  Chris Goertzen, *Fiddling for Norway: revival and identity* (Chicago: University of Chicago Press, 1997), p. 92.
5  An important caveat for this finding is that all fieldwork interviewees were interviewed as adults and were teenagers or older when participating in Fleadhanna during these decades.
6  Another publication in 1971 republished the same guidelines, with little difference between them. *Fleadhanna Cheoil Rialacha* (Dublin: Comhaltas Ceoltóirí Éireann, 1971).
7  Exacting standards for 'the right kind' of performance could also be applied outside of a competitive space. See Ó Laoire's discussion on song transmission and 'ceart' on Tory Island. Ó Laoire, *On a Rock in the Middle of the Ocean* (USA: Scarecrow Press, 2002), pp. 104–14.
8  Judith Blau, 'Music as Social Circumstance', *Social Forces*, vol. 4, no. 66, 1988, p. 888.
9  David L. Oakley, 'Adjudication: a wide scope', *School Musician*, vol. 56, 1985, p. 9.
10 'Rules for Fleadhanna Ceoil' in *Bunreacht* (Dublin: Comhaltas Ceoltóirí Éireann, 1962), p. 1.
11 Kearney, 'More than buzzing', p. 128.
12 Jeff Todd Titon notes this in reference to blues revival. Titon, 'Reconstructing the Blues: reflections on the 1960s blues revival', in Neil V. Rosenberg (ed.), *Transforming Tradition: folk music revivals examined* (Chicago: University of Chicago Press, 1993), p. 221.
13 Larson Skye, 'A Lot of Notes', p. 159.
14 Breandán Breathnach, 'An Appraisal of the Past and Future of CCÉ', *Bliain Iris Comhaltas Ceoltóirí Éireann* (Dublin: Comhaltas, 1968), p. 63.
15 There are frequent inconsistencies published of adjudicators' county identity. At times, the county of residence is listed. Mrs Harrington is identified as from Dublin where she was living, though she was originally from Sligo. Her brother, John Joe Gardiner, is listed as Sligo, but was living in Dundalk for many years in 1952. *Northern Standard*, 6 June 1952.

16 Interview, 5 May 2008.
17 Peig Ryan, interview, 9 June 2008.
18 Ibid.
19 Interview, 12 June 2008.
20 Interview, 8 June 2008.
21 Ibid.
22 Ibid.
23 Goertzen notes the same concern in American fiddling competition discourse. Goertzen, 'The Transformation of American Contest Fiddling', *The Journal of Musicology*, vol. 6, no. 1, 1988, p. 127. In contrast, D.K. Wilgus, in 1968, dismissed a recording of folk singers Ewan MacColl and Peggy Seeger because they sang in 'a revival style' without making any distinction between songs from the American South and North-east. Wilgus, 'Revival and Traditional', *The Journal of American Folklore*, vol. 320, no. 81, 1968, p. 174.
24 Larson Skye, 'A Lot of Notes', p. 245.
25 Sheila O'Dowd, interview, 3 May 2008.
26 Levi S. Gibbs, 'Chinese Singing Contests as Sites of Negotiation Among Individuals and Traditions', *Journal of Folklore Research*, vol. 55, no. 1, 2018, p. 53.
27 Interview, 11 May 2008.
28 Alexander C. Sutton, 'The Composition of Success: competition and the creative self in contemporary art music', *Qualitative Sociology*, vol. 43, 2020, p. 492.
29 Goertzen, *Fiddling for Norway*, p. 92.
30 Allen, 'Old-time Music', p. 73.
31 Goertzen, 'The Transformation', p. 110.
32 Oakley, 'Adjudication', p. 8.
33 Blaustein, 'Rethinking Folk Revivalism: grass-roots preservationism and folk romanticism', in Neil Rosenberg (ed.), *Transforming Tradition: folk music revivals examined* (Chicago: University of Chicago Press, 1993), p. 259.
34 *Clár na Fleidhe 1954*.
35 *Fleadhanna Cheoil: Rialacha* (Dubin: Comhaltas, 1971), p. 4.
36 *Programme of Competitions Centres, List of Adjudicators, Stewards and Hours of Various Competition*, 1954. Personal library.
37 *Fleadh Cheoil na hÉireann Clár 1964*.
38 NPU, SR F23 D11.
39 This kind of tension between local branches and the executive umbrella of the organisation became increasingly overt during the 1960s as the organisation grew and was sharpened by the managerial system of administration in place by 1968. See Méabh Ní Fhuartháin, 'Comhaltas', pp. 159–63.
40 *Fleadh Programme 1962*. Fleadh commemorative programmes, CTMA, FCNE1-12. P. 9.
41 NPU, SR F34 D25.
42 Ibid.
43 Ibid.
44 *Fleadhanna Cheoil: Rialacha*, p. 4.
45 Ó Ceallacháin, 'My Memory of a Fleadh', p. 47.
46 Ibid., p. 48.
47 Ibid.
48 Rooney (ed.), *Eamonn Murray*, p. 2.
49 NPU, SR F33 D23.
50 *Fonn*, vol. 11 no. 7, 1964, p. 9.

51　NPU, SR F35 D15.
52　Interview, 11 May 2008.
53　Interview, 18 May 2008.
54　*Fleadh Cheoil na hÉireann 1955, Clár*.
55　Motion nos 26 & 27, 17th Annual Congress agenda, 1967, personal library.
56　Laura Olsen, *Performing Russia*, pp. 46–51.
57　Peter Cooke, *The Fiddle Tradition of the Shetland Isles* (Cambridge: Cambridge University Press, 1986), p. 210.
58　Rachel Fleming, 'Resisting Cultural Standardization: Comhaltas Ceoltóirí Éireann and the revitalization of traditional music in Ireland', *Journal of Folklore Research*, vol. 41, nos 2 & 3, 2004, p. 245.
59　Blaustein, 'The Organization of Traditional Music Revival', p. 561.
60　Ibid.
61　Ciarán Mac Mathúna made multiple trips to Clare with the Mobile Broadcasting Unit beginning in 1955 and later played those extensively on his radio shows.
62　'Fleadh Cheoil na hÉireann, Clones', 1964, CTMA.
63　The Kilfenora Céilí Band drafted in Mrs Connole and her daughter, Phil who 'trained' the band. Jerry Lynch, interview by Brian Lawlor, 26 June 2001. ITMA, 12079- BL- CDR.
64　Jerry Lynch, interview by Brian Lawlor.
65　Céilí band function and the impetus for céilí band formation expanded beyond playing for dancers at céilithe to include bands put together explicitly to compete at the Fleadh (later termed competition bands). Other céilí bands have developed a concert performance aesthetic, disassociated from social dances, what Vallely describes as listening céilí bands. Vallely, 'Bands–Céilí', in Vallely (ed.), *CITM*, p. 48. These céilí band types can be discrete or overlapping and these categorisations do not preclude a band beginning as one type and adding another function subsequently. For more on contemporary céilí band functions and types, see Kearney, 'More than Buzzing', pp. 126–35.
66　Rooney, *The Spirit of the Reels*, p. 40.
67　The hyperbole is noted in other festive contexts. Gusfield and Michalowicz, 'Secular Symbolism', p. 429.
68　The first 78rpm recording of Irish traditional music was released in New York in 1916, with Ed Herborn on button accordion and James Wheeler on banjo, two decidedly untraditional Irish instruments in the early years of the century. 'The Maid Behind the Bar/ The Rambler's Jig' (Co. 2147, 1916), Richard K. Spottswood, *Ethnic Music on Records Vol. 5* (Illinois: University of Illinois Press, 1990), p. 2784.
69　11 June 1962. ITMA, 160-RTÉ-RR=CD-R-32, A3. Burke's performance of the national anthem embodies in sound the military nature of the anthem's text and sensibility, trumpet-like in its resonance at times.
70　Earle Hitchner, 'Séamus Connolly: a living legend in Irish traditional music', https://connollymusiccollection.bc.edu/exhibits/show/essays/essay-hitchner.
71　Ibid.
72　Ibid. There was a motion in 1971 to formally discontinue this competition. In practice, it had waxed and waned in the intervening years. *Comhdháil Speisialta 1971 Samhain* (Dublin: Comhaltas, 1971).
73　O'Neill, 'Traditional Music, Song and Dance', p. 17.
74　Séamus Connolly, interview, 12 June 2008.
75　Ibid.
76　3 August 1964. ITMA, 126-RTÉ-RR=CD-R-95, A1.

77  Connolly, interview, 12 June 2008. Fiddlers had a wide variety of individual styles in east Clare in the late twentieth century, with clear variations in tempo and ornamentation. Ability and preference intersect with performance context and local repertoire to produce individual styles. For a review of stylistic features of individual fiddlers (and other musicians) from east Clare see Jos Koning, 'Irish Traditional Dance Music', unpublished PhD thesis, Amsterdam University, 1976, pp. 158–71.
78  Collins, 'Mountain Music', p. 40.
79  Tommy Fegen, et al., *The Sweets of May: the céilí band era, music and dance of South Armagh* (Armagh: Ceol Camlocha, 2009), p. 40.
80  *Amharc Éireann*, 2 June 1961, Eagrán 104, IFI IFA. Solo competitions were just that, solo, with no accompaniment allowed. But winners playing in the subsequent winners' concerts frequently played with piano accompaniment, as the stage performance convention of the period.
81  Blaustein, 'The Organisation of Traditional Music Revival', p. 561.
82  Vallely, 'Authenticity to Classicisation: the course of revival in Irish traditional music', *The Irish Review*, no. 33, 2005, p. 63.
83  Goertzen, 'The Transformation', p. 116.
84  Ernst Klusen, 'Differences in Style Between Unbroken and Revived Folk-Music Traditions', *Journal of the International Folk Music Council*, vol. 9, 1957, p. 28.
85  Fleming, 'Resisting Cultural Standardization', p. 242.
86  *Nenagh Guardian*, 3 June 1961.
87  Séamus Connolly, interview, 12 June 2008.
88  *Irish Press*, 23 May 1961.
89  Ibid.
90  *Evening Herald*, 23 May 1961.
91  *Evening Herald*, 23 May 1961.
92  'Rules for Fleadhanna Ceoil', p. 2.
93  Ibid., p. 3.
94  *Irish Press*, 23 May 1961. Double jigs were preferred over single jigs in competition and in fact, a motion brought forward in 1969, 'That the single jig and slip jig be included in the solo competitions' illustrates ongoing confusion about the matter (motion no. 19, *Comhdháil Bhliantúil 1969*, p. 14). The principle of a repertoire regulation being brought to bear on an adjudication remains, regardless of the jig type.
95  Séamus Connolly, interview, 12 June 2008.
96  Draft *CCÉ Annual Report 1957*. NPU, SR F35 D24.
97  Letter announcement of quarterly meeting to all delegates in 1959. NPU, SR F34D44.
98  Vincent Broderick, interview with Brian Lawlor, 23 June 2001. ITMA, 12064-BL-CDR.
99  No. 25, 17th Annual Congress agenda, 1967. Personal library.
100  Joe Burke, interview, 21 February 2006.
101  Breathnach, 'An Appraisal', p. 65.
102  Ibid.
103  Ibid., p. 64. For a description of the institutionalisation process of Comhaltas from 1951 to 1970, see Ní Fhuartháin, 'Comhaltas', pp. 134–7.
104  Fleming, 'Resisting Cultural Standardization', p. 224.
105  Goertzen, 'Balancing Local and National Approaches at American Fiddle Contests', *American Music*, no. 14, vol. 3, 1996, p. 363, p. 364.
106  Interview, 5 May 2008.
107  'Rules for Fleadhanna Ceoil', pp. 1–13. The first Comhaltas *Bunreacht* (constitution) was published in 1956. It went through a number of iterations and republications in the years

that followed including this one in 1962 which included a greatly expanded set of rules for Fleadhanna.
108  The strict rules regarding where judges should be positioned have precedence elsewhere. At some old-time fiddle contests in the USA, judges were required to be in a different building listening to competitors over a P.A. system and without applause. Barre Toelken, 'Traditional Fiddling in Idaho', *Western Folklore*, vol. 4, no. 24, 1965, p. 260; Goertzen, 'Balancing Local and National Approaches', p. 376.
109  'Secretary's Report 1962', CTMA; 'Comhaltas Ceoltóirí Éireann Annual Congress 1967', CTMA.
110  'Secretary's Report 1962', CTMA.
111  Letter to Comhaltas delegates and members of the Executive with agenda of Quarterly Meeting 1959, CTMA.
112  'Secretary's Report 1957', CTMA.
113  Letter to Comhaltas delegates and members of the Executive with agenda of Quarterly Meeting 1959, CTMA.
114  Michael Tubridy, interview, 13 January 2009.
115  Ibid.
116  Rappaport, 'Ritual', p. 254.
117  Peadar O'Loughlin, interview, 5 May 2008.
118  Ibid.
119  *Fonn*, vol. 2, no. 10, p. 52.
120  Ibid.
121  Letter to Seán Reid, 8 December 1960. NPU, SR F34 D63.
122  *Fonn*, vol. 11 no. 7, 1964, p. 2.
123  'Secretary's Report 1967', CTMA.
124  *Nótaí do Mholtóirí* (Dublin: Comhaltas Ceoltóirí Éireann, 1967).
125  CCCÉ press release, 26 February 1969, CTMA.
126  Letter from Liam Glennon to Seán Reid, No date, early 1969. NPU, SR F36.
127  Séamus de Brún, 'The Future of Comhaltas Ceoltóirí Éireann', *Treoir*, vol. 8, 1969, p. 14.
128  *Nótaí do Mholtóirí*, p. 1.
129  Ibid.
130  *Bliain Iris Comhaltas Ceoltóirí Éireann 1968*, p. 11.
131  Ibid., p. 2.
132  *Clár na Fleidhe 1954*, p. 6.
133  Ibid.
134  Ibid.
135  *Nótaí do Mholtóirí*, p. 2.
136  Ibid.
137  Polkas are also found elsewhere. Vallely, 'Polka', in *CITM*, p. 548.
138  Kearney, 'Regions, Regionality and Regionalization', pp. 72–94.
139  No. 15, 'Rules for Fleadhanna Ceoil', p. 2. In a parallel context, at the National Old-time Fiddlers' Contest in Idaho, musicians must play a waltz and a hoe-down, and a third tune of their choice. Toelken, 'Traditional Fiddling in Idaho', p. 260. At Feiseanna during the 1920s and 1930s, each piper had to play the same tunes in any given competition, the better to compare them. O'Neill, 'Piping Contests', p. 3.
140  *Nótaí do Mholtóirí*, p. 2.
141  Jerry Lynch, interview with Brian Lawlor, 26 June 2001. ITMA, 12079-BL-CDR.
142  An adjudication template for dancing at feiseanna was also established by 1951, under the direction of the Coimisiún le Rinnce Gaelacha.

143 *Clár Oireachtas 1904*. NLI, Ir 780941, p. 50.
144 Many early Fleadh adjudicators had previously adjudicated at Feis competitions and were familiar with the system.
145 Goertzen, 'Balancing Local and National Approaches', p. 335.
146 Little change has been made since to the categories outlined in 1967. Larson Skye noted in 1997 that 'the sheets list such criteria as style and ornamentation, command of instrument, rhythm and phrasing, time, tone and tuning'. Larson Skye, 'A Lot of Notes', p. 2.
147 Ibid.
148 *Nótaí do Mholtóirí*, p. 20.
149 Ibid.
150 Ibid., p. 9.
151 John Bealle, *Old-Time Music and Dance: community and folk revival* (Bloomington: Quarry Books. 2005), p. 26.
152 Keegan, 'The Verbal Context of Regional Style in Traditional Irish Music', *Blas: The Local Accent Conference* (Limerick: The Irish World Music Centre and the Folk Music Society of Ireland, 1997), p. 119. The same problem is encountered here in this chapter, where articulations of sound are explained, but using a mixture of prose description and borrowed Western music terminology.
153 Ibid.
154 *Nótaí do Mholtóirí*, p. 3.
155 Christine Beckett, 'Auditory Structural Parsing of Irish Jigs: the role of listener experience', Society for Music Perception and Cognition, annual conference, oral presentation, Rochester, NY, 2011.
156 Bealle, *Old-Time Music and Dance*, p. 26.
157 Séamus Ó Dubhthaigh, interview, 21 April 2008.
158 O'Connor, 'The Cold Chain of Silence', p. 96.
159 The first collated book of Irish songs issued under the auspices of Claisceadal sold 8000 copies by April 1956. See Conchubhar, 'An Chaint sa tSráidbhaile', 1956, p. 30.
160 *Irish Independent*, 27 May 1953.
161 There was inconsistency up to the late 1950s in gendered division of singing competitions. In Longford (1958), the County Longford confined competition of Amhránaíocht Aonair (solo singing) had both men and women listed as competitors, as did the provincial Connacht Bailéadaí i mBéarla (ballads in English) competition. Gendered singing competition also take place at the Oireachtas, though the highest profile Oireachtas competition, Corn Uí Riada, is not gender specific. Gendered singing competitions also feature in other music cultures (for example, tenor or soprano competitions in Western classical music culture).
162 In his article on singing in Ireland in 1956, O'Connor provides many statistics, among them a table in which he asserts confidently that 3 per cent of all children in Ireland were 'tone deaf'. This figure was arrived at from analysis of examinations and records taken from classroom teachers over the course of twenty years, from 1936 to 1956. The 'tone deaf', those he describes as 'the unteachables', he believes would never be able to sing, and furthermore some teachers contend that this group constitutes closer to eight percent in some areas. O'Connor, 'The Cold Chain of Silence', pp. 95–108.
163 *Nótaí do Mholtóirí*, p. 4.
164 Thomas Moore, *Irish Melodies* (London, 1808–34).
165 *Nótaí do Mholtóirí*, p. 4.

166  18 May 1964. ITMA, 1255-RTÉ-RR=CD-R-313. The ban on recording was flaunted all the time and Comhaltas stewards at competitions often facilitated recording. Personal communication, Gearóid Ó Tuathaigh, 13 April 2011.
167  Recorded on 18 May 1964. ITMA 1255-RTÉ-RR=CD-R-313.
168  Ibid.
169  Adjudicators were later accused of being biased against northern styles of singing. The song 'The Free State Adjudicator' written by Joe Mulheran as a 'revenge ballad', referred specifically to this. It was written c.1980 and is well outside the parameters of the discussion here. I am grateful to John Moulden for access to his transcribed interview with Joe Mulheran, conducted in 1998.
170  Robert Dwyer Joyce, *Ballads of Irish Chivalry, Songs and Poems* (Boston: Patrick Donahoe, 1872), p. 367.
171  'The Blackbird of Avondale' first won at the Longford Fleadh in 1957 when Francis McDermot took first prize. Ann Mulqueen later won with the same selection, *The Rambles of Kitty* (Ceoltas, 1968). Nora Butler, 'Where the Mulcair River Flows', 1970.- CTMA, T417. Beyond the competitive Fleadh zone, these songs were hawked outside GAA matches constantly, which also contributed to the dissemination and popularity.
172  Breathnach, 'An Appraisal', pp. 62–3.
173  18 May 1964. ITMA, 1255-RTÉ-RR=CD-R-313.
174  Bridie Gallagher, 'Moonlight on the Shannon River/Noreen Bawn' (UK: Beltona, 1959), 45 rpm, BE2713. For a full biography, see Jim Livingstone, *Bridie Gallagher, The Girl from Donegal* (Cork: Collins Press, 2015).
175  18 May 1964. ITMA, 1255-RTÉ-RR=CD-R-313.
176  Ibid.
177  Bridie Gallagher, 'A Mother's Love is a Blessing', 45 rpm (UK: Beltona, 1959).
178  Donaill Ó Braonáin, 'Bairéad, Riocard', in *Dictionary of Irish Biography*. Web. https://www.dib.ie/biography/bairead-riocard-barrett-dick-a0324.
179  *The Rising of the Moon* (Tradition, 1956, 1959).
180  18 May 1964. ITMA, 1255-RTÉ-RR=CD-R-313.
181  Ibid. Tom Gleeson, who was All Ireland winner in 1962 in Gorey, sang the same selection in Newport later that year at the county fleadh. ITMA, 500- RTÉ-RR=CD-R-150. Cáit Ní Chúis, the Limerick fiddler, played 'The Rocks of Bawn' at the winners' concert in Thurles in 1965. ITMA, 465-RTÉ-RR=CD-R141.
182  Moore writes that he learned the song originally from Andy Rynne in Prosperous, County Kildare. *The Christy Moore Songbook* (Kerry: Brandon Press, 1989), p. 28. It appears on Moore's solo album, *Prosperous* (Tara, 1972) and on Planxty's *The Collection* (Polydor, 1975).
183  Gibbs, 'Chinese Singing Contests', p. 53.
184  Ann Mulqueen, interview, 5 June 2008.
185  Bealle, *Old Time Music and Dance*, p. 24.
186  Blaustein, 'The Oldtime Fiddlers Association Movement: a grassroots folk revival', *Southern Folklore*, vol. 51, 1994, p. 210.
187  Chris Goertzen, "The Transformation', p. 110.
188  Guss, *The Festive State*, p. 9.
189  Interview, 5 May 2008.
190  Interview, 14 May 2008.
191  Interview, 5 May 2008.

## 7. 'Strange Contrasts at the Fleadh'

1 'Strange Contrasts at the Fleadh', Eagrán 159, *Amharc Éireann* (1962), IFA.
2 Harry Belafonte, *Calypso* (RCA Victor, 1956).
3 E. Stapleton, 'From Donnybrook to Mullingar', *Ceol*, vol. 1, no. 2, 1963, p. 4. As an example, Bill Smith, subsequently singer with the Scottish folk group the Corrie Folk Trio, travelled from Scotland to Gorey to listen and learn songs, and recalled being in Mullingar the previous year at the Fleadh. Interview with Bill Smith, available at http://www.theballadeers.com/scots/cft_01.htm, [Accessed 22 July 2022].
4 Ní Fhuartháin, 'Comhaltas', pp. 143–5.
5 Gusfield and Michalowicz, 'Secular Symbolism', p. 429.
6 Picard and Robinson (eds), *Festivals*, p. 12.
7 *Free Press*, 15 June 1962.
8 Rudolf Brandl quoted in Manfred Bartmann, 'Spotlights on Festive History and Communication', *The World of Music*, vol. 43, nos 2 & 3, 2001, p. 197.
9 Kaul, *Turning the Tune*, p. 154.
10 Hall, *A Few Tunes of Good Music: a history of Irish music and dance in London 1800–1980 & beyond* (London: Topic Records, 2016), pp. 569–615.
11 Luke O'Malley interview. ITMA, 125-RTÉ-RR=CD-R39.
12 Frances Morton, 'Performing Ethnography: Irish traditional music sessions and new methodological spaces', *Social and Cultural Geography*, vol. 6, no. 5, p. 666; Hall, *The Social Organisation of Irish Traditional Music Making: the Irish in London after the war* (Cork: Traditional Music Archive, UCC, 1995).
13 Jessica Cawley, *Becoming an Irish Traditional Musician, Learning and Embodying Music Culture* (London: Routledge, 2020), p. 106.
14 Ibid. The term 'session' is also used to describe recording sessions from the 1920s onwards that were subsequently released as albums, for example Blind Willie McTell's, *McTell 1940, the Legendary Library of Congress Session* (Melodeon, 1966).
15 Benjamin Krakauer, 'A "Traditional" Music Scene and Its Fringes: experimental bluegrass of 1970s New York City', *American Music*, vol. 36, no. 2, 2018, p. 168.
16 Though Michael Nicholsen does report session being used is the nineteenth century in Chicago. Nicholsen, '"Auld Sod" and New Turf: entertainment, nationalism and identity in the Irish traditional music community of Chicago, 1868–1999', unpublished PhD thesis, Loyola University Chicago, p. 71. There is no mention of the term 'session' in Ó Riada's *Our Musical Heritage* (Dublin: Dolmen Press, 1982). Though published posthumously, the text is drawn from Ó Riada's radio series of the same name broadcast in 1962 and the accompanying LP releases, suggesting it did not yet have broad currency in Ireland.
17 Hall, *A Few Tunes of Good Music*, pp. 569–615; Augusto Ferraiuolo, *Rites of Spontaneity: community and subjectivity in traditional Irish music sessions* (Newcastle Upon Tyne: Cambridge Scholars Publisher, 2019), p. 26.
18 Hall, *A Few Tunes*, n3, p. 587.
19 Letter, 20 July 1960. NPU, SR F36. *Irish Press*, 6 June 1960.
20 *Irish Press*, 21 May 1956.
21 Motion no. 10, Agenda, 17th Annual Congress, Comhaltas Ceoltóirí Éireann, 17 September 1967; *Fleadh Cheoil na hÉireann Mainistir na Búille 1966*, p. 14.
22 Rooney (ed.), *Eamonn Murray*, p. 50. Cawley also notes this in the new millennium. *Becoming an Irish Traditional Musician*, p. 106.
23 *Anglo-Celt*, 12 June 1954.
24 Vincent Broderick, interview by Brian Lawlor, 23 June 2001. ITMA, 12066-BL-CDR.

25  Patsy Herron, interview, 21 April 2008. Herron also noted that the Comhaltas branch network gave him an immediate social network when his job necessitated moving locations.
26  Deborah Rapuano, 'Working at Fun, Conceptualizing Leisurework', *Current Sociology*, vol. 57, no. 5, 2009, pp. 624–5.
27  Peig Ryan, interview, 9 June 2008.
28  Broderick, interview, 23 June 2001. ITMA, 12066-BL-CDR.
29  *Irish Independent*, 21 September 1964; *Free Press*, 8 June 1962.
30  *Irish Press*, 24 May 1958.
31  *Irish Press*, 21 May 1956.
32  Healy, 'The Fleadh Cheoil', in *Comhaltas 1968 Bliain Iris* (Dublin: Comhaltas Ceoltóirí Éireann, 1968), p. 22.
33  John Burke, interview, 19 September 2009.
34  Rooney, *The Spirit of the Reels*, p. 37.
35  Kaul, *Turning the Tune*, p. 39; Anna Falkenau, '"It Was in the Air": Irish traditional music in Galway, 1961 to 1979', in John Cunningham and Ciaran McDonagh, *Hardiman and After: Galway culture and society, 1820–2020* (Melbourne: Arcadia, 2023), p. 201–3.
36  Peig Ryan, interview, 9 June 2008.
37  Seán Shéamais, 'An mBeidh tú ar an bhFleadh?'.
38  Healy, 'The Fleadh Cheoil', p. 21.
39  *Evening Herald*, 6 June 1960.
40  Ibid. Garech Browne returned from Tokyo to attend the Fleadh. *The Irish Times*, 7 June 1960.
41  *Fleadh Cheoil na hÉireann Lios Tuathail 1970* (Comhaltas, 1970), track 2.
42  *Irish Independent*, 6 June 1960.
43  *Irish Press*, 3 June 1963. *The Irish Independent* reported that 100,000 attended the Fleadh in Mullingar over the course of the three days festivities (4 June 1963). *Irish Independent*, 29 May 1963.
44  'Fleadh Cheoil Clones', 16 May 1964. ITMA, 270-RTÉ-ITMA=3-RTÉ-DVD.
45  In 1955, the *Connacht Tribune* reported with excitement on visiting international media at the Fleadh in Loughrea. 4 June 1955.
46  *People*, 2 June 1962; *People*, 16 June 1962.
47  Ibid.
48  *Irish Independent*, 25 August 1962.
49  *Sunday Independent*, 26 August 1962.
50  Ibid.
51  Ibid.
52  Peillon, 'Irish Festivities', p. 44. Peillon further notes that the disregard for 'normal rules of society' at festivals was particularly demonstrated in drinking alcohol. Ibid., p. 45.
53  Anderton, *Music Festivals*, p. 109.
54  *Sunday Independent*, 26 August 1962.
55  *Irish Farmers Journal*, 29 September 1962.
56  Ibid.
57  Ibid.
58  Carole Holohan, 'Challenges to Social Order and Irish Identity? Youth Culture in the Sixties', *Irish Historical Studies*, vol. 38, no. 151, 2013, p. 390.
59  Letter from Cáit Uí Mhuineacháin to Seán Reid, June 1963. NPU, SR F36 D24.
60  Ibid.
61  *Irish Press*, 3 June 1963.

62  Ibid.
63  Ibid.
64  Stapleton, 'From Donnybrook to Mullingar', p. 3.
65  *Irish Press*, 3 June 1963.
66  Ibid.
67  Ibid.
68  *Irish Catholic*, 20 June 1963.
69  *The Irish Times*, 3 June 1963.
70  *Irish Independent*, 4 June 1963. Letter from Cáit Uí Mhuineacháin to Seán Reid, June 1963. NPU SR F36 D24.
71  Holohan, 'Challenges to Social Order', p. 391.
72  Gibson and Connell, *Music Festivals*, p. 47.
73  *Rural Ireland* (Tipperary: Muintir na Tíre, 1968), p. 27, p. 28.
74  Holohan, 'Challenges to Social Order', p. 392.
75  *Irish Catholic*, 20 June 1963.
76  Turner, *Celebration*, p. 12; *Irish Independent*, 3 June 1963.
77  Gibson and Connell, *Music Festivals*, p. 3.
78  *Irish Catholic*, 20 June 1963. NPU, SR F36 D24.
79  NPU, SR F36 D2.
80  Minutes of the Executive Council, 1959, CTMA.
81  NPU, SR F36 D24.
82  *Irish Independent*, 21 September 1964.
83  *Fleadh Cheoil na hÉireann Dúrlas Éile 1965 Clár*. Fleadh commemorative programmes, CTMA, FENC1-15, p. 6.
84  *Fonn*, no. 3, 1963, pp. 8–9.
85  Ibid., p. 9.
86  Ibid.
87  Conchubhar, 'An chaint sa tSráidbhaile', *Comhar*, vol. 26, no. 6, 1967, p. 23.
88  *Fonn*, no. 3, 1963, pp. 8–9.
89  Ibid.
90  Stapleton, 'From Donnybrook to Mullingar', p. 5.
91  *Fonn*, no. 3, 1963, p. 1.
92  Ibid., p. 3.
93  *Irish Independent*, 19 May 1964.
94  Ibid.
95  *Anglo-Celt*, 23 May 1964.
96  *Irish Independent*, 21 September 1964.
97  *Connacht Tribune*, 26 June 1965.
98  *Irish Independent*, 21 September 1964. Dempsey noted in 1966 that 'the stranger in the house was not always the one to do the mischief'. See *Fleadh Cheoil na hÉireann Mainistir na Búille 1966 Souvenir Programme*, p. 4.
99  *Irish Independent*, 21 September 1964.
100 *Irish Independent*, 21 September 1964.
101 *Fonn*, no. 3, 1963, p. 9.
102 *Irish Press*, 8 June 1965; *Munster Express*, 11 June 1965.
103 *Munster Express*, 11 June 1965.
104 *Irish Independent*, 7 June 1965.
105 *Irish Independent*, 20 September 1965.
106 Holohan, 'Challenges to Social Order', p. 403; *The Irish Times*, 7 June 1965.

107  Sunday Independent, 13 June 1964.
108  Interview, 18 June 2008.
109  Ó Muirí (under the pseudonym Mountainy Man), 'The Fleadh', in Rooney (ed.), *Eamonn Murray*, p. 48. The essay was first published in *Clár na Fleidhe Cúige Uladh*, 1966.
110  Ibid., pp. 50–1.
111  Ibid., p. 51.
112  *Irish Press*, 8 June 1965.
113  Ibid.
114  Dana Gooley, 'The Outside of "Sitting In": Jazz jam sessions and the politics of participation', *Performance Research*, vol. 16, no. 3, 2011, p. 43.
115  *Fleá Ceoil* (Gael Linn, 1967). *Fleá Ceoil* won a Silver Bear at the Berlin Film Festival in 1968.
116  Gooley, 'The Outside of "Sitting In"', pp. 45–6.
117  Motion no. 10, Agenda, 17th Annual Congress, Comhaltas Ceoltóirí Éireann, 17 September 1967.
118  *Fleadh Cheoil na hÉireann Mainistir na Búille 1966*, p. 14.
119  *Irish Press*, 8 June 1965.
120  Motion no. 40, Agenda, 17th Annual Congress, Comhaltas Ceoltóirí Éireann, 17 September 1967.
121  *Anglo-Celt*, 31 May 1968.
122  Ibid.
123  Ibid. This is also noted in Marcus' film, *Fleá Ceoil*.
124  Similar to spontaneous jazz sessions. Gooley, 'The Outside of "Sitting In"', p. 43.
125  *Irish Press*, 4 June 1968.
126  Healy, 'The Fleadh Cheoil', p. 23.
127  *The Irish Times*, 3 June 1968.
128  *Irish Independent*, 20 September 1965.
129  *Enniscorthy Guardian*, 10 June 1967; *Irish Independent*, 31 May 1966; letter to the editor from Sheila Crowe, Secretary, Cashel I.C.A, *Tipperary Star*, 14 June 1969.
130  *Irish Independent*, 2 June 1969; *Irish Press*, 3 June 1969; Conchubhar, 'An Chaint sa tSráidbhaile: An Fleadh', *Comhar*, vol. 7, no. 7, 1969, p. 23; *Irish Independent*, 2 June 1969; *Irish Press*, 3 June 1969.
131  *Irish Independent*, 2 June 1969; *Irish Press*, 3 June 1969; letter to the editor from Sheila Crowe, Secretary, Cashel I.C.A, *Tipperary Star*, 14 June 1969.
132  Ibid.
133  Ibid.
134  *Féach*, 23 March 1970. ITMA, 271-RTÉ-ITMA=11-RT-DVD.
135  Curran, 'Changing Audiences', p. 61.
136  *Kerryman*, 5 September 1970. Comhaltas did not relinquish the calendar weekend of Whit which it had worked so hard to territorialise as an Irish traditional music one. A new festival, the Fleadh Nua (literally, the new festival), was established in 1970 at Whit weekend and held in Dublin, filling the slot. It has been hosted in Ennis annually since 1974.
137  Dobransky, 'City Folk', p. 240.
138  Stapleton, 'From Donnybrook to Mullingar', pp. 3–4.

# Afterword

1  https://fleadhcheoil.ie [Accessed 25 July 2022].
2  Séamus de Brún and Labhrás Ó Murchú, 'Concern for Fellow Irishmen', *Treoir*, vol. 5, no. 3, 1971, p. 3.

3   For a discussion of the Fleadh in Derry and peace building, see Devine, et al., 'Reaching Across the Divide', pp. 363–80.
4   Commins, 'Scoil Samhraidh Willie Clancy', p. 35.
5   Fleadh 2023. https://www.tg4.ie/ga/player/baile/?pid=6333442426112&title=Na%20Comórtais:%20Banna%C3%AD%20Céil%C3%AD%200s%20cionn%2018&series=Fleadh%202023&genre=Ceol&pcode=000018. 3:48:20. [Accessed 29 January 2024.]
6   Turner, *Celebration*, p. 16.
7   Guss, *The Festive State*, p. 6.
8   Picard and Robinson (eds), *Festivals*, p. 16.
9   Ibid., p. 10.
10  Guss, *The Festive State*, p. 3.
11  Vallely, 'Comhaltas Ceoltóirí Éireann', in *CITM*, p. 148.
12  Ó Murchú, liner notes.
13  Ibid.

# Bibliography

### FIELDWORK INTERVIEWS

Brody, Bríd, 13 May 2008, County Dublin
Burke, Joe, 15 June 2005; 16 June 2005; 20 June 2005; 2 February 2006; 7 May 2006; 25 May 2006, County Galway; 29 April 2008 (phone)
Burke, John, 19 October 2009, County Offaly
Butler, Nora, 1 May 2008 (phone), County Tipperary
Connolly, Séamas, 12 June 2008, Boston, MA, USA
Hearns, Vincent, 11 April 2008 (phone); 21 April 2008, County Sligo
Herron, Patsy, 21 April 2008, County Sligo
Horan, Peter, 18 June 2008, County Sligo
Kelleher, Delia, 14 March 2009, County Waterford
Kelleher Jr., Humphrey, 25 February 2009 (phone), County Dublin
Looney, Barry, 5 June 2008, County Cork
Mac Mathúna, Séamas, 11 April 2007, County Dublin
McMahon, Robbie, 14 May 2008, County Clare
Marrinan, Mícheál, 1 May 2008 (phone), County Waterford
Moulden, John, 28 May 2008, County Galway
Mulqueen, Ann, 5 June 2008, County Waterford
Ó Canainn, Tomás, 11 May 2008, County Cork
O'Connor, Mick, 7 January 2009, County Dublin
O' Dowd, Sheila, 18 June 2008, County Sligo
Ó Dubhthaigh, Séamas, 21 April 2008, County Mayo
O' Loughlin, Peadar, 5 May 2008, County Clare
Ó Muinneacháin, Aodán, 9 May 2008 (phone); 4 June 2008; 31 March 2009 (phone), County Westmeath
Ryan, Peg, 9 June 2008, County Limerick
Tubridy, Michael, 13 January 2009, County Dublin
Uí Shé, Lena Bn, 5 June 2008, County Cork

# Bibliography

## NEWSPAPERS

An Claidheamh Soluis
Anglo-Celt
Clare Champion
Connacht Tribune
Dungarvan Leader
Dungarvan Observer
Enniscorthy Guardian
Evening Echo
Evening Herald
Free Press
Galway Observer
Glasgow Herald
Irish Catholic
Irish Examiner
Irish Farmers Journal
Irish Independent
Irish Press
The Irish Times
Irish Weekly Glasgow
Kerryman
Limerick Leader
Longford Leader
Midland Herald
Monaghan Argus
Munster Express
The Nationalist
Nenagh Guardian
Northern Standard
The Observer
People
Sunday Express Reporter
Sunday Independent
Sunday Press
Tipperary Star
Tuam Herald
Waterford News and Star
Westmeath Examiner
Westmeath Independent

## FILM

*Anew McMaster: A Theatrical Life* (RTÉ, 2008)
*Fleá Ceoil*, dir. Louis Marcus (Gael Linn, 1967)
*In the Blood: one hundred years of the Kilfenora Céilí Band*, dir. John O'Donnell (RTÉ, 2009)
*Last Night as I Lay Dreaming* (Comhaltas, 2010)
*Léargas, Good Girl Yourself Mrs Crotty* (RTÉ, 2001)
*Porter Och Pipa*, dir. Lennart Malmer (1966)
'Strange Contrasts at the Fleadh', Eagrán 159, *Amharc Éireann* (Gael Linn, 1962). Irish Film Archive.
*The Job of Songs*, dir. Lila Schmitz (2021).

## COMMERCIAL SOUND RECORDINGS

Belafonte, Harry, *Calypso* (RCA Victor, 1956)
Bothy Band, *Old Hag You Have Killed Me* (Mulligan, 1976)
Canny, Paddy and P.J. Hayes, with Peadar O'Loughlin and Bridie Lafferty, *All Ireland Champions – Violin meet Paddy Canny & P.J. Hayes* (Dublin Records, 1959)
Clancy Brothers and Tommy Makem, *The Rising of the Moon* (Tradition, 1959 (1956))
*Fleadh Cheoil na hÉireann Lios Tuathail 1970* (Comhaltas, 1970)
Kilfenora Céilí Band, *The Fabulous Kilfenora Céilí Band* (Dublin Records, 1959)
Laichtín Naofa Céilí Band, *It's an Irish Dance Party* (Dublin Records, c1961)
Leitrim Céilí Band, *It's Irish Dance Time, Current All Ireland Champions* (Dublin Records, 1960)
McMahon, Robbie, *The Black Sheep* (Robbie McMahon, n.d.)
—, *Last Night as I Lay Dreaming* (Comhaltas, 2012)
—, *Old Man in the Hob* (Comhaltas, 2014)
McTell, Blind Willie, *McTell 1940, the Legendary Library of Congress Session* (Melodeon, 1966)
Moore, Christy, *Prosperous* (Tara, 1972)
Murphy, Paddy, *Paddy Murphy In Good Hands* (Celtic Crossings, 2007)
Murray, Ruby *When Irish Eyes are Smiling* (Columbia Records, 1955)
Ó Riada, Seán with Seán Ó Sé and Ceoltóirí Cualann, *Ó Riada sa Gaiety* (Gael Linn, 1970)
O'Neill, James, *Ireland in Song* (Dublin Records, 1959)
O'Neill, John, and His Irish Dance Band, *Irish Ballroom Dancing* (Dublin Records, 1960)
—, *Irish Folk Music* (Dublin Records, 1958)
Planxty, *The Well Below the Valley* (Polydor, 1973)
Planxty, *The Collection* (Polydor, 1975)
Russell, Micho, *Ireland's Whistling Ambassador* (Pennywhistler's Press, 1997)
—, *The Man from Clare* (Claddagh Records, 2003)
Tulla Céilí Band, *Echoes of Erin* (Dublin Records, 1958)
Various, *Fleá Ceoil* (Gael Linn, 1966)
Various, *Rambles of Kitty* (Ceoltas, 1968)

## OTHER PRINTED SOURCES

Allen, R. Raymond, 'Old-Time Music and the Urban Folk Revival', *New York Folklore*, vol. 7, 1981, pp. 65–81

# Bibliography

Anderton, Chris, *Music Festivals in the UK* (UK: Routledge, 2019)

Bartmann, Manfred, 'Spotlights on Festive History and Communication', *The World of Music*, vol. 43, nos 2 & 3, 2001, pp. 193–206

Bauman, Richard, *Story, Performance and Event: contextual studies of oral narratives* (New York: Cambridge University Press, 1986)

Bauman, Richard, and Patricia Sawin, 'The Politics of Participation in Folklife Festivals', in Ivan Karp and Steven Levine (eds), *Exhibiting Cultures* (Washington: Smithsonian Books, 1991), pp. 288–314

Bealle, John, *Old-Time Music and Dance: community and folk revival* (Bloomington: Quarry Books. 2005)

Beckett, Christine, 'Auditory Structural Parsing of Irish Jigs: the role of listener experience', Society for Music Perception and Cognition, annual conference, oral presentation, Rochester, NY, (2011)

Benjamin, Walter, *Illuminations* (New York: Schocken, 1969)

Berneman, Corinne and Charlotte Petit, 'Festivals and Product Life Cycle: an exploratory study in the Rhône-Alpes region', working paper (2005) http://archives.marketing-trends-congress.com/2006/Materiali/Paper/Fr/Berneman_Petit.pdf

Blau, Judith, 'Music as Social Circumstance', *Social Forces*, vol. 4, no. 66, 1988, pp. 883–902

Blaustein, Richard, 'Grassroots Revitalisation of North American and Western European Instrumental Music Traditions from Fiddlers Associations to Cyberspace', in Caroline Bithell and Juniper Hill (eds), *The Oxford Handbook of Music Revival* (Oxford: Oxford University Press, 2014), pp. 551–72

—, 'The Oldtime Fiddlers Association Movement: a grassroots folk revival', *Southern Folklore*, vol. 51, 1994, pp. 199–217

—, 'The Organization of Traditional Music Revival Activities from the Eighteenth Century On', in Caroline Bithell and Juniper Hill (eds), *The Oxford Handbook of Music Revival* (New York: Oxford University Press, 2014), pp. 551–72

—, 'Rethinking Folk Revivalism: grass-roots preservationism and folk romanticism', in Neil Rosenberg (ed.), *Transforming Tradition: folk music revivals examined* (Chicago: University of Chicago Press, 1993), pp. 258–74

Blaylock, Danielle L., et al., 'From I to We: participants' accounts of the development and impact of shared identity at largescale displays of Irish national identity', *Irish Political Studies*, vol. 36, no. 1, 2021, pp. 92–108

*Bliain Iris Comhaltas Ceoltóirí Éireann 1968* (Dublin: Comhaltas Ceoltóirí Éireann, 1968)

Böll, Heinrich, *An Irish Journal*, 2nd edition (USA: McGraw Hill, 1967)

Boydell, Barra, 'The United Irishmen, Music, Harps and National Identity', *Eighteenth-Century Ireland*, vol. 13, 1998, pp. 44–51

Bradley, John, 'The History of Economic Development in Ireland, North and South', *Proceedings of the British Academy*, vol. 98, 1999, pp. 35–68

Breathnach, Breandán, 'An Appraisal of the Past and Future of CCÉ', *Bliain Irish Comhaltas Ceoltóirí Éireann* (Dublin: Comhaltas, 1968), pp. 62–5

—, 'As We See It', *Ceol*, vol. 2, no. 3, 1965, pp. 59–61

—, 'The Feis Ceoil and Piping', *Ceol*, vol. 8, nos 1 and 2, 1986, pp. 11–24

—, 'The Nomenclature of Irish Dance Music', *Sínsear*, vol. 3, 1981, pp. 12–6

Breathnach, Pádraig, *Ár gCeol Féinig* (Dublin: Browne and O'Nolan, 1920)

—, *Ceol Ár Sinsear* (Dublin: Browne and O'Nolan, 1923)

—, *Songs of the Gael* (Dublin: Browne and O'Nolan, 1915)

Breen, Richard, et al., *Understanding Contemporary Ireland: state, class and development in the Republic of Ireland* (London: Gill & Macmillan, 1990)

Brennan, Helen, *The Story of Irish Dance* (Kerry: Brandon, 1999)

Brown, Roger Lyle, *Ghost Dancing on the Cracker Circuit* (USA: University of Mississippi Press, 1997)

Brown, Terence, *Ireland: a social and cultural history 1922–1985* (London: Fontana Press, 1985)

Browne, Peter, *Tuning the Radio: the connection between radio broadcasting and traditional music* (Cork: Traditional Music Archive, Cork University Press, 2007)

Bruner, Edward M., 'Ethnography as Narrative', in Victor Turner and Edward M. Bruner (eds), *The Anthropology of Experience* (Chicago: University of Illinois Press, 1986), pp. 139–55

*Bunreacht* (Dublin: Comhaltas Ceoltóirí Éireann, 1962)

Byrne Kavanagh, Nóra, *Music and Memories: Waterford City branch of Comhaltas Ceoltóirí Éireann* (Waterford: Nóra Byrne Kavanagh, 2020)

Byrt, Enda, *Sound Your A: the story of the céilí and dance bands of Ennistymon* (Lahinch: Corcomroe Publishing, 2022)

Carolan, Nicholas, liner notes, *The New Demesne: field recordings made by Alan Lomax in Ireland, 1951* (Dublin: ITMA, 2021)

—, 'From 2RN to International Meta-Community: Irish national radio and traditional music', *Journal of Music in Ireland*, vol. 5, no. 1, pp. 9–13

Cawley, Jessica, *Becoming an Irish Traditional Musician, Learning and Embodying Music Culture* (London: Routledge, 2020)

Chanan, Michael, *Repeated Takes: a short history of recording and its effects on music* (London: Verso. 1995)

Cleary, Joe, 'Introduction: Ireland and modernity', in Joe Cleary and Claire Connolly (eds), *The Cambridge Companion to Modern Irish Culture* (Cambridge: Cambridge University Press, 2005), pp. 1–22

Collins, Tim, '"Take Off Yer Boots": céilí bands, 2RN and sounding the nation', *Irish Review*, vol. 54, 2017, pp. 23–34

—, 'Music Mountain: space, place and Irish traditional music practices in Sliabh Aughty', unpublished PhD thesis, NUI Galway, 2013

*Comhaltas Ceoltóirí Éireann Bun-Reacht* (Dublin: Comhaltas, 1956)

*Comhdháil Bhliantúil 1969* (Dublin: Comhaltas Ceoltóirí Éireann, 1969)

*Comhdháil Bhliantúil 1972* (Dublin: Comhaltas Ceoltóirí Éireann, 1972)

Commins, Verena, '"The Crustiest and Most Unbiddable of Instruments": Éamonn Ceannt and the pipes', *An Píobaire*, 2016, pp. 19–22

—, 'Éamonn Ceannt, the "Union" Piper', *Sound Post*, Winter 2016, p. 8

—, 'Locating the Centre: Irish traditional music and re-traditionalisation at the Willie Clancy Summer School', David Doyle and Méabh Ní Fhuartháin (eds), *Ordinary Irish Life: music, sport and culture* (Dublin: Irish Academic Press, 2013), pp. 114–27

—, 'Scoil Samhraidh Willie Clancy: transmission, performance and commemoration of Irish traditional music, 1973–2012', unpublished PhD thesis, NUI Galway, 2013

Commins, Verena and Méabh Ní Fhuartháin, 'Ageing Masculinities and Irish Traditional Music on Screen', in Michaela Schrage-Früh and Tony Tracy (eds), *Ageing Masculinities in Irish Life and Culture* (London: Routledge, 2022), pp. 220–33

Comyn, J.P., 'The Emigrant Isle, a Flight of Fancy', *Capuchin Annual*, 1952, pp. 246–62

Conchubhar, 'An Chaint sa tSráidbhaile: an Fleadh', *Comhar*, vol. 7, no. 7, 1969, pp. 22–3

—, 'An Chaint sa tSráidbhaile', *Comhar*, vol. 26, no. 6, 1967, pp. 23–4

—, 'An Chaint sa tSráidbhaile', *Comhar*, vol. 4, no. 15, 1956, pp. 30–1

Cooke, Peter, *The Fiddle Tradition of the Shetland Isles* (Cambridge: Cambridge University Press, 1986)

Corcoran, Seán, 'Céilí Bands', in Harry White and Barra Boydell (eds), *Encyclopaedia of Music in Ireland* (Dublin: UCD Press, 2013), pp. 180–4

Corcoran, T., 'An Issue Concerning Music', *The Irish Monthly*, vol. 61, no. 720, 1933, pp. 338–40

Costello, Eamonn, 'Oireachtas na Gaeilge and Sean-nós Song Competition, 1940–2012: regionalism, nationalism and Gaelicness', *Éire-Ireland*, vol. 54, nos 1 & 2, 2019, pp. 160–87

Cotter, Geraldine, *Transforming Tradition: Irish traditional music in Ennis, County Clare 1950–1980* (Clare: Geraldine Cotter, 2016)

CSO 1956 https://www.cso.ie/en/media/csoie/census/census1956results/volume1/C_1956_VOL_1.pdf

Cullinane, John, *Aspects of the History of Irish Céilí Dancing 1897–1997* (Dublin: John Cullinane, 1998)

Curran, Catherine, 'Changing Audiences for Traditional Irish Music', in Fintan Vallely, et al. (eds), *Crosbhealach an Cheoil: the Crossroads Conference 1996, tradition and change in Irish traditional music* (Dublin: Whinstone, 1999), pp. 56–63

Curtayne, Alice, 'Review', *The Furrow*, vol. 5, no. 5, 1955, pp. 331–3

Curtis, L. Perry, 'The Four Erins: feminine images of Ireland, 1780–1900', *Éire-Ireland*, vols 33 & 34, nos 3 & 4, 1988, pp. 70–102

Curtis, P.J., *Notes from the Heart: a celebration of Irish traditional music* (Dublin: Torc Press, 1994)

Daly, Mary E., *The Slow Failure: population decline and independent Ireland 1920–1973* (Madison: University of Wisconsin, 2006)

de Brún, Séamus 'The Future of Comhaltas Ceoltóirí Éireann', *Treoir*, vol. 8, 1969, pp. 2–3, pp. 14–5

—, and Labhrás Ó Murchú, 'Concern for Fellow Irishmen', *Treoir*, vol. 5, no. 3, 1971, p. 3.

Dempsey, Thomas P., 'Twelve Years A'Growing', *Fleadh Cheoil na hÉireann 1963 Muilleann Cearr*, Fleadh commemorative programmes, CTMA, FCNE1-13, p. 48, p. 50

'Denis Cox, County Meath Singer, 1930s' https://www.itma.ie/features/playlists/cox-denis

Devas, Nicolette, *Two Flamboyant Fathers* (New York: William Morrow and Company, 1966)

Devenney, Andrew D., '"A Unique and Unparalleled Surrender of Sovereignty": early opposition to European integration in Ireland, 1961–72', *New Hibernia Review*, vol. 12, no. 2, 2008, pp. 15–32

Devine, Adrian, et al., 'Reaching Across the Divide: the role of cultural events in peace building', *Event Management*, vol. 25, 2021, pp. 363–80

Dillane, Aileen, 'Crossroads of Art and Design: musically curating and mediating Irish cultural artifacts in Chicago', *Éire-Ireland*, vol. 54, nos 1 & 2, 2019, pp. 82–109

Dobransky, Kerry, 'City Folk: survival strategies of tradition-bearing organizations', *Poetics*, vol. 35, 2007, pp. 239–61.

Donnelly, Kevin, *The Spectre of Sound: music in film and television* (Ann Arbor: University of Michigan Press, 2005), pp. 4–10

Dorson, Richard, 'Material Components in Celebrations', in Victor Turner (ed.), *Celebration: studies in festivity and ritual* (Washington: Smithsonian Institution Press, 1982), pp. 33–58

Duffy, Michelle, 'Lines of Drift: festival participation and performing a sense of place', *Popular Music*, vol. 19, no. 1, 2000, pp. 51–65

Duffy, Philip, *On the Night: Fleadh Cheoil na hÉireann – musicians and senior céilí band winners, 1951–2021* (Sligo: Philip Duffy, 2023)

Dwyer Joyce, Robert, *Ballads of Irish Chivalry, Songs and Poems* (Boston: Patrick Donahoe, 1872)

Edelman, Katherine, 'Ireland, After Long Absence', *Capuchin Annual*, 1958, pp. 51–5

Ekamn, Ann-Kristin, 'The Revival of Cultural Celebrations in Regional Sweden: aspects of tradition and transition', *Sociologia Ruralis*, vol. 3, no. 39, 1999, pp. 280–93

Falassi, Alessandro (ed.), *Time Out of Time: essays on the festival* (Albuquerque: University of New Mexico, 1987)

Falkenau, Anna, '"It Was in the Air"': Irish traditional music in Galway, 1961 to 1979', in John Cunningham and Ciaran McDonagh (eds), *Hardiman and After: Galway culture and society, 1820–2020* (Melbourne: Arcadia, 2023), pp. 201–11

Fanning, Ronan, 'The Genesis of Economic Development', in John F. McCarthy (ed.), *Planning Ireland's Future: the legacy of T.K. Whitaker* (Dublin: Glendale, 1990)

Federigo and Sebastin, 'The Feis Ceoil Fraud', *All Ireland Review*, vol. 1, no. 26, 1900, p. 5

Fegan, Henry, 'A Feis', *The Irish Monthly*, vol. 31, no. 362, 1903, pp. 463–6

Fegen, Tommy, et al., *The Sweets of May: the céilí band era, music and dance of South Armagh* (Armagh: Ceol Camlocha, 2009)

'Feis', *The Musical Times and Singing Class Circular*, vol. 41, no. 688, 1900, p. 402

Ferraiuolo, Augusto, *Rites of Spontaneity: community and subjectivity in traditional Irish music sessions* (Newcastle Upon Tyne: Cambridge Scholars Publisher, 2019)

Ferriter, Diarmaid, *The Transformation of Ireland 1900–2000* (London: Profile Books, 2005)

Fitzpatrick Dean, Joan, *All Dressed Up: modern Irish historical pageantry* (Syracuse: Syracuse University Press, 2014)

Flanagan, Kathleen M., *Steps in Time: the history of Irish dance in Chicago* (USA: Macatar Press, 2009)

*Fleadhanna Cheoil Rialacha* (Dublin: Comhaltas Ceoltóirí Éireann, 1971)

Fleischmann, Ruth, 'Cork International Choral Festival', in Harry White and Barra Boydell (eds), *EMIR* (Dublin: UCD Press, 2013), pp. 248–9

Fleming, Rachel, 'Resisting Cultural Standardization: Comhaltas Ceoltóirí Éireann and the revitalization of traditional music in Ireland', *Journal of Folklore Research*, vol. 41, nos 2 & 3, 2004, pp. 227–57

Foley, Catherine, *Step Dancing in Ireland: culture and history* (Farnham: Ashgate, 2013)

Foster, Roy F., *Modern Ireland 1600–1972* (London: Allen Lane Penguin Press, 1988)

Geertz, Clifford, *The Interpretation of Cultures: selected essays* (New York: Basic Books, 1973)

Geraghty, Des, *Luke Kelly, A Memoir* (Dublin: Basement Press, 1994)

Gibbs, Levi S., 'Chinese Singing Contests as Sites of Negotiation Among Individuals and Traditions', *Journal of Folklore Research*, vol. 55, no. 1, 2018, pp. 49–75

Gibson, Chris, and John Connell, *Music Festivals and Regional Development in Australia* (Surrey: Ashgate Publishing, 2012)

Gilrane, Thomas, *Just the Way it Was: Tommy Dan Tims, Derrinageer, Ballinaglera, a true story of a traditional farm life in County Leitrim, Ireland* (New York: iUniverse, 2007)

Goertzen, Chris, 'Balancing Local and National Approaches at American Fiddle Contests', *American Music*, no. 14, vol. 3, 1996, pp. 352–81

—, *Fiddling for Norway: revival and identity* (Chicago: University of Chicago Press, 1997)

—, 'The Transformation of American Contest Fiddling', *The Journal of Musicology*, vol. 6, no. 1, 1988, pp. 107–29

Gooley, Dana, 'The Outside of "Sitting In": jazz jam sessions and the politics of participation', *Performance Research*, vol. 16, no. 3, 2011, pp. 43–8

Gusfield, Joseph R. and Jerzy Michalowicz, 'Secular Symbolism: studies of ritual, ceremony, and the symbolic order in modern life', *Annual Review of Sociology*, vol. 10, 1984, pp. 417–35

Guss, David M., *The Festive State* (Oakland: University of California Press, 2000)

Hall, Reg, *A Few Tunes of Good Music: a history of Irish music and dance in London 1800–1980 & beyond* (London: Topic Records, 2016). https://www.topicrecords.co.uk/wp-content/uploads/few-tunes-reg-hall.pdf

—, 'Heydays are Shortlived: change in music-making practice in rural Ireland 1850–1950', in Vallely, et al. (eds), 1999, pp. 77–83

—, *The Social Organisation of Irish Traditional Music-Making: the Irish in London after the war* (Cork: Traditional Music Archive, 1995)

Hamilton, Colin, 'Whistle', in Fintan Vallely (ed.), *CITM* (Cork University Press, 2011), p. 748

Hamilton, Mary, *Kentucky Folktales: revealing stories, truths and outright lies* (Lexington: Kentucky University Press, 2012)

Hast, Dorothea E., and Stanley Scott, *Music in Ireland: experiencing music, expressing culture* (New York: Oxford University Press, 2004)

Healy, John, 'Ennis Welcomes Traditional Musicians', *Irish Press*, 12 May 1956
—, 'The Fleadh Cheoil', in *Comhaltas 1968 Bliain Iris* (Dublin: Comhaltas Ceoltóirí Éireann, 1968), pp. 20–3
Henderson, Stuart, '"While There is Still Time …": J. Murray Gibbon and the spectacle of difference in three CPR folk festivals, 1928–1931', *Journal of Canadian Studies*, vol. 39, no. 1, pp. 139–77
Hennessy, Peter, *Having it So Good: Britain in the 1950s* (London: Penguin Books, 2007)
Henry, Edward O., 'Institutions for the Promotion of Indigenous Music: the case for Ireland's Comhaltas Ceoltóirí Éireann', *Ethnomusicology*, vol. 33, no. 1, pp. 67–95
Hitchner, Earle, 'Séamus Connolly: a living legend in Irish traditional music', https://connollymusiccollection.bc.edu/exhibits/show/essays/essay-hitchner
Holohan, Carole, 'Challenges to Social Order and Irish Identity? Youth Culture in the Sixties', *Historical Studies*, vol. 38, no. 151, 2013, pp. 389–405
Homans, George, 'Foreword' in Alexander Humphries, *New Dubliners: urbanisation and the Irish family* (London: Routledge and Kegan Paul, 1966), iv
Hudson, Ray, 'Regions and Place: music, identity and space', *Progress in Human Geography*, vol. 5, no. 30, 2006, pp. 342–62
Hutchinson, John, 'Cultural Nationalism, Elite Mobility and Nation-building: communitarian politics in modern Ireland', *British Journal of Sociology*, vol. 38, no. 4, pp. 482–501
Janiskee, Robert L., and Patricia L. Drews, 'Rural Festivals and Community Reimaging', in Richard Butler, et al. (eds), *Tourism and Recreation in Rural Areas* (New York: John Wiley and Sons, 1998)
Jarmen, Neil, *Material Conflicts: parades and visual displays in Northern Ireland* (Oxford: Berg, 1997)
Joyce, Sandra and Helen Lawlor (eds), *Harp Studies* (Dublin: Four Courts Press, 2016)
Karlsen, Sidsen, *Festspel i Pite Älvdal: a study on the festival's impact on identity development* (Luleå: Luleå Techniska Universitet, 2005)
Kaul, Adam, *Turning the Tune: traditional music, tourism and social change in an Irish village* (New York: Bergahn Books, 2009)
Keane, Chris, *The Tulla Céilí Band 1946–1997, A History and Tribute* (Clare: McNamara Printers, 1998)
Kearney, Daithí, 'More than Buzzing Bluebottles: new contexts for céilí bands in Ireland', in Liz Doherty and Fintan Vallely (eds), *Ón gCos go Cluas: From Dancing to Listening, Proceedings of the 2012 North Atlantic Fiddle Convention* (Aberdeen: Elphinstone Institute, 2019), pp. 126–35

—, 'Regions, Regionality and Regionalization in Irish Traditional Music: the role of Comhaltas Ceoltóirí Éireann', *Ethnomusicology Ireland*, vol. 2, no. 3, 2013, pp. 72–94

Kearney, Daithí and Kevin Burns, 'Come Enjoy the Craic: locating an Irish Traditional Music Festival in Drogheda', in A. Smith et al. (eds), *Festivals and the City: the contested geographies of urban events* (London: University of Westminster Press, 2022), pp. 231–47

Keegan, Niall, 'Traditional Music in County Clare', in Matthew Lynch and Patrick Nugent (eds), *Clare History and Society: interdisciplinary essays on the history of an Irish county* (Dublin: Geography Publications, 2008), pp. 641–56

—, 'The Verbal Context of Regional Style in Traditional Irish Music', *Blas: The Local Accent Conference* (Limerick: The Irish World Music Centre and the Folk Music Society of Ireland, 1997), pp. 116–22

Keogh, Dermot, *Twentieth Century Ireland* (Dublin: Gill & Macmillan, 2005)

Keogh, Dermot et al. (eds), *The Lost Decade: Ireland in the 1950s* (Cork: Mercier Press, 2004)

Kersnowski, Frank L., 'The Poet and Politics: John Montague', *South Central Bulletin*, vol. 4, no. 32, 1972, pp. 224–7

Klusen, Ernst, 'Differences in Style Between Unbroken and Revived Folk-Music Traditions', *Journal of the International Folk Music Council*, vol. 9, 1957, pp. 28–9

Koning, Jos, 'Irish Traditional Dance Music', unpublished PhD thesis, Amsterdam University, 1976

Krakauer, Benjamin, 'A "Traditional" Music Scene and Its Fringes: experimental bluegrass of 1970s New York City', *American Music*, vol. 36, no. 2, 2018, pp. 163–93

Larson Skye, Cathy, 'A Lot of Notes but Little Music: competition and the changing character of performance', *New Hibernia Review*, vol. 1, no. 1, 1997, pp. 156–67

Lawlor, Helen, *Irish Harping 1900–2010* (Dublin: Four Courts Press, 2012)

Lee, Joseph J. (ed.), *Ireland 1912–1985: politics and society* (Cambridge: Cambridge University Press, 1989)

—, *Ireland 1945–1970* (Dublin: Gill & Macmillan, 1979)

Lee, Joe and Gearóid Ó Tuathaigh, *The Age of de Valera* (Dublin: Ward River Press, 1982)

Lewis, G.H., 'Folk and Traditional Elements in an Emerging Professional Art World: regional music in the American state of Maine', *International Review of the Aesthetics and Sociology of Music*, vol. 21, no. 2, 1990, pp. 207–8

Livingston, Tamara, 'Music Revivals: towards a general theory', *Ethnomusicology*, vol. 43, no. 1, 1999, pp. 66–85

Livingstone, Jim, *Bridie Gallagher, The Girl from Donegal* (Cork: Collins Press, 2015)

Mac Néill, Seán, 'An tOireachtas: smaointe fánacha', *Comhar*, vol. 8, no. 12, 1949, pp. 27–8

Mahon, Marie, and Torsti Hyyryläinen, 'Rural Arts Festivals as Contributors to Rural Development and Resilience', *Sociologica Ruralis*, vol. 59, no. 4, 2019, pp. 612–35

McCann, May, 'Belfast Ceilidhes – the hey-day', *Ulster Folklife*, vol. 29, 1983, pp. 55–69

McCarthy, Marie, *Passing it On: the transmission of music in Irish culture* (Cork: Cork University Press, 1999)

McClinchey, Kelly A., 'Contributions to Social Sustainability Through the Sensuous Multiculturalism and Everyday Place-Making of Multi-Ethnic Festivals', *Journal of Sustainable Tourism*, vol. 29, nos 11 & 12, 2021, pp. 2025–43

McKean, Thomas (ed.), *The Flowering Tree: international ballad studies* (Utah: Utah State University Press, 2003)

McLaughlin, Patrick J., 'Ireland and the World Population Problem', *Capuchin Annual*, 1962, pp. 163–74

McMahon, Timothy G., *Grand Opportunity: the Gaelic revival and Irish society, 1893–1910* (Syracuse: Syracuse University Press, 2008)

Miller, Rebecca, 'Hucklebucking at the Tea Dances: Irish showbands in Britain, 1959–1969', *Popular Music History*, vol. 9, no. 3, 2016, pp. 225–47

Mitchell Ingoldsby, Mary, 'The Cork Pipers Club 1898–1930', in Tomás Ó Canainn (ed.), *Cork Review 1992* (Cork: Triskel Arts Centre, 1992), pp. 29–31

Mitchell, Gillian, 'Visions of Diversity: cultural pluralism and the nation in the folk music revival movement of the United States and Canada, 1958–65', *Journal of American Studies*, vol. 40, no. 3, 2006, pp. 593–614

Mitchell, Pat, *The Dance Music of Willie Clancy* (Cork: Mercier Press, 1976)

Montague, John, *The Pear is Ripe* (Dublin: Liberties Press, 2007)

—, *The Rough Field* (Dublin: Gallery Press, 1972)

—, 'The Siege of Mullingar', *The Massachusetts Review*, vol. 2, no. 5, 1964, p. 365

—, 'We Were Dazzled by the Arc of his Genius and then Stunned to Sorrow by the Signs of his Decline–Seán Ó Riada', *Irish Independent*, 1 August 2019

Moore, Christy, *The Christy Moore Songbook* (Kerry: Brandon Press, 1989)

Moore, Thomas, *Irish Melodies* (London, 1808–34)

Morton, Frances, 'Performing Ethnography: Irish traditional music sessions and new methodological spaces', *Social and Cultural Geography*, vol. 6, no. 5, pp. 661–76

Mullingar Town Band, https://www.mullingartownband.ie

Munnelly, Tom, 'Junior Crehan of Bonavilla', *Béaloideas*, vol. 66, 1998, pp. 59–161

Murphy, John A., *Ireland in the Twentieth Century* (London: Gill & Macmillan, 1981)

—, '"Put Them Out!": parties and elections, 1948–69', in Joseph J. Lee (ed.) (1979), pp. 1–15

Murphy, Michael Mary, 'A History of Irish Record Labels from the 1920s to 2019', in Áine Mangaoang, et al. (eds), *Made in Ireland Studies in Popular Music* (UK: Routledge, 2021), pp. 19–30

Newman, Jeremiah, *The Limerick Rural Survey 1958–1964* (Tipperary: Muintir na Tíre Rural Publications, 1964)

Ní Bhriain, Orfhlaith and Mick McCabe, *Jigs to Jacobites: 4000 years of Irish history told through 40 traditional solo set dances* (Dublin: Independent Publishing network, 2018)

Ní Chaoimh, Máire, 'Journey into Tradition: a social history of Irish button accordion', unpublished PhD thesis, University of Limerick, 2010

Ní Chonghaile, Deirdre, 'Séamus Ennis, W.R. Rodgers and Sidney Robertson Cowell on the Traditional Music of the Aran Island', in Nessa Cronin, et al. (eds), *Anáil an Bhéil Bheo: orality and Irish Culture* (Newcastle Upon Tyne: Cambridge Scholars, 2009), pp. 67–86

Ní Fhuartháin, Méabh, *Chronicles of Comhaltas: narrating authority in Irish traditional music, 1951–1970* (Cork: Irish Traditional Music archive, UCC, 2018)

—, 'Comhaltas Ceoltóirí Éireann: shaping tradition, 1951–1970', unpublished PhD thesis, NUI Galway, 2011

—, 'Dance Halls, Parish Halls and Marquees: building and regulating Irish public dance space, 1897–1957', *Éire/Ireland Journal of Irish Studies*, vol. 54, nos 1 and 2, 2019, pp. 218–50

—, 'Fleadh Cheoil', in Harry White and Barra Boydell (eds), *Encyclopaedia of Music in Ireland* (Dublin: UCD Press, 2013), pp. 388–9

—, 'Genealogies of Irish Dance in Galway, 1922–1992', in John Cunningham and Ciaran McDonough (eds), *Hardiman and after: Galway culture and society, 1820–2020* (Melbourne: Arcadia, 2023), pp. 250–3

—, 'Irish Music in Irish Life: articulating a vision of revival', in John Cunningham and Niall Ó Cíosáin (eds), *Culture and Society in Ireland since 1750* (Dublin: Lilliput Press, 2014), pp. 306–21

—, '"Mise Éire": (re)imaginings in Irish music studies', in Mike Cronin et al. (eds), *Routledge International Handbook of Irish Studies* (New York: Routledge, 2021), pp. 323–34

Nicholsen, Michael, '"Auld Sod" and New Turf: entertainment, nationalism and identity in the Irish traditional music community of Chicago, 1868–1999', unpublished PhD thesis, Loyola University Chicago

*Nótaí do Mholtóirí* (Dublin: Comhaltas Ceoltóirí Éireann, 1967)

Ó Braonáin, Donaill, 'Bairéad, Riocard', in *Dictionary of Irish Biography* (web). https://www.dib.ie/biography/bairead-riocard-barrett-dick-a0324

Ó Ceallacháin, Mícheál, 'My Memory of a Fleadh', in *Bliain Iris Comhaltas Ceoltóirí Éireann 1968* (Dublin: Comhaltas Ceoltóirí Éireann, 1968), pp. 47–9

Ó Dubhthaigh, Séamus, *Survival, Irish Traditional Music and Song: a view* (Dublin: CCÉ, 2009)

Ó Gallchobhair, Éamonn, 'The Cultural Value of Festival and Feis', in Aloys Fleischmann (ed.), *Music in Ireland: A Symposium* (Dublin: Cork University Press, 1952), pp. 210–7

Ó Gráda, Cormac, 'The Irish Economy During the Century After Partition', *Economic History Review*, 2021, pp. 1–35

Ó hAllmháin, Mícheál, 'A Case for the Harp', *Treoir*, vol. 2, no. 3, 1971, pp. 11, 22.

Ó hAllmhuráin, Gearóid, 'Clare: heartland of the Irish concertina', *Papers of the International Concertina Association*, vol. 3, 2006, pp. 1–20

—, *Flowing Tides: history and memory in an Irish soundscape* (New York: Oxford University Press, 2016)

—, liner notes, *Paddy Murphy in Good Hands* (Celtic Crossings, 2007).

Ó Laoire, Lillis, 'National Identity and Local Ethnicity: the case of the Gaelic League's Oireachtas sean-nós singing competitions', in Brian A. Roberts and Andrea Rose (eds), *Sharing the Voices: the phenomenon of singing* (Newfoundland: Memorial University, 1999), pp. 160–9

—, *On a Rock in the Middle of the Ocean* (USA: Scarecrow Press, 2002)

—, *Re-imagining Tradition: Ó Riada's musical legacy in the 21st century* (Cork: Traditional Music Archive, UCC, 2009)

Ó Muirí, Eamon (Mountainy Man), 'The Fleadh', in Mackie Rooney (ed.), *Eamonn Murray: Irish troubadour and mountainy man* (Monaghan: Comhaltas, 2008), pp. 48–51

— 'The Fortunes of Traditional Music', *Clogher Record*, vol. 1, no. 1, 1953, pp. 27–31

Ó Murchú, Liam, liner notes, *Rambles of Kitty* (Ceoltas, 1967)

Ó Riada, Seán, *Our Musical Heritage* (Dublin: Dolmen Press, 1982)

Ó Tuathaigh, Gearóid, 'Cultural Visions and the New State: embedding and embalming', in Gabriel Doherty and Dermot Keogh (eds), *De Valera's Irelands* (Cork: Mercier Press, 2003), pp. 166–184

Ó Súilleabháin, Mícheál, *Ceol na nUasal: Seán Ó Riada and the search for a native Irish art music* (Cork: Traditional Music Archive, UCC, 2004)

O'Brien, John A., *The Vanishing Irish* (USA: McGraw Hill, 1953)

O'Carroll, Aileen, 'Eight Hours for What We Will', in Roo Honeychild and Kate Butler (eds), *Mesh Net* (Dublin: Preject Press, 2023), pp. 5–12

O'Connor, Barbara, *The Irish Dancing: cultural politics and identities, 1900–2000* (Cork: Cork University Press, 2013)

O'Connor, Joseph, 'The Cold Chain of Silence', *Capuchin Annual* (1956/7), pp. 95–108

O'Connor, Mick, 'Dublin Pipers Club', in Fintan Vallely (ed.), *CITM*, 2nd edition (Cork: Cork University Press, 2011), pp. 224–5

O'Donnell, Mary Louise, 'The Bengal Subscription: patriotism, patronage and the perpetuation of the Irish harp tradition in the early nineteenth century', in Sandra Joyce and Helen Lawlor (eds), *Harp Studies* (Dublin: Four Courts Press, 2016), pp. 75–89

O'Donnell, Peadar, 'De Valera's Speech on Emigration', *The Bell*, vol. XVIII, no. 7, 1951, pp. 53–8

O'Donnell, Ruan, 'The Irish Harp in Political History', in Sandra Joyce and Helen Lawlor (eds), *Harp Studies*, pp. 121–8

O'Flynn, John, *Music, the Moving Image and Ireland, 1897–2017* (New York: Routledge, 2022)

O'Gorman, Róisín, 'Addressing the Bones: parades, photography and pedagogy', *Performance Research*, vol. 23, nos 3 and 4, 2018, pp. 232–6

O'Hara, Aidan, *I'll Live Till I Die* (Leitrim: Drumlin Publications, 1997)

O'Herlihy, John, *Footsteps, Fiddles, Flagstones and Fun* (Killarney: Comhaltas, 2004)

O'Neill, Barry, 'Piping Contests at the Feis, 1897–1935', *The Seán Reid Society Journal*, vol. 1, 1999, pp. 1–8

O'Neill, Francis, *Irish Folk Music: a fascinating hobby with some account of allied subjects including O'Farrell's treatise on the Irish or union pipes and Touhey's hints for amateur pipers* (Chicago: The Regan Printing House, 1910)

—, *Irish Minstrels and Musicians: the story of Irish music* (Chicago: Regan Printing House, 1913)

O'Neill, P.S., 'Traditional Music, Song and Dance', *Landmark*, November 1961, p. 17

O'Shea, Helen, *The Making of Irish Traditional Music* (Cork: Cork University Press, 2008)

—, *No Better Boy, Listening to Paddy Canny* (Dublin: Lilliput Press, 2023)

Oakley, David L., 'Adjudication: a wide scope', *School Musician*, vol. 56, 1985, pp. 8–9

Odello, Denise, 'Ritualised Performance and Community Identity: a historical examination of drum corps competition in the United States', *International Journal of Community Music*, vol. 13, no. 1, 2020, pp. 65–79

Olsen, Laura, *Performing Russia: folk music and Russian identity* (New York: RoutledgeCurzon, 2007)

Owens, Gary, 'Nationalism without Words: symbolism and ritual behaviour in the repeal monster meetings of 1843–5', in James S. Donnelly Jr. and Kerby A. Miller (eds), *Irish Popular Culture 1650–1850* (Dublin: Irish Academic Press, 1999), pp. 252–59

Quinn, Bernadette, 'Symbols, Practices and Myth-making: cultural perspectives on the Wexford Festival Opera', *Tourism Geographies*, vol. 5, no. 3, 2003, pp. 329–49

Payne, Basil, 'Review', *Studies: An Irish Studies Quarterly Review*, vol. 57, no. 226, 1968, pp. 209–12

Peillon, Michel, 'Irish Festivities in Comparative Perspective', *The Maynooth Review*, vol. 6, no. 2, 1982, pp. 39–59

Petrus, Stephen and Ronald D. Cohen, *Folk City: New York and the American Folk Music Revival* (New York: Oxford University Press, 2015)

Picard, David M., and Mike Robinson (eds), *Festivals, Tourism and Social Change, Remaking Worlds* (Clevedon: Channel View Publications, 2006)

Pratschke, Mairéad B., 'A Look at Irish-Ireland: Gael Linn's *Amharc Éireann* films, 1956–64', *New Hibernia Review*, vol. 9, no. 3, pp. 17–38

Rappaport, Roy A., 'Ritual', in Richard Bauman (ed.), *Folklore, Cultural Performances and Popular Entertainments* (New York: Oxford University Press, 1992), pp. 249–60

Rapuano, Deborah, 'Working at Fun, Conceptualizing Leisurework', *Current Sociology* 5/57 (2009), pp. 617–36

*Report of the Working Party on Coloured People Seeking Employment in Great Britain*, December 1953, NA, PRO, DO 35/5216

Reynolds, Willie, *Memories of a Music Maker* (Dublin: Comhaltas Ceoltóirí Éireann, 1990)

Ricoeur, Paul, *Time and Narrative*, trans. Kathleen Blamey and David Pellauer (Chicago: University of Chicago Press, 1988)

Rooney, Mackie (ed.), *Eamonn Murray: Monaghan troubadour and mountainy man* (Dublin: Comhaltas, 2008)

Rooney, Ray, *The Spirit of the Reels: the story of the famous Liverpool Céilí Band* (Liverpool: RayRoo Press, 2019)

Rowsome, Leo, 'The Origin of Our Ceilidhe Bands', *Bliain Iris Comhaltas Ceoltóirí Éireann* (Dublin: Comhaltas, 1968), 57–9

*Rural Ireland* (Tipperary: Muintir na Tíre, 1968)

Sadler, A.W., 'The Form and Meaning of the Festival', *Asian Folklore Studies*, vol. 28, no. 1, 1969, pp. 1–16

Scahill, Adrian, 'The Album in Irish Folk and Traditional Music, ca. 1955–70', *Éire-Ireland*, vol. 54, nos 1 and 2, 2019, pp. 17–45

Schaefer, John P.R., 'Frontstage Backstage: participatory music and the festive sacred in Essaouira, Morocco', *Western Folklore*, vol. 76, no. 1, 2017, pp. 69–99

Scholes, Peroy A., 'The Competition Festival', *The Observer*, 11 March 1923

Sealy, Douglas, 'The Sound of a Wound: introduction to the poetry of John Montague from 1959 to 1988', *Irish University Review*, vol. 10, no. 1, 1988, pp. 8–26

Seán Shéamais, 'An mBeidh tú ar an bhFleadh?', *Irish Press*, 12 May 1956

Shanagher, Sean, 'A Dancing Agency: jazz, modern and ballroom dancers in Ireland between 1940 and 1960', vol. 24, no. 2, *Irish Journal of Sociology*, pp. 175–99

Shields, Hugh, *Narrative Singing in Ireland, Lays, Ballads, Come-All-Ye's and Other Songs* (Dublin: Irish Academic Press, 1993)

Silverman, Marylin, 'An Urban Place in Rural Ireland: an historical ethnography of domination, 1849–1989', in Chris Curtin, Hastings Donnan and Thomas M. Wilson (eds), *Irish Urban Cultures* (Belfast: Institute of Irish Studies, 1993), pp. 203–25

Slominski, Tes, *Trad Nation: gender, sexuality and race in Irish traditional music* (Connecticut: Wesleyan University Press, 2020)

Spottswood, Richard K., *Ethnic Music on Records Vol. 5* (Illinois: University of Illinois Press, 1990)

Stapleton, E., 'From Donnybrook to Mullingar', *Ceol*, vol. 1, no. 2, 1963, pp. 3–5

Stoeltje, Beverly, 'Festival', in Richard Bauman (ed.), *Folklore, Cultural Performances and Popular Entertainments* (New York: Oxford University Press, 1992), pp. 261–71

Sutton, Alexander C., 'The Composition of Success: competition and the creative self in contemporary art music', *Qualitative Sociology*, vol. 43, 2020, pp. 480–513

Tansey, Séamus, *The Bardic Apostles of Innisfree* (Belfast: Tanbar, 1999)

Taylor, Barry, 'Junior Crehan of Ballymakea Beg', *Musical Traditions*, vol. 10, 1992, pp. 28–36

—, *Music in a Breeze of Wind: traditional music in West Clare, 1870–1970* (Kilrush: Danganella Press, 2013)

'The Rise of Comhaltas', *Treoir*, vols 2 & 3, 1971, p. 8

Titon, Jeff Todd, 'Reconstructing the Blues: reflections on the 1960s blues revival', in Neil V. Rosenberg (ed.), *Transforming Tradition: folk music revivals examined* (Chicago: University of Chicago Press, 1993), pp. 220–40

Tobin, Fergal, *The Best of Decades: Ireland in the 1960s* (Dublin: Gill & Macmillan, 1984)

Tobin, Tom, 'The Inside Story, the Flop that Needn't Have Been', *Dungarvan Observer*, 15 June 1957

—, 'National Festival "Flopped" in Dungarvan, Thirty Thousand Short', *Dungarvan Observer*, 15 June 1957

Toelken, Barre, 'Traditional Fiddling in Idaho', *Western Folklore*, vol. 4, no. 24, 1965, pp. 259–62

Tovey, Hilary and Perry Share, *A Sociology of Ireland* (Dublin: Gill & Macmillan, 2003)

Tunney, Paddy, 'Comhaltas Ceoltóirí Éireann in Donegal', in *Comhaltas Ceoltóirí Éireann in Donegal* (Dublin: Comhaltas, 1991), pp. 3–10

Turino, Thomas, 'Nationalism and Latin American Music: selected case studies and theoretical considerations', *Latin American Music Review*, vol. 2, no. 24, 2003, pp. 169–209

Turner, Bryan S., 'Introduction–Bodily Performance: on aura and reproducibility', *Body Society*, vol. 4, no. 11, 2005, pp. 1–17

Turner, Victor (ed.), *Celebration: studies in festivity and ritual* (Washington: Smithsonian Press, 1982)

Vallely, Fintan, 'Authenticity to Classicisation: the course of revival in Irish traditional music', *The Irish Review*, no. 33, 2005, pp. 51–69

—, 'Bands–céilí', in Vallely (ed.), *CITM* (Cork: Cork University Press, 2011), pp. 45–9

—, 'Comhaltas Ceoltóirí Éireann', in Vallely (ed.), *CITM* (Cork: Cork University Press, 2011), pp. 145–9

—, 'Polka', in Vallely (ed.), *CITM* (Cork: Cork University Press, 2011), p. 548

—, and Charlie Piggot, *Blooming Meadows: the world of Irish traditional musicians* (Dublin: Townhouse, 1998)

Von Herder, Johann, *Stimmen der Voelker in Ihren Liedern* (1789)

Walkowitz, Daniel J., 'The Cultural Turn and a New Social History: folk dance and the renovation of class in social history', *Journal of Social History*, vol. 39, no. 3, pp. 781–802

Wallace, Anthony F.C., 'Revitalization Movements', *American Anthropologist*, vol. 58, no. 2, 1956, pp. 264–81

Walsh, Brendan M., 'Economic Growth and Development, 1945–70', in Joseph J. Lee (ed.), *Ireland 1945–1970* (Dublin: Gill & Macmillan, 1979), pp. 27–37

Waterman, Stanley, 'Place, Culture and Identity: summer music in Upper Galilee', *Transactions of the Institute of British Geographers*, vol. 23, no. 2, 1998, pp. 253–72

Whelan, Bernadette, *Ireland and the Marshall Plan, 1947–57* (Dublin: Four Courts Press, 2000)

Whelan, Christopher (ed.), *Values and Social Change in Ireland* (Dublin: Gill & Macmillan, 1994)

Whisnant, David E., 'Festivals, Folk Music', in Bill Malone and Charles Reagan Wilson (eds), *The New Encyclopedia of Southern Culture, Volume 12 Music* (Chapel Hill: University of North Carolina Press, 2009), pp. 64–9

Wilgus, D.K., 'Revival and Traditional', *The Journal of American Folklore,* vol. 320, no. 81, 1968, pp. 173–9

Wilkinson, Desi, 'Flute', in Fintan Vallely (ed.), *CITM* (Cork: Cork University Press, 2011)

Williams, Sean, *Focus: Irish traditional music* (New York: Routledge, 2020, 2nd edition)

Wright, Myles, *The Dublin Region: advisory regional plan and final report* (Dublin: Stationary Office, 1967), http://ireland2050.ie/past/transport/

Yeats, W.B., *WB Yeats Selected Poetry* (London: Macmillan, 1962)

Young, Robert, 'The Pipers' Competition at the Feis Ceoil', *Ulster Journal of Archaeology,* vols 3 and 4, 1897, pp. 239–40

# Index

Note: Page locators in **bold** refer to photographs and tables.

accommodation, 96–98
accordion (box), the, 32, 52–53, 75, 143
  (*see also* button accordion, the)
adjudicators and judging, 130–131, 132–141, 142, 147, 148, 150–154, 167
  guidelines and criteria for, 149–150, 153–158, 157–159
  and singing adjudicators, 159–165
  and subjectivity, 133–135, 136
advance registration for competition entrants, 94–95
advertising and branding, 38–39
age division templates, 48, 53, 54
Aherne, Richard, 177
All Britain Fleadh, the, 79–80
*All Ireland Champions Violin, Meet Paddy Canny & P.J. Hayes* (record), 119
Allen, R. Raymond, 18
Ambulance Corps, the, 44
American old-time fiddling, 146
*Amharc Éireann*, 93, 168
*Anglo-Celt* (newspaper), 43, 46, 172
Anglo-Irish Free Trade Agreement (1965), the, 10
appeals procedures, 138–139
arbiting of a discernible Fleadh music style, the, 131, 134–135
  (*see also* range of winning sounds and musical styles, the)
archival research, 3–4
archive recordings, 146
*Arena* (magazine), 128
Athlone (1953), 36, 47, 52, 58, 64, 83, 130, 160, 167
Athlone B Céilí Band, the, 35
attendance numbers and patronage, 94, 98–99, 101, 179, 181, 182, 183, 184, 185, 192–193
Aughrim Slopes Céilí Band, the, 63–64, 65, 82

bagpipes, the *see* war pipes (bagpipes), the
Báiréad, Riocard, 164
*Ballads of Irish Chivalry*, 162
Ballinakill Céilí Band, the, 114
Ballinamere Céilí Band, the, 35, 63
ballroom dances, the, 11
Band of the Ceard Scoil, Cappawhite, Co. Tipperary, **42**
bardic festivals, 25–26
Barron, Pat, 60
Bealle, John, 158–159, 166
Bean de Brún, Bríd, 134
Bean Uí Shé, Lena, 96
Beirne, Leo, 62
Belafonte, Harry
  'Jamaican Farewell, Kingston Town' (song), 168
Belfast Harp Festival (1792), the, 22, 92
Bellaghy Green Cross Céilí Band, the, 62–63
Blau, Judith, 131
Blaustein, Richard, 130, 136, 142, 145
Bobby Casey medal, the, **51**
Böll, Heinrich, 8
Boyle (1960), 79, 121–122, 139, 172, 176–177, 178
Boyle (1966), 149, 188, 190
Breathnach, Breandán, 14, 150, 153, 163
Breathnach, Pádraig
  *Ár gCeol Féinig*, 14
Breffni Céilí Band, the, 63, 83
Brock, Paul, 53
Broderick, Peter, 54
Broderick, Vincent, 53, 57, 105, 112, 172–173
Brody, Bríd, 87, 88
Brophy, Mick, 56
Brophy, Paddy, 56, 133
Brophy, Tom, 56
Brophy Brothers Céilí Band, the, 56
Browne, Garech, 128, 177
Burke, Joe, 32, 53, 69, 143, 149

Burke, John, 75
Burke Sheridan, Margaret, 177
button accordion, the, 15, 32, 143, **157**, 158
  (*see also* accordion (box), the)
Byrne, Eddie, 163

Canny, Paddy, 51, 56, 106, 117, 119, 152, 167
*Capuchin Annual,* the, 7
car and bus hire, 123–124
Carolan, James, 33
cartographical origins of competitors, 57
Carty, Michael, 122
Casey, Bobby, 51–52
Cashel (1969), 135, 190
Castle Céilí Band, the, 124
Catholic Association, the, 118
Cavan (1954), 43–44, 47, 53, 54, 55, 56, 57, 67, 73, 94, 123, 136, 137, 150, 152, 155, 160, 172
Cawley, Jessica, 171
céilí bands, 34–35, 56, 62–65, 72, 77–79, 82–84, 86, 139, 142–143, 170, 195
céilithe and dancing, 83–88
celebrity concerts, 66–67, 68
Chnoic, Padraic an, 138
CIE, 123
Cill na Manach céilí band, the, 82
Claddagh Records, 128
Claisceadal, An, 29, 160
Clancy, Fr, 173
Clancy, Willie, 34, 50, 106, 116, 125, 188
Clancy Brothers, the, 113
  *Rising of the Moon, The* (album), 165
Clare by-election (1828), the, 118
Clareman's Club, Bridge St, Dublin, 87
Clerkin, Monica, 66
Clinch, Maureen, 90
Clones (1964), 97, 126, 138, 162, 163, 165, 178, 184, 185
Clones (1968), 189–190
closed competitions, 49–50, 52, 55
codes of competition, 130, 131–133
Coen, Tommy, **177**
Coleman, Billy, 52
Coleman, Brian, 66
Coleman, Michael, 144–145
Collins, Dan, 50
Collins, Kieran, 105, 114
Collins, Tim, 145
'come-all-ye' narrative song, the, 108, 112, 113, 126
  (*see also* McMahon, Robbie)
Comerford, Liam, 89, 99

Comhaltas Ceoltóirí Éireann, 1, 2, 16, 17, 18, 19, 38, 39, 41, 46, 47, 48, 55, 73, 79, 84, 92, 100, 126, 138, 143, 166, 185, 188, 191
  and administrative growth of, 55–56, 58, 69, 71, 80, 81, 89, 112–113, 149, 175
  and authority, 3
  Craobh and Phiarsaigh (Dublin branch), 186
  *Nótaí do Mholtóirí,* 131, 154, 155, 159, 161, 162
  'Rules for Fleadhanna Ceoil,' 148, 151, 162
Comhaltas Fleadh (US), the, 75
comic songmaking, 110, 112, 125
commercial and trade interests, 98–99, 100
competitions and increasing entries, 55, 69, 72, 75–76, 80, 81–82, 101, 110, 141–142, 149
  and advance registration, 94–95
  and participation levels, 30, 48–49, 52, 54, 56, 76, 93
concertina, the, 59–61, 117, 143
Concubhar, 184–185, 190
*Connacht Tribune* (newspaper), 11, 54, 69
Connell, John, 18
Connolly, Séamus, 51, 133, 144–147, 148
Connors, Jimmy, 61
Conway, Sylvestor, 182
Cooley, Joe, 32, 52–53, 65
costumry directives, 15
  and young attendees with beards and jeans, 186
Cotter, Geraldine, 80–81
County Clare and reputation for traditional music, 110, 115, 116, 119, 142
county fleadhanna, 71, 74, 82, 115, 119, 138, 149, 188
  Donegal, 74–75
  Ennis (1962), 179, 180
  Kilrush (1963), 42
  Miltown Malbay (1957), 74, 124
  Scariff (1964), 144
  Scariff (1965), 168
Cox, Denis, 66, 67
CPU (Cumann na bPíobairí Uilleann), 21, 23, 27, 28, 30, 31, 34, 35, 39, 41, 50, 66, 87, 111, 137
Cranitch, Matt, 135
Crehan, Junior, 60, 62, 77
Crinion, Very Rev. E.A., 24
Crotty, Mrs. (Elizabeth), 106, **107**, 116, 125
Crowe, Sheila, 190
cultural nationalism, 12–13
Cumann Ceoltóirí Éireann, 36

# Index

Currach Day, Salthill, 69
Curran, Catherine, 10
Curtis, P.J., 13

Danagher, Kevin, 47
dance performance, 62
Davis, Thomas
    'West's Awake, The' (poem), 64
de Brún, Séamus, 154
de Valera, Eamon, 8
decline of Irish traditional music in the early twentieth century, the, 11–13
Delahunty, Mike, 113
Dempsey, Thomas P., 80, 180, 184, 186
Derrane, Joe, 32
Derry and Antrim Fiddlers Association, the, 101
Devanney, Andrew D., 10
Devas, Nicolette, 13
Donncha, Seán Ac, 177
Droney, Chris, 61, 106, 117
Dublin Pipers Club, the, 15, 21
Dublin Records, 119
duet competitions, 56, 57
duet recordings, 34
Dungarvan (1957), 31, 47, 68, 72, 89–90, 93, 94, 96, 97–101, 107, **107**, 108, 116, 124, **137**, 145, **177**
*Dungarvan Leader* (newspaper), 97–98
*Dungarvan Observer* (newspaper), 99, 100
Dunne, P., 33

Easter 1916 Rising, the, 128
economic and social change in the 1960s, 10–11, 181, 191
Eisteddfod, the, 17
emigration, 8–9, 10, 13, 20, 62, 65, 115
    and returning for the Fleadh, 175–176, 181, 192
Ennis (1956), 44, 47, 72, 76, 80–82, 83, 85–88, 95, 96, 104, 112, 115, 145, 172, 175
Ennis, Seamus, 21
Enniscorthy (1967), 43, 45, 184
ensemble competitions, 34, 56–57, 62
European Economic Community, the, 10
*Evening Herald* (newspaper), 85, 147
extant melodies and song lyrics, 108

Fahy, Joe, 89
Fahy, Matty, 89
Falassi, Alessandro, 110
Fanning, Ronan, 9

Farrell, Gertie, 43
Farrell, Liam, 75
Farrell, Vera, 43
Fegan, Henry, 16
Feis Athar Maitiú, 15, 32, 58
Feis Ceoil, the, 32
    Feis Ceoil (1900), 14
Feis Ceoil Association, the, 14, 15
Feis Lár na hÉireann, Mullingar, 1, 14, 22, 23, 24–25, 28, 29, 30, 31, 32, 35, 49, 54, 197
Feis Misneach, 16
Feis Shligigh, the, 32
feiseanna (festival competitions), 14–15
Ferriter, Diarmaid, 9
festivals and cultural identity, 1, 18, 46, 68, 69–72
fiddle and violin usage, 32
fiddle competitions, 51–52, 75, 136, **137**, 139, 144, 145, 146–148, 150, 158, 174–175
Fiddler's Club, Church St, Dublin, 87
fieldwork research, 4, 5, 123, 128
finale concerts, 29, 40, 66, 68, 189
*fíor céilí* (true céilí), 84, 85, 86, 87, 88
*First Programme for Economic Expansion* (policy document), 9–10
Fitzpatrick Dean, Joan, 46
flageolet (tin whistle), the, 33–34
*Fleá Ceoil* (documentary), 188
Fleadh Cheoil na hÉireann, 1, 2, 4, 68, 110, 192, 195–197
    and the 'bed bureau,' 96–97
    and county boards, 73, 74
    and cultural tourism, 178–179, 192
    and Dungarvan and Ennis, 72
    and early years, 27, 36–48, 69
    and experience of the event, 102–104, 111–112, 121–123
    and founding in 1951, 6, 11, 20, 21–22, 24–27, 28–34, 35–36, 91
    and long-term impact, 195–197
    reflected in song and poetry, 103–109, 110, 111–117, 120–121, 126–129
    as the standard bearer for traditional music, 131
    (*see also* venues)
Fleadh Nua, the, 194
Fleming, Rachel, 146, 150
flute, the, 53–54
folk music competitions in the Soviet Union, 141
folk music revival, the, 18–19, 111, 113, 128, 146, 171, 178, 181, 191

food and drink surpluses, 99
foreign notes in melodies, 155–156, 163–164
Fox, Mary B., 43, 85
Franciscan abbey, Ennis, 44, 45
*Free Press*, 173–174

GAA, the, 12, 22, 27, 31, 73
Gael Linn, 93
Gaelic aristocracy and the harp, the, 31, 91
Gaelic League, the, 12, 22, 24, 25, 28, 29, 35, 47, 84, 86
    feiseanna, 15–16, 17
Gallagher, Bridie, 164
Galligan, Dr Brian, 47, 75, 85, 105, 112–113
*Galway Observer* (newspaper), 69
Gannon, Seán, 22, 133
Gardiner, John Joe, 22, 133, 136
Garvey, Philomena, 93
Gebruers, Staf, 93
Gentex (General Textiles) Athlone, 35, 57
Gentex Céilí Band, the, 64
Geraghty, Des, 83
Gibson, Chris, 18
Gilrane, Thomas, 9
Goertzen, Chris, 130, 136, 146, 150, 156
Gorey (1962), 97, 138, 143, 168, **174**, 179
Gorman, Michael, 171
Greenall, Billy, 41
Guinness sponsorship, 93
Gusfield, Joseph P., 109
Guss, David M., 2

Hall, Reg, 170
'Hare was in the Corn, The' (jig), 52
harp, the, 90–94, 137
    and the Gaelic aristocracy, 31, 91
harp festivals, 26
    Belfast Harp Festival (1792), 22, 92
harpers, 72
Harrington, Kathleen, 22, 34, 133, 137
Harwood, C.J., 28, 56–57
    'Irish Music in Irish Life' (lecture), 38–39
Hayes, Paddy, 73
Hayes, P.J., 56, 119
Healy, John, 19, 174–175, 189
Herron, Patsy, 123–124, 173
Hewsen, J., 85
Hitchner, Earle, 144
Hodge, Kitty, 177
Hogan, Connie, 61
Holland, J.P., 44, 45
Hope, Willie, 35

Horan, Peter, 13
house dances, 13, 132

ICA (Irish Countrywomen's Association), the, 44, 190–191
IFM (Irish Federation of Musicians), the, 113
indigenous musical instruments at feiseanna, 15
international interest, 57–58
*Irish Catholic*, the (newspaper), 182, 183
*Irish Examiner* (newspaper), 81
*Irish Farmers Journal*, the, 180
Irish harping tradition, the, 31
*Irish Independent* (newspaper), 44, 55, 113, 182
Irish language, the, 16, 17, 52, 55
Irish post-war economy, the, 7–8, 9–10, 11
*Irish Press*, the (newspaper), 69, 90, 97, 147, 179
Irish Recording Company, the, 52
*Irish Times, The* (newspaper), 96
Irish traditional dance competitions, 16
Irish traditional music at the end of the 1960s, 2–3
*Irish Weekly Glasgow Edition* (newspaper), 26

Joe, Din, 67
Jordan, P.T., 33–34

Keane, Andy, 105
Keane, Chris, 56
Keane, Eamon, 67
Keane, Rita, 188
Keane, Sarah, 188
Kearney, Daithí, 132
Keegan, Joe, 177
Keegan, Kevin, 156
Keegan, Niall, 159
Keenan, Thomas P., 164
Kelleher, Humphrey, 89, 90, 93, 139
Kelly, Kieran, 57, 156
Kelly, Paddy (Donegal), 35
Kelly, Paddy (Tyrone), 32
Keogh, Dermot, 9
Kerr, Bobby, 96
Kilfenora Céilí Band, the, 35, 59, 63, 64, 65, 77–78, 81, 82, 84, 85, 86, 116, 142–143
    *Fabulous Kilfenora Céilí Band, The* (record), 119
Killoran, Paddy, 119, 146
Kincora Céilí Band, the, 63, 65
Klusen, Ernst, 146
Knights of Malta, the, 44
Kyne, Rev. Dr., 24

# Index

Lafferty, Bridie, 119
Laichtín Naofa céilí band, 64, 77, 78
    *Come to an Irish Dance Party* (record), 119
Lankford, Cormac, 180
Larson Skye, Cathy, 50, 132, 134
Leary, Joe, 106
lecture presentations, 46–48, 90
Lee, Gearóid, 177
Lee, Joseph J., 9
Leitrim Céilí Band, the, 35, 63, 143
Lemass, Seán, 10
*Limerick Leader* (newspaper), 81
Linnane, Kitty, 59, 81
Lisdoughan Piping Club, 23
Listowel (1970), 191
Liverpool Céilí Band, the, 35, 41, 65, 121–122, 143, 176
*Living With Lynch* (radio series), 67
Livingston, Tamara, 18
local and national identities, 40, 41
London pubs and ensemble sessions, 171
Longford (1958), 19, 46, 77, 79, 98, 125, 133, 149, 176
Longford Chamber of Commerce, the, 98
Loughnane, Dr Bill, 177
Loughrea (1955), 44, 47, 53, 55, 59, 61, 68, 69, 81, 83, 84–85, 95, 156
Lynch, Jerry, 65, 84, 143
Lynch, Joe, 67

Mac Connaic, Art, 30, 35, 37
Mac Mathúna, Ciarán, 68, 106, 107, **107**, 114, 120, 144, 145, 162
Mac Mathúna, Séamus, 78
Mac Néill, Seán, 17
MacMahon, Bryan, 44, 45–46
Magee, Hubert, 33, 34
Magee, Peggy, 44
Maguire, Leo, 29
    'Whistling Gypsy, The' (song), 67
Maguire, Patrick, 139
Maguire, Seán, 66, 133
Makem, Tommy, 113
Malachy Sweeney céilí band, the, 145
Malmer, Lennart, 168
Marcus, Louis, 188
Marshall Aid, 7
*Massachusetts Review, The* (journal), 128
Maunsell, Paddy, 8, 19, 35, 47, 88, 100
Mayglass Céilí Band, the, 64
McAloon, Seán, 50, 51
McAuliffe, Jack, 165
McBride, Neil, 163
McCabe, Martin, 126
McCabe, Maureen, 52
McCann, Frank, 133
McCann, Kevin, 47, 89
McCarthy, Michael, 35
McCarvill, Johnny, 39
McCormack, Count John, 29
McCreesh, Josephine, 138–139
McElvanney, Paddy, 22, 39
McGlinchey, Brendan, 51, 133, 134, 144, 145–148
McGrath, Fr John, 90
McGuinness, Patrick, 52
McKean, Thomas, 104
McKenna, John, 52
McMahon, Bryan, 178
McMahon, Dolly, 177
McMahon, Johnny, 105, 113
McMahon, Robbie, 104, 107–108, 110, 120, 125–126, 167
    'Fleadh Down in Ennis, The' (ballad), 52, 89, 103–107, 108–109, 110, 111–117, 120–121, 129
McMaster, Anew, 45
McNamara, Joe, 56
McNamara, P.J., 85
McNamara, Sean, 13
McNeill, A., 164
McPeake, Francie, 133
McTigue, Frank, 124
Meade, Tony, 191
Meath-Kerry All Ireland Football Final (1954), the, 44
mediating technologies and cultural revival, 118–120
Meehan, Paddy, 54–55
Michallowicz, Jerry, 109
*Midland Herald* (newspaper), 25, 31
miscellaneous instruments competition, the, 58–61, 75
Moloney, Eddie, 105, 114, **177**
*Monaghan Argus* (newspaper), 49
Monaghan town (1952), 38, 39–40, 41, 47, 49, **51**, 53, 54–55, 56, 62, 66, 83, 91, 95, 149, 172
Monks, Bob, 188
Montague, John, 128
    *Patriotic Suite* (collection), 128
    'Siege of Mullingar, The' (poem), 127–128, 129, 181
Moore, Christy
    *Prosperous* (album), 165
Moore, Thomas, 91, 161

Morrisson, James, 146
Moyvore Piping Club, 23
Muintir na Tíre
    *Rural Ireland* (newsletter), 183
Mulcahy, F., 171–172
Mulcaire, Angela, 112
Mulcaire, Jack, 125
Mulhaire, Brendan, 53
Mulhaire, Martin, 119, 156
Mulkere, Angela, 68
Mullaly, Philip, 24, 25, 27, 29, 30, 32
Mullingar (1951), 21–31, 33–37, 38, 39, 47–50, 54–56, 62, 64, 91–92
Mullingar (1963), 127, 169, 181–182, 183, 195
Mullingar (2022), 194
Mullingar Brass and Reed Band, the, 34
Mulqueen, Ann, 16, 133, 134, 165
Mulvaney, James, 176–177
*Munster Express,* the (newspaper), 90, 99
Murphy, Delia, 66–67, 161
Murphy, Denis, 105, 114, 135
Murphy, John A., 10
Murphy, Michael, 68
Murphy, Paddy, 59, 60–61, 117
Murray, Eamonn *see* Ó Muirí, Eamon
music performers and expertise in judging, 153, 154–155, 162
music revivals and the past, 19–20

Na Píobairí Uilleann, 3
Nath, Rolf Dietrich, 58
Nea, Billie, 22
*Nenagh Guardian* (newspaper), 147
New York Feis, 17
Ní Chonghaile, Deirdre, 118
Ní Curtain, Sighle, 66, 67, 92, 93, 137
Ní Sheaghe, Máire, 29, 92
Northern Ireland economy, the, 8
*Northern Standard, The* (newspaper), 38, 39, 41, 47, 49, 52
Norwegian fiddling, 150

Ó Broin, Proinsias, 95
Ó Canainn, Tomás, 135–136, 140, 176
Ó Ceallacháin, Mícheál, 121–123, 139, 186, 190
Ó Domhnaill, Manus, 178
Ó Donnachadha, L., 59
Ó Dubhthaigh, Séamus, 73, 74, 160
Ó Gallchobhair, Eamonn, 14
Ó hAllmhuráin, Gearóid, 72, 118
Ó Laoghaire, Colm, 168
Ó Lubhlaí, Donald, 85

Ó Muineacháin, Áodán, 33
Ó Muineacháin, Éamon, 24, 25, 35–36
Ó Muirí, Eamon (Eamonn Murray), 35, 37, 39, 47, 136, 140, 187
Ó Murchú, Labhras, 179–180
Ó Murchú, Liam, 120, 196–197
Ó Nualláin, Donal, 162–163
Ó Riada, Seán, 3, 34, 128, 135
Ó Súilleabháin, Mícheál, 5
Ó Tuama, Seán Óg, 29, 47, 63
Oakley, David, 131
O'Boyle, Seán, 47
O'Brien, Dinny, 73
O'Brien, John, 9
O'Brien, Paddy, 32, 52, 65, 73, 106, 115, 143
O'Brien, Vincent, 29
O'Connell, Daniel, 81, 106, 117–118
O'Connor, Frank, 127, 128
O'Connor, Joseph, 12, 160
O'Connor, P., 33
O'Connor, Pat, 60
O'Devlin, Fr Eamonn, 47
O'Donnell, Brian, 75
O'Donoghue, Seán, 24
O'Dowd, Joe, 150
O'Dowd, Sheila, 13, 134–135, 140–141, 187
O'Faolain, Sean, 127, 128
O'Farrell, Very Rev. Brother, 24
O'Gorman, Eamonn, 22
O'Gorman, T.A., 95
O'Keefe, Philomena, 93
O'Leary, Johnny, 13
O'Loughlin, Peadar, 16, 117, 119, 123, 124, 144, 150, 152, 166–167
Olsen, Laura, 141
O'Malley, Luke, 170
O'Neill, Barry, 15, 16
O'Neill, James, 119
O'Neill, John, 119
O'Neill, Patrick
    'All Ireland Fleadh, The' (poem), 126, 129
open competitions, 30–34, 49, 50, 51, 55
oral adjudication, 141, 151, 163
O'Reilly, Margaret, 44, 105, 112
O'Shea, Raymond, 135
outdoor sessions, 173–174, **174**, 176, 187–190
overseas entrants, 79

Paddy Con's (New Hall), Ennis, 81, 86–87
parades and pageants, 40–46, 47, 48, 90
    'Breaking of Eire's Chains of Bondage,' 90
    *Pageant of the Fenian Rising,* the, 43, 45

# Index

*Pageant of the Flag*, 45, 46
*Pageant of the Four Green Fields*, the, 44
Pat Brophy and Sons Céilí Band, the, 56
Payne, Basil, 128
Pearse, Pádraic, 44
Peillon, Michel, 180
Philbin, Marie, 54
piano, the, 54, 90
Picard, David M., 20, 170
Pickering, Johnny, 52, 101, **107**
Pipers Club, Mullingar, the, 6, 31, 32
pipes, 25
   (*see also* uilleann pipes, the; war pipes (bagpipes), the)
Planxty, 165
polka, the, 155–156
*Porter Och Pipa* (film), 168
Potts, John, 21
press coverage, 130, 195
   (*see also newspapers*)
press releases, 40
Preston, Mike, 119
Primrose Céilí Band, the, 122
provincial qualifiers for competitions, 50, 76–78, 79–80, 146–147
Public Dance Halls Act (1935), the, 12
public disorder, 127, 179–182, 183, 185, 186–187, 190–191
Purcell, Noel, 29

radio broadcasts, 119–120
Radio Éireann Repertory Company, the, 67
range of winning sounds and musical styles, the, 141–143, 144–146
   (*see also* arbiting of a discernible Fleadh music style, the)
Rappaport, Roy A., 78, 152
Rapuano, Deborah, 173
RÉ (Radio Éireann), 16–17, 39, 62, 67, 68, 107, 114, 119, 120, 162
Rebellion of 1798, the, 45, 164
recalls in competitions, 50–51
recording technology, 118–119
recordings of traditional music, 146
Red Cross, the, 44
Redmond, Br, 24, 35
Reid, Seán, 74, 81, 89, 107, 119, 120, 121, 123, 125–126, 138, 140, 142, 171–172, 181, 184
Reynolds, Willie, 16, 22–24, 34, 50, 51, 66, 137
Ricoeur, Paul, 26
'Rip the Calico' (tune), 124
Robinson, Mike, 20, 170

Rooney, Mackie, 172
Rooney, William, 164
Ross, George, 32
Rowsome, Helena, 155
Rowsome, Leo, 16–17, 22, 29, 32?, 34, 35, 66, 105, 111, 137
Rowsome, Liam, 52, 133–134
Rowsome, Tom, 36
Rowsome, William, 21, 22, 35
RTÉ, 195
   (*see also* RÉ (Radio Éireann))
rules, 58, 76, 77, 78–79, 135, 142, 148–151, 152, 156, 159, 162, 185
   of convention for ensemble bands, 78–79, 82
   for ensemble bands, 78–79, 82
   (*see also* adjudicators and judging)
rural associations with traditional music, 111
Ryan, Joe, 56
Ryan, Johnny, 105
Ryan, Peig, 133, 173, 176
   'She Lived Beside the Anner' (song), 133
Ryan, Seán, 165

Scahill, Adrian, 111
Scholes, Peroy A., 27
Scoil Éigse, 195
Scoil Samhraidh Willie Clancy, 3, 5
Seery, Jim, 34, 35, 133, 137
Seery, Seán, 66, 111, 133, 137
session and ensemble music making, the, 169–177, **174,** 187–190, 191
set dancing, 84–86, 87–88
Shanagher, Sean, 12
Shéamais, Seán, 60, 176
Sherlock, Roger, 13
Shields, Hugh, 108
showbands and sit-down dance bands, the, 113
singing adjudicating, 159–165
singing competition categories, 57
Sligo (1957), 45
Sligo Feis, the, 14
Smith, Raymond, 187
solo instrumental competitions, 32–33, 34, 48, 53, 58–59, 61, 136, **137,** 143
songs and ballads
   'Ballad of Kevin Barry, The,' 46
   'Ballad of Seán Treacy, the,' 162–163
   'Ballyneety's Walls,' 162
   'Blackbird of Avondale, The,' 164
   'Cliffs of Dooneen, The,' 165

songs and ballads (continued)
  'Eoghan Chóir,' 164
  'Men of the West, The,' 164
  'Mother's Love's a Blessing, A,' 164
  'Noreen Bawn,' 163–164
  'Rocks of Bawn, The,' 163, 165
  'Sligo Maid, The,' 177
  'Streams of Bunclody, The,' 163
  'Where the Mulcair River Flows,' 163
St. Louis' National School Choir, 66
St. Macarton's Brass and Reed Band, 41
St. Patrick's Dancing Club, Dundalk, 66
St. Senan, 42
Stapleton, Bill, 52
Stapleton, E., 169, 185, 192–193
state grants, 2
stewarding, 137–138
Stoeltje, Beverly, 1
Stoltenberg, Wolf and Frau, 178
subjectivity in performance adjudication, 133–135, 136
Súgach, Mangaire, 86
*Sunday Express Reporter* (newspaper), 21
Sweeney, Malachy, 85, 101
Swinford (1961), 51, 74, **75**, 133, 144, 145, 146–147, 148
symmetry and the festive experience, 109, 116

*Take the Floor* (radio show), 67
Talty, Martin, 56, 81, 106, 119
Terry, Sir Richard, 14
TG4, 195
'Thatcher's Mallet, The' (reel), 54
Thurles (1959), **42,** 73–74, 96–97, 101
Thurles (1965), 186–187, 190
tin whistle, the, 54
*Tipperary Star,* the (newspaper), 96–97, 190
Tobin, Jack, 89
Tobin, Tom, 99, 100, 101
tOireachtas, an, 17–18, 34
*tomhas port* (tune guess) competition, the, 58
Tóstal, An, 95–96
tourism and state promotion, 95–96
transport and journey narratives, 123–126
Treacy, Dan, 136
Treacy, Paddy, 53
trios, 56
Troubles, the, 194

Tubridy, Michael, 13, 87, 124, 152
Tulla Céilí Band, the, 56, 63, 64–65, 77–78, 81, 82, 115, 139, 142
  *Echoes of Erin* (record), 119
Tunney, Paddy, 57, 74–75, 92
Turner, Victor, 27, 129, 183

Uí Mhuineacháin, Cáit, 24, 25, 35–36, 181, 183–184
uilleann pipes, the, 15, 16–17, 18, 31–32, 33, 34, 48, 49–50, 53, 56, 60, 66, 75, 76, 90, 92, 93–94, 125, 133, 143, **157,** 158

Vallely, Fintan, 145, 196–197
Vaughan, Kevin, 81
venues, 55, 73, 81, 101, 194–195
  (*see also* Athlone; Boyle; Cashel; Cavan; Clones; Dungarvan; Ennis; Enniscorthy; Gorey; Listowel; Longford; Loughrea; Monaghan town; Mullingar; Sligo; Swinford; Thurles)

Wade, Jack, 126
Walderstown Pipers' Club, the, 17, 23
*Walton's Programme* (radio show), 29
War of Independence, the, 163
war pipes (bagpipes), the, 31, 33, 54–55, 56, 90, 110
Ward, Jimmy, 78, 81, 85, 116, 119
Waterman, Stanley, 70
*Westmeath Examiner* (newspaper), 23, 30
Whit weekend, the, 36, 80, 184, 185, 187, 191, 193
Whitaker, T.K., 9
White, Aggie, 150
White, Theresa, 61
Williams, Sean, 27
Williamstown Girls Céilí Band, the, 62, 63, 65
Wyley, E.M., 47, 90
  'Our Native Music Beyond Compare' (lecture), 90

Yeats, W.B., 127
young people and demographic trends in the 1960s, 182–183

Zilliacus, William, 57–58